Property Rights in Outer Space

This book explores the role of private mining rights in the utopian imaginary of space colonisation. It presents a transdisciplinary account of the new and evolving legislative frameworks that have been established in anticipation of commercial exploitation of the mineral resources of the off-world frontier. Written in an engaging style, the book investigates a novel case study in the history of capitalism and 'the commons': the emergence of a nascent space mining industry, undergirded by a contentious legislative framework. In 2015, the US passed laws that would recognise the claims of US corporations to own and sell space resources. This unilateral act of pre-emptive law-making would appear to contravene the terms of the UN Outer Space Treaty (1967), which declared that the exploration and use of outer space should be 'for the benefit of all mankind' and 'not subject to national appropriation'.

Using this central dynamic between privately held mining rights and outer space as a 'global commons', Matthew Johnson constructs an historical sociology of space mining – from the deep historical roots of common and private property to the contemporary networks of neoliberalism that have engaged with the commercialisation of space activity. The anticipatory expansion of private property claims beyond the Earth both resonates with and problematises the 'terrain' of political history, such as the tensions between states and markets, public law and private power, 'the commons' and exclusive property. The emerging cosmopolitics of off-world private property mirrors (and is often explicitly embedded within) neoliberal geopolitics, prompting urgent questions about how we can reaffirm principles of democracy and 'common heritage' in the international laws of Earth and space. This book is compelling reading for anyone interested in the social study of space, law, economics, technology, politics and property rights.

Matthew Johnson was awarded his PhD in 2020 from the University of Technology, Sydney, Australia. He has worked in a variety of academic and public sector roles, and currently lives and works in Sydney.

Routledge Complex Real Property Rights Series

Series editor: Professor Spike Boydell

University of Technology Sydney, Australia

Real Property Rights are central to the global economy and provide a legal framework for how society (be it developed or customary) relates to land and buildings. We need to better understand property rights to ensure sustainable societies, careful use of limited resources and sound ecological stewardship of our land and water. Contemporary property rights theory is dynamic and needs to engage thinkers who are prepared to think outside their disciplinary limitations.

The Routledge Complex Real Property Rights Series strives to take a transdisciplinary approach to understanding property rights and specifically encourages heterodox thinking. Through rich international case studies our goal is to build models to connect theory to observed reality, allowing us to inform potential policy outcomes. This series is both an ideal forum and reference for students and scholars of property rights and land issues.

Compulsory Property Acquisition for Urban Densification
Edited by Glen Searle

Pseudo-Public Spaces in Chinese Shopping Malls
Rise, Publicness and Consequences
Yiming Wang

Property Rights from Below
Commodification of Land and the Counter-Movement
Edited by Olivier de Schutter and Balakrishnan Rajagopal

People, Place and Property Rights
A Political Ethnography of Land in Molo, Kenya
Ulrika Kolben Waaranperä

Property Rights in Outer Space
Mining, Techno-Utopian Imaginaries, and the Privatisation of the Off-World Frontier
Matthew Johnson

Property Rights in Outer Space

Mining, Techno-Utopian Imaginaries, and the Privatisation of the Off-World Frontier

Matthew Johnson

Routledge
Taylor & Francis Group
LONDON AND NEW YORK

First published 2024
by Routledge
4 Park Square, Milton Park, Abingdon, Oxon OX14 4RN

and by Routledge
605 Third Avenue, New York, NY 10158

Routledge is an imprint of the Taylor & Francis Group, an informa business

British Library Cataloguing-in-Publication Data
A catalogue record for this book is available from the British Library

Library of Congress Cataloging-in-Publication Data
Names: Johnson, Matt (Matthew), author.
Title: Property rights in outer space : mining, techno-utopian imaginaries, and the privatisation / Matt Johnson.
Description: Abingdon, Oxon [UK] ; New York, NY : Routledge, 2024. | Series: Routledge complex real property rights series | Includes bibliographical references and index.
Identifiers: LCCN 2023058522 (print) | LCCN 2023058523 (ebook) |
Subjects: LCSH: Commons. | Property. | Space mining--Law and legislation. | Privatization--Law and legislation. | Outer space--Exploration--International cooperation.
Classification: LCC KZD3491.5 .J64 2024 (print) | LCC KZD3491.5 (ebook) | DDC 341.4/7--dc23/eng/20240129
LC record available at https://lccn.loc.gov/2023058522
LC ebook record available at https://lccn.loc.gov/2023058523

ISBN: 978-1-032-22516-6 (hbk)
ISBN: 978-1-032-27662-5 (pbk)
ISBN: 978-1-003-29361-3 (ebk)

DOI: 10.1201/9781003293613

Typeset in Times New Roman
by MPS Limited, Dehradun

For Jasper

Contents

Figures

Acknowledgements

I would like to start by acknowledging the Gadigal people of the Eora nation, on whose lands I have written this work. I pay my respects to elders past and present, and recognise that First Nations sovereignty was never ceded.

It has been a long journey, from commencing my doctoral studies to publishing this monograph. I'd like to thank everyone in the Faculty of Arts and Social Sciences at the University of Technology, Sydney, and I acknowledge that my doctoral research, on which this monograph is based, was funded by the Australian Government Research Training Program.

I am very fortunate to have been helped by many wonderful and patient people. First and foremost, I am indebted to Dr Jeremy Walker, who was a very kind and supportive PhD supervisor, and who imparted a great deal of knowledge and common sense in my development as a research and writer. I am proud of our work on 'mineral sovereignty', which has been instrumental to the avenues of inquiry contained in this book. I would also like to thank Dr Jonathan Marshall, for his support, kindness, and erudite advice while I completed my doctoral studies.

I am particularly indebted to Dr Spike Boydell, series editor, for his ongoing support and guidance. I would also like to thank the Routledge team, in particular Martha Luke and Ed Needle, for their help throughout this process. I am also grateful to Professor Joanne Gabrynowicz who has kindly shared her expertise on recent movements in United States and international space law with me.

This book would not have been possible without my family and friends. To my mother and father, Margaret and John, and my brother and sister, Tom and Natalie – thank you for everything. I'd also like to thank the families Johnson, Green, Harrison, Rajasingham, Minors, Thompson, Marshall and Kerley, and all the other lovable rascals who continue to bring joy to my life. Thank you to the friends I have made while working in academia and in the NSW public sector, for your words of encouragement and lunchtime MarioKart sessions over the years.

I want to give a special thank to my late grandmother Joan, who – when I was about 10 years old – lent me her good binoculars so I could look at

Jupiter and other wonders of the night sky. For encouraging that early infatuation with space, I will always be grateful.

To my beautiful wife, Yasmin – there's no way I would have finished this without you, and I am eternally grateful for your love, kindness, and calmness. Honourable mentions go to our beloved pets, Jet and Dash. Finally, I wish all the love in the universe to our son Jasper, a beautiful boy with stars in his eyes and the world at his feet. I dedicate this work to him.

Foreword

Real Property Rights are central to the economy and provide a legal framework for how society (be it developed or customary) relates to land and buildings. Property rights are both institutional arrangements and social relations. We need to better understand property rights to ensure sustainable societies, careful use of limited resources and sound ecological stewardship of our land and water.

Land conflict is all around us – from corporate and political corruption over land dealings in the developed world to land grab in developing countries, to compromised indigenous property rights and to resource exploitation. At a time where global food security, water security and shelter are paramount, an understanding of property rights is key to sustainability.

Contemporary property rights theory is dynamic and this series strives to engage thinkers who are prepared to step beyond their disciplinary limitations. 'Property Rights' is a broad term that is fundamentally about social relations. Real property rights, obligations and restrictions can be found in and change across the full range of human societies, both in time and space. Property rights research has emerged from a broad range of disciplines including (but not limited to) archaeology, anthropology, ethics, sociology, psychology, law, geography, history, philosophy, economics, planning and business studies. What makes this series special is that it facilitates a transdisciplinary approach to understanding property rights and specifically promotes heterodox thinking.

In '*Property Rights in Outer Space: Mining, Techno-Utopian Imaginaries, and the Privatisation of the Off-World Frontier*' Matt Johnson takes a unique and comprehensive approach to examining the development of national laws establishing private property rights in outer space resources. In the early 21st century, a fledgeling space mining industry emerged, marked by ambitious plans from start-up firms to extract resources from celestial bodies. This book delves into the socio-cultural and political-economic factors that shaped this industry, exploring the broader implications of space mining within an off-world techno-utopian context. Johnson's analysis transcends traditional legal perspectives, advocating for a broader sociological and political-economic understanding of off-world property rights.

Johnson examines the NewSpace movement, scrutinising its ideological and structural parallels to neoliberalism. This inquiry includes an analysis of American spacefaring history and the influence of physicist Gerard O'Neill's vision for space colonisation. The book questions the alignment of private space mining with the broader interests of humanity, in light of the support and endorsement NewSpace has received from neoliberal entities within the Atlas Network.

The work critically assesses off-world private property within the context of political philosophy and history, especially in relation to the Outer Space Treaty (OST). It challenges the NewSpace utopia, arguing that recent legislative efforts in space resource law potentially undermine the treaty's prohibition on national appropriation. Johnson draws on the insights of Karl Polanyi to explore this paradox of private property, which is often secured by government yet stands in opposition to governmental authority.

Drawing on previous work (Walker & Johnson 2018), Johnson deploys the concept of 'mineral sovereignty' to discuss the appropriation of off-world resources, focusing on the US Commercial Space Launch Competitiveness Act (CSLCA). This act represents a pivotal moment in the legal recognition of private ownership of off-world minerals, rekindling the historical interplay between state power and extractive rights. The book illustrates how mineral sovereignty can extend beyond legislative realms, influenced by the historical power of mining industries to shape legal and political environments.

The anticipatory legal and political status of celestial bodies is another focus, exploring the pathway to the OST. Johnson critiques the disjunction between the OST's principles and interpretations favouring private space resource ownership, suggesting that new forms of 'space constitution' might emerge, driven by first-movers in space colonisation and US commercial interests.

The book also delves into the 'geo-mythography' of space exploration, relating it to themes of national sovereignty, private appropriation, and the legacy of colonialism. It examines space colonialism as a potential form of neo-colonialism, driven by legislative guarantees of private mineral rights, yet distinct from historical colonial violence.

Environmental conservation is presented as a justification for off-world migration and industrialism. Johnson critiques the reliance on a 'techno-fix' approach, which defers immediate action on ecological crises in favour of future technological progress. The book explores alternatives to this approach, advocating for pragmatic solutions that ensure sustainable futures both on Earth and in outer space.

In conclusion, Johnson reflects on the historical precedents of capitalist and colonial history to speculate about the future of the cosmic frontier. The book considers whether off-world colonisation will be a space of freedom and socio-political renewal or a continuation of terrestrial political and economic patterns. While the space mining industry itself currently reflects the 'boom and bust' of space entrepreneurialism, Johnson highlights the immediate policy and advocacy goals arising from the current neoliberal challenge to the cosmic commons, pointing to significant issues we face on Earth.

Matt Johnson's work situates the concept of space mining and off-world property rights within a wider socio-political, economic and ecological context. It challenges conventional legal narratives and frameworks, advocating for a more comprehensive understanding of property rights in outer space. The book's transdisciplinary approach provides a unique lens to view the emerging dynamics of property rights in the new frontier of outer space, intertwining legal, sociological and political-economic analyses to address this complex and evolving issue.

Enjoy.

Spike Boydell, General Editor
Sydney, November 2023

1 Introduction

In the first decades of the 21st century, a curious case study emerged in humanity's relationship with the cosmos. Between 2012 and 2019, a nascent 'space mining' industry rose to prominence as actors in the commercial spacefaring domain. A handful of start-up firms announced very ambitious plans to extract resources from celestial bodies in our cosmic neighbourhood, such as asteroids and the Moon. This book describes the sociocultural and political-economic currents that lead to the genesis of the space mining industry, the role that space mining plays within a broader off-world techno-utopian imaginary and the discourses that have been employed by space mining's supporters to justify such an endeavour.

At the time of writing, the space mining industry has encountered financial challenges, such that several of the firms that led the charge towards off-world industrialisation are no longer in operation (Abrahamian 2019). However, some interesting legal frameworks have been left in their wake: domestic laws that recognise a corporation's right to extract, own and use off-world resources. In 2015, the United States became the first nation to adopt laws that would – if a company ever achieved the technological feat of mining a celestial body – entitle US citizens and entities to private property rights over space resources. In 2017, Luxembourg followed suit, as did the United Arab Emirates in 2019 and Japan in 2021. Through the Artemis Accords agreement that the United States established in 2020, and which approximately 30 of its allies have signed in the years since, there is also a movement to clarify and entrench these resource ownership rights in international law.

These efforts to legally recognise the right to own private property in space resources have proven to be contentious. Whether these domestic laws are consistent with international treaties that govern outer space has been subject to robust debate in the diplomatic and academic fora of the space law community (Hertzfeld, Weeden & Johnson 2016; Pace 2017; Kfir & Perry 2017; Israel 2019; von der Dunk 2020; Hobe, cited in Stirn 2020). In this book, however, I present a heterodox approach to space resources law. There are numerous, valuable accounts of how private ownership of space resources may or may not be consistent with the rules and principles of international space law (Tronchetti 2009; Lee 2012; Jakhu, Pelton & Nyampong 2017). While I engage

DOI: 10.1201/9781003293613-1

with legal scholarship on space resources law, my account of private property in the off-world is anchored in a sociological and political-economic perspective. Indeed, when we consider the sheer political power that often undergirds claims of resource ownership, there are limitations to viewing off-world property through a uni-disciplinary lens. By considering the prospect of extractive industry in the cosmos as part of the deep currents of political history, we find several novel avenues for inquiry that take us beyond the letter of the law and into the contemporary policy challenges of our time.

The field of space resources law is evolving quickly and taking place in a largely speculative and anticipatory domain. In the discussion that follows, I have incorporated legal, diplomatic and commercial developments that were current as of early 2023. The United States and China set their sights on the return of crewed missions to the Moon during the latter half of the 2020s and the possibility of longer-term settlement in the 2030s (Wall 2022). As such, there are likely to be further developments in the tale of space mining and the politico-legal forces that support the right to own and use space resources.

As below, so above?

Before I elucidate the book's recurring themes further, however, let us begin with an enduring and evocative image – one which was taken during what proved to be a pivotal year for human activity in outer space. In 1972, on their journey towards the Moon, Apollo 17 astronauts Eugene Cernan, Ronald Evans and Harrison Schmitt took what became known as the 'Blue Marble' photograph (NASA 1972a, overleaf). The image captured Earth as a full globe for the first time, looking down upon the continents of Africa, Asia and Antarctica, with the resplendence and fragility of Earth illuminated against the pitch-black void of outer space. The Apollo Program's images of Earth from space conjure a sense of cosmopolitan reverie and planetary ecological consciousness. The beautiful mosaic of expansive oceans, diverse biomes and dynamic climates renders invisible the social, political and economic antagonisms that reign on the surface (Figure 1.1).

This photo was taken when environmental protection emerged as a global prerogative, in the same year that the United Nations declared that humankind 'bears a solemn responsibility to protect and improve the environment for present and future generations' (U.N. Conference on the Human Environment 1972, p. 4). This 'Apollonian gaze' looking down upon Nature invokes both stewardship and mastery, humility and omnipotence (Jazeel 2011, p. 82; Cosgrove 2001). A marriage of benevolence and belligerence, these first photographs of Earth from space were made possible by the embedding of the Apollo Program within Cold War geopolitics and the American military-industrial complex.

'We came in peace for all mankind …'. So says the romantic, cosmopolitan message inscribed on a plaque left on the Moon by NASA's Apollo 11 mission, three years before the Blue Marble photo was taken. The plaque serves as a

Figure 1.1 NASA (1972a) – the 'Blue Marble' photo captured the Earth as a globe for the first time, as the Apollo 17 mission made its way towards the Moon.

testament to the militarised capitalist-communist rivalry of the Cold War, at least as much as it does to magnanimous pretences of species consciousness or planetary unity. The plaque's egalitarian sentiment is perhaps undermined by its androcentric language and the fact that it reached the Moon through a space agency characterised by a male-dominated, WASP monoculturalism (Mailer 1970). Beneath the names of the Apollo 11 astronauts Neil Armstrong, 'Buzz' Aldrin and Mike Collins, the lunar plaque bears the signature of one Richard Milhous Nixon. Under Nixon's presidency, the United States simultaneously claimed 'soft power' rewards for its Moon landing feat and secretly bombed Cambodia. Aerospace manufacturer Boeing had built both the first-stage booster of the Saturn V rocket that powered Apollo 11 into cosmic hagiography and the ubiquitous B-52 bombers that levelled Indochina. Science communicator Carl Sagan (1934–1996) remarked:

> As the United States was dropping 7 ½ megatons of conventional explosives on small nations in Southeast Asia, we congratulated ourselves on our humanity: we would harm no one on a lifeless rock. (Sagan 1994, p. 170)

Yet Sagan himself had some insider experience with military geopolitics. In the throes of the early Cold War, Sagan's doctoral studies involved work on the unrealised Project A119, an Air Force project that considered detonating a hydrogen bomb on the Moon (Reiffel 1959; Davidson 1999). Project A119 was proposed shortly after the Soviet Union had beaten the United States in launching *Sputnik* into space, the first artificial satellite. A nuclear explosion on the lunar terminator – the horizon where lunar day becomes night – was hypothesised to be visible from Earth and would have served as a bright and toxic 'don't tread on me' in the wake of the first salvo in the Space Race (Davidson 1999).

Yet it was against this backdrop of Cold War nuclear pageantry when the solidarity of all humankind vis-à-vis outer space was first articulated in public international law.[1] By its 50th anniversary, the United Nations' *Outer Space Treaty* (OST 1967) had been ratified by 105 nations.[2] It proclaims that:

> The exploration and use of outer space, including the Moon and other celestial bodies, shall be carried out for the benefit and in the interests of all countries, irrespective of their degree of economic or scientific development, and shall be the province of all mankind.
>
> Outer space, including the Moon and other celestial bodies, shall be free for exploration and use by all States without discrimination of any kind, on a basis of equality and in accordance with international law, and there shall be free access to all areas of celestial bodies. (OST 1967, Art. 1)

The OST regulates the behaviour of state and non-state actors in outer space, and proclaims principles of common interest, free passage, shared use, mutual benefit, reciprocal obligation and the rule of law in the use of outer space. While the precise meaning of this international legal instrument has been disputed, outer space is often considered *res communis*, or common property – from the edge of national airspace to the valuable geostationary orbit and on to celestial bodies like the asteroids, moons and planets of the Solar System.

Common property is one of our enduring socio-cultural and politico-legal institutions, yet one which is perpetually in contest with private property. In *The True Leveler's Standard Advanced* (1649), political activist and philosopher Gerard Winstanley decried the wave of enclosures that took common land and converted it to private property.

> And hereupon, The Earth (which was made to be a Common Treasury of relief for all, both Beasts and Men) was hedged in to In-closures by the teachers and rulers, and the others were made Servants and Slaves: And that Earth that is within this Creation made a Common Store-house for all, is bought and sold, and kept in the hands of a few, whereby the great Creator is mightily dishonoured, as if he were a respector of persons, delighting in the comfortable Livelihoods of some, and rejoycing in the miserable povertie and straits of others. From the beginning it was not so. (Winstanley 1649)

Much like Gerrard Winstanley's view from Saint George's Hill in 17th-century England, the view of Earth from space might reveal a 'common treasury of relief for all', appearing to be void of exclusive ownership, hinting at shared human futures and a common home.

Like the high seas, atmosphere and Antarctica, outer space is a commons – free to explore and open to all, but subject to restrictions on its use (though each of these global commons possesses different legal characteristics and levels of contestation). The Blue Marble imparts a sense of anxiety and foreboding when we consider the health of these Earthly commons. Our 'common treasury' has been plundered during the short, Anthropocene chapter of Earth's 4.5 billion-year history. Earth is presently the only planet known to harbour biological life, and many might sympathise with Bill Bryson's comment that 'if you were designing an organism to look after life in our lonely cosmos … you wouldn't choose human beings for the job' (Bryson 2005, p. 593). Earth is an oasis suspended in the 'great enveloping cosmic dark' (Sagan 1994, p. 7), and is under threat from the irresponsibility of its apex species (or, at least, a handful of thermo-industrial predators). Since the industrial revolution, a level of biodiversity loss has occurred that rivals the mass extinction events of eons past. Anthropogenic carbon pollution is pushing global temperatures towards an imminent 2°C increase, which might tip Earth towards a catastrophic 4–6°C increase by 2100 – beyond this may lie an unliveable 'hothouse Earth' scenario of irreversible planetary warming (Steffen et al. 2018). There are numerous indications that we are already in the midst of severe, dangerous and permanent changes to the atmospheric commons (IPCC 2023, pp. 5–7). Outer space is arguably the last commons to be subjected to some form of degradation, depletion and contestation.

Space mining and the 'NewSpace' paradigm

For advocates in the 'NewSpace' network, however, the space frontier offers a salve for this planetary pessimism. Centred in the United States, NewSpace is a network of activists, entrepreneurs, commercial entities and civil society organisations that share the goal of furthering space exploration and settlement (Valentine 2012; Shammas & Holen 2019). This diffuse network involves pragmatic technoscientific and commercial elements, and a more grandiose belief that civilisation should not be limited by the bounds of gravity, atmosphere and biosphere (McCray 2013). The destiny of the human species is to continue expanding onto celestial bodies like the Moon, Mars and asteroids, even one day moving beyond the Solar System and traversing the expanses of the Milky Way galaxy. This expansive tendency in the NewSpace imaginary is perhaps better reflected in another photograph taken by the Apollo 17 crew – a distant Earth, dwarfed by the barren and cratered expanses of the Moon (Figure 1.2) (NASA 1972b). Many in the NewSpace network want to do more than launch satellites or send robotic probes to Mars. They want to find new homes among this 'magnificent desolation', as Apollo 11's Buzz Aldrin once

Figure 1.2 The view from Apollo 17, looking over the lunar horizon towards a crescent Earth (NASA 1972a).

described it, aspiring for humanity to ascend from its home planet and colonise the 'high frontier' (O'Neill 1977). In the words of NewSpace progenitor Gerard O'Neill, outer space is to be 'humanised' (1977, p. 230).

This book is an investigation into the NewSpace imaginary, which – despite its fantastic and speculative nature – is now grounded in the sovereignty of the United States. In November 2015, under a Republican-dominated Congress, President Obama signed into law the *Commercial Space Launch Competitiveness Act of 2015* (CSLCA). It states:

> A United States citizen engaged in commercial recovery of an asteroid resource or a space resource … shall be entitled to any asteroid resource or space resource obtained, including to possess, own, transport, use, and sell the asteroid resource or space resource obtained in accordance with applicable law, including the international obligations of the United States. (CSLCA 2015, s.51303)

The CSLCA would recognise the future private property claims on resources mined in space by US citizens and commercial entities, and whether the Act is in accordance with the United States's obligations under the OST shall be explored throughout the chapters that follow. There is currently no property to recognise, for there are no realised space mining industries nor does anyone possess off-world minerals mined for commercial gain. More optimistic estimates suggest that the space mining industry is 'probably a good 15 years off revenue' (Boywer, in Cornish 2017). Yet NewSpace's dream of limitless spacefaring is now anchored in the politico-legal authority of the world's reigning space superpower, manifest in this extra-territorial guarantee of mineral rights.[3]

In 2017, Luxembourg, a small European nation known for its generous tax laws, became the second country to introduce space mining legislation. In 2019, the United Arab Emirates introduced its own law which would facilitate, among other forms of space activity, the granting of permits for the exploration and use of space resources, including for 'their acquisition, purchase, sale, trade, transportation … [and] storage' (*Federal Law No. 12 of 2019 on the Regulation of the Space Sector*, Art. 18). In June 2021, Japan became the fourth country to introduce similar legal frameworks that would enable its private entities to own resources they have mined from outer space (*Act on the Promotion of Business Activities for the Exploration and Development of Space Resources (Act No. 83 of 2021),* Art. 5). These laws may yet play a role in realising the NewSpace dream of space colonisation.

Why would anyone want to own private property in space resources? In the NewSpace imaginary, commercial exploitation of the mineral reserves of the Solar System is considered an essential step in space colonisation (OffWorld, n.d.; Lewis 1997). In order to leave Earth's gravity well, contemporary rockets need to achieve an escape velocity of approximately 11.2 km per second or 40,000 km per hour. This feat necessitates large volumes of heavy and expensive rocket propellant. The cost of transporting material from Earth's surface to low-Earth orbit can be as high as US $23,000 per pound of payload (Planetary Resources 2014). Celestial bodies of the Solar System are thought to contain vast amounts of valuable minerals, including the platinum group metals, iron, nickel and even just water ice. Exploiting these reserves in space would negate the need to transport them from Earth's surface. Metals and alloys could be used for building large spacecraft and habitats that could never be launched from the depths of Earth's gravity well. Water ice from asteroids and the Moon could be used as astronaut life supports. If this water was separated into hydrogen and oxygen, it could become rocket propellant – turning asteroids into off-world 'coaling stations' for journeys into deep space. In anticipation of off-world rewards, a handful of space mining start-up firms were established in the 2010s.[4]

NewSpace considers off-world resource exploitation to be more than a means of living out one's sci-fi fantasies (though this still appears to have some appeal). In 1977, Princeton physicist Gerard O'Neill published *The High Frontier*. He developed a detailed schema for space colonisation and justified this off-world expansionist project by drawing on then emerging environmentalist discourses (O'Neill 1977). NewSpace continues to argue that ecological crises caused by overpopulation, unfettered economic growth and resource depletion are surmountable if the space frontier is colonised and industrialised (Orsulak 2018). More recent articulations of NewSpace environmentalism propose the exploitation of helium-3, for example. Rare on Earth but abundant on the Moon, helium-3 is considered a potential ingredient in the elusive technology of controlled fusion reactions – it could enable unlimited clean energy production (Schmitt 2006). Off-world colonisation is also seen by some as a 'Plan B' in the event of planetary apocalypses that aren't self-inflicted, such as a meteor impact (Diamandis, in Hoffman 2010). Through these currently unrealised technologies of off-world industrialisation – space mining, *in situ* resource refinement and microgravity manufacturing – NewSpace believes that society and economy can (and will need to) become independent of Earth.

Apollo 17's 1972 mission to the Moon represented the end of the Apollo Program. Much to the chagrin of many in the NewSpace network, no human has set foot on a celestial body since – there is no one there to read Apollo 11's famous plaque. Since the NewSpace movement's genesis in the wake of Apollo, NewSpace actors have often mounted libertarian or anti-statist arguments that the government-centred legacy of the Cold War should be displaced by a new era of commercial spacefaring, or the role of government reduced to supporting space businesses (Hudgins 2002; *Orphans of Apollo* 2008; NSS 2019). In 2003, when space entrepreneurialism began to challenge the dominance of NASA in the American space sector, Congressional hearings were held on the Future of NASA. Rick Tumlinson, representing NewSpace organisation, the Space Frontier Foundation, testified before the Senate Committee on Commerce, Science and Transportation. The below extract from his opening statement serves as a concise summary of the central themes typical of NewSpace advocacy and rhetoric in the two decades since.

> Our central and driving goal is the large-scale permanent settlement of space as soon as possible, using the resources we find there, and the imaginations we bring to the task.
>
> We believe all people have the 'right stuff' and that everyone will benefit from opening the space frontier. Given the fragility of our planet we also believe that it is vital that we not only preserve the biosphere of earth using the resources of space, but that we expand that biosphere, taking life to worlds now dead. If successful, we see our future as exciting and full of possibility … .
>
> We believe that free people, free markets and free enterprise will become unstoppable forces in the irreversible settlement of this new frontier, and that our world is on the verge of a truly historic breakthrough – access to space for all.

> To make that happen, we are engaged in the transformation of space from a government-owned bureaucratic program – into a new partnership between the public and private sectors – that will lead to a dynamic and inclusive frontier open to all people … . (Tumlinson 2003)

Like the view of Earth from space, NewSpace cosmopolitics is rife with tension and paradox. It offers both an exotic, eschatological vision and a familiar orientation towards government, social obligation and ecological crisis. Planetary constraints to unfettered industrialism can be overcome through the industrialisation of the limitless frontier and the limitless creativity of the technology entrepreneur. It is the commercial incentive of privately ownable space resources – not solidarity with or reciprocal obligations to 'all mankind' – that they believe will propel humanity towards an eternal space-faring future.

Across the chapters that follow, I ask the following questions: are the CSLCA and the subsequent laws of Luxembourg, UAE and Japan consistent with international law? Are there any historical precedents for the allocation of mining rights in extra-territorial spaces? If NewSpace managed to migrate elsewhere in the Solar System, would the rest of us be worse off? What, really, is at stake in a project that may not take place in the next half-century, and would occur *well* beyond the life-sustaining commons of Earth? I will argue that the private property rights guaranteed under the CSLCA actually undermine NewSpace's cosmopolitan, humanitarian and environmentalist impulses. The space mining project would not entail the universal beneficence envisioned in NewSpace discourse, nor will it offer a plausible resolution to the problems we face on Earth. I will demonstrate that NewSpace has numerous ideological, programmatic and social affinities with neoliberalism – a political philosophy fundamentally opposed to notions of common or public goods.

Despite NewSpace's claims to 'newness', the legal-institutional structures emerging in anticipation of space mining evoke a much deeper historical trajectory. The legal guarantee of privately held mineral rights, projected onto a new frontier, conjures the age of maritime colonialism. The United States's imposition of private property law upon the Solar System represents a pre-emptive enclosure of the space commons, where spaces and resources that were once open for public use become the private property of some to the exclusion of others. Yet despite these historical parallels, it represents very different environment for law, politics and economy. Outer space is the last frontier to be subject to the ravages of industrial capitalism. Will we go in peace, or in avarice?

Theory and method

This book is an interdisciplinary engagement with the legal geography of common and private property rights, the political economy of neoliberalism and scholarship in international space law. However, it is primarily a work of historical sociology: my aim is to contextualise the NewSpace commercial-colonisation project within the broader currents of Earthly social and political history, and to explore how this historicisation opens up new and interesting questions for the social sciences.[5] NewSpace may initially appear to present a harmless and discrete utopian imaginary, but I will argue that its contradictory impulses speak to core tensions in the history of (neo)liberal capitalism. I will demonstrate that the anticipatory contestation over the space commons mirrors the more immediate contestation over the global commons of Earth, such as the atmosphere. I will also explore some legal-institutional proposals that might resolve or prevent 'tragedies of the commons' on Earth and in the Solar System (Hardin 1968).

The social science literature on NewSpace is generally sparse, but it is valuable for approaching the subjectivities and social history of this network. However, most of this work has been published prior to the advent of the CSLCA (Michaud 1986; Launius 2003; McCray 2013). Kilgore (2003) appropriately locates the NewSpace imaginary within science fiction literary traditions – Robert Heinlein's libertarian 'boys' novels', for instance. Ormrod's (2007) psychoanalytic approach describes NewSpace justifications for space colonisation as narcissistic male phantasies of mastery and omnipotence. However, the NewSpace imaginary is now supported by domestic public law and, through the CSLCA and domestic laws like it, space futures are now entwined within broader, enduring narratives of political history: the enclosure of common spaces, extra-territorial projections of national sovereignty and the blurred distinctions between state power and private ownership in neoliberalism and broader property law.

There is, perhaps surprisingly, a well-established field of legal scholarship concerning the question of off-world private property (Scheraga 1987; Pop 2000; Cooper 2003; IISL 2016). There are numerous works that have been published since some nations introduced laws to recognise private property on space resources; however, several authors have noted that it is unclear whether this specific law is consistent with the terms of *Outer Space Treaty* (Tronchetti 2015; Perry 2017; Freeland 2017; Hobe & de Man 2017). Some scholars in favour of the CSLCA have argued that it is legal to extract mineral resources in space so long as celestial bodies themselves are not appropriated by private economic interests (Kfir 2016). In my view, these authors have failed to resolve the tension between private resource ownership and the 'non-appropriation principle' of the OST. According to Article 2 of the OST: 'Outer space, including the Moon and other celestial bodies, is not subject to national appropriation by claim of sovereignty, by means of use or occupation, or by any other means' (OST 1967, Art. 2).

Can we demarcate acts of private appropriation from 'national appropriation', if the legal recognition of private ownership claims is grounded in national sovereignty? I explore this question using an institutional political economic approach, detailing the relationship between states and markets that has existed since the dawn of capitalism. Using primarily online archival research, I analyse NewSpace political discourse through a range of texts: company press releases and advertisements; policy recommendations from civil society organisations; and other published communications from NewSpace actors (for example, O'Neill 1977). NewSpace can be seen mirroring several tenets of Silicon Valley start-up culture, particularly the libertarian emphasis on individual rights secured against government interference (Barbrook & Cameron 1996; Parker 2009). NewSpace actors often frame private property, individual liberty and free markets as the freedom *from* government intervention – and do so from a largely ahistorical viewpoint. Prior sociological research into NewSpace has also identified a dominant libertarian or economic liberal ideological strain within the movement (Launius 2003; Ormrod 2009; Parker 2009; Valentine 2012; Shammas & Holen 2019). In order to contrast this evident goal of an off-world libertarian utopia against its apparent reliance on state-backed private property rights, I turn to Karl Polanyi's *The Great Transformation* (2001 [1944]). Polanyi presented an economic history of market capitalism and an anthropology of economic liberalism that revealed 'free' markets to be entirely mythical: capitalistic freedoms are instead reliant on continuous government intervention (Polanyi 2001).

In this light, is it accurate to describe NewSpace as a 'libertarian' movement? Polanyi's work is valuable in approaching the role of the state in neoliberal government, and NewSpace is an intriguing case study in the era of neoliberal globalisation (projected beyond the globe, in this case). 'Neoliberalism' is a term that is often deployed with imprecision or lampooned as a leftist 'political swearword' (Hartwich 2009). For many, neoliberalism might be synonymous with de-regulation, the reduction of 'red tape' and an end goal of 'small government'. However, NewSpace exemplifies what has been described as the 'double truth' or aporia at the heart of neoliberalism (Mirowski 2009; Dean 2014). On the one hand, neoliberal actors espouse an outward hostility towards 'big government' and the reciprocal obligations to society that democratic government entails (for example, taxation, resource rents and the preservation of commons); on the other hand, the neoliberal political project has sought to capture these same public institutions and re-engineer their functions in order to serve private over collective interests.

Neoliberalism is closer to 're-regulating' than de-regulating (Cahill 2014; Block & Somers 2014). Polanyi (2001) had identified capitalism's reliance upon government as early as the first waves of Enclosure laws that swept across the English countryside 400 years ago. This 'statecraft', as he called it, engendered the development of infrastructure, provision of subsidies or seed investments, and the introduction (or removal) of particular legal architectures in order to make corporations profitable. I will provide evidence of NewSpace's reliance on similar institutional supports, primarily through a theoretical investigation of the nature of private property rights and quantitative data that highlights other supports for the nascent space mining industry (FPDS 2023a; FPDS 2023b; FPDS 2023c).

I am not the first to identify ideological and programmatic affinities between the commercialisation of space activity and neoliberalism (Valentine 2012; Rowan 2018; Shammas & Holen 2019). In addition to investigating NewSpace as an expression of neoliberal political-economic theory, however, my project offers a 'networked history' that investigates the extent to which NewSpace cosmopolitics is explicitly embedded within neoliberal political networks – to this end, I draw on Phillip Mirowksi and Dieter Plehwe's volume, *The Road from Mont Pelèrin: The Making of the Neoliberal Thought Collective* (2009).[6] Mirowski, Plehwe and their contributors highlight that – while neoliberalism may sometimes appear to have nebulous or contradictory philosophical tenets, and is realised in diverse and variable socio-political contexts – the neoliberal policy program has been propagated by a consistent and organised collection of individuals and institutions. Founded in 1947 by Friedrich Hayek, among others, the Mont Pelèrin Society is the taproot of the transnational neoliberal collective. Since 1981, this collective has been extended and consolidated in local political forms through the Atlas Network, a coordinated array of over 500 think-tanks, academic departments and other interest groups across the globe (Atlas Network 2023).

By looking at neoliberalism through the institutional nodes and political-economic links of the Atlas Network, we can draw together a range of actors that have evangelised neoliberal ideology or funded its proliferation. As applied in diverse policy arenas, the political infrastructure of the Atlas Network commonly involves: the deployment of 'conservative' or 'free market' lobbying and advocacy organisations, such as the United States's Heritage Foundation or Australia's Institute for Public Affairs (IPA); corporate philanthropy, particularly from industrial magnates who have waged war on environmental policy (for example, the Koch brothers or Gina Rinehart); and the embedding of former Atlas employees within public sector institutions and the chambers of democratic government (such as former Heritage policy wonks employed in ambassadorial positions by the Reagan Administration, or the election of former IPA staffers to the Australian Parliament). Since the neoliberal revolutions of the Thatcher, Reagan and Howard governments (among others), neoliberal policies have removed regulatory and institutional protection for workers, marginalised socio-economic groups, the environment and future generations, while converting public assets and services into privately owned fiefdoms.

To what extent can we treat NewSpace as an expression of neoliberal capitalism, and what points of confluence exist between American NewSpace and the Atlas Network? Using publicly available qualitative and quantitative data, I trace the history of NewSpace and the road to the CSLCA, and identify linkages between this seemingly idiographic techno-utopian network and key nodes in Atlas Network neoliberalism (the Heritage Foundation, Cato Institute and venture capitalist Peter Thiel, for instance). In addition to the above textual sources, I have also used Congressional transcripts, lobbying expenditures collated by the Center for Responsive Politics (for example, OpenSecrets 2023a) and space mining start-ups' (limited) publicly available financial data (for example, Crunchbase 2019a). My primary research has identified moments of confluence between the Atlas and NewSpace networks, such that neoliberal political agency can be seen influencing the passage of the CSLCA and other US positions on international space law – particularly the ill-fated UN *Moon Agreement* (1979).[7] Committed to continuous economic growth, Atlas organisations have played a significant role in the obstruction of coordinated responses to climate change and the entrenchment of corporate rights to appropriate from mineral commonwealths. Links between Atlas and the passage of the CSLCA would suggest that the space commons will be enclosed for the benefit of wealthy 'cosmic elites' (Dickens & Ormrod 2007), not for the 'benefit of all mankind', while also casting doubt on NewSpace's environmentalist claims.

While Polanyi's institutional political economy and the 'neoliberalism as network' approach of Plehwe and Mirowksi are helpful for characterising NewSpace, these theories are unable to convey how momentous the CSLCA may prove to be in political-economic history. Private property rights – the core legal architecture of market capitalism – are being projected into the extra-terrestrial and extra-territorial spaces of the Solar System, a frontier that only 12 American astronauts have ever set foot on. As a way of framing the significance of the CSLCA, I will draw on German jurist Carl Schmitt's *Der Nomos der Erde* (*The Nomos of the Earth*, 2003 [1950]). Reappraising the ancient Greek term for spatial law or order – *nomos* – Schmitt describes the origins of *all* law in the fundamental act of land appropriation. The off-world frontier awaits this foundational act from which both national sovereignty and private property have historically derived.

What is the significance of the CSLCA for the future *nomos* of the Solar System? This is a rapidly developing arena in law and politics. Masson-Zwaan and Palkovitz (2017) note that states' legal practice on space resources law is evolving. Perhaps owing to the sheer practical challenges involved in conducting profitable off-world mining, opposition to the CSLCA has been limited to a handful of state and non-state actors (Masson-Zwaan & Palkovitz 2017, pp. 14–16; Tronchetti & Liu 2018, p. 430, FN 4). In attempting to ascertain exactly what impact the CSLCA will have, sociologists, lawyers and law-makers are inevitably drawn into speculating on how space resources law and the actual practice of space mining will transpire. In contextualising the anticipatory project of space mining within the history of Earthly *nomoi*, I will argue that the CSLCA heralds both a new chapter in the genealogy of international law and a recapitulation of the imperialist projects of centuries past, undermining the OST's fundamental principles of equality and cooperation in the process.

While I engage with legal scholarship on the topic of private resource ownership in outer space, I do so primarily from the perspective of the political and social sciences. I will explore space law interpretations of the OST and CLSCA, while also arguing that the barren expanses of outer space present fertile ground for political economy, resonating with and problematising the 'terrain' of political history. This book investigates what happens when we extend political categories of property, sovereignty and freedom onto a frontier that is devoid of 'land', in the life-supporting sense that it has been known for tens of thousands of years of social history. The legal geographic and political economic questions I investigate are supported by research in the environmental humanities that has approached attempts to sustain human and non-human life in the utterly hostile, abiotic environments of outer space (Cooper 2007; Walker & Granjou 2017). Outer space subverts the environmentalist and social democratic animus that we would normally expect from the granting of expansive mining rights and laws of enclosure. While *terra nullius* was a lie of British colonialism, in space there is no life to destroy and no commoner to evict (as far as we are aware). For NewSpace and neoliberalism, outer space appears to represent an endless, guilt-free frontier for the pursuit of capitalist freedoms. What do traditional defences of 'common rights' mean on an abiotic, frontier environment that has only been accessible to powerful techno-industrial elites?

Outline of the book

In Chapter 2, I present a long-run historical sociology of NewSpace which explains the emergence of the nascent space mining industry and this contentious private property law. I pay particular attention to the *High Frontier* project of NewSpace progenitor Gerard O'Neill (1977). Responding to the first *Limits to Growth* report (Meadows et al. 1972), O'Neill presented space mining and colonisation as a techno-utopian solution to ecological crisis and did so with an anarcho-libertarian political ideology that continues to inform NewSpace. I set NewSpace's political-economic history against the evolution of the neoliberal political network. What ideological and programmatic affinities can we identify in NewSpace and neoliberalism? How does NewSpace cosmopolitics challenge the egalitarianism and fairness envisioned under the OST (1967)?

In Chapter 3, I focus on the legal geography of outer space and the OST's non-appropriation principle (1967, Art. 2). The novelty of space mining and the utopianism of NewSpace mask what is ostensibly a well-worn narrative in human history: the enclosure of 'the commons' through private property rights and sovereign powers of appropriation. In keeping with American libertarianism, NewSpace actors appear to invoke a natural law justification for individual rights to private property (Locke 2005 [1690]). I critique this position by drawing on Karl Polanyi's (2001) institutional political economy of enclosure. The Polanyian account of state-backed private property is helpful in approaching the legality of laws like the CSLCA and the broader questions of economic justice that are at play in the enclosure of the space commons. Yet outer space problematises traditional narratives of enclosure – what do categories of 'land' and 'property' mean in the micro-gravity expanses of the

Solar System? How can we theorise authority and power on the uninhabited and landless frontier?

The CSLCA and laws like it belong to a different political history than private property in land. While mineral rights also derive from the sovereign authority to delegate private ownership within a given territory, the CSLCA evokes the enclosure of a different form of estate – the mineral commonwealth. The history of mining law reveals a much closer relationship between state power and private ownership rights than that of land tenure, and this further undermines claims that the CSLCA is legal under international law. In Chapter 4, I introduce the term 'mineral sovereignty' to excavate the entwined, subterranean genealogies of states, corporations and mineral rights (Walker & Johnson 2018). Mineral sovereignty denotes the constitutional authority to legitimise miners' access to mineral estates, and the apparent ability of mining firms to exert extra-parliamentary power over the jurisdictions in which they operate. What parallels can we draw between the history of mineral sovereignty and the CSLCA – such as sovereign claims to precious metals in pre-modernity or social democratic distributions of benefits from mineral estates of the 19th–20th centuries? What can the passage of the CSLCA tell us about contemporary democracy and the rule of law?

In Chapter 5, I will describe the emergence of international space law – particularly the OST – and legal characteristics of outer space as it emerged in dialogue with comparable regimes in international law, such as those governing the high seas. The OST represents an uneasy compromise between the interests of the United States and the rest of the world in the space commons. Key principles of the OST emerged through the US's Cold War anticipatory geostrategy: the introduction of *mare liberum* ('free seas') rights to freely use global commons effectively safeguarded US corporate and military freedoms within these commons. In exploring the political-legal history of the OST, I describe it as the 'space constitution' – both in the sense that it acts as a foundational legal document from which common rights are derived and that it seeks to constrain the exercise of state power (Gabrynowicz 2004). While the commons of space are yet to be exploited on a material level, the very definition of celestial bodies as commons is being contested beforehand (Hertzfeld, Weeden & Johnson 2016). I argue that NewSpace mining can thus be read as an agent of neoliberal constitutionalism (Schneidermann 2013; Purdy 2014), whereby the commons 'constitution' of UN treaty law is effectively displaced with a pre-emptive and unilateral legal regime predicated on private ownership. NewSpace actors have argued that the universal rights prescribed under the OST actually support private mining operations: the freedom to use and explore space can be exercised by corporations under the competitive logic of market capitalism, nothing in the OST explicitly prohibits private ownership of space resources, and benefits from space mining will 'trickle down' to the rest of humanity in any case (Kfir & Perry 2017). What might this mean for future developments in international space resources law?

In Chapter 6, I position these questions of the space commons within an interesting episode of NewSpace myth-making. 'The frontier' is a particularly potent and well-worn trope in NewSpace discourse: as anomic spaces in which state authority is diminished, frontier myths feed into NewSpace's libertarian patina (Parker 2009, pp. 89–91). The NewSpace anti-statist narrative is most explicit in the documentary, *Orphans of Apollo* (2008), which I analyse as a case study in NewSpace mythology. The movie's promotional material is evocative: the NewSpace protagonists describe themselves as a 'rebel alliance of entrepreneurs', brandishing the Jolly Roger flag of the pirate as they claim to reject government authority on the off-world frontier (Free Radical Productions 2008). There is some irony in invoking the pirate. I argue that the state guarantee of frontier property *does* reflect the age of maritime colonialism, but through the less rebellious figures of the privateer and the charter company – the commercial vanguards of Empire. What does this mean for NewSpace libertarianism? How far can we analogise space mining with the violence of the colonial frontier in the age of seafaring? Is space mining actually a benign form of colonialism, as is claimed in NewSpace narratives?

In Chapter 7, I return to NewSpace's claims of environmentalism and link the off-world commons with environmental law on Earth. Gerard O'Neill's techno-utopian environmentalism is perpetuated by NewSpace advocates and commercial entities, who optimistically reject the claim 'that the advancement of our technological civilization must mean the decline of our ecosystem' (SFF, in Tumlinson 2003; see also Bezos, in Blue Origin 2019). Yet I will argue that NewSpace environmentalism rests upon speculative techno-fixes, in which an off-world deliverance from ecological catastrophe rests upon the utter transcendence of biophysical limits. Consistent with neoliberal environmentalism, space mining will not provide remedies for ecological crisis, but instead offers an elitist escape route from its consequences. How do we counter NewSpace's post-nature fantasies and their undermining of international laws of the global commons? Can we confront planetary ecological crises in a more pragmatic sense, while also working towards more inclusive uses of the off-world commons? I argue that Joseph Sax's (1969) work on the public trust doctrine might help us realise more responsible and equitable futures on Earth and in space (Babcock 2019). A means to go in peace for all Earthkind, as it were.

Notes

1 While 'mankind' is the exact wording of the *Outer Space Treaty* and several other instruments of international law, I have used 'humankind' when not directly quoting from these treaties, declarations and resolutions.
2 Formally, the *Treaty on Principles Governing the Activities of States in the Exploration and Use of Outer Space, including the Moon and Other Celestial Bodies* (1967).
3 Others have tried to introduce off-world property ownership, though without the legal recognition of nation states or international governmental organisations.

Owning extra-terrestrial 'property' might be as simple as visiting the website of Lunar Embassy. For a modest price, one can buy a certificate allocating them an acre of real estate on the Moon, Mars, Mercury or Venus (Lunar Embassy 2024a). The Embassy's owner, Dennis Hope, attempts to reassure any sceptical customers that their extraterrestrial title is recognised and protected by the sovereignty of the 'Galactic Government', of which Hope has declared himself Galactic President (Lunar Embassy 2024b).

4 This book focuses primarily on space mining and space colonisation as these projects appear in NewSpace discourse. However, there are a range of space industries that could be categorised as 'NewSpace', including companies focused on rocket manufacturing and launch services like Elon Musk's SpaceX, space tourism firms like Richard Branson's Virgin Galactic, and highly specialised engineering start-ups like Made In Space (who are developing microgravity applications of 3D printing technology).

5 While I make occasional reference to commercial space activity outside of the United States (in particular to Russia and Luxembourg, the United States' traditional rival in space and the first nation to follow its lead in domestic space resources law, respectively), this book is weighted towards American NewSpace. This is due in large part to NewSpace's American locus and the US's position as 'first movers' in off-world private property rights.

6 I am reticent to use the term 'social network analysis' or network 'mapping', since these methodologies generally involve quantitative analysis or visualisation techniques that are perhaps less appropriate for the diffuse, multi-sector NewSpace network which encompasses entrepreneurialism, 'grassroots' advocacy, public sector space officials and mainstream lobbyist networks.

7 Formally, the *Agreement Governing the Activities of States on the Moon and Other Celestial Bodies* (1979). It is sometimes referred to as the 'Moon Treaty', though I have used *Moon Agreement* throughout.

2 NewSpace and neoliberalism

How have we arrived at laws that recognise a corporation's right to own resources extracted from the celestial bodies of our Solar System? We can attribute the existence of the *Commercial Space Launch Competitiveness Act* (2015) to recent lobbying from a now-defunct space mining firm – Planetary Resources. However, the road to private property in space resources can be traced to older origins, in a rich and compelling narrative that begins with the cosmist philosophy of pre-Soviet Russia and winds its way through several political-economic milestones of the 20th and 21st centuries. This chapter presents a long-run sociological and political-economic account of (predominantly) American spacefaring, entwined with a similar narrative that charts the historical development of neoliberalism. In particular, I will explore the work of physicist Gerard O'Neill (1977), whose work sought to realise a space colonisation project predicated on off-world resource utilisation, and which inspired organisations that, in different ways, would come to shape domestic and international space law. In recent decades, these NewSpace organisations and enterprises have enjoyed the support of the neoliberal Atlas Network. This chapter elucidates ideological, programmatic and structural affinities between NewSpace and the neoliberal political network, with the goal of questioning whether private space mining would proceed for the benefit of all humankind.

First, what is NewSpace? 'NewSpace' is a term of historical periodisation which attempts to demarcate a new epoch of entrepreneur-led space innovation that has or will supplant the 'old' space era of government-centred space programs. The 'NewSpace' label appears to originate in 2004 with the Space Frontier Foundation (SFF), a civil society organisation based in the United States. The SFF is 'dedicated to opening up the space frontier to human settlement' and 'unleash[ing] the power of free enterprise and lead [ing] a united humanity permanently into the Solar System' (SFF 2023a).[1] The term 'NewSpace' makes the distinction with an 'old space' era, which was characterised by Cold War geostrategic imperatives, and massive state patronage and coordination of superpower space activity. Those who self-apply the NewSpace moniker see themselves as breaking the dominance of the National Aeronautics and Space Administration (NASA) and the massive

DOI: 10.1201/9781003293613-2

arms and aerospace manufacturers like Boeing, Lockheed Martin and Northrop Grumman that it frequently contracts – an arrangement the SFF founders characterised as 'the bureaucratic nature of the space program' (SFF 2023b).

Contemporary NewSpace is situated within a larger constellation of actors, beliefs and texts that could be loosely aggregated as 'space enthusiasm'. 'Pro-space' may have been the more widely used label in academic research, an umbrella term that links together diverse forms of space advocacy regardless of their individual ideologies or policy goals (Bainbridge 1976; Michaud 1986; Launius 2003; Dickens & Ormrod 2007; Ormrod 2007). Writing in 1986, historian Michael Michaud suggested that 'pro-space' was essentially 'convenient shorthand' for these inter-related and often competing interests exhibited by a diverse group of advocates:

> It can refer to their support for larger and better government space programs; to a desire to see more activity by individuals, companies, nations, and the human species in the extraterrestrial realm; to a belief that the intelligent use of space offers solutions to national and world problems; or to a philosophical, even emotional conviction that human expansion into space is a natural and desirable next step in the evolution of life of Earth. (Michaud 1986, p. xx)

As I will demonstrate in this chapter, recent space mining firms like Planetary Resources, Deep Space Industries (DSI) and Moon Express are an outgrowth of both the 'pro-space' philosophy and the specific commercial orientation of NewSpace.[2]

While the NewSpace network is diffuse, such that I will refer to it as a 'network' as opposed to 'community' or 'movement', there are unifying precepts. In using the term, I draw on the work of anthropologist David Valentine (2012), who characterises the NewSpace imaginary as the 'more expansive, positive, and indeed, *urgent* orientation toward a future of space settlement, with commercialization seen as the logical path towards this goal' (Valentine 2012, p. 1049, emphasis in original). This future-oriented axiom is shared across a network of entrepreneurs, scientists, engineers, policy wonks, science fiction fans, advocates and the occasional Silicon Valley billionaire (Valentine 2012, p. 1047). In their rejection of the 'old space' model, this vision of space colonisation is often inflected with discourses of individual liberty and economic freedom. To use the words of NewSpace advocate Rick Tumlinson, Newspace '[celebrates] the spirit of exploration and individuality' while seeking to 'harvest the resources of space' (Tumlinson 2003, p. 89). In NewSpace ideology, humanity needs to colonise space and 'big government' is not the way to do it.

Within NewSpace advocacy and discourse, the commercial incentive to use off-world resources is often backgrounded or sidelined by recourse to grander narratives of the off-world civilising mission. For example, as SpaceX was becoming increasingly influential in the American aerospace sector, Elon Musk articulated his motivations as owner and CEO:

> The reason I'm doing SpaceX is not because I think the rocket business is the easiest place to make money, it's an extraordinarily difficult place to make money, and would be pretty low on the list of things you'd want to try if maximizing your wealth was your goal. But … I really want us to become a true space-faring civilization and ultimately be on a path to becoming a multi-planetary civilization and going out there and exploring the stars and making true the things that one sees in sci-fi movies and reads in books about the future. That's my goal for SpaceX … . (2010, cited in Valentine 2012, pp. 1060–1061)

'Making true' the fantasies of science fiction consumed in their childhoods appears to be a prominent motivation for many people engaged in the NewSpace movement (O'Neill 1977, p. 59; Ormrod 2007, p. 264). Robotic rovers or public-sector astronauts shouldn't have all the fun, and the sci-fi inspirations of NewSpace seep into more pragmatic outputs. For example, SpaceX's Falcon series of rockets derive their name from the 'Millennium Falcon', the spaceship of *Star Wars*' smuggler Han Solo, the original renegade entrepreneur of outer space (Musk, in *HitRecord on TV* 2014). Robert Heinlein is a popular author for some NewSpace advocates (Zubrin, cited in Riesman 2013). In Heinlein's *The Moon is a Harsh Mistress* (1966), a tale of lunar colonists revolting against an oppressive command economy, Heinlein introduced the expression, 'there ain't no such thing as a free lunch'. Milton Friedman, neoliberal economist and advisor to the Thatcher and Reagan governments, was a fan of that one too (Friedman 1993, p. 10).

My exploration of NewSpace is indebted to the spacefaring histories of Michaud (1986), Kilgore (2003) and McCray (2013), among others. However, there is a tendency in the literature to focus on socio-cultural understandings of 'The Vision', while the political economy of spacefaring is given less attention. For example, Kilgore's work on 'astrofuturism' is valuable in positioning NewSpace within 'the tradition of speculative fiction and science writing inaugurated by scientists and science popularizers during the space race' (2003, p. 2). As such, his account is weighted towards the intersection of science fiction and the core space projects of the 20th century, and pre-dates the proliferation of commercial firms in the 2010s.

Kilgore's work and other accounts of the politics of spacefaring are worth revisiting following the advent of domestic laws recognising the right to own space resources. Dickens and Ormrod (2007, p. 4) have introduced the apt term 'cosmic elite' to describe how the space entrepreneur is the latest persona to be bestowed with cosmic privilege, like priests and shamans, Enlightenment astronomers and Cold War strategists. Their account of off-world capitalism invokes Marxist geographer David Harvey's (2004) notion of the 'spatial fix' (Shammas & Holen 2019, pp. 5–6). Ormrod's (2007) psychoanalytical approach to broader pro-space movements reveals the narcissism of 'needing' to visit space and the fantasies of omnipotence and conquering that come with it. Writing before the advent of private property and space mining start-ups, he seems to echo one of his NewSpace interviewees who claimed that the harnessing of commercial incentive was merely 'window dressing' for the loftier goal of space settlement (Ormrod 2007, p. 263). Legislative assertions of the right to privately own space resources are now part of the spacefaring zeitgeist – it is now more difficult to accept Ormrod's summation that this movement is 'constituted predominantly of people without any financial or political gain to be made from the success of their lobbying efforts' (2007, p. 262).

My exploration of NewSpace as a manifestation of neoliberalism serves to augment previous research that describes this movement in related but imprecise terms, such as noting its libertarian tenor (Launius 2003; Ormrod 2009, p. 126; Parker 2009) or describing it as one component within 'space capitalism' (Dickens & Ormrod 2007; Shammas & Holen 2019). On this note, Genovese (2017, pp. 77–84) investigates specific case studies that might point to the neoliberalisation of the American space program (and counter-movements against this) – such as the 1973 Skylab astronauts 'strike' against surveillance and efficiency pressures placed on them by NASA. Parker (2009, pp. 90–92), meanwhile, describes the libertarian attacks that space advocates have mounted on NASA and the US state, and draws attention to work of the Cato Institute (Hudgins 2002). However, his description of Cato as a 'libertarian' organisation (Parker 2009, p. 91) is not cognisant of this think-tank's centrality in the Atlas Network. In spite of a 'small government' or *laissez-faire* veneer, neoliberal politics enlists a 'strong state as both producer and guarantor of a stable market society' (Mirowski 2009, p. 435). NewSpace cosmo-politics has similarly invoked a libertarian ethos, and yet the state has been indispensable in supporting space exploration and, through the advent of domestic laws that recognise private property in space resources, is likely to be in the future.

In this chapter, I will argue that NewSpace and private property rights for space resources are manifestations of neoliberalism. This realisation is important for the future of the space commons, rather than merely being 'libertarian' or 'capitalistic' in their outlook and rhetoric. If the first movers into space colonisation have evident social, ideological and programmatic affinities with neoliberalism, it is unlikely that space exploration and settlement would proceed, in the words of the *Outer Space Treaty*, 'for the benefit of all mankind'. Valentine aptly notes the resonance between NewSpace and neoliberal governmentality; he describes how the NewSpace project rests upon a model of government where the state is:

> … reduced to an enabler of private citizens' and corporations' economic objectives, with social good emerging from the activities of private actors (indeed, the removal of government restrictions, taxes and regulation is itself seen as a social good in this framework). (2012, p. 1054)

I will extend Valentine's argument by comparing NewSpace political ideology with specific neoliberal concepts and arguments, such as neoliberal constitutionalism (Hayek 1986), the conflation of social democracy with totalitarianism, public choice theory (Buchanan & Tullock 1962) and the pursuit of market-based solutions to ecological crises (crises that are caused often by the market in the first place).

However, in Phillip Mirowski's words, 'Neoliberalism turns out to be anything but an easily and clearly defined contemporary political philosophy once we venture beyond popular representations' (2009, p. 421). As a way of cutting through the ambiguities and variabilities of neoliberal politics, I follow Mirowski and Plehwe's (2009) 'networked' approach which emphasises that neoliberalism has been propagated through a particular set of individuals and institutions, now coordinated through the global Atlas Network. The entwined narrative I present here – the political sideshow of NewSpace set against the dominant economic paradigm of contemporary capitalism – culminates in the passage of the *Commercial Space Launch Competitiveness Act* (2015), where Atlas neoliberals have supported the passage of US laws that will likely shape human futures in outer space.

1920s–1969: the pre-histories of NewSpace and neoliberalism

We will begin in the 1920s, by exploring the roots of NewSpace philosophy in the utopian writings of early rocket scientists and early neoliberal thought that developed in the same period. From here, we will explore the establishment of NASA in 1958 as a direct coordinator of the American space economy, and close with the climax of the Apollo Program (the first lunar landing in 1969). The immediate post-war period is also when the Mont Pelèrin Society (MPS) is founded by Friedrich Hayek, Milton Friedman and other neoliberal economists – this organisation becomes the fountainhead of the contemporary Atlas Network. The pre-histories I present here are disparate, and the two movements develop through contrasting institutional frameworks. Neoliberalism forms around an opposition to socialism and centralised planning, while the early decades of spaceflight were spurred almost entirely by totalitarian technocracy and centrally coordinated research and development. By discussing early neoliberal thought, we can see ideological parallels between select appeals for 'constrained democracy' that have emerged in NewSpace discourse, and the 'limited democracy' espoused by Hayek.

Freedom and totalitarianism

Early science fiction literature combined the rational calculus of the natural sciences with utopian yearnings for emancipation and social experimentation – much like contemporary NewSpace. Modern space engineering owes much to scientists from the Russian cosmist tradition, predominantly Konstantin

Tsiolkovsky (1857–1935), in addition to American rocket pioneer Robert Goddard (1882–1945) and German physicist-engineer Hermann Oberth (1894–1989). Tsiolkovsky, Goddard and Oberth had all consumed the work of Jules Verne, in particular his *De la terre à la lune* (*From the Earth to the Moon* 1865), which had offered some accurate calculations for potential escape velocities from Earth – albeit using a cannon to fire astronauts to the Moon (McCurdy 2011, p. 16).

Science and technology historian W. Patrick McCray has coined the term 'visioneer' (2013), a portmanteau of visionary and engineer that captures the pragmatic and idealistic impulses exhibited by Tsiolkovsky and Goddard (and later 'old' and 'new' space figureheads like Werner von Braun and Gerard O'Neill, respectively). Technical design of rockets and spacecraft (which, for Tsiolkovsky, pre-dated their actualisation by several decades) merged with speculations on spaceflight's potential for transforming and emancipating society. In his novel *Beyond the Planet Earth*, Tsiolkovsky described outer space as a cornucopia of material abundance and unoccupied space:

> ... how vast and free is the space that surrounds Earth; you know that it is filled with light; you know that it is empty. It's a sad thought that we are crowded on Earth, treasuring every sunny corner where we can raise crops and build our homes and live in peace and tranquility [sic]. While I was wandering in the emptiness about our rocket, it was the vastness, the freedom and lightness of movement that impressed me - that tremendous quantity of solar energy going to waste, uselessly ... Who is there to stop Men from building their greenhouses and their palaces here and living in peace and plenty? ... This will give us the possibility of operating various kinds of solar engines, welding metals and performing a great many manufacturing operations without the use of fuel. (cited in Michaud 1986, pp.63-64)

Tsiolkovsky envisioned off-world 'greenhouses and palaces' – in other words, life-sustaining agriculture and centres of governance. This notion of 'off-worlding' industry and society would become central to the 1970s visioneering of Gerard O'Neill and the genesis of NewSpace.[3]

While Tsiolkovksy's utopia was generally devoid of political polemic, historian Gerard DeGroot has noted that he equated 'weightlessness and liberty', as on the space frontier 'one could find freedom and fulfilment' (2006, p. 5). Tsiolkosvsky yearned to be 'freer than a bird in flight ... [and] unfettered by gravitation', and outer space heralded the 'perfection of mankind and its individual members' (cited in DeGroot 2006, p. 4). Tsiolkovsky espoused a 'Promethean urge to remake everything that surrounds us' and 'brought a messianic and transformative vision to the cause of spaceflight' (Siddiqi 2008, p. 266, 267). After his death in 1935, the Soviet Union would declare him 'the father of cosmonautics' (McDougall 1997, p. 19).

To my knowledge, Ludwig von Mises, Friedrich Hayek and other economists central to the development of neoliberal thought and policy were entirely disinterested in the question of outer space. They were nonetheless Tsiolkovsky's contemporaries, with the seeds of neoliberalism being planted in Europe in the 1920s against a backdrop of emerging socialist government. NewSpace rhetoric has described private property as an essential human freedom (NSS 2019) and has framed centrally coordinated space activity as unfree (Tea Party in Space 2014a). This sentiment echoes principles that emerged in neoliberal thought during this period (Lippman 1938; Hayek 1986).

Pre-war Vienna was the nucleus of early neoliberalism, in response to socialist gains across Europe in the wake of WW1. Communist revolutions in Russia and neighbouring Hungary, and Germany's social democratic Weimar Republic, made clear to those in the intellectual scene of 'Red Vienna' that liberalism was no longer an unquestionable economic or political orthodoxy (Polanyi, in Block & Somers 2014, p. 5). Ascendant trade unionism highlighted that the collective was evidently as important as liberalism's ubiquitous individual, and this individual was neither inherently self-interested nor would the 'invisible hand' inevitably deliver socially desirable outcomes. For Mises and Hayek, among others, the challenge was to restore the credibility of a liberal, *laissez-faire* form of economics in the face of its obvious failure to deliver material well-being and social security for all individuals in society (Plehwe 2009, p. 10).

Neoliberalism and space exploration were spurred (in different ways) by the rise of totalitarianism in Europe. Staying with the former, political economist Dieter Plehwe describes how the 'neo' got into neoliberalism (2009). He notes that the Viennese period was yet to produce a critique of classical liberalism, and still retained a largely negative understanding of the role the state could play in the functioning of markets (Plehwe 2009, p. 11). Plehwe outlines how neoliberal ideas, as we would now recognise them, began to crystallise in the wake of the 1937 publication of American political commentator Walter Lippman's *(An Inquiry into the Principles of) The Good Society* (1938). Lippman mounted an impassioned rejection of what he called 'the cult of the state as provider and savior' (Lippman 1938, pp. 37–38). He railed against both the totalitarianism ascendant in Europe in the mid-1930s, and against planned economies and bureaucracies more generally. Lippman homogenised fascism, communism, Keynesianism and the social liberalism of the Roosevelt Administration's (1933–1945) New Deal, and critiqued these diverse political forms as 'collectivism' and 'directed societies'. He believed 'there is nothing in the collectivist principle which marks any stopping place short of the totalitarian state' (ibid, p. 52). This 'slippery slope' argument was later echoed by Hayek (1986).

Lippman articulated a core ideological tenet of neoliberalism that would later be central to the philosophy of Hayek and the MPS: the defining of 'totalitarianism primarily with regard to the absence of private property, rather than with the more commonplace reference to a lack of democracy or countervailing political power' (Plehwe 2009, p. 13). There are examples where NewSpace advocates have similarly aggregated alternatives to economic liberalism – particularly when they are articulated in international laws seeking to constrain market freedoms in the service of a common, social good – and portrayed them as restrictive, unjust collectivism (NSS 2009, p. 6; Gump 2018). In the words of the National Space Society:

> … private property is one of the principal freedoms guaranteed by our nation's Constitution. Without this protection, individuals also would lose the safety of their persons and political rights. (NSS 2009, p. 3)

Liberal democratic constitutions of course protect a range of civil and human rights. However, NewSpace and neoliberalism disproportionately emphasise the safeguarding of rights to private property – as if private property were important to 'the safety of their persons' in the hostile environs of the off-world.

The Great Depression was an unparalleled socioeconomic catastrophe brought about by unfettered free-market capitalism and its 'animal spirits' (Keynes 1936). Arriving in its immediate wake, Lippmann's critique of state intervention in the market rested upon 'a principle (to say the least) leaning against the wind' (Plehwe 2009, p. 13). While much of the world was leaning into Keynesian macroeconomic management and welfare state protections, Lippman argued instead for a minimal state, confined to the basic provision of law and order such that voluntary, contractual exchange could be maintained:

> In a free society the state does not administer the affairs of men. It administers justice among men who conduct their own affairs. (Cited in Plehwe 2009, p. 13)

Karl Polanyi, also of the Red Vienna intellectual scene (who I discuss in the following chapter), noted that participation in the market was effectively involuntary for those multitudes 'torn from [their] roots and all meaningful environment' by industrial capitalism (Polanyi 2001 [1944], p. 87). This is a fact given less emphasis in neoliberalism's utopian 'free society'. Regardless, Lippman's attempt at revitalising a philosophy of government and law predicated on the preservation of individual economic liberties resonated with liberal economists on both sides of the Atlantic.

In 1938, a year after the publication of *The Good Society*, the Colloque Walter Lippman was held in Paris. It is here where the term 'neoliberalism' was coined: a 'new liberalism' that was apparently a more popular term than other suggestions like *néo-capitalisme* or *libéralisme positif* (Plehwe 2009, p. 13).[4] In Paris, some of the more recognisable tenets of neoliberalism emerged, chiefly the acceptance of the need for a strong and impartial state that respected and safeguarded free enterprise, competition between firms and the operation of the price mechanism – the latter considered the prime coordinator of economic relationships (Plehwe 2009, p. 14). There is a clear aporia already evident in this embryonic stage of neoliberalism, as Mitchell Dean describes: an authoritarian streak where 'a strong state was needed [paradoxically] to promote economic freedom and markets, and to neutralize the pathologies' of parliamentary democracy and the welfare-state demands made within it (2014, p. 155). The neoliberal 'double truth' (Mirowski 2009; Dean 2014) is best encapsulated by German political economist and Colloque participant, Alexander Rüstow, who had summarised the new liberalism as 'Free Economy – Strong State' (cited in Dean 2014, p. 154).

Two strong states had indeed emerged on the continent by the time of the Colloque Walter Lippman – Nazi Germany and the Soviet Union. The outbreak of WW2 postponed the development of an organised and politically active neoliberalism and, returning to our other narrative, the two most powerful totalitarian states in human history gave rise to modern rocketry and the first actualisations of the spaceflight vision. Rather than preserving free enterprise, competition or individual liberties, the National Socialist and Communist dictatorships had increasingly large military-industrial complexes coordinated under varying degrees of command economy.[5] The Allied powers would also rely on central planning as the backbone of their war economies, including the coordination of privately owned arms manufacturers in the United States and the nationalisation of arms and ordinance manufacturers in the UK. However, the American development of rocketry did not begin until after WW2. Core developments in the technologies of spaceflight can instead be attributed to the antitheses of the 'free society'.

The Soviet Union would become the United States' key rival in the main thrust of space research and engineering during what Lippman, writing for *Foreign Affairs*, had dubbed 'the Cold War' (Time Magazine, 1947). Walter McDougall's (1997) research is particularly valuable for approaching this early political history of the 'space race'. The first Russian rocket scientists had formed the All-Union Society for the Study of Interplanetary Communication (OIMS) in 1924, and developed research, outreach and publication practices that were initially independent of the Soviet state (McDougall 1997, p. 27). The OIMS began hosting conferences with the regime's Central Bureau for the Study of the Problems of Rockets soon after, shifting rocket science 'from theory to praxis' and into Soviet wartime technoscience (ibid, p. 27). From 1930 onwards, engineers like Sergei Korolev, Tsiolkovsky's student Fridrikh Tsander and Valentin Gushko worked on rocket and missile design (McDougall 1997, pp. 36–37). Following Stalinist purges, Korolev joined Russian aviation pioneers in the *sharaga* labour camps that imprisoned those with technical expertise, '[resuming] their mental work on behalf of their own masters, despite a miserable climate, meagre rations, and the presence of armed guards' (ibid, p. 38). What began as a Tsiolkovian dream of emancipatory spaceflight became subsumed within an R&D base forged by Stalinisation (ibid, pp. 39–40).

Soviet wartime rocketry was limited to shorter-range missiles. It was through Nazi Germany's coercion of intellectual and physical labour that the first notable rocket program was realised (albeit reaching only the lower boundaries of what could be considered 'outer' space). In inter-war Germany, there was a brief period of amateur rocket science in the form of rocket club Verein für Raumschiffahrt (Society for Space Travel; formed in 1927), which included Werner von Braun, Willy Ley and Hermann Oberth (all of whom became key personnel in the Apollo Program). In late-Weimar Germany, rocket technology and its progenitors were also co-opted into the machinery and bureaucracy of war. Shortly before the Nazi Party took power, the *Reichswehr* army sent members of its ordinance division to visit the VfR 'rocketport' in Berlin and recruited key personnel in Ley and von Braun (McDougall 1997, p. 43; Kilgore 2003, p. 70).[6] As in Russia, 'the rocketeers did not find state support – the state found them' (McDougall 1997, p. 43).

Kilgore describes how early 'astrofuturist' figures like Ley and von Braun would be transformed by the Third Reich from 'a group of idealistic backyard experimenters into the technical managers of a large-scale enterprise that could use slave labour as an efficient means of production' (Kilgore 2003, p. 55). Between 1944 and 1945, the V-2 rocket production lines of Peenemünde were reliant on slave labour from neighbouring concentration camps (McDougall 1997, p. 44; Kilgore 2003, pp. 54–55). In McDougall's words: 'If too weak to work, slaves were left to expire – 150 per day – human sacrifices on the altar of machines and power' (1997, p. 44). In mid-1944, V-2 rockets began to breach the upper atmosphere on their trajectories towards London, Antwerp and a host of other British and European cities. The first rocket-powered flights beyond the atmosphere were conducted in the service of genocidal totalitarianism.

At this point in time, Friedrich Hayek was lecturing at the London School of Economics, which had been evacuated to Cambridge during the war years (Donnelly 2016). It was during this onslaught of Nazi technoscience that Hayek had written what would become one of neoliberalism's foundational texts, the *Road to Serfdom* (1986 [1944]). He had commenced his work by saying that the United States and UK were in danger of repeating the fate of Germany – 'though the road be long, it is one on which it becomes more difficult to turn back as one advances' (Hayek 1986, p. 2). Yet his concern was as much with those social democracies of Weimar Germany or Sweden 'held up by progressives as an example to be imitated' as it was with National Socialism (ibid, p. 3). Like Lippman, Hayek's political economy took aim at collectivism and centralised planning. He was concerned that in Western democracies there was 'the same determination that the organization of the nation we have achieved for purposes of defense shall be retained for the purposes of creation' (ibid, p. 2). Along with the centrally coordinated war economies, Hayek asserted that planning of any kind was problematic, for it was predicated on 'ideals whose realization would lead straight to abhorred tyranny' (ibid, p. 4). Hayek believed that it was only through the distributed decision-making of property-owning individuals could freedom prevail, rather than vesting control in a centralised authority.

> What our generation has forgotten is that the system of private property is the most important guarantee of freedom, not only for those who own property, but scarcely less for those who do not … If all the means of production were vested in a single hand, whether it be nominally that of 'society' as a whole or that of a dictator, whoever exercises this control has complete power over us. (ibid, pp. 103–104)

The Road to Serfdom provided an early conceptualisation of Hayek's notion of 'spontaneous order' – the ideological commitment that 'in the ordering of our affairs we should make as much use as possible of the spontaneous forces of society, and resort as little as possible to coercion' (Hayek 1986, p. 17).[7]

Yet, for a project motivated by the spectre of totalitarianism and dictatorship, *The Road to Serfdom* contained the early seeds of an 'authoritarian liberalism' that would pervade Hayek's later work (Cristi 1984). Consistent with the 'Strong State – Free Economy' disavowal of *laissez-faire* articulated by Rüstow, Hayek believed in 'deliberately creating a system within which competition will work as beneficially as possible' – a legal order benefitting market capitalism that was scarcely 'spontaneous' (Hayek 1986, p. 13). In *The Road*, Hayek hinted that this system should entail 'democracy with definitely limited powers' (Hayek 1986, p. 173). His desire for constitutional limits on democratic power contradicts any concern he may have had about tyranny, and this contradictory position would become realised through the explicit alliances that neoliberal theorists would later forge with dictatorial regimes in the pursuit of trade liberalisation (Mirowski 2009, p. 445; Fischer 2009).

Advocates for commercial activity in space have argued that moving away from government-led programs represents the 'democratisation' of space activity (Lubin, in Planetary Resources 2018; Beck, in Shammas & Holen 2019, p. 3). However, there is some evidence of a Hayekian distrust of democracy within the NewSpace movement, or at least a desire to render the space economy immune from politics. Peter Thiel, an investor in space mining firms, has previously derided 'the unthinking demos that guides "social democracy"' (2009). In milder terms, the National Space Society has noted failings of US space exploration due to governments with 'inherent pressure to think in the short-term and perhaps just to the next election' (2012, p. 6). At face value, this statement reflects NewSpace frustration at the absence of a compelling, long-term vision for American space policy – the NSS also notes that industry is equally capable of such short-termism (NSS 2012, p. 6).

NewSpace's commercial orientation derives in part from the realisation that the priorities of the *demos* (and thus the national budget) may be closer to home than the off-world frontier, but is there more to 'NewSpace democracy' than disquiet about the tyranny of the majority? Consider this provocative edict from Moon Express CEO, Bob Richards:

> ... the U.S. government should in principle enact laws that assure freedom of enterprise in space, making it illegal for the government to deny or restrict private sector space activity. (Richards 2017, p. 4)

Richards makes this statement while arguing for streamlined regulatory processes concerning launch approval and goes on to say that these laws should 'not breach U.S. obligations under international treaties' (ibid, p. 4). However, beneath his concern about bureaucratic inefficiency is the notion that the space economy should be rendered immune from democratic accountability (made during invited Congressional testimony, no less). Is this a case of extra-terrestrial liberty requiring extra-parliamentary freedoms – to be well and truly above any laws that could constrain space enterprise? In Chapters 4 and 5, we will return to questions of 'space democracy' in relation to corporate lobbying and in international law.

The NASA and the MPS

We will now turn to two landmark moments in the history of space exploration and neoliberalism: (1) the establishment of NASA in 1958 and the substantive beginning of the space age (2) the establishment of a transnational neoliberal network through the MPS in 1947, which is the foundation of the modern-day Atlas Network. In the 21st century, the Atlas Network has supported the NewSpace movement and played a role in shaping US space resources policy. The neoliberal creed of the MPS highlights the disjuncture between NewSpace's rejection of centrally planned spacefaring and the Keynesian foundations of the American space program. At this point in our entwined narrative, however, neoliberalism and NewSpace remain disparate projects.

As far as the United States is concerned, post-war neoliberal thought was largely confined to the work of the Chicago School of Economics and would not penetrate economic policy and public discourse until the 1980s (through the Reagan Administration). In 1947, the Volker Fund – managed by the 'strident anti-New Deal conservative' Harold Luhnow – had provided funding for Hayek's temporary position at the University of Chicago (Van Horn & Mirowski 2009, p. 141). With the Foundation for Economic Education, the Volker Fund also assisted the establishment of the MPS, which took its name from the Swiss resort overlooking Lake Geneva where it was first held (ibid, p. 140). Van Horn and Mirowski's archival research into the establishment of both organisations reveals that Hayek and Milton Friedman were keenly aware that – contrary to the detached 'inveterate optimists' or 'curmudgeonly elitists' of classical liberal thought – a neoliberal economic order would need to be consciously constructed (ibid, p. 160).

Core tenets of neoliberalism were established through the MPS and the early years of the Chicago School. The MPS Statement of Aims was deliberated upon during the 1947 meeting and now adorns their website (MPS n.d.).

> The central values of civilization are in danger. Over large stretches of the Earth's surface the essential conditions of human dignity and freedom have already disappeared. In others they are under constant menace from the development of current tendencies of policy. The position of the individual and the voluntary group are progressively undermined by extensions of arbitrary power.
>
> The [MPS] holds that these developments have been fostered by … a decline of belief in private property and the competitive market; for without the diffused power and initiative associated with these institutions it is difficult to imagine a society in which freedom may be effectively preserved. (MPS n.d.)

The orientation of neoliberalism towards the state is evident in the MPS' founding principles, confining its role to the preservation of market freedoms. The neoliberal policy program emerged from MPS work that centred on the 'redefinition of the functions of the state', 'establishing minimum standards by means not inimical to initiative and functioning of the market' and creating and safeguarding an international order of peace, liberty and 'harmonious international economic relations' (MPS n.d.).

I have not discovered a great deal of interest from MPS theorists on America's costly involvement in the space race. Yet the founding of the American space program was predicated on a means of production that was highly coordinated by state agencies, with a much broader scope for government decision-making than the 'diffused power' of market forces envisioned by the MPS. In the wake of the Axis Powers' defeat, the United States commenced its Cold War rivalry with the Soviet Union – a highly militarised clash between communism and capitalism. It did so through a huge injection of public funds in what amounted to a massive public works project facilitated by centralised planning and bureaucracy. In 1958, the Eisenhower Administration (1953–1961) passed the *National Aeronautics and Space Act*, which established a federal 'civilian agency exercising control over aeronautical and space activities' (NASA Act 1958, s. 102). This would, of course, be NASA. The *NASA Act* declared that:

> … it is the policy of the United States that activities in space should be devoted to peaceful purposes for the benefit of all mankind … The Congress declares that the general welfare and security of the United States require that adequate provision be made for aeronautical and space activities. (1958, s. 102)

Its first major program was Project Mercury (1958–1963), which sent astronaut John Glenn into Earth orbit in 1962. As an expression of both 'all mankind' cosmopolitanism and directed towards the 'general welfare' of American society, NASA arrived during an era of Keynesian demand stimulus and social security measures established under Roosevelt and continued under the Republican Eisenhower Administration. NASA was part of 'the largest peacetime public works program in history' that also included the Federal Highway System (Linklater 2015, p. 359).

Historian Joan Lisa Bromberg has emphasised that, from the very inauguration of American space policy, there have always been public-private partnerships – partnership, in a broader sense, implying 'contention as well as concord' (1999, p. 14). While the NewSpace movement has pointed to bureaucratic and regulatory barriers that have stood in the way of space commerce, it is worth noting that NASA has supported private enterprise from the outset. Bromberg notes that '[leaders] of the aerospace industry … were among the Wise Men who in 1958 gave counsel on NASA's conception and birth' (1999, p. 1). Eisenhower appointed T. Keith Glennan to be NASA's first Administrator. Glennan shared Eisenhower's 'philosophy of small government and of giving the maximum possible scope to the private sector' (ibid, p. 17). McCurdy similarly emphasises how, under Glennan's leadership, a pattern was established whereby private firms would produce rocket and spacecraft components to supply NASA's missions, rather than develop any state-owned plants for the production of this hardware (McCurdy 2011, p. 270).

Glennan's 'limited government' approach to managing NASA programs nonetheless resulted in a marketplace that was entirely dependent on the government as a sole purchaser of the technologies necessary for spaceflight. This required a swelling bureaucracy to co-ordinate the development of these technologies. NASA is much more than Cape Canaveral: in addition to the Kennedy Space Center in Florida, there are now research centres in Virginia, Ohio and California (the Jet Propulsion Laboratory and Ames Research Center), and space flight centres in Alabama, Texas and Maryland. All these departments are coordinated by NASA Headquarters in Washington, D.C. Between 1960 and 1963, NASA's total personnel expanded from 10,000 to 30,00 people (Bromberg 1999, p. 62). NASA's workforce reached a peak of 35,680 in 1967 (NASA 1997, p. 28). The number of people indirectly employed through NASA, via contracted aerospace firms across 'gunbelt' states of the south and southwest like Florida, Alabama, Texas, Colorado and California (Markusen et al. 1991), was many thousands more. In his ethnography of contemporary NewSpace, David Valentine cites interviewees who deride NASA as 'a wasteful government "jobs program"' (2012, p. 1047). NASA continues to be viewed as a crucial employer across the United States and the political spectrum (Cruz 2018).

NewSpace often mythologises the unbridled creativity and innovation of the tech entrepreneur, in contrast with the cumbersome state (Hudgins 2011).

The SFF's inspiration for the 'NewSpace' moniker likely derives in part from Michael Lewis' 2000 book, *The New, New Thing* (SFF, in Denis et al. 2020, p. 432). This book lauded the entrepreneurial, 'visionary' culture of Silicon Valley at the onset of the 1990s Internet boom (an important quarter for investment in contemporary space mining ventures). Yet this hotbed of American industry owes a great deal to military contracting in the Cold War period. Historian Thomas Heinrich describes how Santa Clara County, California, produced the majority of transistors, integrated circuits and microprocessors central to early military projects in missiles and satellites (2002, pp. 247–248). A significant event for Silicon Valley was the 1956 relocation of Lockheed Corporation's missile division to the Valley's Moffett Federal Airfield, next door to the NASA Ames Research Center. The renamed Lockheed Missile and Space Corporation eventually became 'the largest industrial employer in Silicon Valley during the Cold War' (ibid, p. 258). In Heinrich's words,

> No account of postwar batch production industries is complete without a close look at the Strangelovian netherworld of defense policy, military procurement, Pentagon-funded research and development, and weapons production. (ibid, p. 280)

More recently, Moffett was home to the corporate headquarters of space mining firm DSI. NASA Ames also includes a number of public-private partnerships, including Singularity University, which is an incubator founded by Planetary Resources chairman and founder Peter Diamandis (NASA 2009). Today, hangars in the publicly owned Moffett Airfield house the private jets of Google's billionaire executives (Lardinois 2014), forming an apt symbol for techno-libertarians' tendency towards an 'inflated sense of their own resourcefulness in developing new ideas … [and giving] little recognition to the contributions made by the state, their own labour force, or the wider community' (Barbrook & Cameron 1996, p. 55). Mazzucato's (2013) *The Entrepreneurial State* thoroughly debunks the myth of the risk-averse public institution and the innovating entrepreneur. Many key ICT technologies were supported and developed through state patronage, representing the 'socialisation of risk and the privatisation of rewards' (Mazzucato 2013, ch. 9).

NASA's co-ordination and management of numerous firms contracted to design and construct rocket stages and spacecraft components represented a highly centralised form of decision-making that is at odds with the emphasis on government failure, and the goal of commercial independence from government directives, that has characterised NewSpace discourse. The landmark achievements of American spacefaring originate with the heavy and very visible hand of the US state, which stands in contrast with the 'new lean, mean set of alternative space firms' that emerged in the late 1990s as part of the NewSpace movement (Tumlinson 2003, p. 12). The ongoing prevalence of public institutions that support private space enterprise might suggest that mining and colonising space through small, libertarian projects is unlikely to become a reality.

The climax of 'old space'

The development of the American space sector accelerated with the orbit of the Soviet *Sputnik* satellite in 1957. *Sputnik* was the opening milestone in a period of space exploration that reached its climax with the fabled lunar landing of Apollo 11 in 1969. For the NewSpace movement, the Apollo period is something of a 'golden age' that is yet to be repeated (*Orphans of Apollo* 2009). Peter Diamandis, founder of space mining start-up Planetary Resources, was characteristic of the NewSpace movement in saying that he had 'given up' on the idea that NASA is capable of repeating the feats of the Apollo era (Hoffman 2010).

The dream of spaceflight, articulated decades earlier by Verne, Tsiolkovsky and others, was realised in this period through a coronation of human ingenuity and mastery of the physical sciences. It was also an off-world projection of volatile Cold War hostilities and the expanding military-industrial might of the superpower rivals. Kennedy's challenge to send an American to the Moon by the end of the 1960s was part of the broader 'freedom doctrine' to challenge the Soviet Union—a strategy of Communist containment that was equally concerned with modernising the American military, providing foreign military and economic aid, and negotiating a comprehensive nuclear test ban (Mazo 2009, p. 226). The Kennedy Administration settled for ratification of the *Partial Test Ban Treaty* (1963), an early UN treaty of the global commons that prohibited nuclear testing in the atmosphere, outer space and under water.

President Kennedy's famous 1962 speech at Rice University oscillated between patriotic exceptionalism and cosmopolitan invocations of 'humanity':

> the eyes of the world now look into space, to the Moon and to the planets beyond, and we have vowed that we shall not see it governed by a hostile flag of conquest, but by a banner of freedom and peace', and yet 'the vows of this Nation can only be fulfilled if we in this Nation are first … the world's leading space-faring nation. (1962)

Jazeel notes that the Soviet Union also 'deployed the rhetoric of universal freedom and common human rights' in service of international competitiveness (2011, p. 82). Upon taking power in 1964, and shortly before expanding the military budget of the USSR, General Secretary Brezhnev declared:

> We Soviet people do not look upon our space exploration as an end in itself, as some sort of 'race'. The spirit of gamblers is profoundly alien to us in the great and serious business of exploring and conquering outer space. We regard this enterprise as a component of the tremendous, creative work in which the Soviet people is engaged, consistent with the general line of

> our party in all areas of the economy, science and culture, in the name of man and for the good of man. (Cited in McDougall 1997, p. 296)

Space was a key domain in which 'competing political universalisms were contested' (Jazeel 2011, p. 82).

Superpower claims to international leadership were mobilised through contrasting discourses of freedom and collectivism, the techno-industrial spectacle of spacefaring serving as proof of each side's virtue and might. There may well have been a transcendent, unifying moment when millions fixed their gaze on the black and white images of Armstrong and Aldrin surveying the 'magnificent desolation' of the Moon's surface. Yet the first Moon landing was undergirded by the violence of military-industrial power. Both the United States and USSR often developed 'dual use' technologies that could serve both civilian and military purposes. For the United States, the development of intercontinental ballistic missile designs occurred alongside the development of booster rockets for human spaceflight, as captured V-2 rockets contributed to the design of new models that were tested in Hunstville and Cape Canaveral (Launius 1995, pp. 14–16). Advancements in long-range rockets could carry the hopes and dreams of their respective peoples to the cosmos, and could also carry nuclear warheads to Moscow or Washington.

Under the Johnson Administration (1963–1969), new NASA Administrator James Webb directed the Agency's spending as a means of building national R&D capacity and as 'an engine for domestic [economic] growth' (Bromberg 1999, p. 61). Bromberg (1999) describes NASA's management of contracts with aerospace firms during the Apollo program. She illustrates how Webb's administration of NASA involved the direct management of contracting firms (often through project management and personnel secondments) rather than trusting in their autonomy and 'forces' of competition.

> Webb saw the private sector, properly used, as a way to provide the government with resources in a flexible manner, as well as an engine for achieving efficiency, rapid results, and low costs ... On the other hand, Webb believed that national space policy should not be turned over to private firms. It was government acting in the public interest that had to determine what should be done, when it should be done, and for how much money. (ibid, p. 61)

Webb saw the potential for distributed NASA procurements to 'spread money to less developed parts of the nation, and serve as a template for other large scale social programs' (Bromberg 1999, p. 61). This resistance to handing-over key responsibilities for publicly funded projects to the private sector marks a crucial point of difference with the neoliberal approach to space policy that was introduced under the Reagan Administration (discussed below).

In addition to economic growth, American exceptionalism and security was also perceived to be at stake. The Apollo Program has been described as 'first and foremost a soft-power effort par excellence, to put down a marker for American prestige' (Mazo 2009, p. 226). The injection of public funding during the 'old space' period owes much to the fact that, prior to Neil Armstrong's 'giant leap for mankind' in 1969, their Cold War antagonists had taken a clear lead in the race to space. A succession of triumphs presented a propaganda coup for the Soviet Union: *Sputnik 1* (launched in 1957) was the first artificial satellite orbiting Earth; Yuri Gagarin (in 1961) and Valentine Tereshkova (in 1963) were the first man and woman in outer space, respectively; and the Luna Program achieved the first landings of man-made objects on the Moon's surface (an impact from *Luna 2* in 1959 and a soft landing from *Luna 9* in 1966). American technological supremacy and its grasp on the ultimate military high ground could no longer be presumed.

Subsequently, the Apollo Program ran from 1961 to 1972 at a total cost of US $25.4 billion (U.S. House of Representatives 1974, p. 1271). NASA funding was at its highest proportion in 1966: 4.4% of the national budget, more than twice the proportion allocated to the Department of Education in that same year (OMB 2019). The 'old space' era underlines the scale of investment and central coordination that were required to achieve the ambitious goal of crewed spaceflight to other celestial bodies.

The *Outer Space Treaty* (1967) also arrived during this sustained period of geopolitical tension and the omnipresent threat of Mutually Assured Destruction.[8] It was a cosmopolitan gesture in international law that aspired for outer space to be used peacefully and equitably, and was negotiated against a backdrop of global anti-communist, anti-capitalist and anti-colonial movements, with the Cold War frequently playing out in proxy conflicts in the global south. Conflicts flared in Europe, Asia, the Middle-East and the Caribbean throughout the 1960s: ranging from the US war with Communist Indochina and anti-colonial movements like those against Israeli expansionism or English occupation of Northern Ireland. However, the *Treaty* asserted that peace would reign in outer space: a host of UN member states 'often in conflict with one another and adhering to widely divergent political philosophies' ratified the *Treaty* in the hope that it would ward against off-world militarism and conquest (Dembling & Arons 1967, p. 420). It can be read as a repudiation of colonial empire (Marboe & Johnson, in IISL 2016, p. 26). The *Treaty* declared that the 'exploration and use of outer space … shall be carried out for the benefit and in the interests of all countries … and shall be the province of all mankind' (OST 1967, Art. 1) and that the space commons were 'not subject to national appropriation by claim of sovereignty, by means of use or occupation, or by any other means' (Art. 2).

The 1969 Apollo Moon landing involved only a symbolic planting of the US flag, and any questions of resource ownership were drowned out by international marvel at NASA's technological feat and the bravery of the Apollo astronauts. When the Apollo mission returned samples of lunar rock, no ownership claim was made over them, and many samples were distributed to the international community (a gift economy that contrasts with the private property model of the CSLCA). For Gerard O'Neill, forebearer of the NewSpace movement, it did raise the question of exploiting off-world resources: from revealing reserves of silicon and aluminium to iron and titanium, he thought Apollo was 'of enormous value for its lunar prospecting function' (O'Neill 1977, p. 57).

1970s: liberty, limits and the dawn of NewSpace

During the 1970s, the American space sector was undermined severely by a rapidly changing political-economic environment. NASA funding receded well below its Apollo peak, the US was humiliated in Vietnam and the American environmentalist movement became cognisant of the limits to economic growth (Meadows et al. 1972). The oil shortages of the 1970s fuelled stagflation and a recognition of resource finitude. Princeton physicist Gerard K. O'Neill responded to these social and environmental crises with a model of space colonisation predicated on off-world manufacturing and the mining of lunar and asteroidal resources (O'Neill 1974, 1977). In addition to formulating technical concepts that are evident in the proposals of recent space mining ventures, O'Neill's work also introduced political-economic and political-ecological philosophies similar to those promulgated in NewSpace discourse. His career trajectory involved a collision with the realities of space funding and policy, and his legacy – in the organisations he inspired and his resort to pursuing space activity through commercial means – was influential in shaping the political orientation of the NewSpace movement. In particular, the L-5 Society, a civil society group inspired by O'Neill, launched a successful campaign against the UN *Moon Agreement* (1979) and, in doing so, established private property rights as a key pillar of the NewSpace vision for space colonisation.

O'Neill's High Frontier *and the limits to growth*

In the same year that Apollo 11 landed on the Moon, Gerard O'Neill – a tenured physics professor at Princeton University – was preparing to teach the undergraduate 'Physics 103' course for the 1969–1970 semester. 'Relatively stiff [and] requiring calculus', the course was a bit dry, given the zeitgeist (O'Neill 1977, p. 233). The civil rights and feminist movements had won hard-fought legal victories, the unpopular Vietnam War continued, and university campuses – Princeton among them – were significant sites for the mobilisation of dissent. Student protests opposed the militarisation of scientific research, as several universities undertook classified research into fundamental physics and chemical weapons on Department of Defence contracts (Stevens 2003, p. 164). Armstrong's footsteps on the Moon may have briefly unified the US electorate in admiration of NASA, but the Apollo Program was frequently derided at the time as a massive misuse of national funds and misplaced political energy (O'Neill 1977, p. 234; Deudney 1982, p. 11).

In this climate of anti-military protest and technological pessimism, Physics 103 would need to 'attack the question of the place of the scientist and the engineer in the society of the next decades' (O'Neill 1977, p. 235). The first question O'Neill asked his students was, 'Is a planetary surface the right place for an expanding technological civilization?' (O'Neill 1977, p. 236). It was of course a loaded question, in the assumption that civilisation can and will inevitably continue expanding (an assumption that prevails in both NewSpace advocacy and neoliberal growth policy).

However, in keeping with O'Neill's commitment to restoring the social value of technoscience, the question reflected those raised by the American environmentalist movement that had gained much momentum in the years prior, of which I present only a brief account here. From 1965, economist Kenneth Boulding argued that Earth 'has become a single spaceship, without unlimited reservoirs of anything, either for extraction or pollution' (1966, p. 7). The term 'spaceship Earth' was subsequently popularised by British economist Barbara Ward, US Ambassador to the UN Adlai Stevenson II and futurist Buckminster Fuller, among others (McCray 2013, p. 23). Garrett Hardin's (1968) paper 'The Tragedy of the Commons' described the tendency towards over-exploitation of common spaces and resources. Paul Ehrlich's (1971) *The Population Bomb* described the dangers of unchecked population growth and the unequal access to food between developed and developing nations. Grassroots environmental activism also emerged: activists in San Francisco held the first 'Earth Day' in 1970, following the 1969 spill from Union Oil's Santa Barbara platform. Public demand for environmental protection was recognised in national legislation when the US Congress passed the *National Environmental Policy Act of 1969* and Federal environmental responsibilities were consolidated into the newly formed Environmental Protection Agency a year later. In 1972, the United Nations Conference on the Human Environment was held in Stockholm and declared 'the need for a common outlook and for common principles to inspire and guide the peoples of the world in the preservation and enhancement of the human environment' (U.N. Conference on the Human Environment 1972, preamble).

In 1967, NASA's ATS-3 satellite returned the very first colour photo of Earth from space. Lower in resolution than the famed 'Blue Marble' photo of 1972, it nonetheless captured a dynamic, life-harbouring world against the pitch-black nothingness of outer space. The photo was soon released by NASA as a result of campaigning from activist Stewart Brand (Bjørnvig 2013, p. 10), who used this image on the cover of the DIY guide to self-sufficiency, the *Whole Earth Catalog* (1968–1972). Kilgore eloquently describes the era: 'for the first time in history humanity saw the true compass of its world, and some understood its small scale and fragility' (2003, p. 153).

In addition to the 'Blue Marble' photo and the final Apollo mission, 1972 also saw the publication of the *Limits to Growth* report, produced by a team of environmental scientists at the Massachusetts Institute of Technology (MIT) led by Donella Meadows (Meadows et al. 1972). With MIT engineer Jay Forrester, the researchers built a computer simulation that processed observable, global trends of 'accelerating industrialization, rapid population growth, widespread malnutrition, depletion of nonrenewable resources, and a deteriorating environment' (Meadows et al. 1972, p. 21). The mathematical model projected that if these trends continued unabated, 'the limit to growth on this planet will be reached sometime within the next one hundred years' (ibid, p. 23). They argued, however, that a 'global equilibrium' state could be reached: every human could have their basic needs met and 'an equal opportunity to realize his individual human potential' under conditions of 'ecological and economic stability' (ibid, p. 24). The *Limits* report claimed that, if the consequences for exceeding the limits to growth were to be averted, society would need to exist in a steady state, with growth decelerated in developed countries and permitted only to raise the living standards of developing countries. Such a feat would require 'concerted international measures and joint long-term planning' (ibid, p. 194).

O'Neill was profoundly optimistic about the potential of technological innovation and rejected the period's 'bleak chic' and the steady-state goal (Michaud 1986, p. 58). His anticipatory research project aimed to bypass – rather than work within – planetary limits. He published two seminal texts that articulated notions of *in situ* resource utilisation, space manufacturing and space colonisation that are now central to NewSpace and its space mining project. The first was published in *Physics Today*, 'The Colonization of Space' (O'Neill 1974), and the second (and more widely known today) was *The High Frontier* (1977) – the culmination of close to a decade of work trying to turn space colonisation into feasible project. Like the early 'visioneers' Tsiolkovsky, Goddard and von Braun (McCray 2013), O'Neill's *High Frontier* was a detailed synthesis of space utopianism and space engineering. It fused mathematical extrapolations and space colony design with frequent appeals to social experimentation and renewal. It was lavishly illustrated with the utopian artwork of Don Davis and Rick Guidice. The cylindrical and torus-shaped habitats he presented ranged from 1 km to 32 km in length and represented the 'most effective geometry' for producing artificial gravity and a day-night cycle, harnessing natural sunlight and creating 'an earthlike appearance' that could abound with living space, parkland, water bodies and agriculture (O'Neill 1974, p. 33). O'Neill had designed and mounted a case for literal, artificial 'spaceship Earths' that he hoped would negate any terrestrial limits to growth.

The Saturn V rocket that carried the Apollo astronauts could carry a payload of 140 metric tons to low-Earth orbit; some of O'Neill's 'islands' would need upwards of 3 million tons of construction materials delivered well-beyond the edge of Earth's atmosphere (O'Neill 1977, p. 127). With that mass, they could never be launched from Earth – the colonies would require mining and processing of resources found outside Earth's gravity well. O'Neill identified the Moon as 'a rich source of both titanium and of aluminium' for building the habitats (1974, p. 33). He engaged his background in high energy physics to design the 'mass driver': a 'recirculating conveyor belt' powered by magnetic propulsion that he imagined could launch '3.6 million tons of lunar material over a six-year period' to the sites of habitat construction (ibid, p. 138). Shipping materials from the asteroid belt would eventually be more cost-effective, he thought, because their lack of mass and lower gravity would reduce the escape velocity for take-off. The prospective space mining industry shares this aspiration to off-world resource extraction and processing.

Space colonisation and off-world industry proposed a solution to planetary ecological limits. This solution was predicated on engineering and innovation, not international governance or economic planning as envisioned by the *Limits* report. In keeping with his original aims with the Physics 103 course, *The High Frontier* involved numerous 'blue sky' speculative engineering proposals. They were 'techno-fixes' that assumed exponential technological progress would remedy endogenous social and ecological crises (Clark & York 2013). Grand 'techno-fixes' like space colonisation would negate the need for curtailing unsustainable industrial growth by opening new spaces for resource exploitation, population growth and waste output.

There is a striking contrast between O'Neill's recognition of the fundamental importance of the biosphere and his optimistic belief that space engineering would render these limits surmountable. The Mercury, Gemini and Apollo missions demonstrated that keeping a maximum of three astronauts alive in space is extremely difficult. In the 40 years since O'Neill's book was published, there have been no successful closed-system biospheres capable of sustaining a human presence in deep space (Walker & Granjou 2017). In keeping with the overall optimism of his work, O'Neill pointed to the asteroid belt as a means of making outer space liveable. He argued that carbonaceous chondritic asteroids could provide key life supports of carbon, nitrogen and hydrogen in abundance (O'Neill 1977, pp. 57–58). O'Neill proposed that each of his artificial biospheres could support over 10,000 people (ibid, p. 92). His hugely speculative calculation was that the 'the ultimate size limit for the human race on the newly available frontier is at least 20 000 times its present value' (O'Neill 1974, p. 32).[9]

O'Neill's off-world expansionism offered a cosmopolitan vision of 'humanising' outer space, yet it rested upon some individualistic, libertarian precepts. It represented more than an escape from ecological limits: it was also an escape from the limits to individual liberty that an economic 'steady state' would entail. O'Neill confessed that he had:

> always felt strongly a personal desire to be free of boundaries and regimentation. The steady state society, ridden with rules and laws, proposed by early workers on the limits to growth was, to me, abhorrent. (Kilgore 2003, p. 159)

Unlike the conclusion reached by the *Limits* researchers, 'freedom and individual worth' could exist in and would indeed require a boundless economic base (ibid, p. 230). O'Neill's version of freedom was what political philosopher Isaiah Berlin (1969) described as 'negative liberty': freedom understood as the absence of imposed constraint, an 'escape from outside interference', in O'Neill's words (cited in Kilgore 2003, p. 168).

For O'Neill and more recent advocacy from NewSpace, individual freedoms require the freedom to expand (Alliance for Space Development 2019, p. 3; Bezos, in Blue Origin 2019). In his belief that 'held by law to a steady state condition, freedom of thought and of inquiry would be dangerous and would probably be suppressed' (Kilgore 2003, p. 159), O'Neill echoed a conclusion reached by the then famous neoliberal economist and MPS co-founder, Milton Friedman. Friedman had argued that '"freedom" in economic arrangements is itself a component of freedom broadly understood … an indispensable means toward the achievement of political freedom' (Friedman 1962, p. 15).

However, O'Neill did not engage in any explicit political discourse and tried to distance himself from the utopian tradition. His project was primarily grounded in maths and physics, and there is no textual citation of libertarian or then-emerging neoliberal philosophy in the *High Frontier*. O'Neill generally 'said nothing about the government of space communities' and claimed to make 'no prescription for social organization or governance' (Kilgore 2003, p. 169). Nonetheless, despite O'Neill's original intentions to use space engineering as a means of addressing the problems caused by industrialism, his solution was instead a means of escaping ecological catastrophe without taking responsibility for it.

Fiscal crisis, budgetary limits and the end of 'old space'

The 1970s saw macroeconomic change that derailed the post-war economic boom and signalled the end of NASA's 'golden age' of state patronage. In addition to O'Neill's work, this era is formative in the emergence of NewSpace ventures and its advocates insistence on independent, commercial space exploration. Prompted by the balance of payments crisis, stagflation and the OAPEC oil embargo, the American economy confronted (and bypassed) the apparent inability to run an unlimited deficit. In this context, O'Neill's advocacy work encountered a political establishment that was disinterested in space colonisation. The Nixon Administration's (1969–1973) abandonment of the gold standard also spurred the development of speculative venture capital (VC) markets that would become influential in Silicon Valley start-up culture and the emergence of space mining firms.

The 1971 balance of payments crisis curtailed US economic growth. The Bretton Woods monetary agreements were put under significant strain with huge deficits run by the United States, due largely to its expenditure on the Vietnam War. Foreign central banks held more US dollars than the value of gold in US reserves; when a host of European countries sought to redeem their dollars for gold, Nixon ended the gold convertibility of the dollar in August 1971. The first oil shock of the decade also damaged the American economy, and simultaneously lent further credibility to the *Limits to Growth* thesis' projections of increased resource scarcity. The US economy was in a state of stagflation, with high inflation and high unemployment coinciding with low economic growth.

While heavy industry stagnated during this period, the techno-utopian concept of the 'knowledge economy' began to enter policy discourse. Political economist Melinda Cooper's (2008) *Life as Surplus* highlights how the twin crises of ecological and monetary limits were instrumental in the development of the 'knowledge economy'. After Nixon's abandonment of the gold standard, the United States became an 'empire curiously devoid of tangible reserves or capital' (Cooper 2008, p. 29). Daniel Bell's (1973) *The Coming of Post-Industrial Society: A Venture in Social Forecasting* was another futurological, techno-optimistic project that gained popularity in the same period as O'Neill's work. Cooper notes how Bell's 'post-industrialism' became influential in right-wing futurists' rejection of limits discourse (Simon & Kahn 1984). Central to the 'post-industrial society' was an innovation-based 'knowledge economy', where the 'creativity of the human mind (a resource without limits) would replace the mass-production of tangible commodities' (Cooper 2008, p. 17). Discourses of the 'post-industrial' society were actively deployed in the Reagan Administration's R&D policy a decade later. The faith in human innovation to surpass biophysical limits has been central to techno-utopian discourse emanating from the NewSpace movement (Zubrin 1994; Diamandis & Kotler 2012).

The financial reforms originating in the 1970s ultimately opened up more capital for speculative 'knowledge economy' investment and led to the accumulation of personal fortunes that were invested in NewSpace start-ups decades later. Following the OAPEC oil embargo, the United States pursued deepened military and economic partnerships with Saudi Arabia. Bilateral agreements and US pressure via Saudi Arabia pushed other Middle Eastern oil exporters to standardise oil sales in US dollars. This meant that the dollar was backed by oil demand, and the huge amounts of 'petrodollars' accumulated by oil producers would be recycled back into US financial markets, creating a huge pool of funds for investment. No longer limited to the bullion of the Federal Reserve, the US stock market became increasingly liquid and mobile: a large pool of funds became available for highly speculative investments in high-risk shares, junk bonds and VC funds (Cooper 2008, p. 27). These VC funds started investing in information and communication firms from the late-1970s onwards – and these investments fuelled further capital mobility through the digitisation of economic exchange. The increased mobility of capital also facilitated the transfer of vast sums of money to lowly taxed offshore principalities – one example being Luxembourg, which was the first nation to follow the United States in introducing domestic space resources law.

In addition to these precipitating these financial reforms, the US fiscal crises of the early 1970s served to reduce the national budget allocation for space science and engineering. Against the backdrop of economic turmoil and falling government revenue, the Nixon Administration gradually cancelled the Apollo missions. In 1969, the year of the Moon landing, the NASA

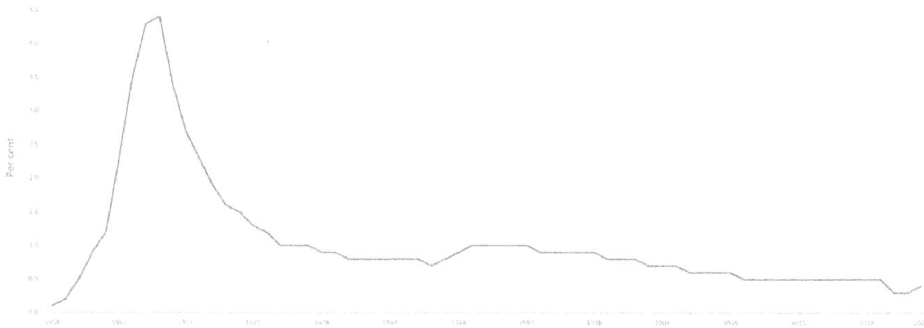

Figure 2.1 Annual NASA funding as percentage of total national budget.

budget had nearly halved from its 1965–1966 peak, down to 2.3% of the national budget (Figure 2.1; OMB 2019).[10] After achieving six crewed Moon landings, Apollo 20 was cancelled in January 1970 and Apollos 18 and 19 were cancelled in September 1970. In 1972, when Apollo 17 marked the last time a human set foot on the Moon – taking its memorable ‘blue marble’ photo along the way – NASA’s share of the national budget had dropped to 1.5% (OMB 2023). In 1975, for the first time since Kennedy’s famous 1962 declaration of intent, it dropped to 1.0% and has not exceeded this level since (Office of Management and Budget 2023).

While early ‘visioneers’ like von Braun had been able to wed their personal, idealistic space aspirations to the national military agenda, O’Neill struggled to gain comparable support from the US Government for his expansive vision (Kilgore 2003, p. 151). Kilgore describes how, in pursuing follow-ups to Apollo, NASA ‘scrambled for political and fiscal survival in congressional hearing rooms’, lacking the broader support of the American voting public for the cause of space exploration (ibid, p. 151). As Michaud recounts, ‘The ordinary voter … saw no point in continuing to pour huge amounts of money into the space program once the prestige and confidence of the United States had been restored’ and the ‘race’ had been won (Michaud 1986, p. 15). Thousands of engineers, technicians and scientists were pushed outside the national space program (Kilgore 2003, p. 151). The golden age of space travel had come to an end.

As far as Gerard O’Neill was concerned, it proved to be an inopportune time to ask the US Government to fund space settlement projects, particularly those that planned scenarios featuring 32-km-long spaceships replete with terrestrial comforts like skiing, sailing and mountaineering facilities (O’Neill 1974, p. 36). O’Neill spent several years taking his ideas to Capitol Hill in search of funding and commitment from legislators to support the humanisation of outer space, which would ultimately never arrive. He had some successes, including NASA Ames workshops that culminated in the *Space Settlements: A Design Study* (Johnson & Holbrow 1975) and the *Space*

Resources and Space Settlement (Billingham & Gilbreath 1977) reports. He was invited to testify at a number of Congressional committee hearings during the latter half of the 1970s. For example, a pro-space organisation reported that he had received a 'good reception' at the 1978 'Future Space Programs' hearings of the House Committee on Science and Technology (Gluckman 1978, p. 5).

There were select 'pro-space' voices in Congress at the time. Michaud's (1986) history of pro-space organisations notes the following: Harrison Schmitt (R-NM; 1977–1983), the former Apollo 17 astronaut-geologist and later lunar mining advocate; Don Fuqua (D-FL; 1963–1987), who proposed an unsuccessful 'Space Industrialization Act' in 1979; Ken Kramer (R-CO, 1972–1987), who in 1982 proposed the creation of a US Space Force (a new branch of the military, recently realised by the Trump Administration); and Newt Gingrich (R-GA, 1979–1999), a consistent libertarian voice in American politics, who advocated for a widely ridiculed Moon Base proposal during the 2012 Republican primaries (Michaud 1986, p. 74, 217, 231). However, broader government support under the austerity budgets of the Carter Administration (1977–1981) was not forthcoming. O'Neill's *High Frontier* proposal was often received with incredulity, most famously by Sen. William Proxmire (D-WI, 1957–1983), who questioned the sheer cost of O'Neill's massive space stations, disputed the likelihood of financial return and emphasised the 'massive problems remaining to be solved here on Earth' (Proxmire, in Gluckman 1978, p. 5).

O'Neill received greater support from sections of America's burgeoning counter-culture movements. The widespread interest in the 'Colonization of space' paper (O'Neill 1974) owed much to the support of Stewart Brand's Portola Foundation, publisher of the *Whole Earth Catalog* and a funding source for O'Neill's 'First Princeton Conference on Space Colonisation' held in May 1974 (Kilgore 2003, p. 161). His work also received free publicity from LSD-advocate Timothy Leary, for whom space settlements could assist in his own millenarian project of human evolution (McCray 2013, p. 11). Leary's endorsement sat uneasily with O'Neill, the tenured Ivy League physics professor, while the financial support of communitarian environmentalists like Brand 'was a last resort' after years of unsuccessful attempts at securing more credible, 'establishment' funding sources (Kilgore 2003, p. 161).

Michaud identifies a three-stage cycle of space advocacy that aptly summarises O'Neill's experiences:

> … first, enthusiasm about the big idea and a desire to communicate it with others. Second, the encounter with the realities of government and politics, leading to frustration. Third, the scaling down of near-term goals and their pursuit by indirect or private means. (Michaud 1986, p. 81)

It is this pursuit of space colonisation and interrelated mining, manufacturing and industrialisation projects through 'indirect or private means' that paves the way for NewSpace mining start-ups. In 1978, O'Neill and his wife Tasha founded the Space Studies Institute through private philanthropy, for the purpose of organising 'small groups of people to develop the tools of space exploration independently of governments and to prove that private groups could get things done enormously cheaper and quicker than government bureaucracy' (Dyson 1993, p. 98). It is an entrepreneurial form with a libertarian ethos, reflecting the neoliberal aversion to centralised planning.

Several key figures in contemporary NewSpace draw their inspiration from O'Neill. One of O'Neill's protégés at SSI was Rick Tumlinson, a torchbearer of the NewSpace movement who co-founded the civil society group SFF in 1988 with former Gingrich staffer James Muncy. Tumlinson has been involved in a number of influential firms, including MirCorp (Chapter 6). He was co-founder and chairman of former space mining start-up DSI in 2013 (DSI 2018). O'Neill was also a mentor to young entrepreneur Peter Diamandis, who founded Students for the Exploration and Development of Space (SEDS) at Princeton in 1980 and co-founded Planetary Resources in 2012 (Michaud 1986, p. 100; Diamandis, in Sheppard 2013; Diamandis, in Phan 2021). Bob Richards, a former Senior Associate at O'Neill's Space Studies Institute, founded SEDS Canada shortly after the Princeton chapter was founded. With Diamandis, Richards later founded the International Space University and Silicon Valley's Singularity University. In 2010, he co-founded the contemporary space transportation start-up Moon Express in 2010.

However, the most famous of Gerard O'Neill's former students is one Jeffrey Bezos, founder of the online retail behemoth Amazon.com and space launch services company Blue Origin. At Princeton, he had seen O'Neill's lectures and, as with Richards and Diamandis, was president of his local SEDS chapter (Gruss 2016). In a May 2019 presentation titled, 'Going to space to benefit Earth', Bezos unveiled Blue Origin's new lunar lander, discussed mining lunar water ice and re-capitulated the O'Neillian imaginary of limitless growth and human settlement in vast orbital colonies (Blue Origin 2019). One of the world's richest individuals – with an estimated net worth of US $118 billion at the time of writing (Forbes 2023) – is spreading the O'Neillian message to a new generation of space enthusiasts. Mirroring his mentor's rejection of the *Limits to Growth* thesis and the curtailment of economic freedom, Bezos asked his audience: 'Do we want stasis and rationing? Or do we want dynamism and growth?' (in Blue Origin 2019).

While Bezos does not appear to have collaborated with Atlas member organisations, he has nonetheless deployed quintessentially neoliberal business strategies in accumulating his staggering wealth. For example, Amazon pays very little corporate tax in the United States, and has made use of offshore jurisdictions like Luxembourg (Abrahamian 2017); it has near-monopolistic control of supply chains stocked with low-wage labourers who have been actively discouraged from unionising (Johnson 2018); it encouraged a 'race to the bottom' between sub-national jurisdictions before deciding on the location of its second corporate headquarters, and many states proposed using taxpayer funded incentives to this end (Wingfield 2018)[11]; and, as the Poynter Institute has discussed, in 2018 the company made political donations to a significant number of legislators with tendencies towards climate denialism and evident voting patterns against environmental protection legislation (Mahadevan 2019). The rationalisation of human labour in the Amazon supply chain has led to fundamental denial of human liberty and biological necessity (Reuters 2021). Despite the libertarian sentiment underpinning his critique of the *Limits to Growth* thesis, O'Neill appeared to make a sincere attempt to address the looming environmental crisis through what appeared to be a well-intentioned, if highly impractical, techno-utopian scheme. It is hard to reconcile the business practices of Amazon – the source of wealth underpinning Bezos's spacefaring endeavours – with the claim that Blue Origin will be 'going to space to benefit Earth'.

Precisely what influence Gerard O'Neill's legacy will have on space colonisation and mining remains to be seen. Of the three NewSpace firms discussed above, only Richards' Moon Express remains in operation (and is focused more on space transportation than resource extraction). Both Planetary Resources and DSI were purchased by other commercial space firms in the late 2010s (discussed further in the Epilogue). So far, Bezos' Blue Origin has been successful in crewed missions to low-Earth orbit (Blue Origin 2022). Meanwhile, *in situ* resources utilisation projects of any kind, let alone something approximating the extravagance of O'Neill's *High Frontier*, are yet to be attempted.

In politico-legal terms, however, O'Neill's ideas have already been quite influential. Perhaps the most significant chapter in O'Neill's legacy will have been through the formation of an advocacy group called the L-5 Society. Through the L-5 Society, private property rights to off-world resources became part of the NewSpace policy program. Their lobbying work may have established a structural link between NewSpace and neoliberalism, as opposition to international treaty law that sought to constrain extractive industry in the global commons found voice in both this early NewSpace organisation and the political organs of Atlas neoliberalism.

The L-5 Society and the defeat of the Moon Agreement

O'Neill's *High Frontier* inspired a group of civilian enthusiasts that banded together as the L-5 Society.[12] Based in Tuscon, Arizona, the L-5 Society was founded by Carolyn Meinel and Keith Henson, a couple who had met O'Neill in the wake of his first *High Frontier* publication (O'Neill 1974; Henson & Henson 1975). Michaud's (1986) social history of American space enthusiasm is particularly valuable in accounting for L-5's emergence between 1975 and 1981 as the most politically active 'pro-space' organisation. Following the cancellation of the final Apollo missions, this period was also one in which the pro-commerce or anti-bureaucratic element of American pro-space organisations started to develop.[13] Following Nixon and Ford, Carter had de-prioritised the space program, and NASA generally pursued goals that were modest compared to their Apollo achievements. Carter entered the White House in the aftermath of economic recession, and a second oil shock occurred in 1979 (following the Iranian Revolution). Yet NASA funding under Carter was not insubstantial, despite the absence of any commitment to manned missions beyond the Moon or any other pathways to the O'Neillian frontier. The Space Shuttle program was announced by Nixon in 1972 as an attempt at more affordable (and reusable) launch services. The first space station, *Skylab*, orbited between 1973 and 1979.

In advocating O'Neill's ideas, L-5 recruited new members with tenacity and were highly organised in lobbying their Congressional representatives during the Carter Administration (Michaud 1986, p. 89; Brandt-Erichsen 1994). A broad array of space enthusiasts was drawn towards the O'Neillian space vision through the work of the L-5 Society, and its early membership included diverse personal and political philosophies (Michaud 1986, p. 86; discussed further in Chapter 7). Anthropologist and Club of Rome collaborator Margaret Mead is one interesting example (*L-5 News*, December 1975, p. 1).

Futurists from the political right were also drawn to L-5 during this period. This included K. Eric Drexler, a founder of the MIT Space Habitat Study Group and later advocate for utopian applications of nanotechnology, and Herman Kahn, a civil defence strategist at RAND (Michaud 1986, p. 83).[14] McCray notes that Drexler was interested in the private property freedoms of Hayek and the 'minimal state' anarcho-capitalism of Robert Nozick, whose *Anarchy, State and Utopia* (1974) was influential in the establishment of neoliberal interest groups in the same period (McCray 2013, p. 173).[15] Kahn represents a particularly intriguing connection between the L-5 Society and neoliberal futurology, having founded the Hudson Institute in 1961 and later been commissioned by the Heritage Foundation and Reagan Administration to provide a pro-growth, right-wing response to the *Limits to Growth* report and the environmental reforms of the Carter Administration (Simon & Kahn 1984; Cooper 2008, p. 17; Granjou, Walker & Salazar 2017, p. 8).

Meinel and Henson had unsuccessfully attempted to get space colonisation on the agenda for the 1976 UN Committee on Peaceful Uses of Outer Space, but continued lobbying Congress in support of O'Neill's space colonisation agenda (Michaud 1986, p. 87). O'Neill's post-Earth environmentalism lived on through L-5. Slogans included, 'Declare Earth a wilderness area' and 'If you love it, leave it' (ibid, p. 89). Alongside this conservationist discourse, L-5 members took increasing interest in the possibility of commercial exploitation of space resources – both as a means of making space colonisation independent from government funding *and* on the level of self-interest. L-5 founder Keith Henson remarked, 'I'm going to be a billionaire. A lot of us are' (Michaud 1986, p. 246).[16]

In 1979, the L-5 Society began its most notable political campaign – a lobbying project that had a significant impact on international space resources law. The United Nations' *Agreement Governing the Activities of States on the Moon and Other Celestial Bodies* was negotiated in the UN from 1972 and opened for signature in 1979 (henceforth referred to as the 'Moon Agreement'). This treaty described celestial bodies and their resources as the 'common heritage of mankind'. The *Agreement* went further than the 'province of all mankind' language of the *Outer Space Treaty* (1967), by explicitly prohibiting unilateral, private appropriations of space resources. Further, it stated that, when off-world mining became technically feasible, the international community would establish 'an international regime … to govern the exploitation of [lunar] resources' and distribute economic and technological benefits to all nations (Art. 11, para. 5). A number of articles published in the L-5 News between 1979 and 1982 highlight the organisation's opposition to the Moon Agreement (e.g. Dula 1979a). There were countervailing opinions evident within L-5 during this period, including a board member's call for restraint in L-5's lobbying activities (Finch 1979).

However, the overall thrust of L-5 communications during this period exhibited marked hostility towards the *Agreement*. A two-part series from lawyer Art Dula warned that US ratification of the *Agreement* posed a threat to the commercial development of outer space. Noting that 'NASA has a monopoly on space transportation', Dula argued that the *Agreement*'s emphasis on central planning of resource exploitation represented the 'antithesis of a free market approach to the exploitation and use' of off-world resources (Dula 1979a, p. 2; Dula 1979b, p. 5). If national governments could no longer be relied on to support large-scale space projects, commercial investment was needed. If commercial entities were unable to privately own space resources, private capital would be discouraged from participating in space colonisation, thus presenting a significant hurdle for the O'Neillian vision. L-5's Keith Henson framed L-5's opposition to the Agreement within the American libertarian tradition, claiming that 'The treaty makes no provisions for the civil rights of those who go to into space', and would 'stifle creative private initiative by prohibiting private property' (Henson 1980). Through the L-5 Society's opposition to the *Moon Agreement*, private property entered the NewSpace policy program largely as a reactive measure against international laws of the global commons.

As much as the L-5 Society (now the National Space Society) has enjoyed counting the defeat of the Moon Agreement among their otherwise limited political triumphs (Hopkins 1982; Brandt-Erichsen 1994), Michaud makes the apt summation that the episode demonstrates 'the value of weak interest groups having more powerful allies' (Michaud 1986, p. 93). The L-5 *Moon Agreement* episode is a watershed moment in space advocacy where – through their opposition to international governance and laws of global commons – early NewSpace moved from being a broader coalition of space enthusiasts, libertarianism directed against an uncooperative national government and into a distinctly neoliberal position where the 'strong state' and the power of mining capital are directed to attack an international legal order attempting to constrain private appropriation in the global commons (see Chapter 4). It is a fascinating transition. In the mid-1970s, the L-5 Society was enmeshed within American counter-culture movements, publishing interviews with Timothy Leary (Robinson 1976, p. 6). By 1981, L-5 had aligned itself with the foreign policy directions of the Reagan Administration. This dispute over the international governance of off-world resource appropriation – resolved in favour of embryonic NewSpace – paved the way for the private property guarantees of the *Commercial Space Launch Competitiveness Act* (2015).

From 1983, O'Neill himself became an entrepreneur, most notably through his GEOSTAR satellite positioning project (Michaud 1986, p. 79). The Reagan Administration 'recognized his status as an advocate of the private sector' and appointed O'Neill to serve on the National Commission on Space (Dyson 1993, p. 98). Part of the Reagan Administration's reappraisal of US space policy, the Commission's 1986 report outlined a 'Pioneering Mission for 21st Century America':

> To lead the exploration and development of the space frontier, advancing science, technology, and enterprise, and building institutions and systems that make accessible vast new resources and support human settlement beyond Earth orbit, from the highlands of the Moon to the plains of Mars. (National Commission on Space 1986)

Following O'Neill's death in 1992, Freeman Dyson – his friend and an ongoing advocate for space colonisation – penned an obituary that described O'Neill as an 'effective and enthusiastic' teacher, who took 'infinite trouble to get the details right' and an outsider prepared to stand up 'against the established wisdom' (1993, p. 98). 'Established wisdom' would change, however. A new neoliberal agenda for the American economy would intensify the commercialisation of US space activity. The strong state and free economy would be projected onto an alternate 'High Frontier' (Graham 1982), re-characterised as the military high-ground in a re-escalating Cold War.

1980–present: the emergence of private property rights and space mining start-ups

This final section focuses on two core developments that bring us to the present day: on the one hand, the development of a neoliberal program in US space policy; on the other hand, the emergence of network of recognisably 'NewSpace' start-ups and civil society groups with an ascendant pro-commerce and anti-statist idiom within them. The Reagan Administration (1981–1989) undertook commercialisation reforms that reconfigured NASA's role in the 'public-private partnership', whereby the government direction of private contractors of the Apollo era makes way for turn towards a more arms-length privatisation of space activity. I argue that the emergence of space mining firms and the passage of the *Commercial Space Launch Competitiveness Act* (2015) is the culmination and synthesis of these two developments. By the 1990s, new entrepreneurs are drawn into the space industry by Reaganite reforms. By the 2000s, libertarian NewSpace appears to secure the backing of the neoliberal Atlas Network (Hudgins 2002; TechFreedom 2015; Lowe 2022). In the 2010s, space mining start-ups emerge with the funding of Silicon Valley fortunes. Now, the high frontier is well and truly open for (state-supported) business.

The high frontier of Reaganite neoliberalism

While the L-5 Society was fighting the *Moon Agreement*, neoliberalism had begun to penetrate public discourse and public institutions. The Thatcher Government (1979–1990) and Reagan Administration (1981–1989) became the first Western neoliberal governments.[17] The 1980s involved a realisation of the ideas established in the MPS and the Chicago School of Law and Economics, with the US and UK governments devolving the state's provision of goods and services to corporate firms. New markets were created for public utilities like energy, water, education, health and public safety. Reagan aggressively pursued economic growth and attacked the social democratic Great Society and New Deal welfare reforms, enacted massive cuts to education budgets and the EPA, and pushed pro-market reforms that included tax cuts for corporations and high-income earners, deregulation of telecommunications industries, expansive granting of oil drilling licenses and the commercialisation of national R&D projects (to name a few). Contrary to the aspirations of 'small government' that mark neoliberalism's public façade, defence spending under Reagan swelled and much public money flowed to large military-industrial contractors engaged in space engineering and NASA procurement. The simmering NewSpace movement found a government willing to restore space exploration to national prestige following its exile during the 1970s, albeit with a renewed emphasis on Cold War geostrategy and a new commercial orientation.

The 1980s also saw the consolidation of the neoliberal thought collective, from a loose array of MPS members into a coordinated transnational political network that began to take an interest in US space policy (among many other policy fields). In 1981, English businessman Sir Antony Fisher had founded the Atlas Economic Research Foundation, now known as the Atlas Network (Fisher founded London's Institute for Economic Affairs in 1964, which became a central think-tank for English neoliberalism under Margaret Thatcher's government). Neoliberal think-tanks like the Heritage Foundation and the Cato Institute became key Atlas nodes in the United States. Today, it is a network amply-funded by corporate and private philanthropy, encompassing over 500 think-tanks globally and committed to a 'vision of a free, prosperous and peaceful world where the principles of individual liberty, property rights, limited government, and free markets are secured by the rule of law' (Atlas Network 2023). Plehwe notes that most of these think-tanks 'have been founded and are run with the help of at least one MPS member' (2009, p. 35, footnote 6). One example is the Reason Foundation. Its monthly magazine, *Reason*, has served as a mouthpiece for libertarian and neoliberal thought, and published articles from leaders within this movement in the early years of the Reagan Administration (Rothbard 1980; Hayek 1981).

Some early examples of NewSpace discourse being communicated through Atlas member organisations appeared in *Reason* during the early 1980s. In 1981, writer James Bennett prescribed the same role for government in supporting space commerce that NewSpace has done in recent decades (Tumlinson 2012).

> For too long advocates of private enterprise have been torn between an admiration for the magnificent accomplishments of space explorers and an uneasiness at the domination of the field by a giant government bureaucracy. The time has come for policy decisions that will move the field of space development forward by getting the government out of humankind's newest arena of endeavor and replacing it with the creative, innovative approach of entrepreneurs. (Bennett 1981)

Bennett offers a clear example of the Hayekian aporia of claiming to 'make as much use as possible of the spontaneous forces of society' while also 'deliberately creating a system within which competition will work as beneficially as possible' (Hayek 1986, p. 13). Bennett asserted that 'the US Government should be doing all that it can, without active involvement, to further the establishment of a commercial, competitive merchant fleet in space' – this included privatising the Space Shuttle, limiting regulatory burden on private space operators and a 'government that stands up for the freedom of commerce and refuses to sign agreements that infringe upon basic freedoms and rights' (Bennett 1981). The right to exploit off-world resources is supposedly one of these 'basic' rights. His call for 'the government [to] clearly oppose any attempts on the part of international bodies to allocate space resources or to otherwise hamper commercial space operations by US citizens' was answered in the Reagan Administration's refusal to sign the *Moon Agreement* (Bennett 1981). Subsequent Atlas interest in off-world resource exploitation appeared in the aforementioned critiques of the 'common heritage' principle (Bandow 1982; Malone 1983).

Key developments in the neoliberalisation of the American space program can be attributed to other nodes in the Atlas Network. The Heritage Foundation also took an interest in American space policy through the *High Frontier: A New National Strategy* report (Graham 1982). This report had originated in the conservative American Security Council Foundation (a military-oriented think-tank that is not an Atlas member), but was sponsored and published by Heritage during Reagan's second year in office

(Michaud 1986, p. 228). The report served primarily as a pre-cursor to the Strategic Defense Initiative ('Star Wars') by introducing the concept of a defensive shield of anti-ballistic missile technology. The Heritage *High Frontier* report appeared to draw on concepts from the O'Neillian high frontier.[18] Space would provide 'zero gravity, near perfect vacuum, unlimited heat absorption, and sterile conditions' to aid commercial and industrial activity, alongside the familiar refrain that 'space also contains inexhaustible supplies of minerals and solar energy' (Graham 1982). The report's author, retired Air Force officer Daniel Graham, fuses the Cold War containment paradigm with American exceptionalism and, like O'Neill, refused to accept any limits to growth.

> The United States is faced with an historic, but fleeting opportunity to take its destiny into its own hands. The ominous military and economic trends which today beset the peoples of the Free World can be reversed, and confidence in the future of free political and economic systems can be restored. To accomplish this, we need only take maximum advantage of one priceless legacy handed down to us by those free institutions – superiority in space technology. We can escape the brooding menace of "balance of terror" doctrines by deploying defensive systems in space. We can confound the prophets of doom by opening the vast and rich High Frontier of space for industrialization. (Graham 1982)

In Graham's view, the 'government's role in opening up the High Frontier of space for economic exploitation is basically the same as it has been with the opening of frontiers of the past: exploration, transportation systems, and security' (ibid). A strong state, making the frontier safe for capitalism.

Reagan's 1984 State of the Union address returned outer space to the national limelight. His speech announced the Strategic Defense Initiative and a new space station program for America, following the modest success of *Skylab*. Predictably, it was to be called space station *Freedom.*[19] Reagan's speech embedded the frontier mythos of outer space within neoliberal prerogatives of market-based competition.

> A sparkling economy spurs initiatives, sunrise industries, and makes older ones more competitive. Nowhere is this more important than our next frontier: space ... Opportunities and jobs will multiply as we cross new thresholds of knowledge and reach deeper into the unknown. (1984)

The space sector was among other 'sunrise industries' like information and communication technologies (ICT) and the corporate life sciences (Cooper 2008). Two success stories from this period were Sun Microsystems of Palo Alto, California and Microsoft in Seattle. During this period, Eric Schmidt (now with Google) and Charles Simonyi were employed by Sun and Microsoft, respectively; more recently, the two were founding investors in space mining start-up Planetary Resources (n.d.-a). The burgeoning US ICT sector was also fuelled by financial reforms, including those that allowed pension funds to invest more speculatively – during the early 1980s, investment into VC funds increased tenfold (Lerner 2002, p. 76).

The 'integration of public science and private profit' is a central element of the neoliberal agenda for scientific research (Lave, Mirowski & Randalls 2010, p. 664). Specific reforms had arrived prior to the Reagan Administration, such as the 'Bayh-Dole Act' which authorised universities and private sector firms to profit from 'inventions arising from federally supported research and development' (*Patent and Trademarks Amendment Act of 1980*, s. 200). In the space sector, the Office of Commercial Programs was created in 1984 and was tasked with advocating commercialisation within NASA and liaising between NASA agencies, industries and university-based institutes (Bromberg 1999, p. 122). Today, this 'public science for private profit' mandate is perpetuated through NASA's Technology Transfer Program, which 'spins-off' intellectual property into the private sector – ranging from image sensors for digital photography to memory foam pillows and nutrient-rich baby formula derived from astronaut food.

The *Commercial Space Launch Act* was passed in 1984, the titular precursor to the recent CSLCA. Whereas rocket boosters like the Saturn V had been built as part of industry-NASA collaboration, the CSLA turned the design and construction of these expendable components over to private business and NASA's role was reduced to that of customer. In the wake of the 1986 *Challenger* disaster, the 1988 'Presidential Directive on National Space Policy' further limited NASA from providing goods or services that could be turned over to the commercial space industry.[20] The Directive stated that:

> Governmental Space Sectors shall purchase commercially available space goods and services to the fullest extent feasible and shall not conduct activities with potential commercial applications that preclude or deter Commercial Sector space activities. (1988)

The neoliberalising of American space policy was eventually confirmed through amendments to the *National Aeronautics and Space Act (NASA) of 1958*. The mandate of the world's pre-eminent space agency would move beyond seeking 'the benefit of all mankind' (*NASA Act of 1958*). In addition to the *Commercial Space Launch Act 1984*, the *NASA Act*'s 'Declaration of Policy & Purpose' would, in 1990, be amended to include that the general welfare of the United States requires that NASA (among other goals)

> … seek and encourage, to the maximum extent possible, the fullest commercial use of space. (*National Aeronautics and Space Administration Authorization Act, Fiscal Year 1991,* s. 107).

The foundations of a neoliberal mode of space exploration would be laid under Reagan. Now, the US state now supports an emerging space mining industry through laws that commodify outer space itself. To this day, military-industrial mainstays like Boeing and Lockheed-Martin have continued their lucrative cooperation with NASA, which implies that the 'old' and 'new' monikers offer only a faulty periodisation.

Globally, the last quarter of the 20th century saw the bipolar superpower duel at the heart of Cold War spacefaring transition into a new, multipolar 'space economy' replete with new state and corporate actors. Commercial satellite activity in low-Earth orbit had proliferated and NASA's Space Shuttle had to compete with international launch service providers. The multinational European Space Agency (ESA) was founded in 1964 and, from 1984, its Ariane Program carried scientific and commercial payloads to low-Earth orbit (LEO). One frequent customer of the Ariane program was the Luxembourg communications satellite company, SES. SES was founded in 1985 with the support of the Luxembourg Government and now has one of the largest satellite fleets in the world. Sky TV, owned by media baron and Atlas member, Rupert Murdoch, was one of SES' first broadcasters (SES 2021; SES n.d.). The recent Luxembourgian space resources law seeks to build on the success of SES and leverage the technoscientific infrastructure the country established in this period. Meanwhile, the Russian Space Agency (renamed Roscosmos in 1999) embarked on a series of privatisation measures that opened up new partnerships with NASA and US corporations.[21] As the 'space age' approached the 21st century, outer space swelled with the advanced infrastructures of globalised capitalism.

Commercialisation 'to the maximum extent possible': the emergence of NewSpace start-ups

As far as the simmering NewSpace movement was concerned, the late 1980s and 1990s proved as disappointing as the Apollo cancellation. During the 1990s and early 2000s an array of civil society organisations and start-ups emerged, and it is during this period where NewSpace's libertarian discourse appears the most pronounced. The commercialisation of LEO did little for the O'Neillian 'humanising' dream of large-scale permanent space settlement. David Chambers, CEO of the late 1990s start-up MirCorp, remarked that the post-Apollo years were so disappointing that 'it's as though the Moon landing never happened' (*Orphans of Apollo* 2008). New organisations like the SFF (founded 1988), Space Access Society (founded 1992) and the Foundation for the International Nongovernmental Development of Space (founded in 1994, now defunct) were founded. In 1987 the L-5 Society merged with the National Space Institute (founded by Werner von Braun) to become the National Space Society. NewSpace civil society groups continue to lobby for more a decentralised and deregulated spacefaring future.

Reagan-era commercialisation reforms had failed to surpass the achievements of the centrally coordinated Apollo Program. Yet NewSpace discourse increasingly deployed an anti-'big government' narrative that attacked NASA more frequently than the corporations it was tasked by Reagan to rely upon. NewSpace advocate Rick Tumlinson testified before Congress and asserted that:

> NASA and its parasitic contractors must no longer be allowed to manage the designing, building and operation of what are essentially glorified government space trucks/vans. Can you imagine if the government had done the same thing with an airline? It is as if the [Federal Aviation Authority] owned our single national air carrier. With no real competition it would never get cheaper, better or more efficient ... and no one would be able to afford to fly on it. That's the socialist monopoly we have in space flight. (Tumlinson 2003)

This equating of the big aerospace lobby with 'socialist monopoly' raises some interesting questions around neoliberalism and concentrated corporate power. *Corporate* monopoly (or oligopoly, more accurately) is institutionalised in the American space industry. The American space economy was a legacy of the WW2 wartime economy: the key firms that supplied aircraft to the government during the war pivoted towards the newly coined 'space industry' (Bromberg 1999, p. 20). Over the ensuing half-century, 'big aerospace' exhibited a consistent pattern of corporate mergers and acquisitions. Today, Boeing and Lockheed Martin have only SpaceX as a notable competitor in the provision of launch services (the most lucrative and high-risk of space industries).[22] In 2006, Boeing and Lockheed Martin merged their space divisions to form the United Launch Alliance, further concentrating monopoly power in the supply of launch services to NASA and the US armed forces – a merger unsuccessfully challenged by SpaceX under antitrust law between 2005 and 2006. In 2018, Orbital ATK was acquired by arms manufacturer Northrop Grumman.[23]

Are there parallels between neoliberal thought and NewSpace anti-statism regarding the acceptability of concentrated corporate power? Some of the earliest projects undertaken by Chicago School neoliberals sought to justify corporate monopoly, notably the Anti-Trust Project (1953–1957). Rob Van Horn describes how Chicago economist Henry Simons had championed the classical liberal view that critiqued corporate monopoly (alongside trade unions and excessive state interventionism) as 'inherently inimical to democracy because ... it undermined a necessary condition for democratic politics to flourish' (2009, p. 204). Following Simons' death in 1946 and publications from Aaron Director, Chicago School neoliberalism began to reconsider monopoly in light of the belief that the 'corroding influence of competition' could 'destroy all types of monopoly', provided government intervention was limited (Director, cited in Van Horn 2009, p. 218).

The 'socialist monopoly' characterisation has been made elsewhere in NewSpace critiques of NASA and its predominant aerospace contractors (Poole 2002). This position initially appears to be in keeping with the classic liberal position advocated by Simons that corporate monopoly has created barriers to entry, concentrated power and thereby undermines competition. However, contemporary NewSpace appears to have an expedient relationship with some of the aerospace monopolies.[24] The space mining start-up DSI co-founded by Tumlinson is one example. The DSI investor prospectus tells potential investors about how the Lockheed-Boeing partnership of United Launch Alliance has offered to become a customer for propellant mined and refined off-world (Deep Space Industries 2016, p. 3; see also Sowers 2017, p. 4). Space mining's relationships with capitalist oligopoly are evident elsewhere. The Google and PayPal behemoths were founded by Larry Page and Peter Thiel, respectively; the personal wealth of these early supporters of Planetary Resources and their capacity to provide seed capital for such speculative investments derives from their ICT oligopolies. Jeff Bezos' Blue Origin owes much to his personal fortune, obviously emanating from Amazon's global e-commerce and media empire. In spite of the NewSpace prerogatives of 'decentralised' spacefaring, concentrated corporate power looms as the more plausible means of actually realising privately operated space mining and colonisation operations. As with the Chicago School's stance on monopoly, NewSpace's activities (as opposed to its rhetoric) suggest they consider the concentration of corporate power as 'not deleterious to the operation of the market' and the power of aerospace oligopolies to be 'attributable to ill-functioning ham-fisted activities of government' (Van Horn 2009, p. 229).

When NewSpace emphasises government as the cause of the 'big aerospace' monopoly problem, they appear to adopt the principles of 'public choice theory'. Public choice theory was developed by MPS economists James Buchanan and Gordon Tullock (1962), and it attempts to explain the behaviour of public officials using the neoclassical economic axiom of the self-interested, utility-maximising consumer. Karen Fischer summarises public choice theory as a theory of 'government failure': policy decisions are made by politicians 'based on their interest in maintaining their positions of power' (2009, p. 324). NewSpace actors have characterised American space bureaucracy as a 'plethora of regulatory agencies whose officials do not even pretend to have been elected by anyone' (Zubrin 1994). The centralised decision-making of NASA is charged with having a bias towards existing contractors (Boeing, Lockheed-Martin and so on), and long-run programs like the Space Shuttle or the (still ongoing) Space Launch System appear in NewSpace discourse as evidence of 'industrial base protectionism and pork-barrelling' (Sarsfield 2002, p. 31). Two writers from the Atlas Network's TechFreedom recently implored Congress to reduce 'opaqueness' in NASA mission authorisation and lamented that 'bureaucrats can still pick winners and losers with impunity' (Dunstan & Szoka 2017, p. 8). According to NewSpace, this short-termism from elected officials reduces the opportunities for the burgeoning entrepreneurial sector – unless, of course, you are one of the winners that receives research grants (see, for example Deep Space Industries 2019).

In NewSpace discourse, these anti-monopoly and public choice arguments served to perpetuate the O'Neillian angst about the US Government's failure to adopt the long-term utopian vision of human settlement. NASA has retained an interest in mining the high frontier since the 1970s, and a number of scoping studies were published during the 1990s. NASA published a series of *Space Resources* reports, which did not represent 'any Government-authorised view or official NASA policy' and were similar in nature to the 'blue sky' workshops that O'Neill had organised NASA's Ames Centre in Silicon Valley at the peak of his popularity (McKay, McKay & Duke 1992, p. vi). The reports proposed mining techniques and hypothesised economic considerations, but the concepts they discussed were never given the multibillion-dollar investments needed for their fruition. NewSpace 'pop science' texts emerged in the 1990s, including some that touted multitrillion-dollar rewards for space miners. In *Mining the Sky,* John Lewis (now Chief Scientist with DSI) made exorbitant claims that asteroid mining could produce wealth 'equivalent to the gross product of Earth for the next thirty thousand years' (1997, p. 112).

NASA and American space policy has had more modest goals, such as Space Shuttle missions to the Hubble Telescope or the *International Space Station* (1998–present). Mars expedition plans came and went under the governments of George Bush, Bill Clinton and George W. Bush. The Obama Administration had established the 2009–2010 *Review of U.S. Human Spaceflight Plans Committee* (the Augustine Commission), which briefly discussed *in situ* resource utilisation and off-world propellant production; the report noted that 'their application appears to be far off' and 'the technology remains to be demonstrated under realistic circumstances' (Review of Human Spaceflight Plans Committee 2010, pp. 101–102). NASA's Asteroid Retrieval Mission was cancelled before its scheduled launch in 2021. NewSpace complaints about government-led spacefaring have been exacerbated by the perception that the United States has been losing ground to foreign competitors (Bigelow 2017). When the Space Shuttle was retired in 2011, the United States no longer had its own means of sending astronauts into space. Until SpaceX's transportation of US astronauts to the ISS in 2020, the only way for American astronauts to reach the International Space Station (ISS) has been NASA procurements of rides in Russian *Soyuz* capsules.[25] For the more patriotic members of NewSpace, NASA and the broader American space industry, this reliance on Russia represented a notable downturn in national prestige.

NewSpace civil society groups continued their advocacy work during this period of change in the international spacefaring landscape. In addition to the SFF, National Space Society and SEDS, further recent examples from the US NewSpace network include the following: the Lifeboat Foundation, Tea Party in Space, Space Renaissance, the Space Development Foundation and Commercial

Spaceflight Federation. The above groups (and more) comprise the Alliance for Space Development (ASD), united in advocating for 'policies that will expedite the growth of the commercial space industry' (Wainscott 2017). The Alliance conducts an annual event on Capitol Hill in which volunteers meet with Congressional staff to discuss their *Citizens' Space Agenda* (ASD 2016, 2019). The ASD continue to advocate for 'public-private partnerships' that resemble Hayek's planned construction of competitive market orders, urging the US Government to support space resources industries, commercial space stations and NASA's existing commercial transport programs (ASD 2016).[26]

Since the late 1990s, NewSpace has been supported by an increasing number of entrepreneurs and venture capitalists. As a culmination of Reaganite commercialisation reforms and a new commercial agenda under George W. Bush (2001–2009), including the *Commercial Space Launch Amendments Act* (2004), new actors were drawn into smaller space projects. VC funds, asset managers and private 'angel investors' saw potential in space investments. Lerner, Leamon and Speen analysed the role of VC in low-Earth orbit (LEO) enterprises, noting a total of US $1.64 billion of VC invested in LEO-operating firms between 1983–2015 (2016, p.90).

Several space mining firms have been established since 2010. While they have attracted investment from numerous quarters, we can attribute their emergence to entrepreneurs within the NewSpace network – such as O'Neill enthusiasts like Tumlinson (DSI) and Peter Diamandis (Planetary Resources). These firms have been supported by VC or angel investment, including numerous Silicon Valley billionaires (Crunchbase 2019a, 2019c, 2019c & 2019d; Planetary Resources n.d.-a, 2016a; Pepis, Evans & de Jong 2018). However, this start-up industry also relies upon the ongoing support of the taxpayer, in the form of research grants, NASA procurements and – in the case of Planetary Resources – a €25 million investment from the Luxembourg Government.[27] In spite of DSI CEO David Gump's claim that his company is 'the working class asteroid mining company' (Gump 2018), the combination of government support and VC suggest that the nascent space mining sector is very much an elite endeavour.

NewSpace, Atlas and private property rights for space resources

During the past 20 years, the NewSpace vision appears to have secured the support of organisations and individuals within the neoliberal Atlas Network. Atlas organisations have mirrored and amplified NewSpace discourse about government failures in American spacefaring and have promoted private, entrepreneurial forces as the preferred means of achieving this expansive project. In addition to Heritage Institute commentary on the common heritage principle and *Reason* writers' interest in commercial space activity during the Reagan Administration (outlined above), a variety of Atlas organisations have more recently advocated for private property regimes in outer space (e.g. Hudgins 1998; Block & Huebert 2008; Salter &

Leeson 2014; Bennett & Grearson 2019; Lowe 2022). Atlas members have taken notice of the space mining industry, and they directly and indirectly supported the passage of the *Commercial Space Launch Competitiveness Act* (CSLCA 2015).

My impression is that most NewSpace advocates arrived at a neoliberal program for space settlement through their disappointment with the lack of progress achieved by NASA, rather than through a concerted engagement with neoliberal theorists. For Atlas writers and policy analysts sympathetic to NewSpace, however, questions of off-world resource ownership and private sector spacefaring are more explicitly couched within neoliberal political philosophy. The Cato Institute's Edward Hudgins, for example, has explicitly drawn on Chicago School theorists in advocating for a neoliberal model for space development and settlement. The Cato Institute is a key node in Atlas neoliberalism and Hudgins (a former Heritage and Cato writer and now Director of Research with another Atlas bastion, the Heartland Institute) has published numerous recommendations in support of private property law for outer space (Hudgins 1998; 2001; 2002; 2011).

In a Cato white paper entitled *Martian law,* Hudgins outlines political-economic arrangements for future off-world economies, predicated on principles of individual liberty and limited regulation (1998). Rejecting the *Outer Space Treaty* and other treaties of the global commons, Hudgins argues that Martian law, regulation and coercion should be limited to enforcing individuals' and consortia's rights to private property and contractual exchange – a view espoused by neoliberals like Lippman (1938) and Ronald Coase (1960). He continues by drawing on the efficient market hypothesis, that 'even with initial mal-distributions of wealth, as long as the free exchange system exists, economic efficiency will win out. That's why establishing markets will be crucial to Martian settlement' (Hudgins 1998). Explicitly invoking Hayek's spontaneous order, he rejects the alleged 'belief among socialists and statists that all-wise, caring bureaucrats can plan and benevolently guide economies to prosperity' – instead trusting that anti-statist free marketeers could benevolently maintain a functioning off-world society (Hudgins 1998).

Hudgins' most significant contribution to neoliberal space advocacy is his compilation of the Cato Institute's *Space: The Free Market Frontier* (Hudgins 2002). This volume resulted from a conference Cato held in partnership with, among others, 'our friends at the Space Frontier Foundation' (ibid, p. v).[28] In Hudgins' volume, space lawyer and advocate James Dunstan offers an example of neoliberal opposition to common property, describing the *Outer Space Treaty* as representing 'the high-water mark of international socialism in its concept that outer space is the province of all humankind' (Dunstan 2002, p. 235). Hudgins and the Cato Institute have elsewhere supported privatising space infrastructure, reducing the role of government in spacefaring to a purchaser of private sector goods and services and the legislating for private property rights legislation for space resources (Crawford 1986; Scheraga 1987; Hudgins 2001; Salter & Leeson 2014).

The relationship between NewSpace and the Atlas Network is likely both networks influencing the other. NewSpace actors can be seen espousing neoliberal-style policies long after publishing with the Cato Institute (e.g. Muncy, Tumlinson & Werb 2002; Tumlinson 2012). One author from Cato's *Free Market Frontier* report now works with a new Atlas organisation – TechFreedom – that has recently testified before Congress in favour of domestic space resources law (Dunstan 2002; Szoka & Dunstan 2017). There are also numerous instances where NewSpace-like discourse emanates from Atlas think-tanks, perhaps suggesting that NewSpace communication has been influential in this 'mainstream' of neoliberal advocacy, and perhaps auguring future entanglements between the two movements. In addition to Cato and Heritage, the Competitive Enterprise Institute, Niskanen Centre, Atlas Society, Foundation for Economic Education, Mises Institute, Reason Foundation, TechFreedom and Institute of Economic Affairs can all be seen supporting off-world private property or the privatisation of NASA (respectively: Simberg 2012; Hampson 2017; Hudgins 2006; Block & Huebert 2008; Murphy 2005; Grearson & Bennett 2019; Dunstan & Szoka 2017; Littlewood 2021). All of these organisations have a social and ideological lineage tracing back to the MPS.

In light of the environmental justifications for space colonisation and off-world resource ownership, it is important to emphasise that nearly all of these Atlas organisations have mounted sustained attacks on climate science, climate scientists and environmental protection law.[29] Through Atlas, NewSpace's post-limits environmentalism becomes bedfellows with neoliberal strategies of climate denial. NewSpace advocacy for the profit-based colonisation of space – a project that began with the O'Neillian rejection of limits to growth and the global environmental governance that came with it – is being amplified by organisations that have opposed action on climate change. In light of NewSpace's evident support from neoliberal think-tanks and the willingness of NewSpace actors to collaborate with these organisations in the past, we need to treat the rhetoric surrounding space mining – such as Planetary Resources' claim that 'we can use the resources of space to save our planet' (Orsulak 2018) – with a degree of scepticism.

However, there are two key differences between NewSpace and neoliberal positions on climate change. First, NewSpace's colonisation project involves a bypassing of Earth's biophysical limits. From O'Neill to the SFF to Elon Musk, most NewSpace members do not deny these limits. Second, Atlas engagement with NewSpace has for the most part been limited to the broadcast of NewSpace discourse through the communication channels of Atlas think-tanks (white papers, blog posts, seminars and so on). I have not found evidence of lobbying for the CSLCA from the Atlas members in the form of campaign contributions or political action committees. This is a point of contrast with the coordinated assault on climate policy conducted by Atlas organisations and their billionaire donors like the Koch brothers and ExxonMobil (ExxonSecrets n.d.). NewSpace's 'March Storm' on

Capitol Hill has, in the past, featured an organisation called the Tea Party in Space (ASD 2017). However, unlike the conservative Tea Party movement spearheaded by Sarah Palin and bankrolled by the Kochs' Americans for Prosperity think-tank (Mirowski 2013), there is no evidence that NewSpace civil society groups are 'astroturf' organisations in receipt of funding from powerful Atlas donors. Neither the SFF nor National Space Society (formerly the L-5 Society), for instance, are Atlas member organisations.

In Republican donor Peter Thiel, however, there are early signs that the NewSpace and Atlas networks are converging on a more material level. Prior to advent of cryptocurrency, Thiel co-founded the PayPal money transfer system in 1998 with a vision of 'a new world currency, free from all government control and dilution – the end of monetary sovereignty, as it were' (Thiel 2009). The sale of PayPal to eBay for $1.5 billion in 2002 expanded the personal fortunes of Thiel and Elon Musk (whose X.com merged with PayPal in 2000). While Musk turned his attention to SpaceX, Thiel backed numerous start-ups and corporations through his Clarium Capital hedge fund and VC Founders Fund (including Musk's SpaceX). Thiel's Founders Fund was an investor in space miners Planetary Resources (Planetary Resources n.d.-a) and Moon Express (CrunchBase 2019b). Founders Fund has also recently invested in the start-up, Varda, which intends to establish automated manufacturing processes in space (Kokalitcheva 2020).

Through the Thiel-Founders Fund investment in Planetary Resources and Moon Express, we can see a material interest from an Atlas member in the passage of the CSLCA. In 2015, Thiel was awarded the Hayek Lifetime Achievement award by the Austrian Economics Center and F.A. v Hayek Institut (Atlas members organisations) in 'recognition of his entrepreneurial contributions to the world economy … as a staunch advocate for free markets and innovation' (AEC 2015). In an article for *Cato Unbound*, Thiel goes beyond the anarcho-libertarian off-worlding of O'Neill into a Hayekian contempt for democracy:

> I no longer believe that freedom and democracy are compatible … the great task for libertarians is to find an escape from politics in all its forms – from the totalitarian and fundamentalist catastrophes to the unthinking demos that guides so-called "social democracy". (2009)

In pursuing the Hayekian immunisation of economy from democracy and the 'escape from politics', Thiel has contributed funding to a number of civil society groups that further techno-libertarian causes closer to Earth. This includes the Machine Intelligence Research Institute, which seeks to augment the human condition through innovations in artificial intelligence and cybernetics, and the Seasteading Institute, which seeks to build offshore island utopias in international waters (Thiel 2009; Quirk 2018; MIRI 2021). Headed by Patri Friedman, grandson of MPS co-founder and neoliberal economist Milton Friedman, the Seasteading Institute is a member organisation of the Atlas Network (2019).

Some of Thiel's other business interests accord with the 'strong state, free economy' aporia of neoliberalism. His Palantir Technologies developed data analytics tools that are used across the United States Intelligence Community.[30] Thiel's business has profited significantly from state surveillance programs, fortifying the sovereign power of the US rather than 'escaping from world politics', as he called it. In terms of ideological inspirations, O'Connell notes how the anarcho-capitalist text *The Sovereign Individual* resonated with Thiel (Davidson & Rees-Mogg 1999; O'Connell 2018). *The Sovereign Individual* described a future where the state becomes obsolete through cryptocurrencies and 'out of this wreckage will emerge a new global dispensation, in which a 'cognitive elite' will rise to power … and will redesign governments to suit their ends' (O'Connell 2018). As an opponent of climate action, Thiel may play an active role in bringing an apocalypse about, but his luxurious doomsday bunker in New Zealand may provide an escape hatch (O'Connell 2018; Becker 2019).

The involvement of an Atlas neoliberal in the space mining sector might foreshadow an off-world plutocracy, drastically at odds with the provisions of the *Outer Space Treaty* and indeed humanity's common interests in global commons. Some further evidence of Atlas involvement in the CSLCA's passage can be found through Rep. Dana Rohrabacher (R. CA; 1989–2018). As Ames notes, Rohrabacher was active in the campus libertarian movement in the 1970s, working with influential neoliberal Robert Lefevre while an activist with Young Americans for Freedom, and was a founding member of Charles Koch's Libertarian Supper Club (Ames 2013, pp. 22–24; see also Konkin 1998). More recently, Rohrabacher was a recipient of campaign funding from Koch Industries (OpenSecrets 2023j).

Rohrabacher was a contributor in Cato's *Space – The Free Market Frontier*, arguing that space corporations should be regulated on a 'zero gravity, zero tax' basis (Rohrabacher 2002). Rohrabacher has more recently supported the NewSpace civil society partnership, the ASD (2016). He introduced the unsuccessful *Space, Exploration, Settlement and Development Act of 2016* (SEDS), which would have amended the *NASA Act of 1958* to prioritise 'the exploration and development of space leading to human settlements beyond Earth' and 'enable America to tap vast new resources' (SEDS 2016, preamble, s. 2; ASD 2016). In May 2015, he lauded pro-commerce legislative reform in the House in the lead-up to the passage of the CSLCA (Congressional Record 2015b, H3517), and was a co-sponsor of a previous attempt to establish domestic off-world private property law (House of Representatives 2014). Through Rohrabacher and Thiel's investment in Planetary Resources, the Atlas-MPS network has played a role in introducing the unilateral assertion of private property rights for US corporations in outer space.

Focusing solely on Atlas neoliberalism perhaps overcomplicates what is a well-trodden path in contemporary representative democracy. The United States' unilateral guarantee of private property in outer space is a direct result of the lobbying conducted by Planetary Resources, who proudly note in their promotional material that they 'successfully lobbied towards the passage of the U.S. Commercial Space Launch Competitiveness Act' (Planetary Resources n.d.-b). The company hired a legal advisor to draft the CSLCA precursor and it paid a lobbying firm that hired former congressmen to directly lobby sitting politicians (Gabrynowicz, in Levine 2015; Edwards, in Cong. Rec. 2015, p.H3520). I discuss the corporate capture of political institutions further in Chapter 4.

At the time of writing, the CSLCA has been emulated by three nations Luxembourg, the United Arab Emirates and Japan, with Luxembourg becoming the first to do so in 2017 (*Law of 20 July 2017 on the Exploration and Use of Space Resources*). Luxembourg's engagement was an interesting development: to the techno-industrial and politico-legal power of the United States we can add a low-tax jurisdiction that is one of the world's primary centres of offshore investment (Zucman 2015). Luxembourg's *SpaceResource.lu* initiative leveraged the nation's existing space industries and associated infrastructures (concentrated in satellite construction and operation) to attract the potentially lucrative space mining industry. The small constitutional monarchy made investments in and established memoranda of understanding with space mining firms (Planetary Resources 2016a). Companies such as Deep Space Industries (recently acquired by Bradford Space) and Japan's iSpace have established offices in Luxembourg (Luxembourg Space Agency 2022). Space miners' engagement with the country's space resources initiative can be read as an effort to 'multi-lateralise' and reframe the US-led private property drive as a 'global endeavour', while still having future property claims anchored in the state authority of the United States (Marquez 2017, p. 4).

Luxembourg has persistently structured its economic policy in order to help multinational corporations avoid their domestic tax responsibilities (Zucman 2015). Here we can see an accord between NewSpace discourses of escape and disavowal of responsibility to society (in the form of preserving commons, paying tax and sharing resource revenue) and these partnerships with Luxembourg. Seeking favourable taxation environments is fairly standard practice in neoliberal globalisation, and space mining firms are not breaking any laws in doing so (though, in Chapter 6, we will explore the proto-NewSpace investor Walt Anderson, who holds one of America's largest tax fraud convictions). However, given that the Luxembourg Government touts its 'attractive corporate tax rate' and 'extensive network of double tax treaties' to foreign companies looking to relocate (Luxinnovation 2017, p. 7), it is not unreasonable to hypothesise that the O'Neillian 'humanising' dream is, in this case, being supported by an escape from domestic, democratic tax obligations. It remains to be seen precisely what role space mining firms will play if and when the 'strong state, free economy' relationship actually materialises on celestial bodies. At this point in time, however, there are strong indications that the freedom to explore and use the province of all humankind will be exercised by an elite few.

Conclusion

We have reached the end of the long road from Konstantin Tsiolkovsky's off-world emancipation to the introduction of laws that recognise private ownership of space resources. For many NewSpace actors, there remains an evident sense of disappointment in how space exploration has transpired since the end of Apollo. The Artemis Project may prove to be a revival of the heights of American spacefaring or yet another ambitious goal that is mired in NASA bureaucracy. As evidenced in Jeff Bezos's plans to 'go to space to save humanity', Gerard O'Neill's *High Frontier* endures as a compelling alternative to the more modest spacefaring activities undertaken by NASA since the 1970s.

While we can trace the origins of off-world private property in the grassroots space enthusiasm, NewSpace ventures now enjoy the support of billionaires like Bezos, Musk and other wealth emanating from Silicon Valley and venture capitalism. Goldman Sachs are no strangers to speculative investment, and they too have taken notice of space mining:

> Space mining could be more realistic than perceived ... According to a 2012 Reuters interview with Planetary Resources, a single asteroid the size of a football field could contain $US25bn- $US50bn worth of platinum ... We expect that systems could be built for less than that given trends in the cost of manufacturing spacecraft and improvements in technology. Given the capex of mining operations on Earth, we think that financing a space mission is not outside the realm of possibility. (Cited in Edwards 2017)

Start-ups like Planetary Resources represent the comparatively sober 'business face' of an emancipatory, transcendent and cornucopian imaginary with roots as deep as the cosmist philosophy of Tsiolkovsky. Yet the 'visioneering' (McCray 2013) of the NewSpace imaginary is now predicated on the accumulation of private wealth; these two elements in NewSpace utopianism will continue to sit uneasily so long as private ownership of space resources is part of the space colonisation agenda.

The NewSpace era has been heralded as a break from the dominance of state-centred spacefaring, and the off-world represents an 'an escape from politics' for the techno-libertarian supporters of the NewSpace movement (Thiel 2009). Yet despite the valorisation of the entrepreneur and rejection of state control of the space economy that has characterised this movement, the libertarian free enterprise dream ultimately needs the strong state to open and enforce its conditions of existence. In the words of the MPS, the supposedly 'diffused power and initiative' of 'private property and the competitive market' actually requires 'fostering' through 'the rule of law' (MPS n.d.). The off-world utopia of individual liberty, economic freedom and limitless abundance is now supported by the recognition of private property rights on space resources. For the very first time in human history, the legal groundwork has been laid for private ownership claims on other celestial bodies. It may prove to be a momentous step in humanity's relationship with the cosmos. Far from 'opening' the space frontier, it is likely to enclose it.

Notes

1 The moniker has assumed an official air through the annual conference of the SFF, which has run annually since 2006 (SFF 2008).
2 Moon Express has outlined plans for off-world resource exploitation; their business model, however, currently leans more towards lunar transportation and landing technologies (Moon Express n.d.).
3 As a further NewSpace precursor, Irish communist, scientist and historian of science and technology JD Bernal had also proposed in 1929 that 'the asteroids would be convenient sources of solid raw materials … . Feeding on sunlight, asteroids, and planetary gases, the space habitations could grow to any desirable size' (cited in Michaud 1986, p. 64).
4 Many of the participants had discussed a 'new liberalism' in Vienna a decade prior – American economists Lionel Robbins and Frank Knight had attended a seminar hosted by von Mises at the Austrian Chamber of Commerce, for instance, and would go on to work in the Chicago School of Economics (Plehwe 2009, p. 11).
5 Nazi Germany had not collectivised private industry in the same manner as the Soviet Union, but had nonetheless coordinated firms like Volkswagen and IBM in the service of the wartime economy.
6 Following the hitherto unparalleled destruction of the First World War, provisions within the Versailles Treaty had limited the development of long-range artillery in Weimar Germany – rocket-propelled explosives presented an appealing work-around for military officials looking to strengthen the German armed forces (Kilgore 2003, p. 70).
7 Hayek refined this into a model of the market as an autonomous, self-regulating and indeed omniscient processor of information (in the form of price signals) – a decentralised authority that was vastly superior to the informationally deficient centralised decision-making of the state (Hayek 1950).
8 The OST and its Cold War origins are discussed further in Chapter 5.
9 I return to NewSpace technofixes and post-limits discourse in Chapter 7.
10 Incidentally, this is also the year when O'Neill was rejected by the US astronaut corps (Michaud 1986, p. 60).
11 Harmes has described this sort of sub-national 'race to the bottom' as 'neoliberal federalism' (2012, pp. 66–67).
12 A brief explanatory note on the 'L-5' moniker is worthwhile. In 1772, the mathematician and astronomer Joseph-Louis Lagrange observed peculiar orbits of 'Trojan' asteroids that share the same path as Jupiter around the Sun. One group was always sixty degrees ahead of Jupiter in its orbit, another always sixty degrees behind (O'Neill 1977, p. 128). He had discovered what became known as 'Lagrange-points' or 'L-points', summarised by O'Neill as 'stable points, near which any object with the correct initial location and velocity would stay forever' (ibid, p. 129). L-points were also evident in the Earth-Moon system, where the confluence of gravitational influence from the two celestial bodies produced stable regions around which an artificial satellite could orbit, trailing behind the Moon in its orbit around the Earth. Gerard O'Neill considered that the L-5 point in the Moon's orbit was 'far enough from Earth and Moon to avoid frequent eclipses, so the community can use free solar power continuously', and he considered this and

other Lagrange points to be suitable locations for his 'islands' in space (ibid, p. 128). Equidistant with the Moon, the L-5 point is approximately 380,000 km away from the Earth, significantly further than the 400-km altitude of the International Space Station – presently the most successful long-term human habitat in space.

13 As a point of contrast, the Planetary Society (founded 1980) was a much larger pro-space organisation that has generally been more interested in the exploration and scientific understanding of space than its colonisation or commercial exploitation.

14 The economics division at RAND Corp contained several Mont Pèlerin Society members (such as Armen Alchian). I discuss RAND's influence on American space policy further in Chapter 5.

15 While they seem to have taken little interest in O'Neill's ideas, the Heritage Foundation (1973) and the Cato Institute (1974) were founded in this period.

16 O'Neill eventually distanced himself from L-5 for fears of his own reputation as a respected physicist, and by 1984 referred to them dismissively as 'those people in Arizona' (Michaud 1986, p. 88).

17 Fischer (2009) describes role of the Chicago School in introducing neoliberal reforms following the 1973 Pinochet coup in Chile, which pre-dated the Thatcher and Reagan governments (which I discuss in Chapter 4).

18 Space sociologist Thomas Ellis describes how O'Neill was incensed that his moniker for peaceful space colonisation could be used for militaristic purposes (2016). Here is an early moment of tension between the humanitarian or cosmopolitan aspirations of NewSpace, and their overarching need for developing the space economy through state support (even when this involves non-peaceful purposes). For more recent examples, we could look to Elon Musk – contemporary NewSpace figurehead – who has evoked the peaceful civilising mission of space colonisation (Musk 2017), while his SpaceX company receives multimillion dollar contracts for launching military satellites into Earth orbit (Ax 2018).

19 Spiralling costs eventually transformed this project into what is now the International Space Station.

20 These commercialisation reforms that emerged in the wake of the widely televised *Challenger* catastrophe could perhaps be considered a form of 'disaster capitalism' described by Naomi Klein (2007), whereby neoliberal policy reforms are introduced while publics are still in shock or mourning (and less capable of organising opposition to these reforms).

21 I discuss this, and the NewSpace privatisation of space station *Mir*, in Chapter 6.

22 Founded in 1916, Boeing bought Rockwell Aerospace and Defense (itself a merger with North American Aviation) and merged with McDonnell Douglas between 1996 and 1997 (Bromberg 1999, pp. 12–13). Founded in 1926, Lockheed Aircraft had competed with Martin Marietta (itself a 1961 merger between the Glenn L. Martin Co and American Marietta, which purchased General Electric's Aerospace division in 1993) until merging with them in 1994 (Bromberg 1999, pp. 12–13).

23 Founded in 1928, industrial chemical manufacturers Thiokol Chemical bought Reaction Motors in 1958 (founded by members of early 'pro-space' organisation, the American Rocket Society) and won numerous contracts for supply of solid-fuel rocket motors (most notably for the Boeing-Air Force designed Minuteman ICBM). Alliant Techsystems – a publicly traded spinoff from Honeywell – purchased Thiokol in 2001 to form ATK Launch Systems (Bromberg 1999, pp. 12–13). In 2015, Orbital ATK was formed through this company's merger with the Orbital Sciences Corporation (founded 1982 and supplier of numerous spacecraft for NASA, the US military and commercial enterprise since).

24 The start-up Made In Space, 'incubated' by Silicon Valley's Singularity University (co-founded by Planetary Resources' Diamandis), is a further example of collaboration between NewSpace and big aerospace. In partnership with arms and aerospace giant Northrup Grumman, Made In Space is developing micro-gravity 3D printing technologies for the Archinaut project, which will attempt construction of large, complex structures in space (Northrop Grumman 2019).
25 SpaceX's recent success can be attributed to the political need to use American space systems capable of transporting crew off-world. While SpaceX was established by the personal wealth of Elon Musk, the company relies upon NASA procurements – such as its $2.6 billion contract for the Commercial Crew Program (Bolden 2014). Musk, figurehead of the NewSpace era, is an exemplary case in the ongoing entwinement of private profit and public money in the space industry.
26 In Chapter 7, we will explore 'NewSpace eschatology' and the role of off-world commerce in averting planetary catastrophe in more detail. Here, it is worth noting that the ASD and other NewSpace actors (such as MirCorp's Walt Anderson) have also advocated for planetary defences in the form of monitoring near-Earth objects (NEOs), like asteroids. Recent endorsement of NASA's NEOCam telescope is one example (ASD 2019, p. 7).
27 I will discuss government supports of the space mining industry further in Chapter 3.
28 The volume features papers covering the scope of the NewSpace network: a pro-private property rights lawyer (White 2002); venture capitalists (Higginbotham 2002); NewSpace civil society advocates (Muncy, Tumlinson & Werb 2002); think-tank professionals, including RAND Corp's Liam Sarsfield (2002); a pro-NewSpace Congressman (Rohrabacher 2002); and former Apollo astronaut Buzz Aldrin (Aldrin & Jones 2002).
29 The Niskanen Center is the notable exception to Atlas' climate denialism, having been formed by former Cato writers who objected to the Koch brothers' takeover of the Cato board and its persistent climate denialism (Gunther 2017).
30 A similar point can be made in relation to Google's Larry Page, who was also an investor in Planetary Resources. Google's early momentum received a significant leg-up from government security initiatives: its search engine was developed with the support of 'the intelligence community' in order to 'find ways to track individuals and groups online' (Nesbit 2017).

3 Enclosing the space commons?

Off-world property through the lens of political history

In the previous chapter, we explored the convergence of neoliberal and NewSpace philosophies. Gerard O'Neill's techno-utopian rejection of the Earthly limits to economic growth is perpetuated in NewSpace discourse, where space is imagined as a frontier of commercial exploitation, individual liberty and limitless expansion. This project is now buttressed by the domestic laws of four nations that have legislated to recognise private ownership claims on resources extracted from celestial bodies. In this chapter, I frame off-world private property within political philosophy and history, paying particular attention to the relationship between common and private property. I argue that NewSpace's utopia beyond the limits of Earth, as supported by recent legislative manoeuvres in space resources law, undermines the principles of the *Outer Space Treaty* (OST) – in particular, its prohibition on national appropriation.

The off-world commerce-colonisation utopia differs markedly from one of the most influential utopian texts that emerged from early modern capitalism. The term 'utopia' originated in the satirical political text by the lawyer and philosopher, Thomas More (1478–1535), which was published during the transition from feudal to capitalist relationships between people, land and law. More's (2005 [1551]) *Utopia* describes the sweeping political and social transformations that began in England in the late 15th century. He wrote during the first wave of Enclosure laws, in which the common lands that provided living space and sustenance for villagers, peasant labourers and the rural poor were gradually and violently converted into land privately owned by wealthy barons, feudal lords and noblemen.

More's critique of the Enclosure laws pointed to the catastrophic social dislocation that they wrought:

> 'But I do not think that this necessity of stealing arises only from [idle men in times of peace]; there is another cause of it, more peculiar to England'. 'What is that?' said the Cardinal: 'The increase of pasture', said I, 'by which your sheep, which are naturally mild, and easily kept in order, may be said now to devour men and unpeople, not only villages, but towns; for wherever it is found that the sheep of any soil yield a softer and richer wool than ordinary, there the nobility and gentry, and even those

DOI: 10.1201/9781003293613-3

> holy men ... not contented with the old rents which their farms yielded, nor thinking it enough that they, living at their ease, do no good to the public, resolve to do it hurt instead of good. (More 2005, p. 12)

Peasants were forced off common lands and were pushed towards proletarianisation through the criminalisation of vagabondage and pulled towards urban wage labour (Polanyi 2001, p. 109). This was authorised and legitimised through the formalisation of private ownership under English law and the extension of sovereign jurisdiction. Traditional forms of land tenure, notably the mutual obligation between feudal lords and peasants, were upended in order to take advantage of commercial opportunities (particularly wool exports to continental textile manufactures) in international trade (Marx 2015 [1887], p. 510). In positing a more just form of social organisation, More described a fictional island where there was no private property and socially essential resources were allocated according to need, in an economy of communal work and the renunciation of greed and competition. Drawing on the Greek term, *utopos* – from *ou* ('not') and *topos* ('place'), or 'nowhere' – he named this idyll 'Utopia'.

Politico-legal enclosures did not of course terminate with the final wave of English *Enclosure Acts* (1845–1882). Commons scholar and activist David Bollier describes contemporary enclosures such as the conversion of developing nations' grazing lands and water supplies into the private property of foreign multinational corporations (2002). Enclosure has also included the commodification of less tangible or visible commons, such as academic knowledge 'paywalled' by oligopolistic publishing houses or genetic material patented by multinational behemoths of agribusiness or biotechnology (Bollier 2002; Bollier & Watts 2002). My analysis in this chapter leans more towards the material or spatial forms of common property. In this sense, the celestial bodies of the Solar System are the last commons to be subject to some form of enclosure.

What parallels can we draw between the legal guarantee of private property ownership proposed under emerging space resources law and the waves of enclosure that have transformed the Earth? The passage of the *Commercial Space Launch Competitiveness Act* (CSLCA) was met with promises that it would 'open up' the space frontier for humanity (Deep Space Industries 2015). NewSpace organisations have described their work as 'opening the frontier for all of us' (Moon Express n.d.). However, I will here argue that the pre-emptive legalisation of private appropriation of hitherto common resources may yield an alternate space future – a form of enclosure that entrenches the neoliberal economic hierarchy, rather than 'opens' it.

At first glance, a discussion about enclosure may appear inappropriate for an assessment of space resources law as it currently stands. Supporters of off-world private property have emphasised that laws like the CSLCA do not enable them to claim land or territory in space – only the resources extracted from celestial bodies (Kfir 2016). However, some NewSpace organisations have previously argued that the US Government should offer land grants to prospective off-world colonists, as a means of incentivising private sector settlements (Wasser & Jobes 2008). The National Space Society, for instance, argues that land grants off-Earth could eventually be 'large enough to make feasible subdivision and resale' (2012, p. 9).

While some writers within the Atlas network have noted that state-endorsed land claims would be a clear contravention of the *OST* (Szoka & Dunstan 2015), others support the ownership of plots of extraterrestrial land (Lowe 2022). In a *Reason* policy paper, for example, Grearson and Bennett (2019, pp. 74–76) note the uncertainty around what companies are able to do in relation to off-world resource extraction, but nonetheless appear to support the notion of privately held title in 'land' off-world in the future. Given that these Atlas writers have expressed concern that companies are unable to use 'land title to extraterrestrial bodies' as collateral for debt financing, the prospect of explicit land enclosures off-world may be a live issue (Grearson & Bennett 2019, pp. 74–75).

Even if we assume that ownership of extracted resources is the extent of private property off-world, and not 'land grabs' on the Moon or Mars and so on, mining operations on moons and asteroids may nonetheless resemble enclosures on Earth. In particular, the exercise of the right to be free from 'harmful interference' may resemble enclosure. In international space law, this term has been understood to mean that, when a nation or private operator exercises their right to freely explore and use outer space as per the OST (1967, Art. 1), they are obligated to 'avoid harmful interference with other spacecraft' (Masson-Zwaan & Palkovitz 2017, p. 8). Consistent with the OST and other space law instruments, such as the Constitution of the International Telecommunications Union, the CSLCA recognises the right of space miners to be free from 'harmful interference' from other parties – much like satellite broadcasters have the right to be free from harmful radio-communication interference from other satellite operators (OST 1967, Art. 9; ITU 1992; CSLCA 2015, s. 51302).

Exercising this right – while still meeting one's OST obligations to ensure other parties' freedom of use and exploration – is problematised in the case of space mining (Perry 2017, pp. 15–17). Tronchetti notes, in the case of the CSLCA, that 'if implemented, the Act could result in the establishment of exclusion/safety zones on the surface of an asteroid so as to protect the activities of US mining companies' (2015, p. 8). Private ownership could produce scenarios in which access and use of celestial bodies will be prevented for anyone who arrived later – first movers could establish semi-permanent mining infrastructure above a valuable mineral reserve on the Moon or Mars, and then exercise the right to be free of harmful interference. This would effectively 'fence off' or enclose surface areas of celestial bodies for the use of space mining firms – analogous to the claiming of 'land' – thereby limiting access for other parties and concentrating the benefits of exploitation in the hands of whichever party mined the resource.

In this chapter, we turn to 'laws of the land' and consider space resources law and NewSpace's colonisation narrative within the wider literature of political and legal geography, in particular the grounding of private property rights in state sovereignty. My analysis in this chapter explores the origins of Anglo-American constitutional laws governing property in land more than it does property in minerals – the evolution of mining rights belongs to a different thread in political history. In the following chapter, we will turn our focus to 'mineral sovereignty' and the close relationship between state sovereignty and private rights to extract from mineral commonwealths (Walker & Johnson 2018). However, it is worth noting here that the 'nearly universal national ownership of minerals today' can be traced to the feudal system's vesting of 'all property in the monarch or sovereign' (Flomenhoft 2018, p. 16).

In exploring the nature and origins of common and private property in Anglo-American legal formalism, I illustrate how the pre-emptive enclosure of celestial bodies both resonates with and challenges the common theoretical frames that scholars have used to approach private property and the political authority in which it is rooted. The CSLCA and subsequent space resources law represent an exclusionary, individually held property entitlement that is supported by the national laws of a sovereign power. By treating outer space as a zone of free appropriation, NewSpace and Atlas supporters of off-world private property generally employ a Lockean 'natural law' description of private property as a self-evident, inalienable right. Thus, the techno-utopian libertarianism of NewSpace takes us to a long-standing paradox of private property – it is secured *by* government *against* government. In developing an approach to this apparent contradiction within NewSpace discourse, I draw on Karl Polanyi's (2001 [1944]) *The Great Transformation*. His historical sociology of capitalism described the emergence of 'free' markets as being the result of continuous government intervention. Polanyi emphasised the role of political and legal institutions in the enclosure of common land, and his work is valuable for revealing the entwinement of sovereign and private appropriation that problematise the validity of national space resources law *vis-à-vis* the non-appropriation principle at the heart of the *OST*.

While Polanyi's history of enclosure is insightful for this discussion, the case study of space mining involves a frontier that does not have land, in the biological, life-supporting sense that has been known for the entirety of human existence. As a way of framing the uniqueness of outer space as a site of political authority and private ownership, I will turn to the ancient Greek term *nomos* – meaning a spatial law or order predicated on the appropriation and division of land – as articulated by the controversial German jurist Carl Schmitt (2003 [1950]; 2015 [1954]). Schmitt elucidates the term *nomos* as part of his account of national and international law, arguing that legal orders and political power derive from the 'terrestrial fundament' of land appropriation, including the *dominium* of private property and the *imperium* of national sovereignty (Schmitt 2003, p. 47). Schmitt's excavation of *nomos* is valuable for framing the sheer unconventionality of the Solar System as a site of state sovereignty and property ownership. Outer space is still awaiting the constitutive act of appropriation. Schmitt and Polanyi both offer unavoidably terrestrial accounts of the *nomoi* of Earth and the deep human history of common property relationships. Yet perhaps the off-world is a literal utopia: with no land to colonise, it is a *utopos* or 'no place' (Carey 1999, p. 1).

What is property?

The terms of the *OST* state that outer space should be 'free for exploration and use by all states ... on a basis of equality ... [and] free access', and is not subject to national appropriation (OST 1967, Arts. 1 and 2). Before we consider the novelty of space as a site of either private or common property ownership rights, I will begin with some basic definitional work – what exactly do we mean by 'property'? Waldron aptly surmises that 'more than most policy areas dealt with by political philosophers, the discussion of property is beset with definitional difficulties' (2016, p. 2). A comprehensive chronology of common and private property arrangements in human history is outside the scope of this chapter. However, approaching off-world private property necessarily involves a discussion of Western, formalist understandings of land law. The questions raised by the NewSpace commercial-colonial project speak to deeper political history and lead us into the legal traditions of ancient Rome, early-capitalist England and post-revolutionary America. On whose authority can one party claim ownership of land to the exclusion of others? What is the moral, political or economic justification for private ownership of things once held in common? Why should private property ownership be conceived of as a fundamental human freedom?

The deep history of common property

Liberal capitalist economies are essentially predicated on the distinction between 'mine' and 'yours', lending private property rights a sense of ubiquity and self-evidence. If we looked for a *vox pop* definition of property, most people might arrive at something synonymous with 'possession': material objects claimed by individuals or groups of people, like dwellings, consumer goods and even immaterial objects like intellectual property. Throughout human history, the 'chattel' property claims of empowered social groups have also been authorised and legitimised through legal statute. Human and non-human life – animals, children, spouses, servants and slaves – can become an individual's private property, and this is still evident in the 21st century.

Property is more than a simple claim by people over objects. It is more accurately described in terms of plural and often fluid relationships *between people in relation to things*. To use legal geographer Daniel Bromley's words, capitalist private property relationships can be defined as 'social relation[s] that [define] the property holder with respect to something of value (the benefit stream) against all others' (1991, p. 2) – a claim to something made by one actor that excludes other actors. More than rights of possession, the entitlements of the CSLCA, for example, include 'component rights' of *jus utendi* (to use property), such as separating asteroidal water ice into hydrogen and oxygen, and *jus disponendi* (to dispose of property), such as transferring ownership rights over off-world minerals to another party through commercial exchange (Cohen 1927, p. 12). They are rights claimed by the property-holder: in legal philosopher Morris Cohen's words, 'the essence of private property is always the right to exclude others' (Cohen 1927, p. 12).[1] Once owned by a space mining firm, the benefits of off-world minerals would flow to the owners rather than to other parties.

Common property also involves relationships between social agents who define rules about places and resources – this time predicated on non-exclusive rights assigned at a community level and defended by the community. Collective decision-making usually results in further codifications on what rights users have, sanctions that the community can impose on users for breaking the rules about using commons and even excluding some groups of people from using commons altogether (such as villagers in a rival town). Elinor Ostrom's (1990, 2012) empirical research outlined the great diversity in 'common pool resource' management schemes across the world, and described multiscalar decision-making units (states, markets and community levels of authority, and combinations of these). All members of a township might have access to a neighbouring pasture to feed their animals or a waterway for fishing, and communal rules might establish limits for the permissible number of grazing animals or the size of a fish catch. These rights sometimes involve principles of open, unrestricted access and these rights are often allocated to much broader, diffuse communities. This is particularly true in the era of UN treaty law and the institutional shift towards international governance, such as rights for states and corporations to access and use global commons like the high seas or outer space.

The OST describes celestial bodies in terms increasingly absent in neoliberal capitalism. Contrary to the normalisation of private property that is evident in NewSpace or neoliberal discourse (Simberg 2012; ASD 2019, p. 3), common property is a social institution that pre-dates market capitalism by many millennia. Private property in land is only as old as capitalism, an approximately 400-year novelty in the grander narrative of human existence. Indeed, communally owned and managed land represented a form of social provisioning that was central to most pre-industrial and indigenous societies (Polanyi 2001, p. 48). Kovel outlines common property arrangements in the laws of ancient Babylonian, Aztec and Islamic societies (cited in Wall 2014, p. 9). Commons scholar Derek Wall, meanwhile, describes indigenous societies in Australia, North America and India in which 'the concept of buying and selling land was alien' (2014, p. 9). It was instead social institutions of rights to use commons and social norms and obligations that *restricted* personal use of life-supporting commons that allowed most societies to continue using them. Common rights to ecological resources, in particular, are indelibly linked to an ethics of care and stewardship that aims to preserve and maintain commons for the use of future generations.

In light of humanity's deep history of common property relationships, there is an inherent absurdity in any claim that future space colonies should be founded on principles of private rather than common ownership, as though exclusive ownership rights were the sole determinant in human flourishing. Even the British jurists and political theorists who helped codify or justify the foundations of private property rights in the Western political canon acknowledged that common property naturally preceded any concept of exclusive ownership (Locke 1690; Maine 2007 [1917]; Blackstone 2019 [1893]). Quoting from the Bible, the jurist William Blackstone said that God gave man 'dominion over all the earth', and that the 'earth, therefore, and all things therein, are the general property of all mankind' – a statement which seems to legitimate common property as the foundational social institution on Earth, albeit from a Judeo-Christian perspective (Blackstone 2019 [1893] , ch. 1, s. 3). Yet it is a neoliberal axiom, one which has been perpetuated in NewSpace discourse, that 'at the basis of all economic prosperity on Earth is the right to private property' (Hudgins 2002, p. xxiv).

Karl Polanyi's anthropological critique of liberal economics is valuable in addressing this ahistorical valorisation of private property ownership. The central thesis of his *Great Transformation* (2001) rests upon a distinction between economic relations of market capitalism and those of non-market or pre-industrial societies. Among other anthropologists, he drew on Malinowski's (1984 [1922]) *Argonauts of the Western Pacific*, which described reciprocal, non-monetised trade among the societies of Melanesia. He noted that fellow historical sociologist Max Weber was 'the first among economic historians to protest against the brushing aside of primitive economics as irrelevant to the question of the motives and mechanisms of civilised societies' (Polanyi 2001, p. 48).

We will return to Polanyi's critique of market capitalism shortly. However, it is worth noting here that his work underlined the fact that communal property arrangements are ubiquitous in human history, while capitalist markets for privately owned resources are a relatively recent social institution. He argued that:

> … man's economy, as a rule, is submerged in his social relationships. He does not act so as to safeguard his individual interest in the possession of material goods; he acts so as to safeguard his social standing, his social claims, his social assets. He values material goods only in so far as they serve this end. (Ibid, p. 48)

The provisioning of essential resources (food production, most importantly) has clearly taken place through alternate allocation mechanisms. Polanyi focused on three alternatives to the ideal of a self-regulating market: reciprocity (mutual obligation, as in the case of the Trobriand islanders), redistribution (or centricity, as was common in ancient empires like the New Kingdom of Egypt and Hammurabi's Babylon) and householding (Polanyi 2001, pp. 49–56; Isaac 2012, p. 17). Polanyi notes that householding – essentially the autarkic production of goods by smaller social units like the family – was described as *oikonomia* in Ancient Greece, the source of the contemporary word 'economy' (ibid, p. 55). Economising and trading were processes embedded in political, legal and cultural institutions. For the majority of human history, trade and exchange for individual profit was close to non-existent, and there was no prior evidence of a society 'even approximately controlled and regulated by markets' (ibid, p. 46). Polanyi noted that Adam Smith's famous declaration of our supposedly innate 'propensity to barter, truck and exchange' rested upon highly selective, short-run historical evidence from the 18th and 19th centuries onwards. The period in which people appeared to have this propensity is precisely when capitalist markets forced them to do so (ibid, p. 47).

Codifying property relationships: from ancient Rome to medieval England

The question of whether national space resources law is consistent with the OST is rooted in western legal tradition, and most scholarship locates the earliest Western formalisation of rules and customs governing common areas in Roman categorisations of property (Rose 2003; Wall 2014; Flomenhoft 2018). Ancient Roman civil law delineated and codified different forms of property ownership in written 'official' forms. Roman common property or *res communes* denoted spaces and material objects that could not be owned exclusively and were to be used by everyone – natural resources like air and water, for instance. *Res communes* was delineated from other types of property, such as privately owned homes and possessions (*res privatae*), publicly owned properties like roads and public services (*res publicae*) and things unowned (*res nullius*), such as the seas outside Roman jurisdiction (Wall 2014, pp. 8–9). Many have noted that non-exclusive property rights have either been 'generally overlooked' (Wall 2014, p. 9) or have 'rapidly [vanished]' in recent centuries (Rose 2003, p. 91). Yet the modern legal systems of Europe, England and the United States are influenced by these Roman precedents.

English social and political history involved several notable shifts in human relationships with the land. Britannic land law traditions were modified drastically by Roman colonisation and then by Anglo-Saxon (5th–6th centuries) and Norman (11th century) conquests. Anglo-Saxon laws of the land were highly localised and customary. These included common rights to use lands and resources, such as rights of usufruct that allowed peasants to extract from the private fiefdoms of local lords and thegns. These ranged from 'pasturage', which allowed for animal grazing in pastures; the right of 'estover' conferred the right to take timber or bracken from forests; 'piscary' granted the right to catch fish in waterways; while 'common in the soil' permitted one to extract minerals, sand and gravel for building rudimentary dwellings (Wall 2014, p. 8). Categories of property rights emerge out of the human need for food, living space and dwellings – in Blackstone's words, 'necessity begat property' (2019, ch. 1, s. 9). Such subsistence-based usufructuary rights contrast with the for-profit, private extractive rights granted under the space resources law of the United States, Luxembourg, UAE and Japan. The comparison between these two forms of property suggests that usufructuary rights will be far more valuable in the hostile environs of space, if off-world mining is to support human settlement.

The year 1066 is transformative in the history of sovereignty: the Norman conquest imposed the feudal system over Anglo-Saxon land law. The invasion created new social hierarchies in England and centralised political authority over land. William of Normandy brought from France to medieval England, Scotland and Wales a system of formal legal order and a social hierarchy that placed the sovereign monarch second only to God. In conquering England, William claimed all land in his name, making it Crown or demesne land and subject to no superior landlord – allodial or radical title, it has been called (Schmitt 2003, p. 47). It was a sweeping declaration of monarchical sovereignty, delegating limited authority to rural landowners while restricting the availability of common space for the commoners. With allodial title vested in the King, grants to feudal baronies were devolved from sovereign authority over the realm. The manorial 'lords of the soil' possessed the right to manage land and extract services from serfs and villeins living on this land. The landed elite transferred these rights to their heirs through inheritance. In the 17th century, Gerrard Winstanley had declared the root of the enclosure problem to be 'the Norman Bastard William', and the longstanding 'pursuit of that victory, imprisoning, robbing, and killing the poor enslaved English' commoners (1649).

The *Magna Carta* represents an important step in the formalisation of property rights to land which, in turn, shaped land law across much of the globe. The *OST* is often described as the *Magna Carta* of space (von der Dunk 2011, p. 4; Smith 2018). Both the OST and the 1215 'Grand Charter of Liberties' established 'the basic rights, duties, and responsibilities' common to all signatories (Smith 2018, p. 50). While both the OST and the *Magna Carta* involved limitations on the exercise of sovereignty, the former evolved out of the anticipatory geopolitics of the Cold War and the latter emerged out of disputes between the Crown and the landowners.[2] The question of private property is (unsurprisingly) answered more clearly in the *Magna Carta*. The *Magna Carta* established that 'no freemen shall be taken or imprisoned or disseised [dispossessed of lawfully-obtained property] ... except by the lawful judgement of his peers or by the law of the land' (Article 39). The legal rights of private landowners were enshrined in what became the foundations of liberal constitutionalism and the very concept of the rule of law.

While the Charter extended some liberties to serfs, it was concerned primarily with the political freedom of wealthy elites who sought to limit the arbitrary power of the Crown through constitutional law. These elites represented themselves in decision-making fora from 1265 onwards, in what became the House of Commons by the 14th century. Parliamentary representation was spurred in large part by the desire of property owners to make decisions about their own property, and parliamentarians were most commonly wealthy landowners. The 'bourgeois state' that Marx critiqued in the 19th century has deep roots: the pace of enclosure in the four centuries prior was testament to the enduring self-interest of empowered landowning elites. The former tenants of common lands were conscripted into wage labour through sovereign powers of legal appropriation, 'the law itself [becoming] the instrument of the theft of the people's land' (Marx 2015 [1887], p. 513). As industrialisation and world trade opened up opportunities for profit, the cultivation and improvement of land was geared less towards subsistence and more towards landowners' accumulation of wealth and national economic goals. National government supplanted the monarch as the sovereign authority of the realm, and the capacity to authorise and legitimise rights to property in land was similarly vested in the new governmental form of the liberal capitalist state.

Property in American traditions of freedom and law

When Britain colonised the 'new' world in the 17th–19th centuries, this 'concept of exclusive property in land, as a norm to which other practices must be adjusted, [extended] across the whole globe, like a coinage reducing all things to a common measure' (Thompson 1993, p. 164). When English common law arrived in North America with 17th-century colonists, the paradox of liberal private property came with it. Protected by the state from the state, the rights of private landowners were secured against arbitrary exercises of sovereign power. Yet the legitimacy and social recognition of their ownership claims were equally dependent on this sovereign power (and its ability to violently appropriate land from traditional custodians). This is the paradox that rests within any libertarian desire for private property-based freedoms.

English colonists were of course neither the first peoples nor the first Europeans to settle the American continent. They were, however, the first to establish legal traditions of private property rights. In Cohen's words, 'property denotes not material things but certain rights' (1927, pp. 11–12) and the language of fundamental rights permeates American political discourse. The *Declaration of Independence* established new independent sovereign states (the Thirteen Colonies) that would legitimise, authorise and protect the rights of individuals (as with the French Revolution, these rights were generally confined to white men). They were rights secured for free men against the tyranny of the British Empire, the sovereignty of a new commonwealth rejecting the monarchical sovereignty of the Crown.

Libertarianism is an enduring philosophy in American politics, one which frames property as a fundamental, self-evident and supposedly inalienable freedom. Thomas Jefferson's famous declaration of individual liberties located the ultimate authority in God, not in the King. Declaring their independence from the Kingdom of Great Britain, the *Declaration* asserted that the men of the Thirteen Colonies were 'created equal' and 'endowed by their Creator with certain unalienable Rights'. Individual liberty is enshrined in the *Constitution of the United States of America* and its first ten amendments under the *Bill of Rights* (both inspired by Britain's 1689 *Bill of Rights*). The US *Bill of Rights* contains some components highly cherished by numerous libertarian movements, in particular the anti-expropriation measures – that no person's 'private property be taken for public use' without compensation (Fifth Amendment). Barbrook and Cameron (1996) identify a Jeffersonian democratic strain that is evident in techno-libertarian movements. Jefferson believed that 'political liberties could be protected from authoritarian governments only by the widespread ownership of individual private property' (Barbrook & Cameron 1996, p. 59). When private property entered the O'Neillian imaginary, via the L-5 Society's opposition to the UN *Moon Agreement* off-world civil liberties are articulated through the right of private possession (Henson 1980).

Jefferson's emphasis on private property was influenced by English liberal political theorist John Locke. Indeed, despite the grandiose vision of space colonisation and the significant technological prowess required to realise it, many arguments in favour of space mining appear to draw on the familiar Lockean proviso, as Gangale (2009) and Pilchman (2015) have identified. In his *Second Treatise of Government* (2005 [1690]), Locke followed Blackstone and Jefferson by commencing his inquiry with recourse to divine gifts of common property: 'God ... has given the earth to the children of men—given it to mankind in common' (2005, s. 25). Locke's challenge was to justify the private ownership of formerly commonly-owned things – effectively, to justify the act of appropriation itself within the Judeo-Christian presumption of common property (Waldron 2016). Locke famously argued that 'every man has a property in his own person ... The labour of his body, the work of his hands ... are properly his' (2005, s. 27). If an actor 'mixed his Labour with' land or natural resources, he 'thereby makes it his property'; so long as 'there is enough, and as good, left in common for others', then appropriators have a justifiable right to private ownership that 'excludes the common right of other men' (ibid, s. 27).

It was an attempt to ground private property ownership in natural law: rights to exclusively own property existed independently of government, they only needed to be enforced by government. In this philosophy, the preservation of private property should be the central aim of government and civil society, and Locke's *Fundamental Constitutions* of the Carolina colonies treated private ownership of land as the basis of membership in political community (Armitage 2004). Locke's theorisation of private property thus promoted individual liberty while justifying the existing social hierarchy of his time (Marshall & da Rimini 2018, pp. 51–52). Locke's justification of property also legitimised private ownership of human beings (and Jefferson was a slave owner). Slaveholders enjoyed 'absolute arbitrary Power, over the Lives, Liberties and Persons of [their] Slaves' while slaves were granted no legal standing let alone the constitutional rights to life, liberty and property enjoyed by white men (Locke, in Armitage 2004, p. 619).

In NewSpace cosmopolitics, space mining becomes an act of Lockean 'original appropriation'. In the words of the then CEO of DSI's David Gump, 'space resources belong to those who show up' (2018). Locke's individualisation of property rights denies the deep human history of co-operation and collaboration in the use of land and resources. Gump's view similarly places greater emphasis on private and not common ownership of resources as the pathway for more expansive human activity in the cosmos, arguing instead that benefits will flow to humanity from the private exploitation of off-world resources (2018).

Locke's project not only justified the racial hierarchy of the Carolina colonies, but it also presented an argument that legitimised the white conquest of the entire American continent. Since he considered that there would always be enough land 'left in common for others', the mass appropriation of land from Native American societies was constitutionally legal and morally acceptable. Much like the *terra nullius* arguments deployed by the British empire, Locke's argument treated 'uncultivated land [as] essentially valueless' and blind to the fact that 'at some point the land must cease to be sufficient to support the pre-existing hunter-gatherer population' (Quiggin 2015).

The prospect of space mining also raises concerns about social hierarchy and over-exploitation, yet these ethical considerations are transformed on the space frontier. The embryonic space mining sector believes it has an inalienable right to own resources extracted from space, because it would be their labour (or at least their capital) that has 'mixed' with asteroids and other celestial bodies, thereby '[removing] it out of that common state nature left it in' (Locke 2005, s. 31). Space is considered a limitless cornucopia of iron, nickel, platinum, gold, water ice, nitrogen and many other minerals, surely enough to satisfy the Lockean criteria of leaving enough 'in common for others'.

However, deploying the Lockean proviso on the space frontier would be a case of equality in rights, but inequality in the exercise of these rights. The 'first come, first served' logic of Locke's labour criterion is likely to perpetuate to Earthly disparities of wealth between and within nations (Pilchman 2015, pp. 142–143). The Solar System has commons of almost unfathomable scale, yet early space miners are likely to pick the low-hanging fruit – the sites of mineral extraction that are easier to reach and more profitable than others. These reserves could be exploited by firms from the world's largest economies, before less developed countries were capable of doing the same (thereby preserving the existing 'space hierarchy'). If the industrial model of *in situ* resource processing and manufacturing is realised, then being the first to exploit lunar resources might make one company more capable of exploiting the minerals of other celestial bodies, such as Mars or the asteroids. The advantages of being first movers could increase exponentially. If the use of space resources became important in the future, would a private property-based scheme for off-world settlement enable leaving 'enough, and as good' in common for future generations, particularly if its proponents are driven by neoliberal tenets of individual economic freedom and market-based competition?

Exactly how individual actors (NewSpace or otherwise) conduct off-world resource exploitation remains to be seen, yet it is obviously true that extractive forms of land use irreversibly deplete resources. Capitalism thus requires new frontiers to extract from. Here, we can turn to the notion of the 'spatio-temporal fix' proposed by Marxist geographer David Harvey (1981, 2004), whose work has previously been utilised in exploring off-world capitalism (Dickens & Ormrod 2007; Shammas & Holen 2019). Harvey elaborated on Marx's understanding of capitalism's crises of overaccumulation: 'an excess of capital in relation to the opportunities to employ that capital productively' which, in the absence of the geographic expansion of capitalist markets, would eventually devalue capital (Harvey 1981, p. 7). As Shammas and Holen surmise,

> Capitalism must regularly discover, develop and appropriate new spaces because of its inherent tendency to general surplus capital ... there is no end point or final destination for capitalism. Instead, capitalism must continuously propel itself onwards in search of pristine sites of renewed capital accumulation. (Shammas & Holen 2019, p. 5)

If capitalism is to be the vehicle by which off-world colonialism is realised, then there will be no inherent upper limit to the appropriation of resources and accumulation of capital, thereby perpetuating Earthly economic hierarchies off-world. The very existence of space mining firms is an expression of the economic inequality that propels the capitalist spatio-temporal fix, as private investment in NewSpace firms 'creates a productive (or valorizing) outlet for excess capital' accumulated by investors like Peter Thiel and Jeff Bezos (Shammas & Holen 2019, p. 5). A Marxist understanding of space mining also serves as a reminder that any profits from corporate mineral exploitation would accumulate with company owners and shareholders – social hierarchies both between and *within* technologically advanced capitalist countries would also be perpetuated.

Returning to our original framing of property as a series of social relationships, the history of property rights reveals clear limitations in a Lockean natural law justification for the private ownership of space resources. Title IV of the CSLCA states that US citizens (including the ubiquitous 'legal person', the corporation) 'shall be entitled to any asteroid resource or space resource obtained, including to possess, own, transport, use, and sell the asteroid resource or space resource obtained'

(CSLCA 2015, s. 51303). One actor (such as an American space mining company) has been entitled by another (the US legislature, in the case of the CSLCA) to take a range of actions in relation to resources extracted from celestial bodies. In Sikor and Lund's words:

> The process of recognition of claims as property simultaneously works to imbue the institution that provides such recognition with the recognition of its authority to do so. This is the 'contract' that links property and authority. Property is only property if socially legitimate institutions sanction it. (2009, p. 1)

Space miners' future claims to space property have been recognised in domestic public law, implying that national legislatures have the authority to allocate private property rights in the extra-territorial spaces of the Solar System. In the case of the CSLCA, this either suggests that the socially legitimate institution for recognising off-world property claims is the US Congress and not the United Nations or any other international decision-making body, or it suggests that the CSLCA is an illegitimate declaration of private property rights. The recent Artemis Accords framework, whereby multilateral agreement between nations with space resources laws (and a handful of their allies) declare that space resource ownership is permissible under the OST, can be read as an attempt to bypass this problem – whereby the authority or legitimacy of space resource ownership is instead grounded in inter-national or bilateral accord rather than wider multilateral agreement in the form of treaty law (Tronchetti & Liu 2021a, p. 5; de Zwart 2022, p. 363).

Common and private property involve power relationships of authority, consent and legitimacy. NewSpace and (neo)liberal discourses that treat private property as an essential human freedom or natural right evade these unavoidable questions of state power and authority. In neoliberal private property discourse, the 'minimal state' defines and enforces property rights – beyond this, the marketplace is considered a more efficient co-ordinator of exchange relationships between people in relation to property. Neoliberal environmentalism has thus entailed 'the creation of private property rights to pollute; the growth of user fees for "public" nature reserves; and the privatisation of all manner of natural resources, from fisheries to forests to water' (McCarthy & Prudham 2004, p. 277).[3] Neoliberal approaches to property involve the authority of a new power, one which is embodied in neither the king's body nor the body politic. The decentralised and omniscient market is treated as sole, legitimate authority for managing property relationships. The power of government (whether democratic or authoritarian) is replaced with the market and its price signal as the arbiter of relationships between people and nature (Mirowski, Walker & Abboud 2013). But could there ever be such a thing as a truly 'self-regulating' market?

'Fictitious' commodification

In Chapter 2, we discussed how the most significant achievements in American spacefaring are due to NASA's central coordination of space R&D and mission planning. NewSpace and Atlas arguments that claim government action has hindered the development of free economies in space mirror those of liberal philosophers from Malthus and Ricardo to Mises and Lippman who claimed that 'power and compulsion are evil, that freedom depends on their absence' (Polanyi 2001, p. 266). We will now turn to anthropologist, historian and institutional political economist Karl Polanyi, who critiqued this version of 'freedom'. His seminal work, *The Great Transformation* (2001 [1944]), arrived in a period when human activity in space was limited to the sub-orbital missile program of the Third Reich and when the Mont Pèlerin Society was yet to convene. Nonetheless, Polanyi's 'fictitious commodities' concept is helpful for approaching the relationship between national and private appropriation, and how private property in space conflicts with the *OST*. Furthermore, Polanyi's work is valuable for critiquing the myths of 'small government' and 'de-regulation' as they appear in neoliberal and NewSpace discourse. Polanyi revealed that contrary to the economic liberal's 'emotional faith in spontaneity', 'regulation and markets ... grew up together' (Polanyi 2001, p. 35, 71). The expansion of capitalist markets represented an attempt to 'subordinate the substance of society itself to the laws of the market' (ibid, p. 75). At stake in laws like CSLCA is the potential embedding of celestial bodies of the Solar System within the market's logic of competition, accumulation and depletion, which I argue will foreclose the possibility of equitable human futures in space.

Von Hayek and von Mises and other neoliberal theorists had aristocratic backgrounds and seemed to write with an ingrained elitism – techno-libertarian Peter Thiel is a contemporary example of neoliberals who share this detached contempt for the *demos* (Thiel 2009). In contrast, Polanyi's academic career reflected his participation in social democratic political movements and an ongoing concern with the fate of the working classes (Polanyi-Levitt & Mendell 1987). Born in Budapest to Austrian parents, Polanyi's life (1886–1964) and career involved a politically active, trans-disciplinary path of 'lawyer turned journalist and economic historian' during one of the most tumultuous periods in European history (Isaac 2012, p. 13). Following Béla Kun's 1919 Communist overthrow of the Hungarian Social Democratic government, Polanyi emigrated to Vienna and soon undertook studies in economics and sociology while also editing the financial newspaper *Der Österreichische Volkswirt* (The Austrian Economist; Polanyi-Levitt & Mendell 1987, p. 13). Here, he would directly engage with liberal economists like Mises by critiquing their faith-like espousal of the 'liberal creed' (Polanyi 2001, ch. 12). His cynicism regarding the Viennese liberal revival was partly fuelled by the 1929 US stock market crash. The Great Depression precipitated the collapse of European central banks like the

Austrian Kreditanstalt in 1931, which he argued had played a role in the rise of fascist movements (Block 2001, p. xx; Polanyi 2001, p. 265). He also witnessed the 'unexampled moral and intellectual rise in the condition of a highly developed industrial working class' under Viennese municipal socialism, and this inspired the social democratic remedies he proposed in *The Great Transformation* (Polanyi 2001, p. 299).

In 1944, Friedrich Hayek published *The Road to Serfdom*, which considered Keynesianism and social democracy to be the first steps that capitalist countries were taking on an interventionist, 'slippery slope' towards fascism and communism. In the same year, Polanyi published a scathing critique of economic liberalism, its *laissez-faire* fantasies and the social consequences of its delusions. Several scholars have recently drawn attention to what was Polanyi's sole major work, because *The Great Transformation*'s focus on the institutional basis of supposedly 'free' markets is as valuable in explaining 21st-century neoliberalism as it was for critiquing 19th- to 20th-century aspirations to *laissez-faire* self-regulation (Block & Somers 2014; Cahill 2014).

Polanyi argued that visions of economic freedom predicated on freedom *from* government were themselves a fantasy. The anarcho-capitalist discourses that have been articulated within the NewSpace movement similarly attempt to frame economic freedom as being independent of government regulation (Orphans of Apollo 2008; Tea Party in Space 2014a). Market freedoms wielded by economic elites are instead enabled and safeguarded by the legal and administrative functions of state institutions. Throughout his history of market society, Polanyi demonstrated that 'the road to the free market was opened and kept open by an enormous increase in continuous, centrally organized and controlled interventionism' (2001, p. 146).

Polanyi was interested in the critique of utopia, but neither a society void of private property like that envisioned by Thomas More (or indeed a Marxist utopia of the 'withering away of the state' via socialist revolution), nor an escape from ecological limits via techno-infinitude (as per NewSpace). *The Great Transformation* is about the 'crusading passion' held by 19th and early 20th-century classical liberal economists (Polanyi 2001, p. 143) for an 'autonomous self-governing entity' that 'cannot possibly be realized' (Block & Somers 2014, p. 9). In Polanyi's words:

> ... the idea of a self-adjusting market implied a stark utopia. Such an institution could not exist for any length of time without annihilating the human and natural substance of society; it would have physically destroyed man and transformed his surroundings into a wilderness. (2001, p. 3)

Polanyi considered free market capitalism to be a 'stark utopia' because there was no such thing as a 'self-adjusting' market – only markets created through 'statecraft' and continuous government intervention (2001, p. 35). For markets to self-regulate via the price mechanism and 'laws' of supply and demand, the key factors of production in industrial capitalism – nature, human beings and money – would have to be 'transformed into commodities in order to keep production going' (ibid, p. 75). Nature, humans and money became land, labour and capital, respectively. Pursuing the liberal economic utopia of self-regulating markets meant allowing 'the market mechanism' to take precedence over other social institutions in directing the fate of humanity and nature (ibid, p. 76).

Polanyi argued that treating land, labour and capital as tradable private property was 'fictitious' because these factors of production predate the formation of capitalist markets and the state-created legal orders that sustain them. Natural resources such as this are thus distinct from 'genuine' commodities that are produced by wage labour for the explicit purpose of market exchange.

> … labor, land, and money are obviously not commodities; the postulate that anything that is bought and sold must have been produced for sale is emphatically untrue in regard to them. In other words, according to the empirical definition of a commodity they are not commodities. Labor is only another name for a human activity which goes with life itself, which in its turn is not produced for sale but for entirely different reasons, nor can that activity be detached from the rest of life, be stored or mobilized; land is only another name for nature, which is not produced by man; actual money, finally, is merely a token of purchasing power which, as a rule, is not produced at all, but comes into being through the mechanism of banking or state finance. (Ibid, p. 75)

Preceding the Western environmental movement by at least two decades, Polanyi explains the fictitious commodities concept with much greater emphasis on labour and capital than on land or 'raw materials' of natural resources (ibid, p. 44). Nonetheless, the state guarantee of private property rights on asteroids and other celestial bodies offers a stark example of fictitious commodification. Some asteroids have been dated to 4.5 billion years old and are as old as the Earth and Solar System: the exo-geological processes that created off-world minerals could not be further in time and space from the origins of market capitalism. Off-world minerals would become private property not through the fictional 'natural' appropriation that Locke described, but through acts of state-supported appropriation.

Polanyi's account of enclosure emphasises how the transformation of common property into formalised private property rights to land and natural resources are grounded in state sovereignty. He describes the waves of enclosure legislation, from the Tudor (1485–1603) and Stuart periods (1603–1714) and onto to the consolidation of global trade networks in the 18th–19th century. The enclosure movement resulted in a 'catastrophic dislocation of the lives of common people' and destruction of 'old social tissue' of village life and its laws and customs (Polanyi 2001, p. 35). In a similar vein to the Silicon Valley and neoliberal elitism propelling the prospective enclosure of the off-world commons, Polanyi notes how the English enclosure movements were 'a revolution of the rich against the poor' and that Parliament 'had been on the side of the enclosers' (ibid, pp. 37–38). Numerous revolutions benefitting wealthy elites have taken place under neoliberal capitalism, from the commodification of public water supplies in Latin America though to the commodification of internet users' personal data – a project supported by ongoing collaboration between Google and the US Intelligence Community, among others (Nesbit 2017).

Polanyi's 'fictitious commodities' concept underlines how the functioning of capitalist markets is utterly dependent on 'deliberate State action' (Polanyi 2001, p. 147). This underscores the limitation of treating the space mining project as ever being a purely 'private sector' exercise. Contrary to the liberal economists' invocations of the 'invisible hand', 'free' and self-regulating markets 'controlled, regulated, and directed by market prices' depended on ongoing intervention of the state and the legal-coercive organs of government (ibid, p. 71, 189). Commodifying nature and thereby ensuring 'predictability in the market for land' necessitated 'sets of rules as to what types of economic activity are permitted in particular localities', and this engendered government administration and regulation in the form of private property rights, land surveys, the creation of localities and their boundaries, and the development of public infrastructure that would enable access to land (Block and Somers 2014, p. 33). Realised through 'legislative action' and 'administrative pressure' as much as they were by 'individual force or violence', enclosures involved deliberate and unspontaneous commodification rooted in the ability of national government to appropriate from the commoners (Polanyi 2001, p. 189). We will return to the connection between violence and the enforcement of private property in Chapter 6. Here I will emphasise that the value of Polanyi's account vis-à-vis space resources law is in his demonstration that – at the birth of market capitalism – national and private appropriations were fundamentally entwined.

The emerge of national laws that recognise private property rights to space resources rest upon an equally blurred boundary between private and national appropriation. That 'private' appropriation of space resources would rest upon ample support of the nation state is also evident when we consider forms of 'statecraft' outside the establishment and enforcement of formal private property rights. Shammas and Holen argue that 'Space libertarianism is libertarian in name only: behind every NewSpace venture looms a thick web of government spending programs, regulatory agencies, public infrastructure, and universities bolstered by research grants from the state' (2019, p. 6). Polanyi emphasises that a broad array of public institutions support 'free' markets, and states' buttressing of the space mining industry is apparent well before any robotic miners are dispatched off-world (and, should that ever happen, they would likely be dependent on publicly-owned launch pads or government-supported space launch firms like

SpaceX or the United Launch Alliance). Data from the Federal Procurements Data System reveals some significant funding in the form of NASA contracts, most commonly for basic research and technology development or the sale of services to NASA. Between 2014 and 2017, Planetary Resources received $1.8 million and DSI received $1.1 million in grants and procurements (FPDS 2023a, 2023b).[4] Moon Express won a $10 million NASA contract under the Innovative Lunar Demonstration Data program in 2010, and is one of the contractors eligible to bid on $2.6 billion worth of NASA's Commercial Lunar Payload Services contracts up to 2028 (Young 2014; NASA 2018a). This public expense is supported by the investment and philanthropy of the private sector, and is dwarfed by the multibillion dollar contracts awarded to Boeing and Lockheed-Martin. Nonetheless, these injections of public funding are crucial to support an industry that is currently incapable of selling its target commodity (off-world resources).

That NewSpace is a neoliberal rather than libertarian project is revealed most clearly by DSI co-founder Rick Tumlinson, who described the continuous intervention of the state into NewSpace enterprises that is essential for their off-world free market utopia to have any chance of success. His article, entitled 'Government and Space: Lead, Follow and Get Out of the Way', includes a list of demands for the US Government:

> Declare that our national goal in space is settlement and resource development … Implement pro-settlement laws and policies … Support the genius of American space enterprise … Purchase goods and services from commercial vendors in every possible area of activity (Buy the ride, not the rocket!) … Become a solid customer for data and information acquisition from space … Move to the edge and build in commercial handoff from the beginning of exploration plans (eg. practice for Mars on the Moon, then hand off the infrastructure needed to do so.) (2012)

Before they can 'get out of the way' of 'the genius of American space enterprise', NASA and Congress are being asked by NewSpace to provide quite an expansive array of corporate 'space welfare' measures: incentives, infrastructures, subsidies and legislative frameworks, while also being a 'solid customer'. NewSpace attacks upon centrally coordinated space agencies resonates with the incongruity Polanyi identified in 'economic liberals [who] must and will unhesitatingly call for the intervention of the state in order to establish' the institution of self-regulating markets (Polanyi 2001, p. 155). The bureaucratic oversight of NASA and the US Government is simply to be replaced with new bureaucracies and state institutions that primarily pursue the commercialisation of space endeavour.

Polanyi's work also points to the fallibility of libertarianism as a coherent philosophy of private property. The Lockean proviso belies the social nature of property and economy, what Polanyi described as 'the reality of society'

(2001, ch. 21). Liberal economics describes an atomised, individualised and frictionless society that bears little resemblance to how political communities – at local, national and international scales – actually work. The liberal individual does not 'create' property out of their own labour. Political and cultural institutions enable, legitimise and authorise property ownership, whether common or public or private property. As Bromley argues, '*all property rights flow from the collective* as opposed to flowing from some alleged 'natural rights' that are claimed to be logically prior to the state' (1991, p. 5, emphasis in original). Corporate freedoms to appropriate from the space commons would be grounded in state power, rendering a natural rights conception of off-world private property unfeasible.

NewSpace has lobbied Congress for legislation that creates a national framework of private property rights in space or, more generally, for Federal funding of their projects. This suggests they understand any space exodus predicated on decentralised, individual freedoms actually needs continuous public support if it is to succeed. So wherein lies the appeal of 'small government' or self-regulating markets? NewSpace actors make the reasonable claim that turning space exploration over to the market would engender new forms of 'public-private partnership' that may reduce taxpayer expense (ASD 2016, p. 4). Yet beneath the disavowal of bureaucratic largesse are some familiar refrains of American libertarianism. Somers and Block summarise Polanyi's appraisal of the 'free' market utopia thus: 'Because politics is tainted by a history of coercion, the idea that most of the important questions would be resolved through the allegedly impartial and objective mechanism of choice-driven, free-market competition has great appeal' (2014).

NewSpace and neoliberalism seek to escape a form of coercion different to the violence of enclosure. This liberal economic utopia means freedom from the consequences of the inequality produced by free market economics – it would be a utopia void of reciprocal responsibility to society in the form of 'coercive' taxation, bureaucracies that oversee and manage taxpayer expenditure, resource rents or limits imposed on what can be appropriated. The libertarian aversion to taxation is noticeable in NewSpace advocacy: NewSpace actors have made clear that, in order to spur the development of commercial spacefaring, they believe space corporations should pay as little tax as possible, while many of the organisations themselves lobby for taxpayer expense while registered as 501(c)(3) tax exempt organisations (Rohrabacher 2002; Tumlinson 2012; Space Renaissance USA 2020 [2011]).

While I have focused on 'real' mining rights rather than intellectual property rights, it is important to note that many of the knowledges and technologies that enable spacefaring rest upon a collective or public form of intellectual property (particularly since so much scientific knowledge is produced by publicly funded educational institutions). In order to leave Earth at all, NewSpace actors would need to 'stand on the shoulders of giants', to use Isaac Newtown's famous expression. The development of scientific knowledge in physics, chemistry, aerodynamics and spaceflight over the centuries forms part of an 'information commons' that (prior to commodification reforms that intensified in the late 20th century, at least) all of us have access to. The Lockean theory of property is further undermined in this sense, because there are often 'no clear boundaries between our own labour and general social labour' (Marshall & da Rimini 2018, p. 52).

Polanyi points us back to the aporia at the heart of neoliberalism: the capturing of state sovereignty to create and fortify economic freedoms for empowered firms and individuals, while – under rubrics of *laissez-faire* and non-interventionism – defeating social democratic claims that would counter the unequal exercise of these freedoms.

> On the institutional level, regulation both extends and restricts freedom; only the balance of the freedoms lost and won is significant. This is true of judicial and actual freedoms alike. The comfortable classes enjoy the freedom provided by leisure in security; they are naturally less anxious to extend freedom in society than those who for lack of income must rest content with a minimum of it. This becomes apparent as soon as compulsion is suggested in order to more justly spread out income, leisure and security … The institutional separation of politics and economics, which proved a deadly danger to the substance of society, almost automatically produced freedom at the cost of justice and security. (Polanyi 2001, p. 263)

Polanyi's argument is that, if markets are underpinned by democratic institutions, then they can be directed towards democratic ends. His work described the potential for compromise between private business and social welfare, in which profit could be made while businesses accepted 'regulatory restraints, taxation, and the steady expansion of social welfare institutions' (Block & Somers 2014, p. 221). Such a compromise between market capitalism and the collective good may be valuable in approaching the future of international space law, and countering the claim that equitable space law engenders some form of unfair redistributionism (NSS 2009; Simberg 2012, p. 6).[5]

Polanyi's account of market capitalism is valuable for theorising private property in space resources as an act of state-backed enclosure, and for framing the NewSpace imaginary within the broader free market utopianism of (neo)liberal economics. It serves to counter the ahistoricity that mythologises capitalist markets as eternal, self-evident and inevitably leading to greater human liberty. However, Polanyi cannot offer much insight into enclosing space commons, when we consider the obvious fact that no prior community will be 'fenced off' from these commons. The OST involves a pre-emptive commoning of celestial bodies and their resources, whereas recent private property laws pre-emptively enclose them. Polanyi's work is unable to convey the unfamiliarity of outer space as a site for the imposition of private property ownership over a common property regime – perhaps no Earth-bound theory of political economy or legal geography adequately can.

Theorising the legal order of the 'landless' frontier: Schmitt's concept of *nomos*

> Every new age and every new epoch in the coexistence of peoples, empires, and countries, of rulers and power formations of every sort, is founded on new spatial divisions, new enclosures, and new spatial orders of the earth. (Schmitt 2003, p. 79)

As a way of framing the novelty of the space frontier in legal geographic terms, we will now turn to the controversial German jurist, Carl Schmitt (1888–1985). Both Schmitt and Karl Polanyi acknowledged the inevitability of politics and power. Yet Schmitt and Polanyi had different views on power, owing in large part to their career trajectories and political affiliations. Polanyi was a 'world citizen' with a 'deep sense of moral responsibility' (Block 2001, p. xxi), while Schmitt became entangled in the racial geopolitics of the Third Reich. Polanyi, a Christian social democrat, saw humanity as a 'brotherhood' of perpetual social bonds and believed the extension of democracy was central to human freedom (2001, ch. 21). Schmitt, the Christian conservative and eventual National Socialist, saw community instead predicated on friend and enemy distinctions (1985 [1922]). Schmitt's scholarly legacy is tainted by his justifications of Hitler's consolidation of power. My intention here is not to mount 'the author is dead' arguments that divorce his ideas from the context in which they emerged. Rather, I will attempt to limit our discussion of Schmittian geopolitics to his etymological investigation of the ancient Greek term '*nomos*' and its value in approaching the genealogy of international law – the most novel chapter of which is the legal recognition of off-world private property.

Nomos has often been roughly translated as 'law' or 'custom'; however, Schmitt's project re-appraised its meaning and ultimately described *nomos* as an explicitly spatial legal order (2003 [1950]). For Schmitt, *nomos* was 'the fundamental process of apportioning space that is essential to every historical epoch' (2003, p. 78). Schmitt's employment of *nomos* went past what he perceived to be the inadequate interpretations of ancient Greek philosophy. Plato's *nomos* represented 'a mere rule' over land (ibid, p. 67), while Aristotle's interpretation did better in communicating *nomos* as an 'original distribution of land' (ibid, p. 68). *Nomos*, for Schmitt, is a 'constitutive act of spatial ordering' (ibid, p. 70).

> The Greek word for the first measure of all subsequent measures, for the first land-appropriation understood as the first partition and classification of space, for the primeval division and distribution, is *nomos.* (Ibid, p. 67)

In Schmitt's *nomos* of the earth, 'land appropriation [is] the primeval act of founding law' (ibid, p. 45). From nomadic societies to the empires of antiquity and through to the liberal international order, Schmitt described how law is 'geographically situated and situating' (Dean 2006, p. 6). The US Government's contentious ability to confer private title or rights on US citizens in outer space derives from successive US governments appropriating from native Americans and rival state powers, thus becoming the supreme political authority over what is now US territory. English common law enshrined the sovereign with powers to lawfully appropriate from natives and commoners, a constitutional power owing to William the Conqueror's appropriation of land from Anglo-Saxon societies, who had claimed the land in the wake of the Romans, who had appropriated it from Celtic tribes, and so on. 'The history of peoples, with their migrations, colonizations, and conquests, is a history of land-appropriation' (Schmitt 2003, p. 328).

Nomos emphasises that *all* laws derive from acts of land appropriation: sovereign authority, political legitimacy and privately owned property all have the appropriation of land at their foundations. *Nomos* thus addresses the question of whether state and private powers over land are interlinked or independent concepts, an 'age-old question' that is now being projected off-world (Pop 2000, p. 275). Perpetuated by Blackstone and Montesquieu in the 18th century, the divide between the public law of sovereignty and the private law of property is a distinction that has directed the course of legal pedagogy (Cohen 1927, p. 8). Private property was treated as a case of civil law, constituting the *dominium* of individuals over things – land, commodities and human and non-human life (ibid, p. 8). Public law, meanwhile, was a case of political power, *imperium:* 'the rule over all individuals by the prince' (ibid, pp. 8–9). However, Schmitt argued that land appropriation is the 'terrestrial fundament' from which both the *dominium* of private law and the *imperium* of political power are derived – it is the 'archetype of a constitutive legal process' (Schmitt 2003, p. 47).

What can Schmitt's *nomos* tell us about outer space? How is political authority in outer space being 'constituted' through appropriation? To Polanyi's emphasis on statecraft in enclosure, we can add Schmitt's argument that – in the very act of settlement – there is a fundamental indistinction between sovereign or national appropriation and the civic laws of private property. To pre-emptively make a legal guarantee of private property ownership is a de facto act of sovereign appropriation. If the allocation of private property rights over space resources derives from the sovereign authority of the US state, then the United States (not just its corporate citizens) is pre-emptively appropriating from celestial bodies – this is the authority from which private resource ownership under the CSLCA would derive. However, it remains to be seen whether an international regime, predicated on multilateral consensus, will regulate private resource appropriations in outer space.

We can also analyse the OST in terms of the Schmittian *nomos*: the 1945 establishment of the United Nations heralded a post-Westphalian international legal order that has more recently been termed 'globalisation', in which the sovereignty of the nation state is thought to be increasingly diminished.

Yet, by taking statehood as its essential membership criterion, the United Nations preserved territoriality – the 'law of the land' – as a key, spatial determinant in international law. The terms of the *OST* effectively project the territorially defined authority of statehood into outer space, while also bringing deliberative politico-legal fora and norms that limit the scope of this statehood. The movement towards private property laws in outer space, most recently articulated in the Artemis Accords, represents an attempt from a handful of UN member nation to realign the norms established by the OST (or, as will be discussed in Chapter 5, entrench a pro-extractivist interpretation of them).

However, *nomos* also problematises any attempt at describing the space frontier in legal geographic terms. The opposite of *nomos* is anomie (*anomos*), or lawlessness. Schmitt deployed *nomos* as a means of explaining the genealogy of international law, taking us from the empires of antiquity to the inter-state relations prevailing in the immediate post-war era.[6] A key step in this process was the concept of 'amity lines', in which the *jus publicum Europeaum* (European international law) of pre-modern European empires made a distinction between lawful warfare on the European continent and a mutually determined 'space of exception' on the anomic colonial frontier.[7] Colonial powers treated the lands of the many indigenous societies as *res nullius* – anomic 'new' worlds, in which the murder and enslavement of indigenous peoples could proceed without legal consequence, providing charter companies with new sources of land, resources and labour in the process. Colonialism or enclosure in outer space may not be as violent as these processes were on Earth. Yet the CSLCA and subsequent private property laws risk treating the off-world as anomic, a space in which to impose a regime of private appropriation on the off-world *nomos*, distorting the fundamental principles of the OST in the process.

Schmitt's excavation of *nomos* inevitably brings us back to his political affiliations. The emphasis on land in understanding *nomos* is consonant with the early 20th century ethno-political entwinement of 'blood and soil', best typified by Freidrich Ratzel's theory of *lebensraum* – the social need for 'living space' that would be used to justify Nazi imperialism in Europe. The O'Neillian dream of new, off-world living space – as fused with private property rights that are anchored in US sovereignty – indeed resembles geographer Isiah Bowman's (1878–1950) call for an 'economic *Lebensraum* that would open up world commerce to American interests' (Smith, 1994, p. 23).

Here, if we can limit our discussion of the Schmittian *nomos* to its more general framing of land appropriation as being constitutive of laws of property and sovereignty, we can see that extending these core political categories into what Buzz Aldrin called the 'magnificent desolation' of the off-world represents a break from millennia of landed human civilisations. Despite the commons-defining 'constitution' of the OST, the Solar System might be considered 'lawless' in that it lacks laws established through new, foundational acts of land appropriation. Yet, like Polanyi's fictitious commodification of land, the agricultural roots of *nomos* are confronted by the complete absence of life elsewhere in the Solar System.

Political theory on a lifeless frontier?

Polanyi and Schmitt offer useful concepts for exploring the off-world colonisation project, yet their accounts of law and politics are problematised by the material characteristics of outer space. Life does not exist in the off-world, as far as we know. There is no soil in which we could grow crops, no air for us to breath and no ecosystems to provide us with nutrients. Human inhabitations of the space around Earth (let alone anywhere deeper into the Solar System) are entirely dependent on technological systems that – at great cost and complexity – can only temporarily imitate the life-supports of our home planet. The Solar System offers not *lebensraum* but *todesraum* – a space of death …

Let us now consider the celestial bodies that may one day be subject processes of extraction and settlement. Earth's Moon has been suggested as a site of habitation in Western science fiction literature as early as Verne's *De la terre à la lune* and in American space policy pre-dating the Apollo Program. More recently, the NewSpace firm Moon Express has its sights on exploiting what it calls 'Earth's 8th continent' (Moon Express n.d.). The Moon has temperatures that oscillate from −180°C to 130°C (Faure & Mensing 2007, p. 154), days and nights that last a fortnight, no atmosphere to provide breathable air, no magnetosphere to prevent the carcinogenic effects of cosmic radiation, and reduced gravity, which may prove difficult for maintaining human bone density during an extended stay. In December 2018, the Chinese Lunar Exploration Program transported the unmanned 'Lunar Micro Ecosystem' aboard the Chang'e 4 spacecraft to the far side of the Moon. Cottonseeds were successfully germinated inside the 3-kg capsule, but the plants died once the lunar evening commenced and the external temperature dropped towards −170°C (Devlin 2019). At 38 million km^2, the Moon has a surface area less than that of the Asian continent (Sharp 2022). With significant technological innovation – like caves dug into lunar bedrock and enclosed in protective 'bubbles' – the Moon might have space to live in, but not 'living' space as we know it.

Heading from Earth towards the Sun is the planet Venus. Elon Musk describes its extreme temperatures (averaging 464°C) and atmosphere of 97% carbon dioxide as being 'not at all like the goddess' (Musk 2017, p. 46). It serves better as a forewarning of runaway climate change scenarios than as a potential site of colonisation. Heading from Earth in the other direction is more inviting. Mars is highly appealing in space colonisation narratives due to being 'resource rich' and having comparable temperature ranges to Earth and similar land mass to colonise (Musk 2017, p. 46). On Mars, temperatures range from −140°C to 20°C, in part due to a very thin atmosphere (Faure & Mensing 2007, p. 24). According to Musk and many others who have advocated for terraforming Mars, 'It is a little cold, but we can warm it up'

(Musk 2017, p. 46). Vastly speculative 'terraforming' proposals have been hypothesised to be capable of yielding a breathable atmosphere on Mars (Sagan 1973). Such a project would require far superior technologies of spaceflight and 'geoengineering' than scientists possess today, and would likely take many thousands of years if it were to succeed at all (considering that the natural evolution of Earth's atmosphere required over a billion years of work from oxygen-producing cyanobacteria). Until then, a healthy Martian colony would be as utterly technologically dependent as anywhere else beyond the relatively lower altitudes of Earth's atmosphere.

Beyond Mars lies the asteroid belt. A handful of missions to minor celestial bodies have been completed, and the Japan Aerospace Exploration Agency's 2003–2010 mission to asteroid 25143 Itokawa and NASA's 1999–2006 mission to comet Wild 2 have returned small samples. While Mars, the Moon or other large celestial bodies might offer a reasonably straightforward analogy to Earth as planetary 'land', asteroids and comets are very different. Many have very weak gravity, meaning that only low escape velocities would be needed to depart the surface of an asteroid – an attractive prospect if you were hauling ore or water ice to an off-world refinery or smelter. The physicist Freeman Dyson, a friend of Gerard O'Neill, once predicted that 'We shall learn to grow trees on comets' and men will one day 'take their ease among the tree trunks' (Carey 1999, p. 469). Minor celestial bodies might become sites of mineral appropriation, but recreating an atmosphere on comets and asteroids traversing the vacuums of deep space is of course entirely implausible.

The planets and planetoids beyond the asteroid belt are less promising as sites for either settlement or commercial exploitation. Jupiter and its moons are the next stop on the outward journey from Earth past the asteroid belt. *Voyager 1* managed a fly-by after 546 days of travel; entering its orbit would require a much slower speed and a longer journey (NASA 2023). Technical challenges aside, this distance alone would put the outer planets outside the reach of profitable exploitation for the present century (at least), and they subsequently do not feature prominently in the NewSpace imaginary. Outward from Jupiter on the final stops on this tour of the Solar System are the other gas giants Saturn, Uranus, Neptune and their moons, followed by Pluto and Eris, the former recently demoted to the status of 'dwarf planet' or 'trans-Neptunian object', and a host of other planetoids – asteroids, comets and 'centaurs'. Between these celestial bodies are vast expanses of interplanetary space. It is not too bold a prediction to say that human agency in the off-world commons of outer space will be limited to the Solar System, if not the space between Earth and the asteroid belt, for a long time to come.

In lieu of an actualised space mining industry, the only real sites of commercial exploitation in the Solar System are much, much closer to home. The orbital bands stretching from 160 km above Earth (below which atmospheric drag will bring any object in orbit back to Earth) and lower than 36,000 km from Earth's surface (beyond which human use is mostly limited to scientific research) are sites of advanced scientific, military and commercial infrastructures. High-earth or geosynchronous orbit (GEO) is particularly valuable. At approximately 35,786 km above sea level, inclined directly above the Equator and having an orbital period matching one-day (thus, moving eastward at 11,000 km per hour), satellites with these orbital elements will match the Earth's rotation and can thus be positioned above the same place on Earth at a height that enables transmission to 42% of the planet (Kelso, cited in Collis 2009, p. 47). The allocation of rights to use GEO is governed by the International Telecommunications Union, where – among other rules – 'a satellite's owner must register first with the ITU, which then checks that the slot positioning is acceptable in relation to other satellites, and then assigns that slot and its frequency to the satellite' (Collis 2009, p. 2). Yet these quasi-private property arrangements are distinct from the *nomos* of space mining and the extractive rights granted under laws for private ownership of space resources.

It is worth emphasising just how difficult it would be to realise the NewSpace colonisation plan. The International Space Station is in low-Earth orbit – humanity's doorstep to space – and is the furthest extent of sustained human inhabitation on the off-world frontier. It is a symbol of international scientific cooperation (if we ignore the US-led exclusion of the Chinese National Space Administration, and prohibitive costs for involvement from developing nations). As a research facility, the ISS provides insight in microgravity living and scientific and commercial experimentation, albeit at the modest distance of 400 km above the Earth's surface. The annual operating cost of the ISS is approximately $3 billion (NASA Office of Inspector General 2021, p. 1). It is one of the most expensive public works project ever undertaken, for the seemingly modest task of keeping less than ten people alive in space.

Sustaining a human colony beyond Earth's atmosphere engenders utter dependence on technologies of life support. The spaceship or the space suit represents an existential bubble that shields the human organism and from the outer space environment (Sloterdijk 2013; Walker & Granjou 2017). In *Dialogues on New Space* (2015 [1954]), Schmitt makes some brief observations on outer space. 'For me, the human is the son of the earth, and so he shall remain as long as he remains human' (Schmitt 2015, p. 81). This statement links both Earth (the home planet) and earth (the soil) as 'the mother of all law' (Schmitt 2003, p. 42). In *Dialogues*, he remarks on the elemental distinctions between land and sea:

> … the midpoint and core of a terrestrial existence – with all its concrete orders – is the house. House and property, marriage, family and hereditary right, all that is built upon the foundation of a terrestrial mode of being … On the contrary, at the core of a maritime existence there sails the ship, which is already in itself much more and much more intensely a technological means than the house. The house is rest, the ship is movement. Even the space in which the ship moves is other than the space of the landscape, in which the house stands. (2015, pp. 73–74)

The household was the centre of production until the Industrial Revolution. In ancient Greek, the household or *oikos* was primarily an agricultural estate – the verb for governing or organising the estate was *oikonomos* or *oikonomia* (*oikos* + *nomos*), the word from which we derive the modern-day 'economy' (Polanyi 2001, p. 55; Schmitt 2003, p. 339). The very concept of economy thus contains an 'immanent measure' related to biological, life-supporting land (Schmitt 2003, p. 340), implying that laws of property and sovereignty are grounded in the lifeways of the common land.[8] Outer space awaits the foundational act of land appropriation that constitutes *nomos*, yet would only ever be *nomos* without *oikos* – a legal order supporting a landless economy.

In some ways, space colonisation would represent a realisation of the 'landless economy' of neoclassical economics. The intellectual heritage of many Mont Pèlerin Society members – notably founders like Friedrich Hayek and Milton Friedman – includes a formal economists' education in neoclassical economics (though neoliberalism cannot be elided with neoclassical economics). In neoclassical economics, capitalism and nature are effectively separate systems – as a result, the economy is not bound to any natural, planetary limit. Rees has noted the 'near doctrinaire position among neoclassical economists that technology can substitute for both resources and environmental functions' (1999, p. 208). Cirillo, meanwhile, notes how neoclassical economist Leon Walras had essentially removed land from a neoclassical model of economic exchange, reducing 'the economy' to a two-factor model of capital and labour (Cirillo 1980). Land and natural resources become simply a form of capital. If nature is infinitely convertible into other forms of capital, then innovation, wealth accumulation and industrial pollution can increase exponentially (Walker 2007, p. 176, 178). NewSpace's expansionism represents a realisation of the 'landless' neoclassical-neoliberal economy by moving industry to a place where there is no land, no biological nature and an infinite 'sink' for pollution outputs.

Conclusion

Private property has been described in NewSpace discourse as a beneficial force for universal prosperity. This is a well-worn trope in neoliberal capitalism, one which obscures the actual history of private property in land and natural resources. In the famous words of Sir William Blackstone,

> There is nothing which so generally strikes the imagination, and engages the affections of mankind, as the right of property; or that sole and despotic dominion which one man claims and exercises over the external things of the world, in total exclusion of the right of any other individual in the universe. And yet there are very few that will give themselves the trouble to consider the [origin] and foundation of this right. Pleased as we are with the possession, we seem afraid to look back to the means by which

> it was acquired, as if fearful of some defect in our title; or at best we rest satisfied with the decision of the laws in our favour, without examining the reason or authority upon which those laws have been built. We think it enough that our title is derived by grant of the former proprietor, by descent from our ancestors, or by the last will and testament of the dying owner; not caring to reflect that … there is no foundation in nature or in natural law [or] why a set of words upon parchment should convey the dominion of land … . (Blackstone 2019, ch. 1, s. 2)

Blackstone's evocative description of (private) property as 'that sole and despotic dominion' resonates with the advent of off-world private property. If a space mining firm exercised the rights of private ownership, use and dispossession that are guaranteed under the recent laws, the exclusionary nature of corporate property may undermine NewSpace's humanitarian or cosmopolitan justifications for space mining. State parties to the OST have collectively agreed that the governance of outer space would be guided by principles of free access, equality and community-wide benefits. Yet the laws of the United States, Luxembourg, UAE and Japan introduce individual rights to extract from and irreversibly change the space commons. Potential community benefits afforded by celestial bodies and resources would be enclosed from non-spacefaring nations and from future generations.

Yet, as a pre-emptive act of enclosure on a lifeless frontier, these laws are far removed from the enclosures described by More, Blackstone and Polanyi. Polanyi's description of property in land as a fictitious commodity mirrored Schmitt's pre-occupation with a telluric understanding of law and order:

> land and labor are not separated; labor forms part of life, land remains part of nature, life and nature form an articulate whole. Land is thus tied up with the organizations of kinship, neighbourhood, craft and creed … . (Polanyi 2001, p. 187)

The NewSpace commodification-colonisation project can be read as an exercise in severing the social-ecological ties between land and sovereignty, projecting mythic, 'self-evident' property rights onto an abiotic frontier.

We have now discussed the legal foundations of property in land. Yet the recent space resource laws assign ownership right to resources extracted from their environment, not land title. Schmitt, Polanyi and Locke were concerned primarily with pre-industrial modes of production and took little interest in mining rights. In the 21st century, the 'enclosure' of mineral estates similarly involves the devolution from common or public property into private hands. Yet, with industrial pollution threatening all of Earth's ecosystems and its inhabitants (so much so that NewSpace continues to argue that space mining and colonisation should be considered an important pillar of Earthly environmentalism), there is much more at stake in the enclosure and combustion of mineral commons than the local, agrarian commons of medieval Europe. Whereas property in land rests upon a paradoxical relationship between private freedom and politico-legal power, the history of mining rights involves a different entanglement of state sovereignty and private property – which we will explore in the following chapter.

Notes

1 Whether we approach property from either a sociological or legal perspective, the 'bundle of rights' concept is a helpful starting point for considering property relationships. Originating with English jurist and legal historian Sir Henry Maine (2007 [1917]), the 'bundle' referred to rights to own property, and commonly involves a set of privileges *and* duties or obligations, rather than unfettered and outright ownership. Owning real estate entails the right to own and sell a house, for instance, but owners are also required to register their ownership with a property registry, pay land tax, adhere to zoning laws and respect the rights of their tenants, among other responsibilities. As Waldron notes that it is 'probably a mistake ... to insist on any definition of private property that implies a proprietor has absolute control over his resources' (2016, p. 6). As far as the CSLCA is the concerned, these reciprocal rights are expressed through Title IV's assurance that these rights would somehow be 'in accordance with applicable law, including the international obligations of the United States' (CSLCA 2015, s. 51303). These obligations refer, of course, to the articles and principles of the OST – ensuring freedom of use for all State Parties (and their corporations), exploring and using space through peaceful means and maintaining other parties right to freedom from harmful interference, among others. Whether the individually held property rights of the CSLCA would (and could) be curtailed for the benefit of external parties (domestic or international) is the subject of much conjecture and is discussed further in Chapters 4 and 5.

2 Andro Linklater's history of ownership notes that in Roman law, 'rights of property went with the land, rather than existing separately' (2015, p. 30). Roman law inscribed a system of mutual obligation between sovereign and landowner, whereby landowners guarded land on behalf of the ruler and if 'an estate be confiscated, or its inheritance disputed, the contract of mutual obligation disappeared and with it the rights of ownership' (ibid, p. 30). In limiting dues and loyalties that landowners were bound to pay to the Crown, the *Magna Carta* represented a break from Roman concepts of mutual obligation in land (in addition to mutual obligation under feudal tenure).

3 We will return to NewSpace as an expression of neoliberal environmentalism in Chapter 7. Here it is worth noting that off-world private property rights are, as they are currently proposed, at least, a divergence from neoliberal approaches to the commons. The commodification of nature is central to neoliberal claims to environmental conservation: it has been argued that the social and environmental costs of pollution ('externalities') can be internalised through private ownership. Ronald Coase (1960) of the Chicago School had proposed that such 'problems of social cost' could be resolved through clearly defined property rights and negotiation between contracting parties. The 'Coase theorem' has been influential in neoliberal environmentalism, which has enshrined private property-based markets as the mechanism to address questions of atmospheric pollution, among other examples (Keohane 2009, p. 43). NewSpace similarly proposes private property rights as a means of reducing centralised (state) decision-making in the future space economy, but not under any pretence of internalising pollution in the space commons. NewSpace has generally treated private property as an incentivisation measure for private investment in space mining enterprises, rather than as a means

of resolving potential tragedies of the space commons (Hardin 1968). NewSpace actors claim that exploiting outer space will conserve the resources of Earth, but outer space is not itself a site for resource conservation.

4 Data produced using 'Contractor search' in the Federal Procurement Data System (FPDS 2023a).

5 We will return to Polanyi in Chapter 7. His concept of the 'double movements' – a destructive commodification movement followed by protective counter-movements (unemployment benefits, environmental protection and so on) – is interesting for discussing how new international laws of outer space might pre-emptively counter the unilateral, profit-based appropriations anticipated through the CSLCA.

6 He thought perpetual peace would be based on a friend-enemy distinction at the level of regional blocs: US dominance of the Americas, and presumably Nazi Germany in Eurasia (2003, p. 355).

7 I will return to the *nomos/anomos* distinction when arguing that space resource appropriation bears several resemblances to maritime piracy and privateering in the expansion of the British Empire (Chapter 6).

8 In Chapter 4, I will revise Schmitt's concept of *nomos* in terms of mineral (not land) appropriation.

4 On mineral sovereignty[1]

State-corporate appropriation and the power of mining capital

Several nations have now established a legal framework of private property rights in anticipation of private claims to space resources. The sovereign's ability to confer rights of property ownership upon their citizens cannot be explained without a history of constitutional laws of property in land. However, enclosing the 'mineral commons' (on Earth and in space) is different to enclosing the lifeways of landed community. What is the difference between private property in minerals and property in land? How do we theorise the relationship between the state and markets vis-à-vis mining law? What parallels can we draw between the private appropriation of mineral wealth in outer space and what has come before on Earth?

Property in land emerged from the reliance of humans upon their land for subsistence. Property rights in minerals emerged more recently, beginning in the 16th–17th centuries and accelerating alongside industrial capitalism and the reliance of states upon metals, ores and combustible fossil fuels in order to administer the national economy and compete in international trade and war. Whereas villagers, serfs and rural wage labourers tended the land, the scale and complexity of enclosing mineral commons involves the delegation of authority to mine to parties who have the requisite skills and capital to do so (Walker & Johnson 2018, pp. 59–60).

In relation to minerals, we often speak of mineral 'estates' or 'commonwealths'. 'Commonwealth' 'literally means common property or riches', but the distinctions between communal, public and private property in minerals are often unclear (Flomenhoft 2018, p. 1). Flomenhoft notes that constitutional law may assign ownership of minerals within a territory to 'the people', yet in practice mineral commonwealths are more often administered by national government and exploited by incorporated entities (2018, pp. 11–12). In his comparative study of 199 nations, Flomenhoft determined that the state or crown retained ownership of minerals in 142 nations (ibid, p. 11).

For the majority of human history, rights to own and use the land engendered modes of production and consumption that were predicated on cultivation, stewardship and inheritance (to varying extents). It is no good over-exploiting your land if you and your heirs will have to live on it. Mineral rights, however, are extractive rights: a party is granted access, they take what

DOI: 10.1201/9781003293613-4

minerals are profitable and then move on to the next reserve. Dahlin and Fredriksson describe 'extractivism' as a fundamentally colonial practice, where 'both the resource and the profit it generates tend to be exported' (2017, p. 255). Resources are 'unbundled' from their context (e.g. an oil reservoir), and transported elsewhere such that they can threaten other commons (a marine estuary or the atmosphere, among others) that are distant from the initial act of extraction and enclosure (Dahlin & Fredriksson 2017, p. 264).

The stakes are thus higher in the enclosure of terrestrial mineral commonwealths than in the agricultural enclosures discussed in the previous chapter. If left unchecked, the carbon intensive extraction of minerals and the combustion of fossil fuels constitute nothing less than an existential threat to all life on Earth. The realisation that we live in an age of 'the Anthropocene' – whereby humanity itself represents the supreme geological force and the present geological epoch is characterised by the wholescale exercise of this force – was arrived at much earlier than O'Neill or the Club of Rome, and indeed much earlier than Paul Crutzen's (2002) proclamation of an Anthropocene epoch. Vladimir Vernadsky (1863–1945) was a Russian mineralogist, biochemist and, with NewSpace precursor Konstantin Tsiolkovsky, a philosopher in the cosmist tradition. Vernadsky is widely considered the founder of Earth systems science, and was one of the first to articulate what would become the essence of the Anthropocene thesis:

> … in our geologic era … – the era of reason – a new geochemical factor of paramount importance appears … Man has introduced into the planet's structure a new form of effect upon the exchange of atoms between living matter and inert matter … With man, an enormous geological power has appeared on the surface of the planet. (Vernadsky [1924], in Guillaume 2014, p. 138)

Vernadsky coined the term 'biosphere' (1926) and described the ancient, solar-bio-energetic processes which human industry was now exploiting (Walker & Johnson 2018, p. 56). He stated that humankind 'does not transcend the bounds of living nature, since the primary source of the electrical and steam energy [driving civilisation] is that same living matter or … past living organisms which have transformed through geological processes' – namely, coal and oil (Vernadsky 2012 [1938], p. 27). Techno-scientific, thermo-industrial civilisation transforms ever more of the Earth into 'the economy' and has fundamentally altered the biogeochemical structure of the Earth's enveloping spheres in this process – biosphere, atmosphere, hydrosphere and cryosphere (Walker & Johnson 2018, p. 57). Were space mining to materialise, human dominion over nature would extend into the off-world, as an exercise in 'exo-geological' power.

However, as Malm and Hornborg (2014) have noted, the concept of the Anthropocene is not easily transferable into the social sciences. In the Anthropocene narrative, it is the abstraction of 'humanity' that wields geological power. Responsibility for the exercise and consequence of geological power are diffused across the 'species', which effectively de-politicises our understanding of the Anthropocene (Malm & Hornborg 2014). Geological power is clearly unevenly distributed, whether we consider disparities in fossil fuel combustion between developed and developing nations or the disproportionate influence of mining interests on climate policy. In the US refusal to sign the *Moon Agreement* (1979) or indeed the passage of the CSLCA, we can see that anticipatory, exo-geological power is similarly concentrated in the developed world and wielded by neoliberal actors.

In the nascent space mining industry, Silicon Valley, aerospace manufacturing and the resources sector become curious bedfellows. The delicate, lightweight construction of spacecraft seems far removed from Earthly extractivism. Mountaintop removal, earthmovers, bucket-wheel excavators and 200-wagon coal trains – the sheer scale and destructiveness of the contemporary resources industry stands in contrast to the intricacies and fragility of aerospace innovation. This contrast is heightened when we consider that many of the venture capitalists and 'angel investors' funding space mining have made their fortunes in the fetishised (Marx 2015) and disembodied 'knowledge' industries – an incorporeal economy seemingly at odds with terrestrial mining's capacity to irreversibly alter the material world. Yet these personal fortunes from ICT entrepreneurialism – whether Musk, Page, Bezos or Thiel – require geological power, in the form of copper phone lines, tantalum capacitors and lithium-ion batteries, to name but a few minerals upon which both the 'knowledge' and NewSpace economies are dependent.

In this chapter, I deploy the term 'mineral sovereignty' as a means of approaching the appropriation of off-world resources (Walker & Johnson 2018). Mineral sovereignty explores how geological power becomes geological agency: the political capacity of specific social subjects to act intentionally, perhaps against the will, interests or rights-claims of others. 'Sovereignty' – one of the most basic concepts in political theory – is lacking a grounding in the politics of the subterranean. Mineral sovereignty is a hybrid term that denotes the general politico-legal field of the extractive, pyrotechnical and metallurgical industries. It describes the co-constitutive powers of state and corporation that are manifest in mineral rights, which I argue are now being projected off-world through private resource ownership laws. Mineral sovereignty is evident in the formal state power to confer legality and legitimacy upon mining operations. As a term of historical method, mineral sovereignty underscores the implausibility of demarcating acts of private appropriation from claims of national sovereignty, and thus it further highlights how the CSLCA and subsequent laws from other nations are incommensurate with the terms of the *Outer Space Treaty* (OST).

I focus here on the US *Commercial Space Launch Competitiveness Act* (CSLCA), the first legal framework signed into national law that permitted the private ownership of off-world minerals. The CSLCA re-animates what I will argue is a deep historical relationship between state power and extractive rights, and the challenges extractive capital presents for popular sovereignty. NewSpace actors have claimed that their project is about 'democratising' outer space (Lubin, in Planetary Resource 2018; see also Rocket Lab's Robert Beck, cited in Shammas & Holen 2019, p. 3).[2] The age of the space bureaucrat and the public servant astronaut is over, they claim, for it is 'the people [who] have "the right stuff"' (Tumlinson, in Orphans of Apollo 2008). In keeping with American frontier exceptionalism, NewSpace treats outer space as a site of political renewal and reinvention (Zubrin 1994; ASD 2019, p. 3). However, the role of corporate lobbying in the passage of the CSLCA suggests that 'NewSpace democracy' deserves closer scrutiny.

We can attribute the passage of the CSLCA to the lobbying of space mining start-up Planetary Resources. As a case study in mineral sovereignty, I trace the passage of the CSLCA using Congressional records (for example: U.S. House of Representatives 2015a) and the OpenSecrets database of federal campaign contributions and lobbying activity, the latter collated from the Senate Office of Public Records and data from the Federal Election Commission (for example: OpenSecrets 2023a; OpenSecrets 2023b). 'Mineral sovereignty' renders the concept of the rule of law ambiguous. It points to the question of power – mineral sovereignty can also be extra-parliamentary, evident in the historical capacity of mining capitals to shape the political environment and legal architectures of the territories they operate in, including state capture, regime change, transgression of international law and corporate donations. This chapter uses mineral sovereignty to highlight how the private property guarantees of the CSLCA became public law through a process that, while commonplace, is discordant with Abraham Lincoln's famed edict that democratic government should be 'of the people, by the people and for the people'.

Rethinking sovereignty

For the CSLCA to be commensurate with the principles of the OST, space miners have claimed that they can appropriate minerals from celestial bodies without there being any territorial or sovereign claim of the United States embedded within these acts of private appropriation (for example: Kfir 2016). The exercise of sovereignty in outer space is generally confined to governments' jurisdiction over their own spacecraft and astronauts – this is distinct from the exercise of jurisdiction over mineral resources as it has occurred in capitalist history. What would 'state sovereignty in space' mean, if it was applied through the permanence of industrial extractivism and the political and technological infrastructures that come with it? Moreover, what does 'sovereignty' actually mean, when we consider this Earthly mining history?

Space law scholars have noted that 'sovereignty is very limited in outer space' (Masson-Zwaan and Palkovitz 2017, p. 8). Article 8 of the OST states that a 'State Party to the Treaty on whose registry an object launched into outer space is carried shall retain jurisdiction and control over such an object, and over any personnel thereof, while in outer space or on a celestial body' (OST 1967) – much like the way in which colonial seafaring vessels brought the laws of their motherland with them, the Empire was contained and floating upon the high seas like a piece of 'moving territory' (Heller-Roazen 2009, p. 180). Perry notes that the CSLCA has avoided discussing this 'active personality' concept, such as whether the extra-territorial mining rights of the CSLCA represent a permissible extension of the state's ability to 'assert sovereignty over its nationals even when its nationals are outside the country' (2017, p. 9). Hobe and de Man also interrogate this point from a space law perspective, and conclude that the active personality principle does not mean 'that a State can regulate … the status of this [extra-territorial] environment itself' (2017, p. 468). Private property law involves state powers changing the status of off-world mineral resources to being ownable as private property.

In space and on Earth, 'sovereignty' is a contested term – particularly when we look to its application in the field of mining. Sovereignty is among the most basic and controversial of concepts in political theory and international law, yet most conventional narratives of sovereignty lack a sense of materiality beyond two-dimensional, cartographic understandings of territory. A conventional genealogy of sovereignty might start with Ernst Kantorowicz's (1957) *The King's Two Bodies.* Kantorowicz described how the concept of the King's body gradually fused with 'the Kingdom', leading to the modern understanding of the 'body politic' (Kantorowicz 1957). In medieval monarchy, the 'sovereign' connoted both the power to rule and the ruler herself; the modern body politic represented 'an authority that was bundled into a single entity', which 'held supremacy in advancing the interests of the polity' and was 'confined within territorial borders' (Philpott 2014, p. 2). 'Popular sovereignty' emerged from democratic revolutions in England, France and America which gave the power to decide on rulers to the *demos.* Enlightenment philosophers like Thomas Hobbes, John Locke and Jean-Jacques Rousseau developed social contract theories of sovereignty, where (to varying degrees) it was argued that the legitimacy of government authority and the rule of law ought to be grounded in the consent of the governed.

The French jurist Jean Bodin (1530–1596) is credited with the earliest secular theory of the state, in which he also noted the ambiguities in sovereignty. In his *The Six Books of the Commonwealth* (1967 [1576]), Bodin said:

> The first attribute of the sovereign prince … is the power to make law binding on all his subjects in general and on each in particular. But to avoid any ambiguity one must add that he does so without the consent of any superior, equal, or inferior being necessary. If the prince can only make law with the consent of a superior he is a subject; if of an equal he shares his sovereignty; if of an inferior, whether it be a council of magnates or the people, it is not he who is sovereign. (Book 1, Chapter 10, p. 42)

On the one hand, sovereignty is the power that gives law its authority, force and legitimacy in a given nation and territory, binding and constituting the rulers and ruled as a political community. On the other hand, sovereignty is the power presumed to be constrained by constitutional limitations upon executive authority, such as the separation of powers under the American Constitution, or its provisions against the expropriation of private property. Yet the sovereign power is revealed most clearly when the declaration of an exceptional threat to security justifies the *suspension* of these constitutional and juridical norms (Schmitt 1985). To use Carl Schmitt's phrase, which Hitler put into practice in assuming dictatorial powers, 'Sovereign is he who decides on the exception' (Schmitt 1985, p. 5). The aftermath of 11 September offers a contemporary example of the constitutional power to suspend the constitution, in which the fortification of the surveillance state and abrogation of citizens' freedoms has been justified with discourses of 'national emergency'.

The concept of sovereignty also appears ambiguous when viewed through the prism of neoliberal globalisation. In an increasingly interconnected world of transboundary capital flows and movements of goods, services and people, the political unit of the nation state is thought to be de-territorialised, its sovereignty diminished. Luxembourg has been described as a tax haven which 'sold its sovereignty' to the global financial industry (Zucman, in Abrahamian 2017). Its *Law of July 20th 2017 on the exploration and use of space resources* outlines the authorisation of missions to appropriate space resources, for European companies with offices registered in Luxembourg (2017, Art. 4). In places, this resembles the 'flag of convenience' used in maritime law, such as when shipping companies register operations in jurisdictions such as Panama. Both DSI and Planetary Resources established legal entities in Luxembourg (Government of the Grand Duchy of Luxembourg 2016). Luxembourgian space resources law involves an exercise of sovereignty that supports the political and economic goals of *foreign* sovereigns and empowered elites, by removing 'borders' for transnational movements of capital. 'Off-shore' tax jurisdictions such as Luxembourg illustrate how neoliberal globalisation and the global 'race to the bottom' on national economic policy can obfuscate the exercise of state sovereignty.

Meanwhile, neoliberal and neoclassical economic theories hold that the power of the sovereign decision is diffused into 'the market' – a spontaneous aggregator of the countless instances of free choice exercised by supposedly rational, autonomous individuals. 'Consumer sovereignty' was a theory proposed by William Harold Hutt, a neoclassical economist and MPS member. He framed sovereignty within the 'laws' of supply and demand, claiming that the 'ultimate power' in an economy was the consumer, and the producer was ultimately subject to their 'demands' (Hutt, in Egger 1994, p. 113). Hutt's consumer sovereignty theory evades the question of 'producer sovereignty' that is so ubiquitous in neoliberal capitalism: the countervailing power of large corporations 'to serve their own goals' often by capturing the state – the 'power that is inherent in institutional position', to use Galbraith's formulation (1970, p. 475). While it acknowledges the role of the state, Galbraith's critique of 'consumer sovereignty' also serves to illustrate the absence of materiality in standard theories of sovereignty.

Clearly, there is a mineral aspect to the question of sovereignty: whether accessing metals to build the technologies of war or securing fossil fuel reserves to power national industry, geological power is the taproot of military and economic power. As Stuart Elden (2013) observes, customary understandings of territorial power are well-expressed in the military command to 'secure the area': a cartographic view of land and territory as a flat space. Sovereignty, understood in this sense, underplays the imperative to secure strategic three-dimensional spaces, or 'volumes', to think of 'height and depth instead of surfaces, three dimensions instead of areas' (Elden 2013, p. 35). It is surely vital to political accounting to estimate the volume of oil and gas in the mineral estate, and to wield 'vertical power' over geological strata. Whether state-owned or state-owning, it is often the most vertically consolidated of corporations running the business of mining.

In this sense, the control of mineral wealth can be said to be constitutive of the political. From the police cell to the presidential palace, the conditions of energy exploitation frequently translate into the political conditions of the nation as whole, and in turn its regional and international relations. Angola, Azerbaijan, Bahrain, Bolivia, Chechnya, Congo, East Timor ... Saudi Arabia, Venezuela, West Papua. We need not list more nations where mineral extraction and the distribution of resource rents are key factors in exceptional histories of revolution or counter-revolutions of constitutional order. This is also true of 'politically stable' jurisdictions like Australia, Canada and the United States, where governments are frequently unable (or unwilling) to reign in the ambitions of fossil capital. National government often appears as the executive arm of mining capital, legislating for 'energy security' and against movements for carbon taxation, renewable energy, Indigenous land rights or environmental conservation.

We thus need to revise our understanding of 'sovereignty' by returning to the question of how law relates to the base materiality of planet Earth – *nomos*. Schmitt's (2003) account of terrestrial order began with the following statement on the primacy of land in *all* law and order, not just that explicitly concerning title in land and natural resources. For Schmitt, the earth, 'the soil', is 'the mother of law':

> ... the earth is bound to law in three ways. She contains law within herself, as a reward of labor; she manifests law upon herself, as fixed boundaries; and she sustains law above herself, as a public sign of order. Law is bound to the earth and related to the earth. (2003, p. 42)

In the pre-industrial legal traditions I discussed in Chapter 3, rights to land, soil, water and other life-sustaining resources originate in social obligations to the common interest in land and food production. Yet the administration of the modern industrial order – dependent on minerals ranging from gold and coal to copper and tantalum – cannot be understood in terms of attachments to the soil.

In light of the significance of sovereign claims to the *sub-soil*, let us revisit Schmitt's claim that 'land appropriation [is] the primeval act of founding law, [the] terrestrial fundament' from which both the dominium of private law and the imperium of political authority are derived (2003, pp. 45–47). Schmitt's statement that 'the constitutive process of a land-appropriation is found at the beginning of the history of every settled people, every commonwealth, every empire' could be equally significant in terms of mineral appropriation (2003, p. 48). As I will demonstrate in the following section, mineral appropriation is a process constitutive of nation and empire. This further emphasises that the recognition of private ownership claims off-world is an anticipatory extension of state sovereignty and national powers of appropriation, rather than a libertarian transcendence of it. Mineral appropriation (rather than land appropriation), under the terms of recent national laws for off-world resource ownership, may become the founding act of a neoliberal *nomos* of outer space. One possibility is that off-world mining corporations themselves become nation states, making laws and protecting their property on the off-world frontier as they see fit. At the very least, a mineralised conception of sovereignty suggests that any dichotomy between 'national' and 'private' acts of appropriation is highly problematic.

Mineral sovereignty in political history

'Sovereign is she who decides the state of extraction' ... who decides the access rights, labour conditions, and revenue obligations of mining concessions, and responsibility for the consequences of pollution. The history of mineral sovereignty reveals an entwined genealogy of the public laws of empire and nation state, and the private law of property rights, where distinctions between the formal political power of government and the economic power of transboundary corporations cannot be presumed. In this section, I will explore mineral sovereignty in three eras: the formation of the industrial state and empire in the age of 'royal metals'; the nationalisation and democratisation of mineral exploitation in the 19th–20th centuries; and the rise of neoliberalism as a movement re-privatising mineral sovereignty. Each of these case studies offers some insight into how mineral sovereignty may materialise in outer space.

Royal metals: mineral sovereignty and empire

Cuius est solum, eius est usque ad coelum et ad inferos. According to this Latin maxim dating to the 13th century, 'the owner of the soil has a prima facie ownership of everything reaching up to the very heavens and down to the depths of the earth' (Gray 1991, p. 253). The *ad coelum* doctrine would be enshrined in English legal commentary by Sir William Blackstone in the 18th century.

> Land hath also, in its legal signification, an indefinite extent, upwards as well as downwards … whatever is in a direct line, between the surface of any land and the centre of the earth, belongs to the owner of the surface; as is every day's experience in the mining countries. So that the word 'land' includes not only the face of the earth, but every thing under it, or over it. (2019, ch. 2, para. 18)

In the 20th century, access to airspace and outer space would place upper limits on the *ad coelum* understanding of property rights as vertically extendable. Yet the *ad coelum* doctrine remained influential in American mining law into the 20th century, in select jurisdictions. Some states allow landowners to claim select minerals beneath their properties (fossil fuels often being a notable exception) and ultimate title is not vested in state or federal government (Flomenhoft 2018, p. 5). National laws recognising private resource ownership in space would be a distortion of the *ad coelum* principle, where mineral rights can be possessed by individual owners without ultimate title resting in state sovereignty *and* without there being any private ownership of the surface 'land'.

Long before the legal revolutions that would abolish feudal titles and establish markets in land as exclusive private property, there were sovereign exceptions to landholders' rights in the subterranean. Flomenhoft notes that ancient Roman law 'established the rights of mineral to states' (2018, p. 5). John Nef describes the *Regale,* the claim of the sovereign to authority over land bearing precious metals (1964, p. 16). Frederic Barbarossa (1155–1189) claimed the regale as an attribute of his imperial sovereignty, and pressed claims for a share of all gold and silver mines in the Holy Roman Empire. In many jurisdictions, the right of the overlord to claim ownership over metals was to become supreme over the rights of the manorial 'lords of the soil'. Sovereign claims to 'royal metals' of gold and silver surpassed feudal rights to collect agricultural rents and enjoy usufructuary privileges. But in practice this required negotiation and the delegation of authority: rents or 'royalties' could not be set so high as to discourage industrial activity that royals themselves were not interested in doing.

There are only brief and isolated examples of what can be called 'free mining'. In ancient Rome, most mining was performed by slaves. By contrast, medieval mining involved relatively autonomous companies of highly skilled miners, with their own charters, rights and privileges often greater than those of towns emerging around textiles and other non-metal manufactures (Nef 1964, p. 60). In England, the charter of the ancient demesne Forest of Dean enabled common rights to exploit minerals, 'whereby men who were born in the [administrative division] of St Briavels and who have worked in mines for a year and a day, have the right to exploit coal and iron ore' (Foundation for

Common Land 2016). In Germany, where the techniques of mining and metallurgy were most advanced, the word for 'mountaineer' and 'miner' was the same (Nef 1964). Envied by serfs bound to labour for the 'lord of the soil', the miners travelled to wild places, seeking exposed surface ores of silver, copper, gold, iron, and abundant forests to cut for fuelwood and charcoal for small-scale open-air smelting. Patterns of 'settlement' in Europe owed much to the migrations of German miners: 'The movement to colonize and to mine went hand in hand' (Nef 1964, p. 12). Lewin notes how gold mining in western American states in the 19th century similarly involved settlements of 'free miners', 'who looked to themselves for the drafting of laws that would suit them best' (1931, p. 247).

'Free mining' is an isolated form of mineral ownership and exploitation because the development of mining, metallurgy and associated pyro-technologies (smelting, coal combustion, the steam engine and so on) became closely related to the emergence of core institutions of capitalism and the development of the nation state. As the scale of production increased, mining works became less *ad hoc*, more capital intensive and less mobile. The financing of larger and more permanent smelting and battery works, and of deeper mines deploying grander drainage and ventilation systems, demanded ever larger sums and combinations of investors. Nef (1964) links the evolution of mining technologies to the emergence of specifically capitalist forms of industry, predicated on the division between capital and labour. Shares in mining companies were once held by and exchanged between miners themselves (Nef 1964, p. 17). Eventually, the ownership and management of mines were transferred to more powerful players, such as wealthy absentee owners, a class of professional mine managers and royal revenue collectors. The miners themselves were increasingly cheapened to wage labourers with no rights in their product or share in the profit.

Mining also became essential to monetary sovereignty and, by extension, modern state formation. *Regalian* rights to mineral ownership were closely related to regal privileges to mint, to be the sole coiner of currency, and thus to administration of the treasury and the management of national economy. While Blackstone's influential *Commentaries* had enshrined the *ad coelum* doctrine in English common law, Lewin notes that 'Blackstone upheld the King's prerogative right' to claim minerals 'for the coinage of money and to promote commerce' (1931, p. 345). English monarchs would reassert their *regalian* rights in the 1556 'Case of Mines' (*R v Earl of Northumberland),* in which the Court of the Exchequer Chamber decided in favour of the Crown, Elizabeth I, stating that:

> by the law all mines of gold and silver within the realm, whether they be in the lands of the Queen, or of subjects, belong to the Queen by prerogative, with liberty to dig and carry away the ores thereof, and with other such incidents thereto as are necessary to be used for the getting of the ore. (Cited in Colman 2010)

In the wake of the Case of Mines decision, the Crown extended its dominion over metals by establishing royal monopoly through two charter companies: the Society of Mines Royal and the Company of Mineral and Battery Works. The granting of letters-patent to skilled miners aimed to benefit the imperial economy, developing productive industry while raising revenue through the collection of rents (Hyde Price 1906, pp. 14–16).

Mineral rights were frequently delegated to privateers, joint-stock companies and corporations – privately owned, for-profit extensions of the sovereignty of the Crown, the vanguard of world Empire. The organisation of corporate forms of private property, risk bearing, joint-stock capital and mercantile enterprise also emerged through the royal charter companies. Whereas the above letters patent would codify forms of mineral sovereignty in England, charters with privateers and companies would extend royal claims to precious metals into the New World. For example, Elizabeth's charter for the exploration of Virginia, granted to the privateer Walter Raleigh, would grant the right to 'holde, occupie, and enioye to him, his heires and assignes, and euery of them for euer, all the soile of all such lands, territories, and Countreis, so to bee discouered and possessed [sic]' (Thorpe 1909, p. 54).[3] But as for royal minerals, the Crown would:

> [reserve] always to us our heires, and successors, for all seruices, duties, and demaundes, the fift part of all the oare of golde and siluer, that from time to time, and at all times after such discouerie, subduing and possessing, shal be there gotten and obtained. (Thorpe 1909, p. 54)

With the colonial conquest of the New World and Asia, mineral rights became a political-economic institution that traversed and irreversibly changed the Earth. The English gold sovereign coin is an apt illustration of the combined powers of mineral and state sovereignty: stamped with the face of the sovereign monarch, it embodied the undivided claim of the sovereign state to be the sole issuer of currency, to tax, make law, declare war and extend Crown control into new territories.

The colonial expansion of European mineral sovereignty offers some parallels with the provisions of the CSLCA. The CSLCA can be read as a neoliberal 'letters patent' to the then emerging American space mining industry. 'The President, acting through appropriate Federal agencies, shall … discourage government barriers to the development in the United States of economically viable, safe and stable industries for commercial exploration for and commercial recovery of space resources' (CSLCA 2015, s. 51302). In the name of national industry and economic growth, the sovereign delegates to the market the authority to mine the 'high frontier'. Lunar helium-3 or asteroidal platinum may or may not become as vital to the energy and resource security of the United States in the same manner as oil or gold.

Yet, reminiscent of maritime empires past, it appears the United States is pre-emptively extending a sovereign claim to the mineral resources of the

Solar System, asserting jurisdiction over minerals through the arms-length entity of the merchant corporation or, prior to the recent downturn in the nascent space mining industry, at least, the start-up company. Instead of the privateer or the charter company, the libertarian quarters of NewSpace have evoked another figure from maritime colonialism – the pirate (Orphans of Apollo 2008). This case study in NewSpace self-representation is discussed further in Chapter 6. Here, it is important to emphasise that, under the auspices of the CSLCA, the space mining project would extend national sovereignty into frontier spaces through the state-sanctioned appropriation of mineral resources. Without this legal guarantee, no private business would anticipate investing in mining the space frontier.

Mineral sovereignty and social democratic claims to mineral estates

Conflicts over the exploitation of mineral resources and distribution of mineral wealth are central to geopolitical history. In particular, the development of global commodity chains of carbon-based mineral energy brought with it sites of struggle, contestation, class-compromise and violence, both within the territorial space of established industrial powers and in the colonial frontiers of imperial expansion. Mineral sovereignty was tamed, in places, in order to meet the needs of the *demos* and the social democratic welfare state. What benefits could be derived from off-world mining if it were similarly directed towards universal human welfare?

In the 19th century, Freidrich Engels had seen the debilitating conditions in which English coal miners worked for wages below levels of subsistence. He said, 'this is not the steerage of an American slave ship, it is the dwelling of freeborn Britons!', implying the dominion of mineral sovereignty over life and labour (1998 [1887]). Yet new forms of economic, social and labour organisation emerged alongside coal-fired industry that facilitated key political movements in the late 19th and early 20th centuries. In his 'carbon democracy' thesis, Timothy Mitchell describes how coal-fired steam and electricity lead to mass urbanisation and the proliferation of manufacturing firms, which lead to an unheralded concentration of labour in cities – this, in turn, facilitated the organisation of labour movements and unionisation (2009). The infrastructure of coal distribution, most commonly through railroads, meant that large volumes of vital carbon energy flowed through narrow channels – chokepoints that could be disrupted through industrial action (Mitchell 2009, p. 403).

Mitchell's 'carbon democracy' thesis illustrates that, with the support of democratic institutions, mineral sovereignty can be domesticated and made to serve broader social interests. Coalminers in Germany, Britain, Australia and the United States went on strike frequently, prompting labour reforms and welfare state demands at the turn of the century. From the bowels of coal mines emerged nascent forms of electoral democracy and the welfare state. English miners achieved numerous class compromises, such as the reduction in hours in a working day and the prohibition of child mine workers. Half a century later, Keynesian governments in the West and anti-colonial nationalists in the developing world sought to nationalise resource industries and tax resource rents for social distribution. For example, the British Labour Party had deposed Winston Churchill in the 1945 election. The new Prime Minister, Clement Atlee, had funded expansive welfare state reforms through the nationalisation of the coal and steel industries, in addition to rail and electricity infrastructure.

Could space mining be guided towards similar social democratic ends, if it ever eventuated? The terms of the *OST* state that the 'exploration and use of outer space … shall be carried out for the benefit and in the interests of all countries, irrespective of their degree of economic or scientific development' (1967, Art. 1). This article of the Treaty offers less precision than, say, the Vietnamese Constitution, which declares that minerals are 'public properties, coming under ownership by the entire people represented and uniformly managed by the State' (Flomenhoft 2018, p. 11). However, the Treaty's declaration that the use of outer space should be for universal benefit could be interpreted in more concrete, social democratic terms.

One possibility is the development of an international mechanism for the equitable distribution of taxes collected on off-world mining profits or super-profits. If space mining becomes as profitable as some estimates have suggested it might (Goldman Sachs, in Edwards 2017), then a redistribution of resource rents could be of significant value for nations and peoples unable to access space. Levine proposes a social democratic space mining policy: a 'Galactic Wealth Fund' 'to manage the proceeds of outer space resources on behalf of all human beings' (2015). Levine's proposal is similar in concept to sovereign wealth funds, such as the Norwegian Government Pension Fund, which has over US $1 trillion in funds deriving from the nation's oil and gas revenue. In lieu of an equivalent fund in international governance institutions, Levine draws parallels between his proposal and the Alaska Permanent Fund, which distributes an annual US $1–2000 dividend in oil royalties to Alaskan residents (Levine 2015; Flomenhoft 2018, p. 10). Levine believes the galactic version could be managed collectively 'beyond the traditional confines of the nation state' and this fund could 'provide the basis for a truly universal basic income' (Levine 2015). Idealistic as it may be, there would be a sense of justice in a sovereign wealth fund that provided universal basic income across the globe by distributing rents from space mining. Many of the advanced economies now pursuing resource appropriation on the space frontier have benefitted from the exploitation of other nations through colonialism – there would be an element of intergenerational, reparative justice if such a mechanism were to share economic benefits with de-colonised nations.

However, terrestrial history provides frequent examples of how mining capital has responded to social democratic reform, and particular chapters in this history might instead give us cause for pessimism, as far as mineral sovereignty in space is concerned. Mitchell's (2009) account also describes the extent to which the interests of transnational fossil fuel corporations have been protected through regime change – victories for carbon despotism over popular sovereignty. Oil is perhaps the clearest case study in the link between mineral sovereignty and violent, interventionist foreign policy – a neo-colonialism in which developing countries' sovereignty over natural resources is undermined by more powerful state-corporate partnerships.

US and UK foreign policy has not only involved securing particular mineral reserves or supply chains but also the protection of international trade monopolies and the hegemony of the US dollar in the global oil market (Mitchell 2009, p. 415; Doran 2012, pp. 71–73). One example is the Trans-Arabian Pipeline, in which Western oil corporations and despotic client government colluded to control resource markets. The use of post-war Marshall Plan funds for construction of oil transportation facilities in the Middle East was a direct response to the militancy of European coal miners (Mitchell 2009, p. 406). This formed part of a geopolitical strategy to shift Europe's energy consumption towards oil-based sources, favouring Anglo-American oil corporations and reducing the influence of industrial unions in European political economy. This included the US-Saudi push for the post-OAPEC embargo agreements that assured oil sales would be conducted in US dollars (Doran 2012, pp. 76–77).

The 'Tapline' extended from the oilfields of Saudi Arabia to the Mediterranean via northern Syria. The Trans-Arabian Oil Company (a partnership between Exxon, Chevron, Texaco and Mobil) enjoyed monopoly concessions and royalty-free operations in neighbouring Palestine. When the Syrian parliament proved uncooperative in their negotiations with the Company, 'the CIA [organized] a coup to put a more accommodating colonel in power' and the military government of Husni al-Za'im 'suspended parliament and the constitution and completed the pipeline agreement' in May 1949 (Mitchell 2009, p. 411). 'Sovereign are they who decide the state of extraction' (Walker & Johnson 2018). The Tapline and its journey through Syria required the legal-political institutions of a newly independent state being suspended in the service of US oil multinationals and a US economy increasingly dependent on oil consumption and trade.

The Tapline was constructed by the Bechtel Corporation, the world's largest engineering firm. In 2013, asteroid mining start-up Planetary Resources announced a strategic partnership with Bechtel (Planetary Resources 2013a). Among other forays into resource imperialism, Bechtel received a no-bid contract worth over $2 billion from USAID in 2003 for the rebuilding of Iraqi infrastructure after the US invasion, in spite of the company's past collaborations with Saddam Hussein's government (Doran 2012, p. 158).

Through Bechtel, there is also a connection between Earthly resource conflict and the high frontier. In the late 1990s, Bechtel also collaborated with militias in the Democratic Republic of Congo who were fighting for control of the region's coltan reserves (Montague 2002, p. 110). Coltan is a mineral composed of columbium and tantalum, the latter element being central to the production of tantalum capacitors. The Congo-Zaïre region is plagued by the 'resource curse', as it possesses the largest coltan reserves in the world (Montague 2002). Dena Montague (2002) describes the global supply chain of this essential component in the global electronics and aerospace industries (key pillars of NewSpace investment). Montague notes how Bechtel had purchased NASA satellite studies that provided both infrared data on the region's mineral reserves and military intelligence that assisted the invading Alliance des Forces Démocratiques pour la Libération du Congo-Zaïre in suppressing local uprisings (Montague 2002, p. 110).

We will return to Planetary Resources and mineral sovereignty later. Here, I will underline that the most influential of space mining start-ups was part of a corporate partnership that offered an ominous portent for the space commons. While Planetary Resources is no longer a discrete corporate entity, it demonstrates that – in order to achieve the ambitious goal of mining resources in outer space – firms may seek partnerships with the heavyweights of the Earthly resources sector, some of which have shown little regard for human welfare. Bechtel is well versed in the relationship between state capture, violence and the power of mining capital to disrupt and overturn democratic norms.

The neoliberal capture of mineral sovereignty[4]

In Chapter 2, I illustrated how the neoliberal network has extended into the NewSpace network and how NewSpace policy has been endorsed and amplified by Atlas think-tanks. Mirowski and Plehwe (2009) described the criterion for membership of the 'neoliberal thought collective' as an affiliation with the MPS or the organisations comprising the Atlas Network. This is an effective means of determining 'what is neoliberalism?' or 'who is a neoliberal?' without attempting to define what is at times a contradictory or ambiguous set of philosophical principles. However, Mirowski and Plehwe's genealogy of neoliberalism also lacks a material and mineralogical dimension. This is in keeping with the broader literature on neoliberalism which has generally taken more interest in the neoliberal policy programme for finance, health, education and carceral policy (Harcourt 2011) more than it has in the extractive and combustive industries. We will here consider 'Atlas mineral sovereignty'.

The ascent of neoliberalism has, in part, involved the reclamation by private capital of the powers of mineral sovereignty, for a time subordinate to the egalitarian ideals of popular sovereignty and social democracy. Neoliberalism, as an economic philosophy and as a project in state capture, developed in response to the nationalisation or socialisation of mineral commonwealths and infrastructures. These include Friedrich Hayek's temporary position at the University of Chicago, which had been established through the philanthropy of John D. Rockefeller, owner of the immensely profitable Standard Oil Corporation; the Thatcher Government's re-privatisation of the same mineral and energy-based industries and infrastructures that the Atlee Government had nationalised, which included recurring heavy-handed police responses to the strike actions of coal miners;[5] and the role of MPS economists in Chile following the CIA-supported overthrow of the socialist Allende Government, inspired in large part by the nationalisation of copper mines previously owned by US multinationals Kennecott and Anaconda, and Canadian miners, Noranda.[6]

During the 1970s, there existed the possibility of an alternate, more equitable international politico-legal order to the international neoliberal institutions that we are now familiar with (e.g. the World Trade Organisation). In 1974, the *Declaration on the Establishment of a New International Economic Order* was adopted by the U.N. General Assembly with the support of the G-77 caucus of developing nations (Res. 3201 (S-VI)). The New International Economic Order (NIEO) platform involved the assertion of the 'permanent sovereignty of every State over its natural resources and all economic properties' and 'equity, sovereign equality, interdependence, common interest and cooperation among all states' (U.N. General Assembly 1971, Res. 3201 (S-VI), p. 3, 4). For the most part, the NIEO stood in opposition to the appropriating practices of foreign transnational corporations within national borders (such as the dominance of US copper multinationals in Chile), rather than frontier appropriations of natural resources. The NIEO caucus members sought to protect the mineral commonwealths of newly independent nations that were once the frontier of empire.

Here, we return to the UNCLOS III and *Moon Agreement* negotiations that took place in the United Nations during the 1970s (as discussed in Chapter 2). These negotiations were influenced by the NIEO movement. Brazil, Colombia, Venezuela and several other Latin American nations had considered the *Moon Agreement* as an effective part of the NIEO (Gangale 2009, p. 68). Both treaties introduced the legal concept of the 'common heritage of mankind': distinct from the more general 'province of all mankind' phrasing of the OST, the 'common heritage of mankind' principle asserts principles of non-appropriation, benefit sharing, non-militarisation and environmental stewardship of global commons and, as a corollary, was eventually articulated in treaties which proposed the management of these commons through international regulatory bodies (Baslar 1998, pp. xx–xxi). The concept of the 'common heritage of mankind' was first expressed in 1967 by Arvid Pardo, the Maltese delegate to the United Nations – it then appeared in a 1970 General Assembly declaration on rights to the sea-bed and ocean floor, before being expressed in the 1979 *Moon Agreement*, the final *Law of the Sea Treaty* and a 1982 declaration on Antarctica (Baslar 1998, pp. ix–xx). More recently, the common heritage principle has been expressed in the draft agreement of the UN's Intergovernmental Conference on Marine Biodiversity of Areas Beyond National Jurisdiction (2023, Art. 5).

The *Moon Agreement* and UNCLOS III involved similar codifications and management regimes for the 'common heritage of mankind' in their respective environments. The *Moon Agreement* included articles that codified the free and equitable use principles first ratified under the OST, heralding a commons management schema that aimed to deliver benefits to all humanity (if space resource exploitation were to eventuate). Unlike the OST and more general phrasings like the 'province of all mankind', more concrete restrictions and prohibitions on unilateral natural resource appropriation were made in the *Moon Agreement*. The Agreement begins by stating that the provisions it makes for the Moon are equally applicable to all celestial bodies. Article 11 then states:

> The Moon and its natural resources are the common heritage of mankind ... Neither the surface nor the subsurface of the Moon, nor any part thereof or natural resources in place, shall become property of any State, international intergovernmental or non-governmental organization, national organization or nongovernmental entity or of any natural person. (*Moon Agreement* 1979)

In the eventual UNCLOS treaty (1994), meanwhile, Part XI makes provisions regarding the management of the ocean floor outside national jurisdiction – referred to simply as The Area. The Area is also the 'common heritage of mankind' (UNCLOS 1994, Art. 136), and the non-appropriation principle to both states and any 'natural or juridical person' (Art. 137). It required state parties to engage in technology transfer from developed to developing nations, in addition to distributing a share of resource profits obtained from mining deep, international seabeds (Art. 140). The International Seabed Authority is the organisation created through the UNCLOS Part XI agreement: its major role thus far has been to grant exploratory licenses for private mineral extractors, but no deep sea mine has successfully been realised as yet.

The *Moon Agreement* episode may have involved confluence between the then embryonic Atlas and NewSpace networks. The Carter Administration was prepared to sign the *Agreement* and Congressional hearings on the Moon Agreement were held from September 1979 (Henson 1980). In its strategy to oppose the Moon Agreement, the L-5 Society (inspired by Gerard O'Neill, and – at the time – unique as the most politically active supporters of space colonisation and commercialisation) became part of a broader pro-mining coalition that was primarily concerned the UNCLOS treaty.

As part of its opposition to the Agreement, the L-5 Society retained the services of lawyer-lobbyist Leigh Ratiner (Brandt-Erichsen 1994). Ratiner's career during the 1970s–1980s alternated between work as a public official and as a lobbyist representing private interests. Prior to L-5's interest in the *Moon Agreement*, Ratiner was head of the Department of the Interior's Ocean Mining Administration in 1975–1976, and was the United States's lead negotiator at that stage of the Law of the Sea conference (Burnett 1981). While retained by L-5, Ratiner was a partner in the Washington-based law firm Dickstein, Shapiro and Morin (Ratiner & Wright 1978, p. 773, footnote). At this point in time, Ratiner was also employed to lobby against the

UNCLOS mining provisions by a consortium of international mining firms, including Kennecott Copper (Burnett 1981; Michaud 1986, p. 91; Ratiner n.d.). In 1979–1980, Ratiner had successfully mobilised opposition to the Moon Agreement, through an alliance of Republican and Democrat legislators who also opposed the Treaty, and his work was influential in the Carter Administration's decision to suspend action on signing the *Agreement* (Burnett 1981; Michaud 1986, p. 92).

In addition to fomenting opposition to the Agreement under Carter, Ratiner may have also been influential in ensuring that the incoming Reagan Administration did not sign it either. Shortly after the Reagan Administration took office in 1981, Ratiner was hand-picked for the US negotiating team for the third convention of the UNCLOS III by James Malone, Reagan's newly appointed Assistant Secretary of State for Oceans and International Environmental and Scientific Affairs (Burnett 1981). As part of a consistent foreign policy platform across the two treaties, the Reagan Administration (and ensuing US governments) refused to sign the *Moon Agreement* and did not recognise the mining provisions of UNCLOS III. The *Moon Agreement* was politically less significant than the UNCLOS restrictions on deep sea bed mining (which was considered more feasible and profitable at the time). By 1982, the L-5 Society reported that the Reagan Administration considered the Moon Agreement to be a 'dead issue' and would not 'submit the treaty for ratification to the Senate' ('UN Moon Treaty falling to US opposition groups 1982'). The Agreement was only entered into force in 1984, once five nations had signed it.

Through Ratiner, however, we can see a potential connection between the early networks of NewSpace and American neoliberalism. The fact that the Reagan Administration refused to ratify the *Agreement* is likely to have involved some cross-pollination between the concerns of the L-5 Society and those of the US's UNCLOS III negotiating team. Prior to joining the Reagan Administration, Malone had written for the Atlas think-tank the Heritage Foundation (Huberty & Malone, 1981). In addition to Reagan-appointee Malone, Doug Bandow was on the UNCLOS negotiating team (see, for example, 'Telegram from the mission to the United Nations to the Department of State' 1981). Prior to working for Reagan, Bandow was a columnist for *Reason* magazine, mouthpiece of the Atlas organisation Reason Foundation (Bandow 1980). Shortly after his stint on the UNCLOS negotiating team, Bandow worked as a policy analyst for another leading Atlas organisation, the Cato Institute (Bandow 1982).

Writing for Cato, Bandow later remarked that 'space entrepreneurs, whose numbers are growing, would face increased uncertainty' under the *Moon Agreement* (Bandow 1985, p. 4). Mirroring the concerns raised by L-5 several years prior, Bandow offered a Hayekian elision of distributive international governance with the tyrannical authoritarianism of the Soviet Union: 'The philosophy of world socialism logically requires the creation of large-scale coercive institutions – like "international authorities" to regulate the seabed and outer space...' (ibid, p. 2). Malone, meanwhile, had authorised Ratiner's UNCLOS consulting fees, which raised eyebrows on Capitol Hill (Miller 1982). One Senator noted the blurring of public and private power that guides neoliberalism, remarking that Malone 'was warned repeatedly about the impropriety of serving industry clients and State Department policy makers simultaneously' (Cranston, in Miller 1982).

In the wake of UNCLOS, Malone noted concerns about 'the grave danger of legitimising this socialist concept' of 'the common heritage of mankind', because doing so meant that it could be 'applied in other areas such as the Antarctic and outer space' (Malone 1983, p. 31). These apparent working relationships between Ratiner and former think-tank staffers employed by the Reagan Administration would suggest that the L-5 Society had (perhaps inadvertently) drawn upon neoliberal political connections in their assault on the *Moon Agreement.* At the dawn of American neoliberal government, an attempt to codify common property arrangements in outer space was severely undermined.

The restrictions on private mineral appropriation envisioned under the UNCLOS treaty, the *Moon Agreement* and NIEO were anathema to the 'liberal international economic order' supported by neoliberal actors (Bandow 1985). We have discussed how the Reagan Administration was the first American neoliberal government – it adopted neoliberal rhetoric of 'freedom' and 'small government' and employed numerous personnel with links to Atlas think-tanks. The terms of the *Moon Agreement* had been reached through the consensus of UNCOPUOS meetings during the 1970s, in which the United States was a participant (Popova, in IISL 2016, p. 5). However, it is essentially a 'failed treaty': the Reagan Administration and ensuing US Governments rejected the *Moon Agreement* in its entirety, and most spacefaring powers followed suit. ESA member states Austria, Belgium and the Netherlands have ratified it, while France and India have signed but not ratified it. To this day, only 18 states are party to it, meaning that '91.7 percent of the membership of the United Nations … have refrained from becoming a party to it for over three decades' (Marboe & Johnson, in IISL 2016, p. 33).[7] Officials from the Reagan Administration appear to have provided little public justification for the rejection of the *Moon Agreement.* An official line on the Administration's opposition to Part XI of UNCLOS comes from the then Ambassador James Malone: '[The] political, economic and ideological assumptions which underlay the treaty are essentially antithetical to American values [and promote] a thinly disguised world collectivism' (Malone, cited in Hufford 1983, p. 127).

The US refusal to sign the *Moon Agreement* can be read as part of a broader neoliberal foreign policy agenda that involved protecting corporate freedoms to extract from the global commons (and domestic oil and gas commons). The Heritage Foundation was influential across this extractivist foreign policy platform. For every incoming Republican president following Reagan's 1981 inauguration, the Heritage Foundation has published a series of reports called *Mandate for Leadership.*[8] In the *Mandate* series, this lead organisation of the

Atlas-MPS network provides a highly specified agenda and list of policy recommendations, many of which have been implemented by Republican governments of the past four decades. Among the first edition's 1,100 pages of policy mandates, Heritage writers implored the Reagan Administration that a '"resource war" is very much a possibility when one considers the power the Third World is trying to assert' through the 'common heritage of mankind' principle and the NIEO (Heatherley 1981, p. 553).

Outside the question of extra-territorial mineral sovereignty, the neoliberal mobilisation against the NIEO has had immense ramifications for the politico-legal institutions of the global economy. The NIEO prompted a counter-revolution in neoliberal development policy that would instead prioritise 'macroeconomic stabilization, liberalization, and privatization as the prescription for the developmental cure' (Bair 2009, p. 348). From the 1980s, neoliberal forms of rule were globalised in the form of the Washington Consensus imposed upon developing nations by the IMF and the World Bank in the form of 'structural adjustment policies', leveraging a shift from national welfarism and import substitution to export-led development and foreign direct investment. Bair (2009) has documented the role of MPS economists and Heritage Foundation personnel in defeating a key instrument of the NIEO: a code of conduct to be observed by multinational corporations operating in developing countries, requiring they respect the political sovereignty and laws of those nations.

Ultimately, the contest over the space commons is reflecting the contest over global commons on Earth. Neoliberal mineral sovereignty is at play in both the organised obstruction to international climate treaties and the NewSpace-neoliberal rejection of the *Moon Agreement.* In America, Atlas think-tanks like the Heritage Foundation and the Cato Institute have been supported by corporate philanthropy, with significant funding from the petrochemical billionaire Charles Koch (Walker 2020, pp.29-30). Greenpeace has published a list of organisations funded by ExxonMobil to spread climate science denial and oppose international climate treaties (ExxonSecrets n.d.). The American components of that list are effectively identical to the American member organisations co-ordinated through the Atlas Network.

One policy analyst with Heritage asserted that the United States should continue 'to resist pressure to sign the Moon Treaty' and also 'consider withdrawing its financial support' from the United Nations Committee on the Peaceful Uses of Outer Space (Copulos 1985). This language mirrors the stance that Heritage and other neoliberal organisations would take with multilateral negotiations seeking the just and equitable management of climate change – as is clear from the first attempts at developing treaty law to limit atmospheric carbon pollution at the 1992 Rio Earth summit. As I have discussed, James Malone's career involved a revolving door between Heritage and the Reagan Administration. In his later stint as a Heritage policy writer, he outlined a position for the US delegates to Rio that became the default goal of many US climate negotiations: 'Do not draft a detailed plan for reducing specific quantities of "greenhouse gases" by a set date' (Gacek & Malone 1992, p. 8). The neoliberal political project has thus involved capturing state power through a coordinated network working to preserve the geological agency of multinational energy and resources companies, preventing citizens and governments from bringing mineral sovereignty under democratic control.

Extra-parliamentary, exo-geological power: the making of the *CSLCA*

In Chapter 2, I described the origins of off-world private property in the O'Neillian tradition and the gradual alignment of NewSpace commercial-colonisation discourses with neoliberal policy and advocacy. The Reaganite commercialisation agenda lead to the establishment of well-funded space mining start-ups. In this section, I will describe the lobbying work conducted by the space mining start-up Planetary Resources, to which we can directly attribute the passage of the CSLCA (2015) into law.[9] I present here a detailed case study in extra-parliamentary mineral sovereignty, in which a (space) mining firm can be seen shaping the legal architecture of the US state. This legislation was a critical step in the emergence of similar laws in Luxembourg, the United Arab Emirates and Japan. I will demonstrate Planetary Resources' influence on domestic public law, chiefly through the firm's lobbying expenditures (OpenSecrets 2023a & 2023c).[10] The passage of this act reflects broader challenges to contemporary democracy both within and outside of the United States, when economic power is transferred into politico-legal power.

The first attempt at domestic space resources law: lobbying for the ASTEROIDS Act

Following a re-branding (from Arkyd Astronautics), Planetary Resources announced themselves to much fanfare in 2012. With high profile backers like Google's Larry Page and Eric Schmidt, film director James Cameron and O'Neillian techno-utopian entrepreneur Peter Diamandis, the company told the world it was going to mine the high frontier.[11] A legislative guarantee of private property rights was essential for attracting additional capital, as it heralded the prospect of returns on risky seed investments. Its core commodity would be mining water ice from asteroids and providing combustible energy off-world (in the form of rocket propellant), with mining metals for off-world manufacturing something of a stretch-goal. Between 2012 and 2016, Planetary Resources raised US $53 million in investment (CrunchBase 2019a).[12] In addition to Page, Schmidt and Cameron, investments came from other wealthy ICT entrepreneurs like Atlas affiliate Peter Thiel (through his Founders Fund), Charles Simonyi (Microsoft) and a series of venture capital funds (Planetary Resources n.d.-a). In 2016 (after the passage of the CSLCA), the firm also received a €25 million grant from Société Nationale de Crédit et d'Investissement, the public investment bank of the Grand Duchy of Luxembourg (Planetary Resources 2016a).

Planetary Resources hired personnel in a manner consistent with the 'revolving door' that often occurs between the public service and the terrestrial resources industries. The company employed a range of experienced US government space professionals. Some of Planetary Resources' senior management and advisory staff held high-profile US Government appointments. Science advisor Dante Lauretta was chief investigator of NASA's Lockheed-Martin built *OSIRIS-Rex* asteroid sample retrieval mission (2016–2023) while engaged by Planetary Resources. Peter Marquez was the company's Vice President of Global Engagement. He was Director of Space Policy under the George W. Bush and Obama administrations and he authored the 2010 US National Space Policy (Planetary Resources 2013b). General Counsel Brian Israel had previously represented the United States in the UN's outer space Legal Subcommittee, and between 2012 and 2016 was 'the U.S. Government's lead lawyer for international legal aspects of outer space' (Planetary Resources n.d.-c). In her history of the American space industry, Lisa Bromberg cites a joke from a former NASA executive: 'the definition of an entrepreneur here in Maryland was somebody who used to work for the government and now sells to it' (Bromberg 1999, p. 117). Based outside Seattle, Planetary Resources offers a West Coast example of former government employees now engaged in private sector employment. A neoliberal model of space exploration risks further 'hollowing out' of public sector expertise, as it is transferred to the private sector.

The road to the passage of the CSLCA began with the *American Space Technology for Exploring Resource Opportunities in Deep Space Act of 2014*, commonly abbreviated to the *ASTEROIDS Act* (H.R. 5063; henceforth, 'the *ASTEROIDS* bill'). The *ASTEROIDS* bill was introduced to the US House of Representatives on July 10, 2014, by Rep. Bill Posey (R-FL; U.S. House of Representatives 2014). It contained provisions that would guarantee private ownership of off-world minerals but used language that rendered the relationship between national and private appropriation entirely unambiguous. It stated that the President shall 'facilitate the commercial exploration and utilization of space resources to meet national needs' and that the 'district courts of the United States shall have exclusive jurisdiction' of any legal action brought by an (American) space mining firm against a rival party for interference in resource exploration and utilisation (ASTEROIDS Act 2014, s. 51301-2). The *ASTEROIDS* bill was a clear contravention of the OST's non-appropriation principle: it attempted to authorise 'exclusive jurisdiction' for US courts and legalise the exploitation of celestial bodies to meet 'national needs'. It nonetheless enjoyed bipartisan support: 11 Democrats and 9 Republicans either sponsored or co-sponsored the Bill (U.S. House of Representatives 2014). In this light, it would be remiss to treat neoliberal space law as though it were limited to the US Republican Party – there is an evident bipartisan neoliberalism in many jurisdictions, in which the 'centre' of the political spectrum is pushed further towards economic liberalism.

Planetary Resources made a concerted effort to push this bill into US public law by purchasing lobbying expertise. There is ample evidence of the start-up's direct influence on the introduction of the *ASTEROIDS* bill to Congress. The bill's original cosponsor was Derek Kilmer (D-WA), the Representative for Washington state's 6th Congressional District – this District neighbours Planetary Resources' head office in Redmond. Public disclosures under the *Lobby Disclosure Act of 1995* reveal that Planetary Resources spent a total of $210,000 in 2014 on the services of the law firm K&L Gates (OpenSecrets 2023d). Of this total, K&L Gates made a $5,500 contribution to Kilmer's 2014 Congressional campaign (OpenSecrets 2023d, b). Planetary Resources – through K&L Gates – was the sole organisation registered to lobby on this bill (OpenSecrets 2023c).[13] While fellow space miners DSI expressed support for the CSLCA when it was signed into law (Deep Space Industries 2015), they appear not to have spent any money on lobbying. Moon Express, a space transportation company that has expressed interest in the resources of the Solar System, was also active in lobbying Congress during this period (OpenSecrets 2023h).

As is common in political lobbying, K&L Gates' work for Planetary Resources was aided by their employment of a number of former Congressmen turned lobbyists (OpenSecrets 2023d). Of those who lobbied on behalf of Planetary Resources in 2014, Bart Gordon (D-TN, 1985–2011), Slade Gorton (R-WA, 1989–2001) and James Walsh (R-NY, 1993–2009) have all served as either Congressmen or Senators. This mirrors the revolving doors and 'golden escalators' that exist between public office and the terrestrial mining industries. Adam Lucas describes these professional networks in the Australian resource sector, noting that the mining industries court 'individuals who hold public office in relevant portfolios as potential allies and future employees' (2018). This is a commonplace practice in contemporary democracies. Yet when former parliamentary or Congressional representatives are employed by lobbying firms to act on behalf of corporate clients – exploiting the personal and professional networks they established when working as democratically elected representatives – the prospect of governing 'for the people' has been undermined.

In an early setback for the space mining industry, the *ASTEROIDS* bill never proceeded beyond consideration by the House Subcommittee on Space (of the Committee on Science, Space and Technology). Hearings on the bill were held in September 2014. Public hearings with invited expert testimony are an important part of democratic law-making in the United States: they enable legislation to be scrutinised in a public forum which makes the legislative process transparent, regardless of whether the legislature heeds expert opinion and amends legislation accordingly. Gabrynowicz (2014) was one expert invited to testify before the subcommittee, and she described the problem of national appropriation raised by the bill's declaration that US courts would have 'exclusive jurisdiction' over potential disputes. She stated that 'it should be expected that there would be both legal and political challenges to its terms' (Gabrynowicz 2014, p. 10). Another witness pointed to the absurdity of such legislation: that 'there can be no commercial enterprise without a market. For water, there is no market [in space] that exists today' (Sykes 2014, p. 11). Implementing the *ASTEROIDS* bill seemed contentious and premature to Committee members. Following these Hearings, Planetary Resources would go back to the drawing board and the *ASTEROIDS* bill itself was abandoned.

The second attempt: the road to the CSLCA

Between 2014 and 2015, Planetary Resources continued to lobby for revised bills featuring private property rights to mined space resources (OpenSecrets 2023a). Republican control of Congress became instrumental in pushing an off-world mineral resources bill over the line. In the November 2014 mid-term elections, the Republican Party recorded its largest House majority since 1929. This huge loss for the Democrats was spurred, in part, by conservative interest groups who attacked the *Patient Protection and Affordable Care Act* ('Obamacare') – the Koch brothers and Atlas think-tanks being particularly vocal opponents. One co-sponsor of the new space resources bills (discussed later) was Jim Bridenstine (R-OK), who would become President Trump's choice for NASA Administrator, and Dana Rohrabacher (R-CA; U.S. House of Representatives 2015a, 2015b). Among a massive lobbying outlay in which most Republican candidates received contributions from Koch Industries, Bridenstine ($5,000) and Rohrabacher ($2,500) received small contributions from these petrochemical benefactors (OpenSecrets 2023e).

The *ASTEROIDS Act* bill and its guarantee of private mining rights were re-packaged as the *Space Resource Exploration and Utilization Act of 2015* (H.R. 1508; henceforth the *Space Resource* bill). This new bill was introduced to the House in March 2015. Planetary Resources are again listed as a lobbying organisation for H.R.1508, joined on this occasion by aerospace and military contractor United Technologies Corporation (OpenSecrets 2023f). Their 2015 lobbying outlay, shared between three hired lobbying firms, totalled $430,000 (OpenSecrets 2023a). The *Space Resource* bill retained the problematic 'national needs' language and the assertion of US district courts' exclusive jurisdiction on any disputes (H.R. 1508, s. 51302–3). An identical Senate companion bill (S.976; 2015) was introduced by Patty Murray (D-WA) of Planetary Resources' home state, in order for the legislation to be discussed in the other chamber. It was co-sponsored, among others, by influential Republican Senator Marco Rubio (R-FL; US Senate 2015a).

The final legislative manoeuvres leading to the legal guarantee of off-world mining rights involve the amalgamation of several bills (Gabrynowicz 2017). During these legislative steps, additional political actors are drawn into the process, including space resources and transportation start-up Moon Express, and heavyweights of the 'big aerospace' lobby, like Boeing and Northrop Grumman (OpenSecrets 2023g). Figure 4.1 outlines the various

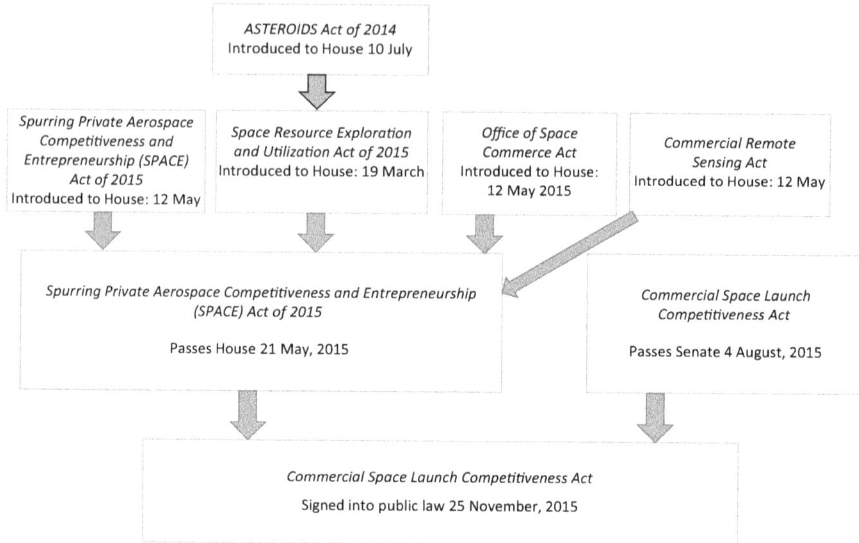

Figure 4.1 The legislative pathway to the Commercial Space Launch Competitiveness Act.

bills that eventually became the *CSLCA*. Through this amalgamation of pro-space commerce reforms, a broader array of conservative or neoliberal politicians are drawn into supporting legislation that contains recognition of off-world private property rights. In addition to Rubio's involvement, far-right Republican Ted Cruz (who is frequently endorsed by Atlas organisations) introduced a bill titled the *Commercial Space Launch Competitiveness Act* to the Senate on May 12, 2015 (S. 1297; U.S. Senate 2015b). The provisions of this bill were aimed at US aerospace corporations much larger than space mining start-ups (such as those in Rubio and Cruz's constituencies) and are now also public law. Cruz's bill afforded 'big aerospace' some reductions to the 'maximum probable loss' in insurance claims made against private space launch providers, while also deferring reporting on 'voluntary industry consensus standards' and creating other generous self-regulatory 'learning periods' (CSLCA 2015, s. 102, s. 111). For O'Neillian space mining advocates who have bemoaned the centrality of the big aerospace lobby in the US space sector, the realisation of off-world mining rights appears to have depended on the political clout of large aerospace firms.

In the House, the *Space Resource* bill and other pieces of legislation amenable to space commerce were merged into the *Spurring Private Aerospace Competitiveness Act* or SPACE Act (H.R. 2262), which passed a House vote on 21 May. The CSLCA bill passed a Senate vote on 4 August, 2015. Having passed both chambers independently, in November 2015 the provisions of the House *SPACE* Act and the Senate *CSLCA* were signed into law as the CSLCA – which now contained provisions for private property rights on space resources.

In spite of all these manoeuvres, the space resources provisions of the CSLCA remained problematic in terms of international law. Under Senate Amendments in October 2015, the 'national needs' language had been watered down to direct the President to 'facilitate commercial exploration for and commercial recovery of space resources by United States citizens' (CSLCA 2015, s. 51302) and the 'exclusive jurisdiction' provisions are dropped entirely. Yet a 'Disclaimer of Extraterritorial Sovereignty' is added to say, 'It is the sense of Congress that by the enactment of this Act, the United States does not thereby assert sovereignty or sovereign or exclusive rights or jurisdiction over, or the ownership of, any celestial body' (ibid, s. 51303). 'It is the sense of Congress' is a non-committal, 'illusory' phrase (Gabrynowicz 2019, pp. 5–6). Its inclusion appears to reflect lawmakers' own uncertainty of the CSLCA's consistency with the terms of the OST.

The long road to the passage of the CSLCA also illustrates how problems in representative democracy can emerge amid the 'busy work' of the legislative process. This has consequences for international law. Despite this apparent uncertainty among some lawmakers about whether resource ownership provisions of the CSLCA were consistent with the United States's treaty obligations, stages of the Congressional legislative process were pushed aside to bring this bill into public law. The strong Republican majority in both chambers afforded some degree of influence over the Congressional schedule (Edwards, in Cong. Rec. 2015, H3512). At least some of the actors involved appear concerned about encountering the scrutiny of expert witnesses (that lead to the demise of the *ASTEROIDS Act*), because no expert witnesses were called to testify on the question of private space resource property rights that appeared in the follow-up bills that led to the CSLCA (House Committee on Science, Space and Technology 2015a).

The standard legislative process involves a 'mark-up' session that follows a hearing, yet this was bypassed in the passage of the CSLCA. Mark-up is a longstanding tradition in which congressional committee members would debate, amend and 'mark-up' any changes needed for the legislation to progress further. Usually this process takes place with warning and ample time for consideration. The CSLCA bill was referred to the House subcommittee on May 12, 2015, and an abrupt mark-up session was held the following day (U.S. House of Representatives 2015a, in Gabrynowicz 2018, pers. comm., 12 June). Eddie Bernice Johnson (D-TX) had written the Minority View statement in the House Committee Report on the *Space Resources* bill, stating that:

> There has been no legislative hearing on this bill, or even a subcommittee markup, nor have we gotten the views of the Administration, including those responsible for tracking our international treaty obligations … . (House Committee on Science, Space and Technology 2015b, p. 20)

At least some Congressional representatives were concerned that the space resources provisions were inconsistent with international law. Yet traditional democratic processes were clearly subverted during this process, possibly to avoid scrutiny of the CSLCA-OST issue. When the amalgamated *SPACE Act* was discussed on the Congressional floor, House Minority Leader Donna Edwards noted that 'with the backdrop of meeting the majority's floor schedule as the top priority, there was insufficient time given to negotiate a compromise before last week's full committee markup' and that

> it would also be prudent, Mr. Chair, to hold hearings on these issues and on this legislation, as well as to have a subcommittee markup, what we sometimes refer to as regular order. (Congressional Record 2015a, H3512)

The passage of the CSLCA through two Republican chambers of Congress does not represent anything as stark as a Schmittian suspension of the constitution, yet there was a clear suspension of regular process that amplified the voice of the commercial space lobby. While private expenditure on lobbying is commonplace, it nonetheless permits corporate actors to shape and influence the legislative process. In this case study, the transferral of private economic power into political capital will have ramifications for international space law and the future of human activity on celestial bodies.

Subsequent developments in US space law: industry committees and the Artemis Accords

Since the passage of the CSLCA, there have been other developments which indicate that commercial space actors continue to exert influence on the development of domestic and international space law. In addition to corporate lobbying as a tool for state capture, 'industry committee reporting' is another state-corporate interface in the legislative process. A long standing committee in US space policy is the influential Commercial Space Transportation Advisory Committee (COMSTAC), an advisory board of the Federal Aviation Administration (FAA) – which is part of the Executive Branch. In the same period as the public *ASTEROIDS Act* Hearings, Planetary Resources' Peter Marquez and Brian Israel (then with the Department of State) presented before the COMSTAC Business and Legal Working Group (Kunstadter 2014, p. 2). The COMSTAC Working Group recommended that the FAA support the *ASTEROIDS Act* (Kunstadter 2014, p. 8). This meeting is an example of the less public fora that can give commercial space actors a voice in the legislative process.

Efforts have been made to establish additional industry advisory committees in the area of aerospace law. Planetary Resources also lobbied for the *American Space Commerce Free Enterprise Act* (ASCFE 2017, H.R. 2809; OpenSecrets 2023i).[14] The ASCFE proposes a new 'Private Space Activity Advisory Committee'. This committee is intended to 'provide recommendations to the

Secretary and Congress on how the United States can facilitate and promote a robust and innovative private sector that is investing in, developing, and operating space objects' (ASCFE 2017, s. 80109). The ASCFE stipulates that 'Members of the Committee may not be Federal Government employees or officials', and that

> Members of the Committee shall include a variety of space policy, engineering, technical, science, legal, and finance professionals. Not less than three members shall have significant experience working in the commercial space industry. (ASCFE 2017, s. 80109)

Rather than scrutinising domestic space law in public hearings or chambers of Congress, industry committee reporting opens up a less transparent window of influence for pro-industry voices into the reform process. Gabrynowicz points to the consequences of creating new legislation that creates new industry advisory bodies which, in turn, can shape further legislation:

> The formula consists of the generous use of technical legal terms of art that do not create law; numerous calls for studies and reports on topics and issues rather than addressing the actual substance of the topics and issues; and the establishment of advisory committees whose work is to be integrated into the ongoing research and reporting. The reports are to be sent to specific Congressional committees for further action. Together this establishes an interconnected mechanism among agencies, advisory committees, and Congressional committees in which lobbying, advocacy, and the legislative process become interchangeable. (2019, p. 5)

The ASCFE passed the House in April 2018, but progressed no further than the Senate Subcommittee level. A bill with similar provisions, also called the *American Space Commerce Free Enterprise Act of 2019*, was introduced to the House the following year. While efforts to pass such bills have subsided recently, they demonstrate the potential for domestic law-making to have ramifications for international laws of the commons. Likely reflecting debate surrounding the OST, the ASCFE contains the brazen proclamation that 'Notwithstanding any other provision of law, outer space shall not be considered a global commons' (ASCFE 2017, s. 80308). Consistent with opposition to the *Moon Agreement* and the seabed mining restrictions of the UNCLOS treaty, this bill is indicative of the US state's consistent efforts on behalf of mining capital to undermine international efforts to preserve global commons.

More recent developments in space resources law have centred around the Artemis Accords. Drafted under the Trump Administration and endorsed by the Biden Administration, the Artemis Accords are a set of principles regarding human activity on the Moon. Among other goals, the Accords seek to provide greater legal certainty regarding the exploitation of space resources under the terms of the OST, affirming that resource extraction and utilisation do 'not inherently constitute national appropriation under Article II of the Outer Space Treaty' (*The Artemis Accords: principles for cooperation in the civil exploration and use of the Moon, Mars, comets and asteroids for peaceful purposes*, s. 10). When first adopted in October 2020, eight nations had signed the Accords, including those countries with domestic legislation recognising private ownership of space resources (Artemis Accords 2020). At the time of writing, 33 nations have signed the Artemis Accords . The choice of 'accords' as the terminology reflects the fact that it is not an international treaty registered with the United Nations, but rather an agreement between particular spacefaring countries, with the United States as its anchor.

The Accords are not purely the outcome of the Trump Administration, but nonetheless arrived in the aftermath of a Presidential decree that noted – in a similar vein to the unsuccessful ASCFE – that 'the United States does not view [outer space] as a global commons' (Executive Office of the President 2020). For our purposes here, establishing a framework for commercial extraction of space resources was a key priority of the Accords, and commercial interests informed the drafting of the Accords. The Accords were developed in consultation with the NASA Advisory Council's Regulatory and Policy Committee under the chairmanship of Mike Gold, a former executive and general counsel in the commercial space sector (NASA 2021; The Planetary Society 2022; Smith 2020). Membership of the Regulatory and Policy Committee was dominated by the commercial sector, and included Sagi Kfir, former General Counsel to DSI, in addition to large aerospace firms like Boeing, SpaceX and Lockheed Martin (NASA Advisory Council Regulatory and Policy Committee 2019). While the Accords state a desire to adhere to the principles of the OST, they nonetheless affirm the right to extract from the space commons by asserting that Signatories believe that 'the extraction of space resources does not inherently constitute national appropriation under Article II' of the OST (Artemis Accords 2020, Section 10(2)).

Conclusion

The passage of the CSLCA is a case study in the influence of mining capital (and venture capital) influencing local political institutions. Regardless of how 'NewSpace democracy' might transpire in future space colonies, the CSLCA demonstrates that sovereignty, the power to make political and legal decisions, is exercised by extractive capital, such that democratic norms and legal institutions of the global commons are undermined. If an individual or organisation can spend US $1,050,000 on lobbying, as did Planetary Resources between 2013 and 2018 (OpenSecrets 2023a), they will clearly enjoy a greater level of access to lawmakers and greater influence in the legislative process than does the average citizen. It represents a transfer of power in one sphere (such as economic power resulting from resource profits or digital technologies) to another – political power that can direct government policy and public law (Brown 2015).

Moreover, the history of mineral sovereignty indicates that mining rights could never be commensurate with the terms of the OST and the legal norm that outer space 'is not subject to national appropriation by claim of sovereignty' (OST 1967, Art. 2). To reframe these terms, we can say that private resource claims under the CSLCA would constitute an act of state-corporate appropriation by sovereign claim – in both the sense that the CSLCA represents a corporate capture of the US state, and that the authorisation, legitimisation and protection of mining rights have historically been anchored in the sovereignty of nation state and empire.

The elite fantasy of refuge in space from social obligations and an increasingly inhospitable Earth may yet be just that – a fantasy – but it serves to illustrate the point that mineral sovereignty is inherent in the deep genealogy and cosmic imaginary of political power. Familiar terrestrial concerns are at stake in the enclosure of the off-world mineral commonwealth: state-corporate prerogatives of accumulation and growth are to be secured through assertions of mineral sovereignty, in direct collision with the claims of popular sovereignty or international law to manage the common wealth with laws of the people, by the people and for the people. In anticipation of actual acts of mineral appropriation in space, and due to the need to provide certainty for private investment in space mining ventures, supporters of the CSLCA have argued that unilateral space resources law is in fact legal under the terms of the OST. We will turn to these arguments and their role in pre-emptively 'de-commoning' celestial bodies in the following chapter.

Notes

1 This chapter has been modified from a publication co-authored by myself and Dr Jeremy Walker (Walker, J. & Johnson, M. 2018, 'On mineral sovereignty: towards a political theory of geological power', *Energy Research and Social Science*, vol. 45, pp. 56–66). It is reprinted here with permission.

2 To reiterate a point from the previous chapter, NewSpace advocates often deploy a Lockean conception of constitutional democracy founded on private property rights, which is melded with a cosmopolitan imaginary of the human species and its eternal prosperity. For example, the National Space Society (which traces its lineage to the O'Neill inspired L-5 Society) has a 'Statement of Philosophy' which says 'space development and settlement will occur most efficiently, and humanity's survival and growth will be best ensured, if every human being is allowed the opportunity to own property in space', and 'if the fundamentals of democracy are applied to and incorporated by space settlements' (NSS 2019).

3 Sovereignty over gold and silver was not limited to the British Empire, of course. Focusing on the Potosí silver mine of Peru, Moore (2010) describes how the violent exploitation of New World silver by the Spanish Empire in the 16th century would radically transform the social-ecological systems of the Americas, accelerating the development of the broader capitalist world-system. Silver inflows from the Americas become a vital stream of income for the Spanish Crown, ultimately leading to imperial decline through a protracted period of agricultural crisis, inflation and rising national debt. American silver was also vital in

maintaining monetary-stocks and money-capital formation across Europe (Moore 2010, pp. 64–65, 59). Potosí silver would become the cash-basis for the Dutch Republic and its East India Company, providing the momentum for multiple European sovereigns' dominion over ever larger expanses of territory.

4 Excerpts from this section were first published as Johnson, M. 2018, 'Privateering on the cosmic frontier? Mining celestial bodies and the 'NewSpace' quest for private property in outer space', in J. Arvanitakis and M. Fredriksson (eds.), *Property, Place and Piracy*, Routledge, Abingdon, pp. 123–139.

5 Thatcher had expanded police powers to disrupt industrial action and had even considered declaring a 'state of emergency' (the Schmittian exception) and a military deployment to quell discontent (Lyons 2014). Legitimising and facilitating 'free' markets clearly involves highly illiberal forms of coercion.

6 Socialist President Salvador Allende continued the previous Montalva government's acquisition of the largest US-operated copper mines, which were fully nationalised in 1971 following a unanimous vote on a constitutional amendment in Chile's Congress. At the time, the US war machine in Indochina absorbed 10% of all copper used in US industry, up from 1.5% in peacetime (US Office of Technology Assessment 1988, p. 13). Supporting the interests of mine owners Anaconda and Kennecott, the CIA (with explicit approval from Nixon and Kissinger) actively destabilised the Allende government, culminating in the 1973 Pinochet coup. MPS law-and-economics theorist James Buchanan was influential in the Junta's 1980 rewrite of the Constitution of Chile (Fischer 2009). The revised constitution involved neoliberal reforms such as the privatisation of national education and social security systems, and illegalisation of trade unions and collective wage bargaining (Fischer 2009). The Chilean constitution was an extension of Buchanan's long-term project, the Virginia School of constitutional political economy – this was discretely bankrolled by the petrochemical billionaire Charles Koch, a fellow MPS member and Atlas Network donor (MacLean 2017).

7 This does not mean that the *Moon Agreement* is irrelevant to discussion on space resources law. Space lawyer Steven Freeland (Freeland 2017; IISL 2016, pp. 35–38) highlights how the *Moon Agreement* represents subsequent state practice on the issue of space resources exploitation – it is an interpretation of the OST that can be construed as providing guidance on how to further interpret the OST's principles when they have not yet been realised in practice. Freeland suggests that the *Moon Agreement*'s undertaking to establish a regime for equitable exploitation implies that exploitation would one day be permissible. Moreover, the appropriation prohibitions are on property rights, or ownership: it might still be permissible to establish 'extra-terrestrial exploitative rights' – akin to terrestrial mining rights – so long as they were granted under this international regime and to the terms of the *Agreement,* rather than through an extra-territorial extension of national sovereignty or without the consensus of the international community (Freeland 2017). This is of course under the terms of an international agreement that has not been ratified by any spacefaring power – however, subsequent state practice on the *Moon Agreement* is discussed further in Chapter 7.

8 The first iteration of the Heritage *Mandate* was clearly consistent with the neoliberal philosophy of MPS members like Hayek: 'the free market, operating as a vehicle for millions of individual decisions, is a more efficient allocator of resources than government and leads, therefore, to greater production and higher real income for all workers' (Heatherley 1981, p. 958). Reagan had reportedly distributed the first report with evangelical zeal, enacting 60% of its recommendations in his first term (Blasko 2004). The 7th Mandate report was published immediately after the election of Donald Trump.

9 I am indebted to the advice of Professor Joanne Gabrynowicz in compiling this section, particularly for pointing me towards the increasing role of 'industry committee reporting' in US space law and some of the finer details of the Congressional record.

10 The data I present here reflect what has been disclosed to the Senate Office of Public Records or discussed in Congressional transcript. The lobbying interfaces that emerge from 'stalking the corridors of power', as it were, commonly involve less visible and documented forms of political influence.

11 Peter Diamandis is the company's co-founder. He is a serial NewSpace entrepreneur and a former L-5 Society member (Michaud 1986, p. 100). Eric Anderson is another Planetary Resources co-founder: previously he founded Space Adventures, a company which has organised visits to the International Space Station for wealthy tourists at roughly $20 million a trip.

12 Their 2016 lobbying expenditures (after the CSLCA was passed) appear to be focused on the *American Space Commerce Free Enterprise Act of 2017* (OpenSecrets 2023i).

13 The lobbying activity conducted by Planetary Resources is of course legal, and the sums involved pale in comparison to the lobbying outlays of other corporate interests. For example, Koch Industries, the petrochemical conglomerate owned by Atlas Network allies Charles and the late David Koch, spent over $20 million in campaign contributions and lobbying in that same 2014 mid-term election cycle (OpenSecrets 2023e).

14 There are other NewSpace attempts at lobbying for pro-colonisation and commercialisation laws (e.g. *Space, Exploration, Settlement and Development Act of 2016*) which are outside the scope of this analysis.

5 Making and re-making the 'space constitution'

The common heritage of humankind or neoliberal constitutionalism?

Thus far, I have explored the relationship between private and national appropriation in terms of neoliberalism's state-supported corporate freedoms (Chapter 2), the enclosure of commons through sovereign powers of lawful appropriation (Chapter 3) and the politico-legal field of mineral sovereignty, in which the distinction between state and private appropriation is often opaque (Chapter 4). Here I will broaden my analysis to focus on international laws of the global commons, and delve more deeply into the contents, history and interpretation of the *Outer Space Treaty* (1967).

The space resources laws of the United States, Luxembourg, UAE and Japan project private property law onto the novel frontier of outer space, and I have drawn parallels with the historical development of property rights in land and the sub-soil. Now we will progress to new elemental categories beyond land, by considering the laws of the air and sea. Space law evolved from international laws of the high seas and the concept of national airspace. Much like the ship and airplane before it, the spacecraft opened up a new domain of extra-territorial space, and international law developed alongside this technological change. Schmitt's genealogy of international law began with the primacy of land appropriation in law and order (2003 [1950]). Yet he was equally concerned with the sea as a 'space of exception', where a different order prevailed to the terrestrial order of the European continent (Schmitt 2003; Minca 2005).

> The sea knows no apparent unity of space and law, of order and orientation ... On the sea, fields cannot be planted and firm lines cannot be engraved. Ships that sail across the sea leave no trace. 'On the waves, there is nothing but the waves' ... The sea is free. (Schmitt 2003, p. 43)

In the 17th century, the Dutch jurist Hugo Grotius (2004 [1609]) mounted an influential legal argument that similarly described international waters as the 'free seas' (*mare liberum*) – the high seas were open to all and not subject to national appropriation. Like outer space, the high seas are a *res communis* global commons.

The legal status of outer space was formulated in the supranational, post-Westphalian order of the United Nations, amidst the political

DOI: 10.1201/9781003293613-5

contestations of the Cold War. The OST and *Moon Agreement* are legal frameworks that sought to establish the status of celestial bodies as 'the province of all mankind' and to codify the collective benefits that could be derived from off-world extractivism, respectively. As discussed in the previous chapter, the *Moon Agreement* has only been ratified by a handful of countries, owing in part to the opposition of US governments since Reagan, with the think-tanks of Atlas neoliberalism and NewSpace organisations prominent among the Agreement's critics. The OST has been much more widely ratified: on the 50th anniversary of its entry into force, 105 states had become parties to the OST (U.N. General Assembly 2017, Res. 72/78).

The OST has been described as 'quasi-constitutional' (Gabrynowicz 2004, p. 1042; Israel 2019, p. 114). It incorporates the UN Charter, extends international law into outer space, establishes fundamental principles and rights for the use of space and forms the backbone of all international space law. Nations take cues from the OST in developing their domestic space laws (Gabrynowicz 2004, p. 1042). Much like liberal constitutions the world over, the OST is concerned primarily with defining and limiting the scope of government action. All nations with launch capabilities (and many without) have ratified the Treaty. The OST is thus 'the cornerstone of the international legal regime governing outer space activities' and 'constitutes' an international political community vis-à-vis outer space (U.N. General Assembly 2017, Res.72/78, p. 15).

Like the liberal constitutions of Earth, the OST is an unstable political framework – in relation to space resource ownership, at least – and is open to interpretation, often along ideological lines. The emergence of national laws facilitating private resource ownership has precipitated widespread discussion as to what the OST actually encourages and prohibits (Hobe & de Man 2017; Babcock 2019; Israel 2019). Many space lawyers have pointed to the potential incompatibility of space mining with the Treaty's core tenets – in particular, whether the CSLCA's ownership provisions would be in keeping with American OST obligations to ensure that its use of outer space was for the 'benefit of all mankind' (Tronchetti 2015; Hobe & de Man 2017; Freeland 2017). These tenets describe space as a commons: it should be governed through collective decision-making on principles of freedom of access, non-appropriation and the global common interest in peaceable, co-operative use of space. However, as many scholars of space resource appropriation have asserted, the OST's precepts are vague or unclear (Lee 2012; Wasser & Jobes 2008; von der Dunk 2012). There is no explicit prohibition on mineral resource appropriation in the OST and it does not specifically discuss this potential mode of 'using' outer space (IISL 2016, p. 34; Masson-Zwaan & Palkovitz 2017, p. 8). Yet, as I have argued, it is not self-evident that the 'non-appropriation principle' can effectively demarcate national from private appropriation, or that neoliberal accumulation via off-world mining rights will 'be carried on for the benefit all peoples irrespective of the degree of their economic or scientific development' (OST 1967, preamble).

Legal and business representatives of space mining start-ups have asserted that private mining rights are commensurate with a *res communis* understanding of outer space (Kfir 2016; Marquez 2017; Kfir & Perry 2017). Some have explicitly voiced support for the OST, arguing that it provides 'stability and predictability' for the changing needs of space commerce (Marquez 2017, p. 4). Its terminological ambiguity regarding the 'province' of humankind and silence on the question of space resource ownership may be beneficial for those seeking to own and use the off-world commons for private benefit. Outer space's status as a commons has also been disputed (Hertzfeld, Weeden & Johnson 2016; Pace 2017). Hertzfeld, Weeden and Johnson note that 'the noun, commons, never appears in any space treaty', only 'descriptors' like 'common interest', 'common heritage', 'common procedure' and 'common understanding' (2016, p. 17). These authors, one of whom has worked for Planetary Resources, highlight that the OST does not provide 'any direct guidance for the future handling of space resources' (Hertzfeld, Weeden & Johnson 2016, p. 17). Scott Pace, a former RAND Corporation analyst and President Trump's appointee to head the National Space Council advisory body, offered this pugilistic and nationalistic interpretation of the OST:

> … outer space is not a 'global commons', not the 'common heritage of mankind', not 'res communis', nor is it a public good. These concepts are not part of the Outer Space Treaty, and the United States has consistently taken the position that these ideas do not describe the legal status of outer space … To unlock the promise of space, to expand the economic sphere of human activity beyond the Earth, requires that we not constrain ourselves with legal constructs that do not apply to space … As with past frontiers, it is those who show up, not those who stay home, who create the rules and establish the norms in new areas of human activity. (Pace 2017, p. 4)

Despite claiming that the terms of the OST can be interpreted in favour of US corporate interests, Pace ultimately invokes a Schmittian understanding of the neoliberal *nomos* that awaits in the off-world. International treaty law is treated as less important than the rules created 'by those who show up' – an argument that it should be the appropriators who make resources law in space.

In advance of any constitutive act of mineral appropriation taking place, the legal and political status of celestial bodies is being contested in an almost entirely anticipatory arena. In this chapter, I explore the pathway to the OST – the *res communis* 'space constitution' – by looking at parallels with the *mare liberum* principle, the challenges that rocketry posed to assertations of sovereignty in national airspace, and the OST's roughly parallel emergence with other international treaties of the global commons. I argue that there is a disjuncture between the overarching principles of the OST and NewSpace interpretations of the treaty that have favoured private space resource ownership (Kfir 2016; Marquez 2017). Claims that national legislation like the *Commercial Space Launch Competitiveness Act 2015* is consistent with the

OST can be read as an anticipatory project in neoliberal constitutionalism (Gill 2002; Schneidermann 2013; Purdy 2014). I discuss how an entirely different 'space constitution' may emerge in anticipation or in the wake of space mining – one which favours first movers in the space colonisation project, and which seeks to bypass international treaty law in favour of multilateral agreement predicated on US commercial interests. The recent signing of the Artemis Accords, a multilateral agreement between the US and its allies which seeks to legitimise private resource ownership as an accepted norm in international space law, may prove to be a crucial step on this path.

The making of the space commons

In this section, I describe how the OST became the foundation of international space law. The concept of 'free space' is a central pillar of the OST: outer space and celestial bodies 'shall be free for exploration and use by all States, on a basis of equality and in accordance with international law, and there shall be free access to all areas of celestial bodies' (Art. 1). As open-access commons, the legal status of celestial bodies inherit the *mare liberum* principle first outlined by Hugo Grotius (2004; Storr 2020, p. 7). 'Free space' refers to the absence of national jurisdiction in space and subsequent freedom of passage for all spacefaring parties, and it was first realised as an accepted norm in international space law through US responses to the question of satellite overflight (McDougall 1997; Launius 2000, p. 28). This lends some credence to Scott Pace's claim that it is the first movers 'who create the rules and establish the norms in new areas of human activity' (2017, p. 4). The broader *res communis* space constitution, however, involved compromise between the United States, USSR and developing nations (von der Dunk 2011, pp. 1–2). At the request of the United States, the final wording of the Treaty was ambiguous concerning private ownership rights in space (McDougall 1997, pp. 417–418). Nonetheless, the pervasive principles of the Treaty are still consistent with what we would understand as a commons regime (Tronchetti & Liu 2021a, p. 5).

Hugo Grotius and mare liberum

The OST treats the celestial bodies of outer space as global commons: they lie outside the sovereign borders of any territorially-defined political community and restrictions on their use have been deliberated in democratic fora. UN publications have described global commons as essentially resource frontiers – 'natural assets outside national jurisdiction such as the oceans, outer space and the Antarctic' (United Nations Statistics Division 2016). Each of these global commons has, to varying extents, involved contestation regarding sovereignty and appropriation, largely as a result of creeping state-based jurisdictional claims. For instance, the UN conferences on the *Law of the Sea* in the 1980s eventually recognised state's rights to extend 'their political economic jurisdiction ... to 200 nautical miles' offshore, by which point approximately 30% of the world's oceans and 95% of global fish stocks had been 'enclosed as state property' and exploited through state-appointed commercial fishing licenses (Mansfield 2007, p. 66). As a further example, tradable carbon permits introduce private property into the atmosphere, using state or intra-state mechanisms (in the case of the EU) to introduce markets for pollution rights as a means of reducing pollution in the atmospheric commons. The UN's definition above is thus potentially misleading: nation states *have* extended their political reach into global commons in the recent past and are likely to do so in the future.

The legal framework for global commons originates in the earliest days of modern international law, through the *mare liberum* principle developed by Dutch jurist Hugo Grotius in his influential book of the same name (2004).[1] While *mare liberum* literally means 'the free sea', it essentially describes a legal principle of free passage, unrestricted access and non-exclusive use. Prior to the 1609 publication of *Mare Liberum*, Grotius had been requested by a division of the Dutch East India Company (VOC) to provide a legal opinion regarding the company's seizure of a Portuguese ship as a prize of war (Armitage, in Grotius 2004, p. xii). Portugal had claimed ownership of the seas in which the vessel had been captured, and Grotius refuted this with a *res communis* argument. He later remarked in *Mare Liberum*:

> ... those things which cannot be occupied or were never occupied can be proper to none because all propriety hath his beginning from occupation. The other is that all those things which are so ordained by nature that anyone using them they may nevertheless suffice others whomsoever for the common use are at this day (and perpetually ought to be) of the same condition whereof they were when nature first discovered them. (2004, p. 24)

Those things that could not be occupied could not be owned, and nature 'has given *all* things to *all* people' (Baslar 1998, p. 31, emphasis in original). Kemal Baslar argues that Grotius had effectively grounded a natural law principle – 'that the existence of moral and legal principles acquire their validity and authority from the natural conditions of the existence of humanity, the natural order of the universe or the eternal law of God' (ibid, p. 14) – in the norms of state practice, 'the positive law of nations rooted in custom and treaties' (ibid, p. 31). This is a feat that the *Moon Agreement*, at least, failed to achieve.

In his argument, Grotius had drawn on the ancient Roman philosopher Cicero to underline that an ethics of fairness and justice was entwined with common property (Grotius 2004, p. 24). Cicero positioned common property as central to the moral obligations that maintained society and 'common bonds' of justice and charity. In his *De Officiis* (On Duties), Cicero asserted that:

> The first office of justice is to keep one man from doing harm to another, unless provoked by wrong; and the next is to lead men to use common possessions for the common interests, private property for their own. (1913, Book I, VII, para. 21)

Yet *mare liberum* in the global commons has frequently produced inequity and injustice. Schrijver (2016) notes that Grotius' *mare liberum* concept has significant limitations in practice. Firstly, Schrijver affirms that 'Grotius's argument that the use of oceans was not prejudicial to their use by others would have to be seriously qualified today' (Schrijver 2016). From community-supporting fisheries pillaged by commercial 'supertrawlers' to oil spills in heritage listed marine parks, it is clear that one actors' exercise of *mare liberum* rights can preclude another's. This is essentially the dilemma described in Garrett Hardin's 'tragedy of the commons' thesis (1968). Secondly, *mare liberum* quickly 'digressed into "first come, first served" advantages for industrialised nations' (Schrijver 2016). Both of these issues could materialise on the space frontier.

With legal rights to freely use and access global commons comes the freedom to conduct business and to conduct war. In introducing the *mare liberum* principle to the jurisprudence of international commons, Grotius effectively treated the high seas as a 'mercantilist, international, inexhaustible space' (Connery 2001, p. 178). He did so for the less magnanimous purpose of protecting Dutch national and corporate interests. That the seas were unownable helped secured dominance for the Dutch Empire (1581–1795) and the corporations it had chartered to navigate, trade, establish colonies, raise armies and navies, and wage war – the VOC and Dutch West India Company. The neoliberal think-tank network provides us with a contemporary parallel to Grotius' work for the VOC. In the 2017 iteration of the *Mandate for Leadership* series, the Heritage Foundation linked US national security with national economic growth, emphasising 'freedom of movement within the global commons: the sea, the air, cyberspace, and the outer space domains in which the world conducts business' (Heritage Foundation 2016, p. 27). There is an evident tension here between opening and enclosing, as protecting freedom of movement in global commons enables the resources within these spaces to be claimed as private property.

From airspace to 'free space': rockets, RAND and the early Cold War

Technological change forces law and politics to play catch-up. Between 1945 and 1957, 'free space' emerged as a precedent in customary international space law. When the V-2 rockets of Nazi Germany reached the edge of the atmosphere during WW2, outer space was an entirely anomic frontier, devoid of norms and rules for its use (though international law did not constrain Hitler's imperial project, in any case). As WW2 ended and the Cold War began, the space technologies of the United States and Soviet

Union increased in sophistication, and rockets and spacecraft reached further into space.

At this time, the emerging field of space law was plagued with uncertainty as to how the off-world should be juridified. Following a 1949 rocket launch that reached a height of 400 km, the international aviation lawyer John Cooper was prompted to ask: 'Did it pass out of the territory of the State below when it left the airspace, and re-enter that territory on returning; or was it at all times within the territory of the State below?' (1951, p. 414). Aerospace and communications lawyer Andrew Haley lamented, with an eye to the distant future, that 'we have about as clear a vision of the space law that will prevail one or two centuries from now as Hammurabi in the 22nd Century B.C. might have had of our private and public international law of the present day' (1956, p. 951).

In addition to maritime law and Roman understandings of property, space lawyers of the 1950s also took cues from aviation law (Cooper 1951). This initially seemed intuitive, since spacecraft needed to pass through the atmosphere before reaching low-Earth orbit, and because spaceflight and aviation were technologically similar. However, legal understandings of national airspace were themselves a work in progress. The juridification of airspace began with the 1919 Paris *Convention Relating to the Regulation of Aerial Navigation* and was further developed with the 1944 *Convention on International Civil Aviation* held in Chicago. The Chicago Convention had stated that, 'The contracting States recognise that every State has complete and exclusive sovereignty over the airspace above its territory' (Article 1, cited in Cooper 1951, p. 414). Crucially, the Convention had failed to address the vertical limits of this 'complete and exclusive' sovereignty, retaining the vertical expansiveness of the *ad coelum* doctrine (Gangale 2009, p. 10; On the Commons 2007). Interestingly, the boundary between national airspace and outer space is still discussed in international legal fora – the highest altitude that planes or balloons can reach is the effective practical delineation between national airspace and extra-territorial outer space.[2]

For the first space lawyers, an infinite extension of sovereignty beyond the atmosphere presented obvious problems: with the orbit of the Moon around Earth, and the apparent movement of planets and stars in the night sky, celestial bodies would pass through copious national jurisdictions below. The space writer Thomas Gangale describes how early scholars of international space law 'recognise[d] the absurdity of national sovereignty reaching to infinity, because in such a system a spacecraft would constantly pass through the legal jurisdiction of one subjacent state after another' (2009, p. 10). Among the first legal scholars to consider the status of outer space, Oscar Schachter, Alex Meyer and C. Wilfred Jenks argued that the extent of state sovereignty was limited to the atmosphere: 'airspace' required air, and outer space 'is [thus] a separate legal environment' (ibid, p. 11).

'Free space' became an accepted norm in superpower relations through the question of satellite overflight. *Mare liberum* or 'free space' norms in outer space can be attributed to competitive state motivations in the form of high-altitude surveillance. The Eisenhower Administration established NASA in 1958 after the USSR's *Sputnik 1* (1957) confined the United States to the ignominy of second place in the race to launch an artificial satellite into orbit – this event was widely considered to be the spark that started the space race. However, as space historian Roger Launius remarks, 'the tantalizing possibility exists that perhaps a part of [US] space policy of the 1950s was predicated on allowing the Soviet Union to orbit a satellite first' (2000, p. 28).

This brief yielding of American claims to superiority appears to originate with the RAND Corporation, founded in 1948 by the Douglas Aircraft Company. RAND (short for 'research and development') was 'a hybrid organisation emerging in the interface between the US Air Force and its avionics contractors' (Granjou, Walker & Salazar 2017, p. 8). Eisenhower's space policy essentially followed the advice provided by the newly inaugurated RAND Corporation in its report, *The Satellite Rocket Vehicle: Political and Psychological Problems* (Kecskemeti 1950; McDougall 1997). RAND was essentially the 'first strategic "think tank"' and, according to McDougall, this report was an anticipatory text of geopolitical strategy that 'deserves to be considered the birth certificate of American space policy' (1997, p. 108).

In the Cold War context, satellite surveillance was considered vital to American national security (Gangale 2009, p. 11). The USSR's state-run media and the travel restrictions it imposed on its citizens limited the United States's capacity for traditional espionage (ibid, p. 11). Satellite-based surveillance of the Soviet intercontinental ballistic missile program became an imperative for the United States. The RAND report had identified that establishing a legal right to use a reconnaissance satellite was important for avoiding Soviet provocation or retaliation and returned to the issue of airspace that had been unresolved in the 1944 Chicago Convention on aviation. The United States had accepted the principles of 'freedom of the air', but the USSR had not (Gangale 2009, p. 15; McDougall 1997, p. 108). Subsequently, the passage of an American surveillance satellite would likely be construed as a 'consummated violation of sovereignty' by the Soviet leadership (Kecskemeti 1950, p. 15). This could have prompted Soviet litigation in the International Court of Justice, some degree of armed retaliation or interference in US reconnaissance (ibid, pp. 15–17). As a result, it was vital for US military strategy that satellite overflight be made legal: 'free space' needed to be established in customary international law. The RAND report argued that establishing 'free space' would help establish America's military freedoms in the off-world commons. The freedom to conduct military surveillance, in this case.

The RAND report was laced with the anticipatory, predictive language of game theory. Game theory has been an enduring intellectual project for RAND scholars and, through John Nash, a source of the mathematical and behavioural predilections of 20th-century neoclassical and neoliberal economics (Mirowski 2002). RAND strategists argued that a preliminary scientific satellite could be used as a trial run while 'work on perfecting techniques of receiving and analysing [surveillance] data' occurred simultaneously (Kecskemeti 1950, p. 23).

> Our objective is to reduce the effectiveness of any Soviet counteraction that might interfere with the satellite reconnaissance operation before significant intelligence results are secured ... Perhaps the best way to minimise the risk of countermeasures would be to launch an 'experimental' satellite on an equatorial orbit. Such a satellite would not cross Soviet territory and, hence, would not provide the 'consummated aggression' on which effective counteraction could be based ... If the results obtained during the test period are satisfactory, the decision may be taken to launch a second 'work' satellite ... It would be distinctly advantageous if the second satellite could be kept black [classified] ... . (ibid, pp. 21–22)

The RAND report argued that the United States ought to be first to launch a satellite into space, but this satellite should be for non-military purposes.

US satellite strategy and international norms of freedom of passage in outer space were thus shaped by RAND's futurological policy brief. In 1955, both the United States and USSR had announced their intentions to launch scientific satellites into space.[3] McDougall describes the 'free space' scenario succinctly:

> ... there were two ways the legal path could be cleared for reconnaissance satellites. One was if the United States got away with an initial small satellite orbiting above the nations of the earth 'for the advancement of science' – and had no one object to it. The other was if the Soviet Union launched first. The second solution was less desirable, but it was not worth taking every measure to prevent. (1997, pp. 123–124)

The first option was explicitly advocated by RAND; the second is what materialised with the *Sputnik* launch in 1957. Yet RAND's intervention had in any case shaped this eventual outcome. The United States actually had the capacity to be the first nation to reach Earth's orbit via a repurposed *Redstone* missile, a short-range ballistic missile designed for the US Army by Werner von Braun's Huntsville team, with its warhead to be replaced with a satellite (McDougall 1997, p. 122; Gangale 2009). The Department of Defense had established the Stewart Committee in 1955 for the purposes of selecting the United States's first satellite from contending proposals. It had opted for the US Navy's *Vanguard* program, which had a longer development schedule than the *Redstone* but had been designed largely for scientific purposes. While this might initially suggest that freedom of passage in space was established through peaceful scientific purposes, McDougall concludes that the Stewart committee had been briefed by RAND and 'instructed to keep in mind the importance of a nonmilitary, scientific image for the enterprise … their decision was ideal from the political, if not technical, standpoint' (1997, p. 122). *Sputnik* represented a substantial dent in American post-war exceptionalism, but the episode diffused anxiety around the legal basis for satellite surveillance (Launius 2000, p. 28). In Gangale's words, 'the right of orbital overflight, recognized from the very beginning by the two original launching states and not objected to by any other states, became a customary norm virtually instantaneously' (Gangale 2009, p. 13).

For 'official use only' and advocating for classified satellite surveillance, the RAND report exemplifies the uniqueness of space as a commons in a politico-legal sense. The early Cold War diplomatic environment was eclipsed by the superpower rivalry between the United States and USSR, with Western Europe rebuilding from WW2 and many developing nations engaged in post-colonial independence movements. The 'global' commons of outer space thus had bilateral origins. The principle of 'freedom of space' became a norm in state practice with the help of classified think-tank research on geopolitical strategy, against a backdrop of swelling military budgets and counter-mobilisations of potential violence.

The **res communis** *space constitution*

There is, of course, more to global commons than this fundamental *mare liberum* right to freedom of passage and shared usage. Here, I will briefly re-visit some of the points I raised in Chapter 2. Commons are governed through collective decision-making and involve some form of management regime that ensures shared use, a community-wide distribution of benefits – and, crucially – long-term preservation. They are 'governed by rules whose point is to make them available for use by all or any members of the society' (Waldron 2016, p. 3). Wall notes that 'prior to European colonialism, commons were the rule rather than the exception across much of our planet' (2014, p. 9). While essential to capitalism, private property is aberrant in the deep historical trajectory of social, political and legal relationships between people and their environments (Polanyi 2001, ch. 4).

It is fitting, then, that when the first human beings ventured forth into outer space, the Solar System was juridified in international law with *res communis* status. The OST is one of several treaties negotiated in the 1950s–1970s that declared international common rights in global commons and expressed a desire for international cooperation, in response to the ongoing likelihood of inter-state violence. The preamble to the OST reflects the anxieties of the Cold War: negotiating parties noted the desire to use 'outer space for peaceful purposes', to 'contribute to broad international cooperation in the scientific as well as the legal aspects' of exploring and using space, and that 'such cooperation will contribute to the development of mutual understanding and to the strengthening of friendly relations between States and people' (OST 1967, preamble). These sentiments were also expressed in other international laws of the global commons that were ratified after WW2. In 1956, the UN held the first Convention on the *Law of the Sea* (UNCLOS I). This began a process of formalising and codifying principles of non-territoriality and free passage in international waters that had been established customarily over centuries. In 1959, the first *Antarctic Treaty* was ratified; it declared that 'No new claim, or enlargement of an existing claim, to territorial sovereignty in Antarctica shall be asserted while the present Treaty is in force' (U.N. Antarctic Treaty 1959, Art. 4).[4]

This period marks a trend towards international laws of cooperation, and multilateral efforts at constraining unilateral state actions in global commons. The post-war phase of international law contrasts with the eras of colonial and world wars, which were characterised by laws of mere co-existence rather than cooperation (Fassbender 2003). Outer space was juridified through the post-Westphalian political community of the United Nations, during the post-WW2 movements towards globalisation. It has always been a fragile community and was embroiled in East-West divisions for over three decades (post-colonial movements and global inequality introduced an additional North-South divide, as exemplified in the contest between the New International Economic Order (NIEO) platform and ascendant neoliberalism in the 1970s). The OST nonetheless emerged from this movement away from 'an essentially negative code of rules of abstention to positive rules of co-operation' that the international community had deemed necessary in the wake of global conflict (Freidman, cited in Fassbender 2003, p. 118).

The space commons were juridified during a succession of agreements between 1958 and 1979. These were initially negotiated as bilateral agreements between the United States and USSR but progressed into UN General Assembly resolutions which, in turn, were eventually amalgamated into the articles of the OST. The negotiation of the OST was foreshadowed by nuclear non-proliferation agreements, which began with Eisenhower's 1953 'Atoms for Peace' speech to the UN General Assembly and the formation of the International Atomic Energy Agency in 1957. These concerns about the nuclearisation of space would be articulated in prohibitions ratified under the OST. In 1958, Eisenhower had instigated bilateral talks with the USSR, proposing 'an agreement to prevent an arms race in space and assure that space be used for only peaceful purposes' (Cooper 2003, p. 111).[5] Later that year, the United States and USSR presented guiding principles of peace and 'common interest' to the Thirteenth Session of the United Nations General Assembly. The Assembly subsequently recognised 'the common interest of mankind in outer space' and 'that it is the common aim that outer space should be used for peaceful purposes only', with the desire to 'promote energetically the fullest exploration and exploitation of outer space for the benefit of mankind' (U.N. General Assembly 1958, Res. 1349, preamble). This Resolution also led to the establishment of the UN Committee on the Peaceful Uses of Outer Space (UNCOPUOS), which continues to provide a forum for diplomatic discussions regarding the implementation of and adherence to space treaty law.

The path towards a multilateral space accord that featured the non-appropriation principle was beset with bilateral antagonism and anticipatory geostrategy, much like customary rights of free passage. In 1961, a *Resolution on International Cooperation in the Peaceful Uses of Outer Space* was adopted by the General Assembly. It extended 'international law, including the Charter of the United Nations, to outer space and celestial bodies' and – presaging Article 2 of the OST – proclaimed outer space and celestial bodies to be 'free for exploration and use by all states in conformity with international law and are not subject to national appropriation' (U.N. General Assembly 1961, Res. 1721). Cooper notes that President Johnson 'took up the issue [of an international space treaty] in order to forestall Soviet placement of nuclear weapons in space or claims to celestial bodies' (2003, p. 111). The United States supported the non-appropriation principle as a way of preventing Soviet territorial claims to the Moon, should they arrive there first (which had seemed likely in the early 1960s).

In July 1966, the OST was negotiated in the Legal Subcommittee of UNCOPOUS convened in Vienna. The United States actively pursued a non-committal wording of the Treaty's *res communis* elements. The Treaty's final wording reflected a compromise between the space superpowers, and seemingly between the United States and the rest of the world. The United Arab Republic (now Egypt) proposed amendments to Article 1, such as the following qualification to the 'benefit to all mankind' provision:

> States engaged in the exploration of outer space undertake to … provide possibilities to the non-space Powers, to enable them to participate in and to draw benefit from the exploration and the use of outer space for the aim of deriving practical benefits related to their economic and social development. (U.N. Committee on the Peaceful Uses of Outer Space 1966, p. 6)

Other countries had pushed for more general recognition that spacefaring should be 'for the benefit of all mankind', such as Brazil (McDougall 1997, p. 416). The US State Department had instructed its UN Ambassador Arthur Goldberg 'to avoid raising the issue of ownership of lunar resources' (ibid, p. 416). McDougall reports that the United States 'acceded to [the more general wording] so long as specific references to property or economic rights were excluded' (ibid, p. 417). Goldberg testified before the US Senate ahead of the Treaty's ratification by the United States in 1967. Senators were concerned about what concessions America was making to the world – property is about power, ultimately. Goldberg reassured them that the Treaty made only vague commitments to delivering benefits to non-spacefaring countries – this was a 'goal subject to further refinement' (McDougall 1997, p. 418). The US position on the OST effectively opened the door towards private property legislation like the CSLCA, while also prompting developing nations to seek codification of 'benefits to all mankind' in later sessions of the General Assembly. These codifications would be proposed a decade later within the *Moon Agreement*, which the US state and other global powers would ultimately reject.

In spite of these points of contention that arose during negotiation, the OST was widely ratified when opened for signature in 1967. The OST is, in Marboe and Johnson's words, 'aspirational in nature, forward-looking and expansive', in that it envisioned a unique legal environment in which benefits from use should extend to nations incapable of reaching space (International Institute of Space Law 2016, pp. 28-29). It has been described as 'quasi-constitutional' in binding State parties to a foundational set of principles for the governance and use of outer space (Gabrynowicz 2004, p. 1042; Israel 2019, p. 114). Waluchow describes how constitutions are distinct from common law because, although both laws and the constitutions from which they derive place restrictions on behaviour, constitutions are 'heavily entrenched' in a society's political and social life and are meant to provide 'continuity and stability in the basic framework' of law-making and policy (2017, p. 24). Robinson and White (1986) have emphasised the OST's declaration that astronauts are the 'envoys of mankind' (1967, Art. 5) and thus suggest the OST ought to serve as a literal constitution for potential space societies. The constitutional nature of the OST is further highlighted by the fact that, as Gabrynowicz recounts, 'President Lyndon Johnson believed that the OST was important enough to the United States national interests to ask then Supreme Court Justice Arthur Goldberg to step down from the Supreme Court in order to negotiate it for the United States' (2004, p. 1042).

The OST effectively 'constitutes' – in the sense of bringing together or giving form to – an international community vis-à-vis the use and exploration of outer space. Global commons like outer space involve what legal theorist Hans Kelsen (1967) called a *grundnorm*: a 'basic norm' or underlying order from which subsequent norms derive. The *grundnorm* of international law has generally presumed state sovereignty as the basis of membership in the international community; the United Nations (1945–present), like the League of Nations before it (1920–1946), is 'composed of states whose membership is in turn defined territorially' (Philpott 2014, p. 4). This is reflected in the *OST*, which is an instrument of international public law and is ratified by 'State Parties'. Precisely what this political community is bound to under the terms of the OST has been highly contested with the emergence of space mining start-ups and the passage of domestic space resources law.

Neoliberal constitutionalism

The principles of the OST focus on freedom, common interest and non-appropriation, strongly suggesting that outer space has the legal status of a global commons in international law – regardless of whether the term 'global commons' appears in the Treaty itself. However, law is a socio-political construct and, as discussed in Chapter 3, property is a social relationship – there are never empirical or immutable 'facts' on what is or is not common property. To declare the mineral resources of space to be either communally owned or open for private or national appropriation invariably involves political claims and strategies. Viewing space mining through the lens of 'mineral sovereignty' illustrates that the act of making laws is an expression of power – a power that is unevenly distributed, given the hierarchies of political power both within and across nation states (Chapter 4). In this section, we will further explore how the 'rule of law' can be ambiguous, particularly in light of the varying interpretations of the OST's terms.

When space mining emerged within the NewSpace start-up landscape, its proponents advocated that the CSLCA be accepted as consistent with international law, presumably in order to provide certainty and project legitimacy to potential investors. These advocates formed interpretations of the OST that portrayed private, state-backed extractive rights as commensurate with the laws of the space commons (Kfir 2016; Marquez 2017). I will illustrate here that these arguments rested upon generous interpretations of the OST that obfuscated its terms and intentions, and will make the case that pro-extractivist interpretations of the OST are analogous with what has been described as neoliberal constitutionalism (Gill 2002; Purdy 2014). Such a neoliberal 'constitution' for use and access to celestial bodies may be realised through the Artemis Accords (2020), which appear to entrench the US interpretation of the OST in state practice, and raise the prospect of the democratic chambers of the UN being bypassed.

Interpreting the OST

In viewing international space law through the lens of constitutional theory, we return to the 'strong state, free economy' double truth of neoliberalism. Constitutionalism is a philosophical, moral and political belief that government power or sovereignty should indeed have limits placed on it, 'and that its authority depends on its observing these limitations', be they formal charters of civil rights, procedural mechanisms that shape how that power is exercised, or other 'checks and balances' that separate legislative, executive or judicial power (Waluchow 2017, p. 3). In the OST, the limitations on state sovereignty are made abundantly clear with the non-appropriation principle (Art. 2) and the anti-militaristic precepts of Article 4, among others.

In light of the CSLCA, NewSpace might appear to be in a predicament: do they support the limitation of government sovereignty in international space law (in keeping with their rejection of government authority in commercial spacefaring), or do they endorse an extension of US state sovereignty into the global commons so that their private property claims can be recognised under US law? As Carl Friedrich surmised during the first decade of the neoliberal Chicago School of Law and Economics, neoliberalism sees the state 'as a central source of authority; yet at the same time, the state must not interfere in all kinds of [business] activities' (1955, p. 512). The projection of state power into the global commons is commensurate with NewSpace's understanding of economic liberty, so long as state authority enhances rather than curtails the ability of space miners to extract from the commons.

We have discussed Hayek's notions of limited democracy (Chapter 2) – that the rule of law should protect individual liberties and rights to own private property (as defined in liberal constitutions) from extensions of democratic power (such as the constitutionally defined power of a state to raise corporate taxes, or the freedom of assembly as expressed through union demands for wage increases). The jurist Joseph Raz notes that the 'rule of law' had traditionally signified that 'people should obey the law and be ruled by it', but a Hayekian interpretation leads to:

> a narrower sense, that the government shall be ruled by the law and subject to it. The ideal of the rule of law in this sense is often expressed by the phrase 'government by law and not by men'. (Raz 1979, p. 212)

As discussed in Chapter 2, we can detect hints of Hayekian constitutionalism in Moon Express CEO Bob Richards' plea that the 'U.S. government should in principle enact laws that assure freedom of enterprise in space, making it illegal for the government to deny or restrict private sector space activity' (2017, p. 4).

Scholarship in neoliberal constitutionalism has recently focused on select US Supreme Court decisions (Purdy 2014; Teachout 2014; Brown 2015), in particular *Citizens United v. Federal Election Commission* (2010).[6] In the *Citizens United* case, constitutional rights to free speech were effectively extended to corporations investing in political campaign spending. The Supreme Court majority deemed that restricting the amount a corporation could spend on political advertising represented an unconstitutional restriction on corporations' alleged freedoms of 'political speech'. Arriving under the conservative Roberts Court, these decisions have involved doctrinaire neoliberal interpretations of the Bill of Rights. In Jedediah Purdy's words, these decisions 'constitutionally protect certain transactions that lie at the core of the economy' and make 'unequal economic power much harder for democratic lawmaking to reach' (2014, p. 202). Precedents were also established during the Gilded Age of economic liberalism, in the *Lochner v. New York* (1905) case.[7] Neoliberal constitutionalism attempts to insulate the market from democracy, expanding 'a set of available constitutional arguments' that would support future Supreme Court decisions (Purdy 2014, p. 208).

Are the NewSpace arguments surrounding the CSLCA creating new 'constitutional' arguments that will legitimise and protect corporate extractivism in the space commons in the future? While the OST is not a literal constitution, it is helpful to consider interpretations of the OST through the lens of 'originalist' and 'living' schools of constitutional theory (Waluchow

2017). An originalist interpretation of the OST would treat it as 'fixed' in its positing of a set of non-negotiable moral and political commitments. In Waluchow's words, originalist interpretations seek to:

> replace controversial moral and political questions with historical questions about the intentions of constitutional authors in creating what they did, or about how the language they chose to express a constitutional requirement was publicly understood at the time it was chosen. (Waluchow 2017, p. 14)

Living constitutionalism, meanwhile, argues that constitutions require evolving interpretation to suit changing social, political and economic circumstances. The OST is a product of the Cold War and some have subsequently considered it anachronistic in the new era of commercial spacefaring (even though the state remains a key player in the contemporary space economy). For example, Planetary Resources' Peter Marquez argues that the OST should be interpreted in light of 'evolving circumstances' such as the emergence of space mining start-ups – largely because a US withdrawal from the OST or pursuit of amendments to it would increase uncertainty for potential investors in the space mining industry (Marquez 2017, p. 4; see also Dunstan & Szoka 2017). Both the originalist and living schools of interpretation are at play in NewSpace arguments in favour of the OST; however, a 'living' interpretation is dominant.

Space miners have made selective 'originalist' interpretations of the OST. Marquez says that 'it is the unbroken consistency of the United States' interpretation of the Treaty … that is the key to our credibility in [introducing the CSLCA]' (2017, p. 3). Much like Scott Pace's comment that 'the United States has consistently taken the position that these ideas do not describe the legal status of outer space' (2017, p. 4), this position essentially prioritises the authorial intentions of US negotiators and subsequent Congressional interpretations of the Treaty over those of other national delegations, as though the United States was a sole judge on a treaty ratified by most of the world. Dunk notes that the USSR 'was squarely against any private activities in most economically relevant areas of society, but certainly so in an area of such strategic concern as outer space' (2011, p. 1). Space lawyers have also pointed to comments made by the Belgian delegation in the OST's *traveaux préparatoires* (Pop 2000, p. 176; Tronchetti 2009, p. 199). Tronchetti identifies that the Belgian delegate had 'stated that notice had been taken of the term "non appropriation" advanced by several delegations' that it effectively covered and prohibited 'both the establishment of sovereignty and the creation of title of property in private law' (Tronchetti 2009, p. 199). The OST's final wording – a comprehensive prohibition on 'national appropriation by claim of sovereignty, by means of use or occupation, or *by any other means*' (Art. 2, emphasis added) – would support an originalist interpretation *against* the legality of private ownership rights through national legislation.

CSLCA supporters have also attempted to present 'evolving' interpretations of the non-appropriation principle by shifting the focus onto the distinction between celestial bodies and minerals extracted from them (Kfir 2016; Perry 2017). Space miners are not seeking ownership of Mars, the Moon or a particular asteroid – only the minerals contained therein. Nor are they claiming 'land grabs' through the CSLCA. If we read the OST's Article 2 literally – 'outer space, including the Moon and other celestial bodies, is not subject to national appropriation' – it is outer space *in its totality* that is not subject to appropriation, including the resources contained within those celestial bodies. NewSpace lawyers have avoided such an interpretation, and have instead looked to *mare liberum* analogies between space mining and fishing. The following example is from Sagi Kfir, the then General Counsel at Deep Space Industries:

> Much like fishing trawlers going to sea, the fishermen have the right to keep the fish that they catch, but have no ownership rights to the sea itself. Similarly, the U.S. space resource utilization industry is not claiming any ownership or right to the asteroid or space resource itself, just the right to retain the material extracted from such resources. (2016)

Hugo Grotius' defence of the unownable nature of the oceans is also invoked in defence of space mining – that 'the sea is the common property of all, but that fish are the private property of him who catches them' (Grotius, cited in Perry 2017, p. 6). It is a problematic analogy. Grotius' proclamation of the common status of the seas rested upon the assertion that 'those things which cannot be occupied … can be proper to none' because 'all propriety hath his beginning from occupation' (2004, p. 24). The exercise of mining rights – a body of law associated with 99-year leases and irreversible alterations to the physical environment – surely involves a claim to property through occupation. The analogy with the law of the 'free seas' is limited in this sense: surely asteroids are closer to 'islands' in the interplanetary 'seas'. Mining operations on asteroids or larger celestial bodies (planetoids, moons and planets) would likely constitute semi-permanent occupations of physical space not unlike terrestrial mines.

If we move beyond this 'constitutional' analogy and the evolving or originalist schools of interpretation, the *Vienna Convention on the Law of Treaties* (VCLT) contains several provisions on treaty interpretation that are relevant to the OST-space mining debate (1969, Art. 31). As Marboe and Johnson note, the draft texts and records of negotiation contained in OST *travaux préparatoires* 'are only supplementary means of interpretation' (IISL 2016, p. 27). The *Vienna Convention* states that treaties 'should be interpreted in good faith in accordance with the original meaning to be given to the terms of the treaty in their context and in light of its object and purpose' and that this interpretation should include the whole text of the treaty, 'including its preamble and annexes' (VCLT 1969, Art. 1, para. 1–2). It is true that, in order for treaties' aims to be comprehensively realised, ratifying nations often need to pass domestic law that codifies their citizens' responsibilities under these treaties (a key example being ineffective domestic implementations of international de-carbonisation targets of the Kyoto and Paris agreements). Establishing 'a domestic legal framework is a concrete method to give effect to a state's international treaty obligations' and a nation's interpretation of the OST is an intractable element in this process, in lieu of binding international legal instruments that explicitly regulate space mining (Marboe & Johnson, in IISL 2016, p. 34). Kfir notes that each nation 'has the right as a sovereign nation to interpret and implement its treaty rights on a national level' (Kfir 2016). Szoka and Dunstan of TechFreedom, a smaller Atlas think-tank, take this interpretive logic further: 'Effective space property rights are not only consistent with international law, they are *required* by it' (2015 p. 1, emphasis in original).

Yet state practice in interpreting the OST and questions of what constitute a 'good faith' interpretation underline the fact that international law – like the concept of sovereignty itself – is also a contestable socio-political construct. A sizeable interpretive jump is being made in the arguments that domestic implementation of the OST necessarily involves the recognition of private mining rights. It is true that the 'province of all mankind' wording of the OST's preamble and Article 1 clearly leaves much open to states' interpretation – as was the intention of the US's OST delegation, who had ensured that a discussion of off-world property and other economic rights did not inform the Treaty's negotiations (McDougall 1997, pp. 416–418). The Institute for International Space Law has recently remarked that the 'formulation that the use of outer space and celestial bodies shall be "the province of mankind" raises difficult questions in the legal assessment of outer space', given that 'the Outer Space Treaty nowhere explains this concept' (Marboe & Johnson, in IISL 2016, p. 32). However, it is also widely accepted in legal scholarship that the articles of international treaties should not be read in isolation but in conjunction with each other (as per the *Vienna Convention*). Space is 'the province of all mankind' and the right of State Parties and their corporate entities to freely 'use and explore' outer space is clearly limited by the non-appropriation principle (Hobe & de Man 2017, p. 463). The inverse is also true: for whatever disagreement exists about the extent of the non-appropriation principle (Art. 2), any use of off-world resources should work towards 'benefits to all mankind' (Tronchetti 2015, p. 8; IISL 2016, p. 41).

There are several areas in which a holistic reading of the OST renders space resources law problematic. For a time, proponents of off-world private property rights had attempted to demarcate national activities in space from private activities in space, arguing that Article 2 presented a loophole for private appropriation (Lunar Embassy 2019b). Article 6 of the OST puts paid to this idea:

> States Parties to the Treaty shall bear international responsibility for national activities in outer space, including the Moon and other celestial bodies, whether such activities are carried on by governmental agencies or by non-governmental entities, and for assuring that national activities are carried out in conformity with the provisions set forth in the present Treaty. (OST 1967)

National governments would be responsible for the conduct of any of their space mining companies, thus binding space miners to the same principles that states are bound to uphold. Freeland notes that this 'includes an adherence to the fundamental principles associated with non-appropriation of outer space' (2017).[8] A presentation from Brian Israel (a former State Department official who was subsequently employed by Planetary Resources) to the COMSTAC working group noted that 'fixing the Article 6 problem is crucial' to US private property law for space resources (Kunstadter 2014).

Further points of contention arise from the case of asteroid mining and the *mare liberum*-style provisions of the OST. The distinction between an asteroid and a mineral resource is perhaps ambiguous. The Treaty or the CSLCA offer no clarity as to whether there are lower limits to what constitutes a celestial body. Is a smaller asteroid with a 500-m diameter effectively a large chunk of unprocessed ore drifting through space? It is plausible that space miners could extract one mineral from a small asteroid and discard regolith or other minerals that were not useful or profitable, akin to terrestrial mining's removal of 'overburden' like soil and vegetation. Except, in asteroid mining, this extraneous debris and dust would be dispersed into the vacuums of outer space. An asteroid could be mined of one mineral to the extent that its mass was reduced and its entire structure altered. As cited earlier, Freeland offers one hypothetical scenario that space mining may produce – that these small celestial bodies could be 'mined "out of existence"' (2017). Returning to the Grotian line of argument, extracting fish from the sea does not *necessarily* involve radical, material changes to the sea itself. Is mining an asteroid for all its resources an acceptable exercise of a space mining firm's freedom of use rights, given that a later scientific mission (studying asteroid composition, say) could be prevented from exercising the same rights? If there 'shall be free access to all areas of celestial bodies' (OST 1967, Art. 1), would a space mining firm pack up its multibillion-dollar infrastructures and vacate a celestial body so a rival company can similarly make use of it?

In addition to Earthly parallels in the 'freedom of use' provisions that have informed the legal status of the high seas, the OST describes outer space as a unique legal environment that is predicated on common interest, co-operation and benefits to all humankind. Scholars with the International Institute of Space Law have duly noted that 'These purposes of the treaty reflect *the spirit of the law*, which is just as important as the letter of the law' (Marboe and Johnson, in IISL 2016, p. 29, my emphasis). It is problematic, then, that NewSpace interpretations of the OST's 'freedom of use' provision have descended into anachronism and invoke the pre-UN era of 'strong state' unilateralism in the high seas (White 1998; Wasser & Jobes 2008, p. 47; Kfir 2016). For example, Kfir states 'it is abundantly clear that no international space law or treaty explicitly prohibits the commercial use and extraction of space resources' (Kfir 2016). There is nothing that explicitly endorses it either – only the general right to 'use' outer space. The lawyers and scholars who claim that states can interpret treaty commitments as they see fit are essentially evoking an era of international law predicated on the sovereign independence of nations, as Jakhu has argued (2006, pp. 41–44).

Doing so is at odds with the principles of state self-limitation that permeates most of the OST and the political climate that it emerged in (Fassbender 2003). Hobe and de Man (2017, p. 466, footnote 33) note that 'permissive' arguments that a state would have jurisdiction over off-world space resources appear to invoke the 1927 *Lotus* case in the Permanent Court of International Justice (the judicial branch of UN precedent, the League of Nations).[9] The 'lotus principle' that emerged from this case has been interpreted to mean that 'all that is not prohibited is permissible' – or that 'in the absence of a clear normative proscription the state whose conduct is being reviewed should retain some freedom of action' (Shany 2005, p. 912, 925). This decision was contentious at the time and is considered problematic in legal opinion on space resources law (Jakhu 2006, p. 41; Hobe and de Man 2017). Furthermore, citing case law that predates the United Nations is discordant with an international legal framework that, at least in principle, is predicated on co-operative deliberation on and negotiation of the rules of the space commons. It is self-defeating to invoke the 'lotus principle' while arguing that the CSLCA complies with UN treaty law.

There are further areas in which viewing one article of the OST in isolation engenders interpretations that are against the 'spirit' of the Treaty. NewSpace discourse is littered with invocations of common interests, common needs and common destinies, from O'Neill's (1977) grandiose salvationist project through to Planetary Resources' claim that it intends to 'expand humanity's resource base' (Lewicki, in Planetary Resources 2012). Arguments that space mining projects predicated on private property law are in service of 'all mankind' generally point towards 'positive externalities' (Kfir & Perry 2017, pp. 165–166) or some commercially available 'spin-offs' for the rest of society (Marboe & Johnson, in IISL 2016, p. 35). Kfir and Perry argue that benefits for humanity might flow indirectly once 'space resources technology allows the cost of operations in space to decrease' – such as using off-world propellant refineries to reduce the cost of rocket launches – thereby allowing 'space exploration [to fit] within the budgets of many more countries than it does at present' and '[adding] to the total stock of resources available to humanity' (2016, p. 166, 167). In order to provide benefits from private mining rights to non-spacefaring countries, space mining firms may one day establish partnerships with developing nations, offering them a stake in profitable ventures or reduced prices for off-world propellant.[10]

However, the language of 'positive externalities' resonates with how neoliberalism often frames the question of alleged societal benefits for pro-corporate economic reform. Grow the cosmic pie, and the benefits will surely trickle down like starlight. Yet the whole purpose of private resource rights, in the words of NewSpace corporations, is to enable companies to 'enjoy the fruits of their labor' rather than to share them with others (Bigelow, cited in Foust 2013). Moreover, there is an evident tendency in the American space industry towards monopoly power, and an obvious predilection in American foreign policy to put national or US-based corporate interests first. It is difficult to imagine how private resource appropriation in the off-world might in practice deliver 'benefits to all mankind'.

If we return to the 'OST as constitution' analogy, Waluchow notes the risk of 'living' constitutional interpretations. They can render

> all talk of constitutional interpretation, properly understood as the retrieval of existing meaning, utterly senseless: constitutional interpretation becomes nothing more than unconstrained, constitutional creation or construction masquerading as interpretation. (2017, p. 26)

While there are limits to analogising international treaty law to a national constitution, the way states interpret and implement treaty obligations can serve to establish 'precedent' in subsequent interpretations. In international law, this is different to *stare decisis* precedent that guides common law jurisdictions (such as in the US Supreme Court decisions discussed earlier).[11] Space lawyers Masson-Zwaan and Palkovitz assert that national laws like the CSLCA may neither 'promote or prevent' the development of international space law, but they nonetheless acknowledge that 'the adoption of national laws … undoubtedly can have the effect of producing "state practice" and "*opinio juris*" on existing or perceived gaps in international law', and thereby 'may form international customary law' (2017, p. 5).[12]

State practice in interpreting and implementing treaties can be significant in informing future treaty interpretations. This, in turn, guides the evolution of the principles of customary international law that – in a legal positive sense – bind all countries. 'Soft law' instruments are also an aspect of state practice that guide the evolution of customary international law: this includes declarations, resolutions and codes of practice. Statements and submissions by national delegations within UN committees are also indicative of state interpretation of the OST and state acceptance of the CSLCA (Masson-Zwaan & Palkovitz 2017, p. 5). Other states' non-acceptance of the CSLCA is significant in this regard. In the 2016 meeting of UNCOPUOS's Legal Subcommittee, Russia has accused the United States of violating the non-appropriation principle, while Belgium expressed concern regarding the potential for global economic inequality to be exacerbated by space mining (Masson-Zwaan & Palkovitz 2017, pp. 14–15). Tronchetti and Liu also note opposition from Belgium, Germany and Russia in the 2017 Legal Subcommittee meetings (2018, p. 430, footnote 4). Greece and

Belgium proposed the creation of a working group committed to devising an international regime for space resource utilisation – including the assertion that 'Outer space is a common space regulated by international law' (UNCOPUOS 2019, A/AC.105/C.2/L.311, p. 2). This may be indicative of an overall 'counter-movement' towards international cooperation in the development of an international regime for space resource exploitation, predicated on realising tangible benefits for 'all mankind' and the preservation of multilateral consensus-making in space law (I discuss this further in Chapter 7).

However, the Luxembourg, Japan and United Arab Emirates space resources laws can be read as an effort to build upon the precedent established by the United States – that codifying 'freedom to use' in national law as the freedom to privately and irreversibly extract from outer space is an interpretation of the OST that is accepted in state practice (von der Dunk 2020). Linking 'free use' with 'exclusive occupation' becomes a legal argument that could be used by other states to justify their own laws of appropriation. Or, if other states support the measures taken by these first movers, new national laws could be implemented by the United States that take private property claims even further – off-world land grabs, for instance (see also Chapter 3, p. 69). The actions of the first movers in space resources law could well serve to legitimise the actions of additional nations – such as the United States's superpower rivals like China or Russia – similar to how the Soviet launch of *Sputnik* cleared the pathway for freedom of passage in orbital flight. There are thus parallels between 'NewSpace law' and legal scholarship in early modern Europe. Scholars like Grotius, Franciso de Vitoria and Alberico Gentili probed ancient Roman law in order to find ways of justifying imperial expansion (Benton & Straumann 2010). More than just conquest, it was an attempt at 'acquiring empire by law' (Benton & Straumann 2010). Here, we reach the boldest declaration on the OST's meaning, contained within the recent *American Space Commerce Free Enterprise Act of 2017*: 'Notwithstanding any other provision of law, outer space shall not be considered a global commons' (ASCFE 2017, s. 80308). Endorsed by the same politicians that co-sponsored the CSLCA and lobbied for by space mining firms, this recent legislation appears part of a concerted and persistent effort to prevent the commoning of outer space.

Neoliberal multilateralism v. the common heritage of humankind

> "The preservation of an effective competitive order depends upon a proper legal and institutional framework. The existing framework must be considerably modified to make the operation of competition more efficient and beneficial" – draft principles of the Mont Pèlerin Society. (Cited in Plehwe 2009, p. 23)

We have discussed the ascension of neoliberal economic policy in the late 1970s and 1980s. Neoliberal capture of mineral sovereignty has involved the corrosion of democratic law-making and the deployment of the state's legal, administrative and coercive functions to legitimise and protect private access to national and global mineral estates. In this section, we will briefly return to the limited ratification of the *Moon Agreement* and what the CSLCA may mean for future multilateral projects. If the CSCLA-friendly interpretations of the OST are effectively acts of 'constitutional' creation 'masquerading as interpretation' (Waluchow 2017, p. 26), then the United States's refusal to sign the *Moon Agreement* was, to use the words of the Mont Pèlerin Society's draft principles, the 'considerable modification' of an international framework envisioned by the NIEO.

I have argued that the US rejection of the *Moon Agreement* and the NIEO was an example of neoliberal 'strong state' support for privately-held mineral rights in the global commons. In recent decades, neoliberal think-tanks and NewSpace organisations have both painted the *Moon Agreement*'s 'common heritage' provisions as ideologically anathema to the market society envisioned by neoliberalism. If '[private] property is explicitly banned', says a Cato Institute white paper, then the 'model for this Treaty is the old Soviet constitution' (Hudgins 1998, p. 3). The National Space Society, meanwhile, lamented that the *Agreement* would have created 'a centralized, government-managed economy dedicated to distributing any benefits or profits from space resources' to nations other than the United States' (NSS 2009, p. 4). This was the intention of the *Moon Agreement*, and for this reason it has not been ratified by the United States. Russia, the UK, Japan and most other nations followed suit. Under the Trump Administration, the United States has renewed its opposition to the *Moon Agreement*; a recent Executive Order has warned the international community that 'the Secretary of State shall object to any attempt by any other state or international organization to treat the Moon Agreement as reflecting or otherwise expressing customary international law' (Executive Office of the President 2020).

An NIEO constitution for the off-world failed. Stephen Gill was the first scholar to describe a 'new constitutionalism' of neoliberal globalisation that 'limits democratic control over central elements of economic policy and regulation by locking in future governments to liberal frameworks of accumulation predicated on freedom of enterprise' (Gill 2002, p. 47). The defeat of the *Moon Agreement* may not 'lock' future governments into adhering to pro-corporate trade agreements or neoliberal interpretations of the OST, as have the mandates of the Washington Consensus and domestic legal interpretations like the *Citizens United* case. Yet it prevented a mineral commonwealth for celestial bodies from taking root in international political institutions and opened the door for the CSLCA.

Might we see neoliberal constitutionalism take root in space resources law in a more concrete or codified way? Schneidermann (2013) has demonstrated that neoliberal constitutionalism is being globalised in the form of a new investment rules regime, realised most nefariously in investor-state dispute settlement (ISDS) provisions being incorporated into international trade agreements.

ISDS clauses allow foreign corporations to seek damages from governments that have introduced policies that may affect their expected profits (an anticipatory claim to damages beyond real private property). These cases are often tried in largely unaccountable and undemocratic international arbitration courts. One example of mineral sovereignty being protected through ISDS litigation is the *Lone Pine Resources v. Government of Canada* suit, in which an American oil and gas company sought US $119 million in damages following Quebec's moratorium on fracking and the revocation of Lone Pine's exploration license (*Lone Pine Resources Inc. v. Government of Canada*). ISDS clauses thus become part of a supranational 'supraconstitution that can supersede domestic constitutional norms' (Schneidermann 2013, p. 3).

We can only speculate about whether anything similar to ISDS multilateralism will enter the space law and policy field in the future. However, there is some evidence that NewSpace actors and Atlas neoliberals are exploring the possibility of multilateral resource appropriation agreements outside of the terms of OST or the fora of the United Nations – as articulated in a recent report from the Reason Foundation, for example (Grearson & Bennett 2019, p. vii, 76). In drawing this discussion to a close, let us consider that the OST preamble states a desire of State parties to 'contribute to broad international *cooperation* in the scientific as well as the legal aspects of the exploration and use of outer space' (OST 1967, my emphasis). Space miners and their legal teams appear conscious of the problem of unilateral declarations of rights to private property ownership in the global commons. Some have made optimistic assertions that:

> The birth and passage of the first national space resource utilization legal regime is the first step toward further international cooperation in space and it will ultimately benefit all mankind. With similar legislation being drafted in other nations, bilateral and multilateral agreements will develop between like-minded nations that see the economic, environmental, and social importance that space resource utilization will bring to their respective countries. (Kfir 2016)

'Like-minded' economically elite and technologically advanced nations could draft agreements governing the space commons, before most of the rest of the world gets a foot in the door. Hertzfeld, Weeden and Johnson appear to be supporting a 'sidestepping' of the OST and the UN, proposing a 'system of arbitration' embedded in national laws, predicated on the assertion that 'there is no compelling argument that all issues in such [extra-jurisdictional common] areas need to or can be resolved through one organisation or one agreement' (2016, p. 25, 24). Writers with the *Cato Journal* have also made the suggestion that space firms could even 'choose the law they want to apply to their agreement in the event of dispute' by one day working through international arbitration courts (Salter & Leeson 2014, p. 593). Salter and Leeson outline how private parties may one day develop multilateral conventions through which appropriation and the enforcement of property rights are managed between groups of appropriators, without the oversight of external regulatory bodies (ibid, pp. 593–594).

The recent emergence of the Artemis Accords points towards the side-stepping of the OST in a more immediate sense. The Accords effectively entrench the United States' pro-extractivist interpretation of the Treaty in an agreement signed between the United States and its allies, in advance of NASA's renewed efforts to revisit the Moon as part of the Artemis Program. Some scholars have argued that the Artemis Accords may not prove to be particularly revolutionary in the development of international space resources law. For example, Delplano argues that the Accords are a non-binding innovation and 'present themselves as a starting point for further discussion of an international framework on space resource activities' (2021, p. 819). However, is it important not to discount the fact that the Accords were developed by the United States, with US commercial interests in mind. Similarly, von der Dunk argues that the Accords may serve as 'an effort on the part of the United States to convince those countries that have not yet openly condoned its approach to now do so, at least for the sake of participating in the Artemis programme' (2020). Hobe also states that 'The Americans always want to lay down the rules of the game. Only then may many other countries be asked to cooperate' (cited in Stirn 2020). The work of the United States and its Artemis Accord allies represents a key step in 'hollowing out the Outer Space Treaty' (Hobe, in Stirn 2020).

Conclusion

Concerns about the future of the space commons are ostensibly defences of the rule of law, a familiar problem in the genealogy of jurisprudence and justice. Who decides the law? Who does it really benefit? How flexible should legal interpretation be? Space mining advocates simultaneously ascribe legality to the CSLCA and irrelevance to the OST, as part of a (US-centric) neoliberal constitution for outer space. Their interpretations of 'freedom to use' and 'benefits to all mankind' are weighted heavily towards corporate freedoms. The rule of law is predicated on the stability of laws (Raz 1979, ch. 11), yet legal adjudication and interpretation often push the law 'in novel and unexpected directions' (Bottomley & Bronitt 2012, p. 50).

While correct in pointing to central ambiguities in its wording, defenders of domestic private property law for outer space are employing a mode of 'constitutional' interpretation of the OST that essentially ignores its fundamental tenets (non-appropriation and universal benefits, in particular). If legal precedent shapes subsequent behaviours, then the justification of domestic space private property within the *res communis* provisions of the OST effectively becomes a 'constitutional argument' to justify further consolidations of corporate rights to exploit the off-world commons. NewSpace-sympathetic writers with the Atlas Network's

TechFreedom think-tank have testified before Congress, strategising precisely on this goal:

> In the future, after the U.S. has shown its world leadership by establishing a domestic regulatory approach that encourages private sector advancement into space while protecting the core values of the OST, then the U.S. will be able to negotiate a future treaty from a position of strength, as by that time U.S. entrepreneurs will already have established themselves as the 'first movers' in a huge new economic arena … . (Dunstan & Szoka 2017, p. 6)

To be the 'first movers' on a new frontier, what precedents do we have for the corporate appropriation of off-world mineral resources through unilateral private property law? In the next chapter, we will continue on the high seas, and explore the pre-modern history of the colonial frontier in more detail. Here, in the age of the pirate and the privateer, we can find precedents for powerful states granting powers of mineral sovereignty to their commercial vanguards, cloaked under the mythologised virtues of the colonisers.

Notes

1 Schmitt's *Nomos of the Earth* points to the birth of international law in antiquity: the 1279BC treaty between the Hittites and Ramses II's Egypt, which Schmitt describes paradoxically as the 'first treaty of peace, friendship and alliance' that was also 'the founding of a "dual hegemony" of two empires' that were less peaceful in their imperial expansion into other territories (2003, p. 52).
2 This issue has been on the agenda of the Legal Subcommittee of UNCOPUOS since 1967 (the year the OST was opened for signature). UNCOPUOS' Working Group on the Definition and Delimitation of Outer Space has sought consensus on this question, as the boundary between airspace and outer space represents the point at which national sovereignty ceases and the 'principles of the freedom of use of outer space and of non-appropriation' commence (UNCOPUOS 2020, A/AC.105/769/Add.1, 2).
3 Organisers of the International Geophysical Year of 1957–1958 (IGY) had pushed for nations to launch satellites for scientific research. The IGY encouraged participating governments to launch satellites into space in the name of international scientific cooperation – a gesture of scientific diplomacy, predicated on openness and communalism (McDougall 1997, p. 118). It would thus be remiss to treat the emergence of US satellite policy solely as an act of Cold War antagonism and distrust.
4 However, a key point of difference between the *Antarctic Treaty System* and the OST is that the existing Antarctic territorial claims of select nations are recognised, rendering it less restrictive than the OST.
5 Article 4 of the OST prohibits placing 'in orbit around the Earth any objects carrying nuclear weapons or any other kinds of weapons of mass destruction' or placing these weapons on celestial bodies or space stations. So much for Werner von Braun's suggestion that a space station could be 'an extremely effective atomic-bomb carrier' (cited in Kilgore 2003, p. 68). Article 4 also prohibited the 'establishment of military bases, installations and fortifications, the testing of any

type of weapons and the conduct of military manoeuvres on celestial bodies'. Project Horizon, the lunar military base proposed to the US Army (by von Braun's Army Ballistic Missile Agency), would have been illegal. As would creating 'asteroid forts' for anti-ballistic missile defences, which was one of many 'wild speculations' proposed by Keith Henson, co-founder of the L-5 Society (1979, p. 1).

6 The *Citizens United* decision deemed corporations' political advertising and donations to be acts of 'political speech', thus protected under the First Amendment rights to freedom of speech. It meant that 'for Congress to limit corporate campaign spending was just as unconstitutional as banning a flesh-and-blood person from arguing for or against health care reform' (Purdy 2014, p. 199).

7 The *Lochner* decision ruled invalid a state law that had set maximum daily and weekly hours for bakers on grounds that it 'violated constitutionally protected "liberty of contract", the freedom of employees to make whatever agreements they saw fit' (Purdy 2014, p. 196).

8 Much to the chagrin of select NewSpace libertarianism, this means that all launches and activities are subject to government approval. In lieu of any equivalent 'spacefaring authority', the FAA oversees the activities of American private space corporations in tandem with the Federal Communications Commission (regulating commercial satellites) and the National Oceanic and Atmospheric Administration (regulating remote sensing satellites, such as those recording climatological data), all of which ensure the compliance of US' public and private space activity with the OST (SFF 2019). For instance, Moon Express was granted 'mission approval' to land on the Moon by the Federal Aviation Authority. The Space Frontier Foundation subsequently bemoaned the need to get permission to go to the Moon: 'Long term, this is not an ideal solution, and Congress will need to develop law that codifies a process that is simpler than what Moon Express had to use' (SFF 2019). The author argues in support of 'an in-space or on-orbit authority whose mandate covered all of space including surface activities on planets, active interactions of docking spacecraft and so on' (SFF 2019). A neoliberal model of re-regulating in favour of the market, rather than de-regulating (Cahill 2014).

9 In 1926, the French *SS Lotus* collided with the Turkish *SS Boz-Kourt* in international waters, killing 8 people aboard the *Boz-Kourt*. When the *Lotus* arrived in Constantinople, criminal proceedings were launched by Turkish officials against the vessel's French captain. The French and Turkish Governments asked the Court whose jurisdiction the vessel's owner should be tried under – was it legal for the captain to be tried under Turkish law? French lawyers in the Court had tried to argue that they should retain jurisdiction over a vessel bearing the French flag, yet the Court decided in Turkey's favour that there was no principle in international law to that effect; therefore, Turkey's actions were permissible (*S.S. Lotus (Fr. v. Turk.)*, 1927 P.C.I.J.).

10 Similar agreements have emerged in the case of seabed mining, as per the 'common heritage' mandate of exploratory licenses granted by the International Seabed Authority (discussed in Chapter 4). One example is the Canadian start-up Nautilus Minerals, which made plans to mine deposits of valuable minerals off the coast of Papua New Guinea. In 2014, the PNG government had purchased a 15% stake in the company's proposed Solwara mine (Kero 2014). While this is only one example within a similarly nascent and speculative mining industry, it perhaps serves as a cautionary tale for any developing nation seeking partnerships with start-ups of the global North. In 2019, Nautilus filed for bankruptcy, rendering a return on the national treasury's $115 million investment unlikely (Kero 2014; Stutt 2019).

11 The legal principle of *stare decisis* (literally, 'to stand by decisions') refers to the judicial practice of precedent. It is the foundation of adjudication in the domestic courts of common law jurisdictions, yet legal precedent is still significant in the arbitration courts of international law (Bhala 1990).

12 *Opinio juris sive necessitatis* (usually translated as 'opinion of law or necessity') represents the belief that an action was undertaken as a legal obligation, such as the view that states are obligated to introduce their own resources law for outer space.

6 Privateering the cosmic frontier

Empire, myth and the violence of property[1]

There is an intractable link between national sovereignty and private property (Chapter 3), particularly as manifest in mining rights (Chapter 4). A neoliberal paradigm is emerging in international law that fortifies corporate rights to extract from and pollute the global commons, as Atlas organisations pressure sovereign states to undermine alternate legal orders that recognise collective rights and responsibilities. NewSpace's 'constitutional' arguments attempt to create a legal justification for private off-world resource appropriation in advance of this speculative project being realised (Chapter 5). In this chapter, we will move further into the realm of the anticipatory, as I discuss how state-corporate appropriation on the cosmic frontier might transpire.

I will do this by counter-posing my own speculations against an episode in NewSpace myth-making, a tale of off-world privatisation. The now-defunct NewSpace start-up MirCorp had briefly privatised the Russian space station *Mir* – this was essentially NewSpace's first and only corporate outpost in space. The story of MirCorp is told by NewSpace protagonists in the documentary film, *Orphans of Apollo* (2008). This text is a stark example of the network's anti-statist and anti-bureaucratic mythos: it is a paean to NewSpace entrepreneurialism that implicates NASA and the US Government in the failure of MirCorp, while simultaneously absolving speculative capital. The documentary invokes the figure of the pirate – the original extra-territorial anarcho-libertarian – and in doing so, it opens up further questions about the tension between national appropriation and private mineral ownership that are at the heart of this book. I will use the *Orphans*' pirate imagery as a heuristic for establishing precedents for space mining in the age of maritime colonialism (returning to themes I raised in Chapter 5). I posit that the state-backed space mining firm bears a closer resemblance to the privateers and charter companies of maritime colonialism: pirates for hire and commercial vanguards for empire, pushing back the frontier.

Places or spaces are generally categorised as frontiers to highlight their geographic characteristics: 'the frontier' can describe the furthest extent of a civilisation, the periphery at spatial remove from the core (Wallerstein 1974). It can also denote areas that are particularly difficult to access, like mountainous regions, jungles, deserts and outer space (Hall 2013, p. 53).

DOI: 10.1201/9781003293613-6

As Derek Hall notes in his political economy of land, 'frontiers are areas where states fall well short of exercising administrative control' (2013, p. 52). Yet using physical or political-geographic terms to describe frontiers is to neglect their cultural characteristics and their mythoi. The future studies scholar William Kramer (2014) reports on the ongoing use of frontier metaphors in NASA mission planning and lists the adjectives that can accompany frontier discourses and the role of the valorous pioneer within them. The frontier can be:

> unknown, vast, lonely, godless, godforsaken, virgin, barren, unbroken, untamed, heathen, wild, desolate, savage, unforgiving, cold, hostile, foreboding, limitless, dangerous, uncivilized and even angry. These, then, contribute to the suite of terms that describe aspects of pioneers' relationship to that frontier, such as fear, battle, challenge, assault, conquering, conquest, subduing, civilizing, and taming. (Kramer 2014, p. 181)

To varying extents, frontiers are anomic or lawless (*anomos*; discussed in Chapter 3) – at least from the perspective of colonisers. Frontiers either lack a *nomos*, or there is an older, indigenous *nomos* that is displaced by a new colonial *nomos* through state-sanctioned violence (Walker 2013, pp. 399–400). To tame, to conquer and to subdue – more than mere geophysical marker, 'the frontier' indelibly connotes the violence of colonialism.

'The frontier' has always been a central trope in NewSpace discourse, one in which discourses of individual freedom or deregulation merge with the inherent patriotism of the US-centred movement. The Tea Party in Space is a small NewSpace civil society organisation which has participated in the 'March Storm' or 'August Blitz' lobbying events organised by the Alliance for Space Development (Alliance for Space Development 2017, p. 1). In their policy platform, they state:

> Only through fiscally responsible policy, which limits government bureaucracy and stimulates the free market, will the United States expand on its leadership in space. By removing barriers of entry to the utilization of the solar system, new business models become viable. This sound free-market-based approach will create new sectors of the economy and strengthen America as the vanguard of freedom and opportunity as we spread throughout the solar system. We will carry forth the American values that made our nation great. The United States will settle space as it settled the American continent. The days of Lewis and Clark, and Apollo, are over. This is the Oregon Trail space policy. (Tea Party in Space 2014b)

The Tea Party in Space's platform invokes some historically durable motifs. In addition to neoliberal edicts of 'fiscal responsibility' and removing barriers to entry, the Tea Party in Space's platform is, in their words, 'grounded in American exceptionalism' (Tea Party in Space 2014b).

This exceptionalism is expressed through the spatio-historic lens of the frontier. NewSpace will 'carry forth the American values that made our nation great' onto unsettled celestial bodies like the civilian pioneers westward bound on the Oregon Trail. In this trope, it is the exceptional, valorous entrepreneur who is skyward bound as 'the vanguard of freedom and opportunity' – America's destiny manifests in a union with free-market capitalism. Parker (2009, pp. 89–90) has noted the synergy between the westward frontier and the libertarian space frontier. Henry David Thoreau (1817–1862) had said, 'Eastward I go only by force; but westward I go free' – on the frontier, one could 'forget the Old World and its institutions' that lay across the Atlantic, because 'we go westward as into the future' (2008 [1862]; Parker 2009, p. 89). For libertarian space advocates, beyond the atmosphere lies an open expanse of extra-territorial liberty, an endless frontier in which to exercise one's inalienable right to private property ownership, with the grasp of terrestrial polity or regulation weakened as they venture from Earth.

However, unacknowledged in the frontier romanticism of Thoreau and the Tea Party in Space is the fact that the Oregon Trail had been blazed, in large part, by the Hudson's Bay Company (Douthit 1992). This British charter company was incorporated by King Charles II in 1670 for the purpose of 'finding some Trade for Furs, Minerals, and other considerable Commodities … [from which] there may probably arise very great Advantage to Us and Our Kingdom' (*Royal Charter of the Hudson's Bay Company*, HBC Heritage 2016). The Company was granted powers of de facto government and had exercised the rights bestowed by the Crown 'to send either Ships of War, Men or Ammunition … unto any their Plantations, Forts, Factories, or Places of Trade aforesaid, for the Security and Defence' of the land it had claimed along the fabled 'pioneer' trail from Missouri to Oregon (HBC Heritage 2016). Also missing in the above frontier mythologies is the fact that the American continent had been pioneered millennia before the arrival of early industrial civilisation. The indigenous societies that lived and worked the land prior to the Oregon Trail were often key sources of trade for Anglo-American wagon trains and, through disease and violence, were frequently killed through contact with white settlers. Far from forgetting the institutions of the Old World, 'free from all worldly engagements' (Thoreau 2008 [1862]), the frontier freedoms of white pioneers were enabled by European monarchical sovereignty – often expressed and solidified through colonial violence.

Myth-making is abundant in NewSpace. By myth, I mean both what may be perceived to be a falsehood, and also myth as 'legend' that 'still powerfully conveys some important moral and social lesson' regardless of its veracity (Christman 2014, p. 3). The mythic frontier appears in the policy platforms of NewSpace organisations. It appears in the promotional material of prospective space prospective space start-ups: Moon Express, for example, looks to new colonial horizons and core-periphery relationships when asserting that 'The Moon is Earth's 8th continent, a new frontier for humanity with precious resources that can bring enormous benefits to life on Earth and our future in space' (n.d.). The frontier trope is also evident in the private property advocacy formulated and published by neoliberal think-tanks. For Edward Hudgins of the Cato Institute, the off-world frontier promises commercial infinitude and boundless capital accumulation, so long as it is tamed through private property rights.

> In the past patriots fought to establish political and economic conditions of free exchange and private property rights. These conditions opened commercial frontiers on Earth and allowed us to create material wealth and technical capacities never dreamed of. By establishing these conditions throughout the solar system, we will open boundless new commercial frontiers. (Hudgins 2002, p. xxv)

Hudgins claims private property will open new frontiers, rather than enclose them or establish new barriers to open access. Much like the Tea Party in Space, Hudgins fuses together the heroic narrative of American nationalism with neoliberalism's omniscient market and the trailblazing entrepreneur.

This chapter explores the 'geo-mythography' (Connery 2001; Dean 2006) of the frontier and its role in NewSpace's political imaginary, particularly as it relates to the themes of national sovereignty, private appropriation and the legacy and prospects of colonialism, past and future. I begin by discussing *Orphans of Apollo* and its invocation of the pirate, before moving into a discussion of the privateer – an alternate figure in maritime colonialism that brings us closer to a precedent for state-backed frontier mineral rights. I focus primarily on the CSLCA in this chapter, more so than subsequent national laws from Luxembourg, the UAE and Japan, as the relationship between national power and force is clearer when off-world mining rights have been introduced by one of the world's military superpowers.[2]

To what extent would the NewSpace mining project mirror the frontier appropriations of the privateer and the joint-stock company? On the one hand, I venture that the legislative guarantee of private mineral rights represents the first, pre-emptive step in a neo-colonial entwinement of US resource imperialism and NewSpace's humanising mission. In the off-world, there is an unrealised, anticipatory violence lurking behind the promise of property ownership – such as the Trump Administration's 2019 establishment of a US Space Force that would (among other geostrategic priorities) protect American commercial interests in space (DoD 2018). On the other hand, NewSpace colonialism is discordant with the piratical and imperial violence that has plagued the frontiers of Earth. For NewSpace, the Solar System represents the guilt-free frontier – a benign colonialism. To use Hegel's words, it is an attempt to escape from the 'slaughter bench' of history (2001, p. 35).

Piratical NewSpace: parables of frontier libertarianism

We have discussed NewSpace's apparent desire to escape collective responsibility and its espousal of libertarian political philosophies at numerous places in earlier chapters (O'Neill 1977; Henson 1980; Zubrin 1994; Tumlinson 2003; Gump 2018; ASD 2019), as has also been discussed in sociological studies of NewSpace (Dickens & Ormrod 2007; Parker 2009; Valentine 2012; Genovese 2017; Shammas & Holen 2019). In the documentary film *Orphans of Apollo* (2008), NewSpace anti-statism is at its most virulent – particularly in the rhetoric of Walt Anderson, an earlier ICT billionaire who provided financial backing for the MirCorp start-up at the turn of the millennium. MirCorp's brief privatisation of the ailing space station *Mir* proved that raising the Jolly Roger flag on the off-world frontier was premature. Walt Anderson was later convicted for tax evasion, which provides an interesting example in drawing parallels between the off-world, as a site of 'piratical' freedoms, and the economic freedoms presented by the off-shore jurisdiction.

MirCorp and the Orphans of Apollo

For NewSpace and neoliberal actors in the 1990s, Russia's post-Soviet economic frontier held much promise. Following the dissolution of the Soviet Union under Mikhail Gorbachev in 1991, the Yeltsin Government enacted sweeping privatisation reforms that Naomi Klein (2007) describes as 'shock therapy'.[3] The 1993 constitutional crisis resembled the Pinochet Coup that preceded neoliberalism's Chilean laboratory (discussed in Chapter 4, note 6). The Russian Parliament had resisted an increase in the executive powers of Yeltsin and faced shelling from tanks positioned across the Moscow River. Yeltsin's voucher privatisations and 'loans for shares' scheme involved the sale of state assets to favoured individuals at heavily discounted prices – a process that left the country in the grip of financial crisis and famine, giving rise to the oligarchy and cronyism that persists to this day. Mischa Glenny describes the anomic character of the Russian economy at this point and draws comparison with the 'Chicago Boys' – albeit while neglecting the role of the 'Harvard Boys' in this shock therapy (Wedel 1998; see also Andrews 2014, p. 110).[4]

> The collapse of the Soviet Union is the single most important cause of the exponential growth in organised crime that we have seen around the world in the last two decades. Almost overnight, it provoked a chaotic scramble for riches and survival. From the bitter wars of the Caucasus to the lethal shoot-outs in towns and cities, this was a deadly environment as a new class of capitalist exploited the vacuum of power by seizing whole industries and raiding state coffers. Accompanied by an orgy of consumption and decadent behaviour, the like of which was last witnessed a century ago under Tsar Nicholas, it sucked every citizen into its vortex of violence [...] Russia's economy became a giant Petri-dish of Chicago-school market economics, but among the cultures they were busy cultivating was a Frankenstein that slipped out through the door of their laboratory almost unnoticed. (Glenny, cited in Andrews 2014, pp. 109–110)

Amidst this economic turmoil, the Russian Space Agency and its newly decentralised administrative and mission control centres were operating under a limited budget. The Russian Government had already made financial, technological and diplomatic commitments to participate in the upcoming *International Space Station* (ISS). Under this fiscal pressure, the nation's publicly owned rocket manufacturing agency had been partially privatised as a state-owned corporation called RSC Energia (Office of Technology Assessment 1995, p. 33). By the late 1990s, the Space Agency began pursuing new relationships with commercial actors, particularly those in the United States. The Space Agency sold seats on *Soyuz* crew transport missions to a handful of wealthy tourists, while also launching private satellites. In 1999, Pizza Hut paid the Russian space agency $1 million to print their logo on a Proton rocket (Parker 2009, p. 88; see Kochetkov 2000). The image of hundreds of Muscovites queuing outside the city's first McDonald's restaurant is an enduring image of Russia's birthing into capitalism – to this, we can add a spacefaring fast food company as further evidence of US corporate penetration into the formerly communist state.

We can also see linkages between post-Soviet space privatisation and NewSpace actors within contemporary space mining. Planetary Resources co-founders Peter Diamandis and Eric Anderson were co-founders of Space Adventures, a space tourism company that from 1998 had found customers for these privatised Russian launch services. Their first repeat customer was Charles Simonyi, the billionaire and former Microsoft programmer, who flew to the ISS on 2007 and 2009 *Soyuz* flights. Simonyi was one of Planetary Resources' backers in its early funding rounds (CrunchBase 2019a).

Central to this tale is a team of early NewSpace entrepreneurs who had visited Russia in the late 1990s. They were given an armed escort as they met with government officials in Moscow, and one member remarked that it was 'totally the Wild West' (Tumlinson, in *Orphans of Apollo* 2008). The group included Rick Tumlinson, founder of the SFF and co-founder of space mining firm Deep Space Industries, and the anarcho-capitalist Walt Anderson. Anderson was a telecommunications multi-millionaire and the venture's largest financial backer. He once confided to Russian space official Yuri Semenov: 'I have to tell you about my utopia idea. We have to build a very big rocket and we allow all the bureaucrats in the world a free trip to space [in] one direction' (in *Orphans of Apollo* 2008). Like the frontier pioneers, the NewSpace team could sense opportunity.

Their goal was to privately operate space station *Mir*. From 1986 to 2001, *Mir* was a site of scientific research and experimentation and was capable of housing three people at once. While the United States had the Apollo Program and the first manned lunar landing, *Mir* was the pride of the Soviet bloc. Towards the end of its lifespan, Russia began plans to de-orbit the space station. The posse of entrepreneurs had an alternative plan: if they could somehow privatise *Mir*, it could remain in orbit and become the first privately operated space station. Leasing the ailing station from the Russian government would allow *Mir* to remain in orbit with reduced budgetary burden on constrained Russian coffers. The word '*mir*' means 'peace'; it was also the name used colloquially by Russian serfs for democratic fora that governed the collective distribution of land (Linklater 2015, p. 142). There is thus some irony that '*mir*' was the namesake of NewSpace's first corporate outpost on the space frontier.

MirCorp was incorporated to undertake this privatisation, but it would only be a fleeting realisation of the NewSpace dream. In 1999, an agreement was reached between the NewSpace group and RSC Energia, the partially state-owned corporation overseeing *Mir*'s operation. MirCorp was incorporated as a partnership between the two parties: Energia owned 60% of MirCorp and oversaw technical management of the orbital station itself, while the American investors would own 40% and manage the business operations (Hudgins 2002, p. xix). The corporation would lease the station from the Russian space agency, by then renamed Roscosmos. The business plan included: flying-in wealthy space tourists; contracting *Mir* as a laboratory space; testing zero-gravity manufacturing projects; filming a reality TV programme; and the space station becoming a staging post for deep space mining projects (Chambers & Gardellini, cited in *Orphans of Apollo* 2008). In April 2000, MirCorp launched its one and only mission, paying for Russian cosmonauts to complete repair work on *Mir* and boosting it to a higher orbit. But this was as far MirCorp would go: in December 2000, Roscosmos had finally decided to de-orbit *Mir* and, in March 2001, it broke-up in the atmosphere and the wreckage sank to the depths of the Pacific Ocean.

NewSpace actors have narrativized the decision to de-orbit *Mir* in a manner consistent with the aversion to bureaucracy and emphasis on individual liberty and economic freedom that pervades their political imaginary. Protagonists on the American side of MirCorp have claimed that NASA and the US State Department pressured Roscosmos to drop this new venture in favour of meeting Russian commitments to the ISS (Tumlinson & Chambers, cited in *Orphans of Apollo* 2008). They also allege that the export license for an American-made 'tether' technology, which they believed would keep *Mir* in orbit more cost-effectively, was deliberately delayed by the State Department until after the de-orbiting decision had been made. The *Orphans of Apollo* documentary filmmakers offer a modest $1000 reward for anyone who can find definitive proof of US Government interference in MirCorp's project ('*Smoking Gun Memo $1000 Reward*', n.d.).

The exploits of MirCorp are recounted in the documentary film *Orphans of Apollo* (2008). The film tells the MirCorp story in a sympathetic light. The title harkens back to the era of Gerard O'Neill, the post-Apollo funding cutbacks and the disappointments of the Space Shuttle. Jeffrey Manber, MirCorp's legal officer who was instrumental in drafting the *Mir* leasing agreement, describes post-Apollo spacefaring as 'decades of dreams never realised, decades of false expectations, decades of government interference in what the private sector does best: opening up a new frontier' (Manber, in

Villaneda 2009). Manber ignores the role of government in opening the space frontier, here offering a revisionist history of the American space programme.

The film and its promotional material elucidate the NewSpace-neoliberal aporia that I have discussed throughout this dissertation (Free Radical Productions 2008). The film's advertising features a trio of symbols with conflicting ideas about the state – piracy, communism and anarchism – and the tagline, 'A rebel alliance of entrepreneurs dared to open up the final space frontier' (Free Radical Productions 2008). In this evocative image, the contradictory impulses of NewSpace and neoliberalism are clear: the anarchists circled 'A' rejecting authority, the pirate flag as symbol of freedom and violent appropriation, unbounded by legal regimes; and the national flag – by my analysis, the symbol of the state power in which property rights are grounded and where the colossal expense of space infrastructure generally accrues.

Against what authority does this 'rebel alliance' brandish the flag of the pirate? While Disney-fied and infantilised since, the pirate flag was originally a symbol of opposition to the empires of the pre-modern era. The libertarian 'Orphans' use the pirate flag here to conflate NASA and the State Department with a similar level of oppression. Michael Potter, the film's director, would later surmise that: 'The real drama was that the U.S. didn't want these entrepreneurs, these anarchists to buy the Russian space station, because they wanted to have the monopoly on everything in space' (cited in Villaneda 2009). This 'US monopoly on space' would, presumably, be NASA. In the wake of the space station's demise, MirCorp's supporters have blamed public sector inefficiencies and spouted free-market triumphalism. According to Hudgins:

> MirCorp struggled heroically to convert a money losing relic into a private, moneymaking success. Its tragic failure was due in part to NASA officials who seemed more comfortable with a Soviet space model than a free market one. (Hudgins 2002, p. xx)

NASA's alleged interventionism in *Mir*'s fate and the size of its bureaucracy now, supposedly, makes it a bastion of collectivism and redistribution, with NASA's greater interest in the ISS is framed as engaging with the 'Soviet space model' that dared to hinder the invisible hand of economic liberalism. This is a curious assessment of NASA, given its centrality in the Cold War and its ongoing support of the privately owned firms of the US military-industrial complex.

Beyond the protagonists' allegations of government intervention, this allusion to the pirate myth reveals the contradiction at the heart of NewSpace: the state is often portrayed as the enemy of freedom (to explore, to conquer and to trade) and yet so much of the NewSpace strategy relies on the participation of said state, one way or another. Hudgins' quip regarding the 'heroic struggle' of the free market (2002, p. xx) conveniently underplays the presence of RSC Energia, the former Soviet rocket manufacturer turned state-owned corporation, as a majority participant in MirCorp. This vision of free-market homesteading rested upon ailing 'big science' infrastructure built by the polar opposite of the free market, the Soviet Union, and was still owned by the Russian state. MirCorp supporters downplay the governmental origins and composition of Energia. Muncy, Tumlinson and Werb note that it was only a 'partially publicly held firm' (2002, p. 217), while Hudgins states that it was 'over two-thirds privately owned' (2002, p. xix).

An alternate reading of the MirCorp case study would be to point to the US entrepreneurs' inability to be credible capitalists. For NewSpace, this is obviously a more rhetorically and ideologically inconsistent proposition than a narrative of government failure. Roscosmos's space budget was split between *Mir* and the soon-to-be-launched ISS; NASA officials were concerned that Russian rocket manufacturing would not support both the ISS and a new phase of *Mir* occupation (Harland 2005, p. 281; *Orphans of Apollo* 2008). Failures in key systems and a series of accidents a number of years prior had also increased the technological challenges facing MirCorp. When the company missed a payment in December 2000 – shortly after it had announced an initial public share offering for the following year – Mir's fate was sealed (Harland 2005, p. 283; Hall & Shayler 2003, p. 363). In the Orphans' anarchic narrative, less convenient targets are given less attention – chief financial backer Walt Anderson in particular. MirCorp's inability to meet financial obligations to Roscosmos owes much to the dot-com crash of 2000 and a substantial loss in Anderson's personal fortune – implicating speculative capital in MirCorp's demise more so than the meddling of government agencies.

Tax evasion and the off-shore

Anderson was an interesting figure in the NewSpace network. He was an early supporter of the SFF and, with Peter Diamandis and Bob Richards (founders of NewSpace firms Planetary Resources and Moon Express, respectively), was a backer of the International Space University, and has also advocated for investment in monitoring asteroids for planetary defence (Hilzenrath, Leonnig & Noguchi 2005; The Space Show 2017). According to MirCorp CEO David Chambers:

> Walt's view of the government, of state control, is completely resonant with that of people in what's known as the NewSpace movement. That is, the loose agglomeration of anarcho-libertarian utopians who would like to get away from what they see as the intractable mess down here. (in *Orphans of Apollo* 2008)

For Anderson, escaping that 'intractable mess' involved a more immediate goal. In 2006, Anderson pleaded guilty to offshoring around US $365 million in income between 1995 and 1999 in an attempt to avoid approximately $200 million in personal income tax – at the time, it was America's largest tax evasion case (Hilzenrath 2005). As part of a plea bargain to limit jail time, he admitted to 'using aliases, shell companies, offshore tax havens, secret accounts and drop boxes' in the Netherlands, Panama and British Virgin Islands (Weiss 2006). One holding company was named 'Gold & Appel Transfer' – a reference to the 'golden apple' motif in the *Illuminatus!* libertarian sci-fi conspiracy novels (Weil 2000).

The *Orphans* invocation of piracy is telling, as it conjures notions of extra-territoriality and the 'off-shore' – a place to escape. The offshore, in the contemporary political-economic sense, of course, refers to foreign jurisdictions that help wealthy elites escape societal obligations in the form of taxation. Hudson posits 'offshoreness' as a fundamental component of the international economic order, where 'jurisdictions beyond the regulatory reach of onshore regulatory authorities' play an important role in 'the changing relationship between the geographies of globalization and sovereignty' (2000, p. 269). The emergence of Luxembourg as the second nation to introduce private property law in space is significant in this sense. Luxembourg has been described as 'the tax haven of tax havens, present at all stages of the financial industry' (Zucman, cited in Abrahamian 2017). As discussed in Chapter 2, Luxembourg's *SpaceResources.lu* initiative has culminated in the *Space Resources Act* and a fund for investment in space mining start-ups (Luxembourg Space Agency 2019). Planetary Resources, Deep Space Industries and Japanese space miners iSpace have all established offices in the tiny constitutional monarchy (Planetary Resources 2016a). It would appear contemporary NewSpace is perpetuating the 'tax aversion' established by Anderson, though not to the degree of tax evasion Anderson was charged with. Anderson has claimed that the money was being stored in low-tax jurisdictions before being given away as part of a large philanthropic fund, in which space exploration was but one component (Hilzenrath, Leonnig & Noguchi 2005). If this can be taken at face value, Anderson also serves as an example of how NewSpace actors have attempted to reach lofty, humanistic ends through contradictory, self-defeating means.

Moving past the Anderson case study, the oceans – the literal offshore – also have appeal for wealthy libertarians. MirCorp's project of a self-contained haven for tech-savvy, monied elites has also been proposed for the aquatic frontier. Zalik notes that the 'marine zone offers space freer from public disruption and constant forms of social accountability than on land' (2015 p. 173). Indeed, there are many similarities between the privatised space station and the nascent project of 'seasteading'. Seasteading involves the use of 'islands' as libertarian utopias that exist outside the sphere of government influence, ranging from retrofitted oil platforms and (hypothesised) purpose-built floating islands, to cruising vessels permanently at sea. Steinberg, Nyman and Caraccioli (2012) surmise the views of the San Francisco-based Seasteading Institute:

> ... the seastead is promoted simultaneously as the apotheosis of and an antidote to globalization, an insular and uncorrupted city-state where capitalism can regain its originary energy and where the spirit of human entrepreneurship can flourish. (Steiberg, Nyman and Caraccioli 2012, p. 1533)

Peter Thiel – venture capitalist, Atlas supporter and financial backer of Planetary Resources and Moon Express – forms an interesting link between seasteading and 'spacesteading'. Thiel was an active supporter of the Atlas Network's Seasteading Institute, which is headed by Patri Friedman (grandson of the Mont Pèlerin Society founder, Milton Friedman). Friedman has spoken of 'start-up countries': independent city-states founded beyond national borders with no territorial allegiance (Friedman 2018). As with Walt Anderson's vitriolic mistrust of NASA and the US Government, seasteading appears to attract rich individuals with a resentment for the state's capacity to enforce tax obligations and impose other regulatory constraints.

Anomie on the frontier and (neo)colonial violence

> We were the privateers – it was all about being rebels.
> (MirCorp co-founder Rick Tumlinson, cited in *Orphans of Apollo* 2008)

Charged with stealing the wealth of the American people and hoarding it in tropical hideaways, MirCorp's Walt Anderson essentially gave the *Orphans* tale its own pirate of the Caribbean. Yet the *Orphans*' rebellion is probably closer to Disney's Jack Sparrow than to 'Calico Jack' Rackham (1682–1720), the infamous English pirate who was hung for his crimes in Port Royal, Jamaica. MirCorp's Rick Tumlinson notes that the invocation of piracy in the MirCorp story was tongue-in-cheek fun – a Jolly Roger flag was even sent with the two cosmonauts to *Mir* (in *Orphans of Apollo* 2008). The pirate's capacity for unrestricted violence in plundering treasure from rival vessels undoubtedly highlights the limits of a direct analogy between the aquatic anarcho-libertarians of yesteryear and those of spacefaring, techno-utopian futures.

Nonetheless, the pirate remains a useful heuristic for approaching legal geographic questions of the frontier. Supporters of space mining have looked for precedents that portray the anticipated appropriation of frontier resources as peaceable, legal and harmonious. Writing in Cato's *Space – The Free Market Frontier*, space lawyer James E. Dunstan (2002) refers to the 842 pounds of lunar material collected by the Apollo missions. Dunstan argues that 'customary international law precedent has been established for the proposition that ownership can be exercised and claimed over pieces of celestial bodies' (2002, p. 228). NASA claims 'ownership' of these Moon rocks, uses them for public display, experimentation and inter-governmental loan, having exchanged some of these samples for samples obtained by the Soviet Union during their *Luna* robotic missions. Perhaps the Moon rocks do establish a precedent that things can be 'owned' in space – albeit in their original state, with no destructive extraction method or for non-profit, scientific purposes (Tronchetti 2015, p. 8). However, as Fabio Tronchetti has noted, 'it is simply not true that there is practice in the exploration and utilisation of extraterrestrial resources, at least not in the form and content envisioned' by US space mining law (Tronchetti 2015, p. 8).

In this section, I will argue that alternate precedents can be found much earlier than the 'old space' period. The age of maritime colonialism tells us much about both the mythology and legal geography of frontier spaces and frontier resources, and how they are often 'tamed' through a union of national and private appropriation. It is instead the colonial privateer and the charter company that offers more realistic historical precedents for the state-backed appropriation of space minerals.

From pirate to privateer: appropriation at arm's length

> 'Beyond the equator there are no sins.'
> – 17th century maxim (in Policante 2015, p. 53)

The pirate, as frontier libertarian of the colonial seas, was both anathema to and fundamentally constitutive of the international legal order that began to emerge alongside the 'juridification of the oceanic commons' (Policante 2015, p. xii). The pirate of the pre-modern world was a violent appropriator exploiting the 'free' spaces outside the sphere of state power. From oceans of ancient Rome to modern Somalia, the pirate has held the status of *hostis humani generis* – the enemy of all humanity, an unlawful combatant akin to the terrorist. Paradoxically, efforts to eradicate piracy solidified the role of European colonial powers as protectors of the oceanic commons and global commerce, simultaneously strengthening the state's monopoly on legitimate violence on the frontier (Policante 2015, p. xii; Heller-Roazen 2009). The political theorist Amedeo Policante notes that these 'exceptional spaces navigated by the lawless freebooter and anarchic buccaneer progressively [disappeared]' alongside the death throes of the 'Golden Age of Piracy' (1650s–1720s) and the emergence of an international legal order that protected the oceans as a space for commerce (Policante 2015, p. 73).

This juridification of the seas often involved pirates being employed directly by colonial powers through the arms-length institutions of privateering and charter companies. This represented a commingling between piratical lawlessness and the extension of state power, an imposition of a colonial *nomos* on the anomic frontier. To achieve this, a transformation in the pirate's legal standing occurred between the 16th and 18th centuries.

During the European Wars of Religion, a 'state of exception' (Agamben 2005) became solidified in customary law and treaty agreements beginning with the *1559 Treaty of Cateau-Cambrésis.* 'Amity lines' were drawn to separate the emergent 'law of nations' between continental powers and an anomic space 'beyond the line', where 'treaties, peace and friendship applied only to Europe, to the Old World, to the area on this side of the line' (Schmitt 2003, p. 92). The amity lines ran east-west along the Equator or Tropic of Cancer to the south and a line of longitude running north to south near the Azores Islands, off the African coastline (ibid, p. 90). To the other side was an anomic 'space of exception' exploited by the pirate, buccaneer and privateer.

It is within this anomic space beyond the inter-state order of continental Europe where the pirate became employed by the state: those who held a *lettres des marque et de représailles* (letter of marque and reprisal) were authorised to plunder enemy vessels and treasure without any limit on hostility. The pirate was transformed from lawless freebooter to state-sanctioned privateer: resources appropriated beyond the line were shared between privateers and state coffers, and the privateer became fundamental to European state-building (Policante 2015, pp. 61–67). For example, Walter Raleigh's charter for Virginia reserved one-fifth of any 'royal metals' for the Crown (Lewin 1931, p. 245). Raleigh and Francis Drake, two cherished figures in English history, were both privateers – heroes to one nation, pirates to another.

Royal charters were also given to privateers and joint-stock companies for the extraction of mineral resources and the claiming of territory. In addition to the examples I discussed in the history of mineral sovereignty (see Chapter 4), James I (1566–1625) authorised the *First Charter of Virginia* in 1606, and reserved one-fifth of all gold and silver and one-fifteenth of all copper mined 'within any Part' of the colonies for the Crown, alongside provisions granting the colonies the authority to 'establish and cause to be made a Coin' (cited in Thorpe 1909, p. 3786). In the 1632 *Charter of Maryland* , Baron Baltimore was granted fairly expansive provisions to:

> all Veins, Mines, and Quarries, as well opened as hidden, already found, or that shall be found within the Region, Islands, or Limits aforesaid, of Gold, Silver, Gems, and precious Stones, and any other whatsoever, whether they be of Stones, or Metals, or of any other Thing, or Matter whatsoever. (cited in Thorpe 1909, p. 1678).

One-fifth of all these precious metals were to be delivered to Windsor Castle (Charter of Maryland, cited in Thorpe 1909, p. 1679).

Charter companies were the commercial vanguards of Empire and were granted monopolies over foreign (and domestic) sources of resource wealth. While Pacific territorial claims in the late 18th and early 19th centuries involved annexation of territory for Britain from First Nations peoples, territories and resources of the Americas, Caribbean, Central Asia and Africa were often claimed under the arms-length entity of the charter company. Key charters included: the East India Company (1600), Virginia Company (1606), Somers Isles Company (Bermuda; 1615), Royal Africa Company (1660), Hudson Bay Company (1670) and through to the Royal Niger Company (1886), which merged with the Oil Rivers Protectorate in modern-day Nigeria in 1900. That the Sun never set on the British Empire at the turn of the 20th century is testament to the role of chartered, joint-stock companies – the first corporations – in ensuring England's imperial competitiveness: 'it may be said that in England, "monopoly" formed the connecting link between "mercantilism" and "protection"' (Hyde Price 1906, p. vii). The charter companies de-commoned the lands of the 'new' world, spreading capitalism by appropriating the lands and resources of indigenous populations.

Extending state power onto the cosmic frontier

What parallels can be drawn between the frontiers of the pre-modern seas and those of a possible spacefaring future? Might the frontier beyond the atmosphere comprise a similar state of exception, where the physical distance from the 'concrete order' (Schmitt 2003 [1950], p. 65) of terrestrial legal and political norms results in an extra-legal or anomic space, free for plunder? While outer space cannot be considered 'lawless' (International Institute of Space Law 2016; Freeland 2017), the breadth of interpretations of the OST would suggest that the pre-emptive juridification of outer space retains an anomic character – existing 'beyond the line'.

Schmitt's philological work identifies that the word 'pirate' is derived from 'the Greek *peiran*, meaning to test, to try, to risk' (2003, p. 43) – a contemporary definition of 'entrepreneur' might use similar terms. Indeed, Roth describes tech start-ups like Spotify and the Pirate Bay as 'pirate organisations' (2014, p. 402). NewSpace's aspirations to 'disrupt' the American space industries might have loose resonance with contemporary formulations of piracy as entrepreneurship (Roth 2014). Yet we must return to *nomos*, and the intractable connection between acts of appropriation and the establishment of law (Schmitt 2003). While the CLSCA would not entail the American flag being planted on the surface of an asteroid or celestial bodies, the United States is tacitly claiming some level of jurisdiction via acts of corporate appropriation. Acts of piracy involving intellectual property may represent 'a revolutionary act to confront property rights that ruptures the neoliberal ideology' (Arvanitakis & Fredriksson 2016, p. 140). Yet space mining laws clearly extend and rely upon state power rather than challenge it – the 'piratical' space mining firm is brought within the empire as if given a letter of marque. While many NewSpace actors may see off-world, private property-based colonisation as an act of protecting the future of the human race, the CSLCA has also been interpreted as an act of plunder (e.g. Oduntan 2015).

As a unilateral guarantee of private mining rights, the CSLCA essentially positioned the United States in opposition to other nations – spacefaring or otherwise – seeming to contradict the *res communis* nature of the OST. The

United States would recognise and enforce its citizens' resource claims on the space frontier in the name of '[developing] in the United States ... economically viable, safe and stable' space resource industries' (CSLCA 2015, s. 51302). This exploitation of the frontier as a 'state of exception' is an act of economic competition and, as the first move to establish private property over space resources, the CSLCA bears some resemblance to the royal charter or the letter of marque – minus the licensing of armed plunder of rival vessels. Resources claimed in outer space will generate tax revenue and further political prerogatives of economic growth (jobs, infrastructure and so on), akin to the role of privateering and joint-stock companies in European state-building. The space mining firm becomes the commercial vanguard, enabling an indirect form of 'accumulation by dispossession' (Harvey 2004; Dickens & Ormrod 2007) – a piratical act of pre-emptively stealing resources owned by all.

As we discussed in the previous chapter, NewSpace lawyers have made legal argumentation that resemble the 'acquiring empire by law' justifications of pre-modern jurists like Grotius (Benton & Straumann 2010). In seeking precedents that show how private property law could be commensurate with the OST, an early supporter of off-world private property pointed to an intriguing case study in the history of charter companies – one which inadvertently weakens the case that national appropriation could be demarcated from private mineral appropriation. Appearing in Cato's *Space – The Free Market Frontier*, space lawyer Wayne White admits that 'traditional real property rights are inconsistent' with Anglo-American constitutional law which 'dictates that [a] government must have sovereignty over territory before it can confer title on its citizens' (White 2002, p. 84). Elsewhere, White has proposed that a solution to the sovereignty problem is for terrestrial governments to confer 'functional' – as opposed to real – property rights, whereby the owner is granted use of an area without the right of exclusion that would accompany real property rights.

> Functional property rights permit free access to all areas of outer space and celestial bodies because they do not necessitate territorial sovereignty and its consequent appropriation of large areas of space ... The regime is attractive because it is so easy to implement. Nations can unilaterally enact legislation, and they can tailor that legislation to conform to their existing property laws. (White 1998)

He provides few examples to support this proposal, acknowledging that 'terrestrial governments have never actually conferred or recognized property rights predicated on functional rather than territorial sovereignty' (White 1998).

White employs the case of the (once) unclaimed Spitsbergen Island off Norway's coast, in which the establishment of coal mining and whaling operations briefly involved a functional sovereignty arrangement between a handful of nations. In 1613, the chartered Muscovy Company had claimed the island for England after commencing whaling operations. The Denmark-Norway union empire had also claimed it in 1616. Russia had begun coal mining in the late 19th century. Uninhabited Spitsbergen was effectively treated as *terra nullius*. As the US Secretary of State proposed as a negotiator for the 1920 Spitsbergen Treaty, the region could involve 'political sovereignty' (sovereignty over settler whalers and miners) rather than territorial sovereignty over the island itself. For White, Spitsbergen implies that it is possible to for states to grant functional rather than territorial property rights outside of their jurisdiction, and therefore, there would be some precedent for states granting private property rights on celestial bodies in a manner consistent with the OST.

However, the advent of World War I ended the prospects of negotiation. In 1920, the Spitsbergen treaty was signed granting:

> … sovereign power over Spitsbergen to Norway while guaranteeing rights of commerce and fishing to all interested parties. It thus ended the state of anarchy while permitting the continuation of existing mining interests. (Fitzmaurice 2014, p. 315)

A counterpoint to White's argument is provided by Pop (2000, pp. 277–279). Discussing both Spitsbergen and Jan Mayen Island, Pop demonstrates that in areas of 'non-sovereign resource exploitation' 'eventually a State sovereignty was superimposed over the private appropriation of the real estate' (p. 278). This suggests a precedent that the granting of mineral rights eventually leads to more formal territorial sovereignty. The establishment of a political community of whalers and miners was important in this: whether something similar happened in outer space might be contingent on whether off-world mining took place through robotics or through human habitation. In any case, the establishment of mining interests had occurred under inter-state recognition of *terra nullius* rather than *res communis* provisions like those established under the OST.

The Spitsbergen scenario – where the flag followed the mine – is but one historical case study that illustrates how sovereignty can devolve from private mineral rights on the frontier. Given the colossal expense of space mining, it is more likely that it will be conducted by the behemoths of the US military-industrial complex than small Silicon Valley style start-ups (perhaps Lockheed-Martin's government contracting will help them afford space mining operations). In this case, the comparison with the charter companies of maritime colonialism would be more overt, should the corporation lead the way in establishing national interests off-world. Alternatively, we could look to case studies in 'free mining', such as the Californian gold panners who briefly formed semi-autonomous political communities in the 19th century. Yet – if we return to the *Orphans* yearning for more immediate pirate utopias – the fundamental reliance on the state's legislative apparatus underscores the implausibility of having a truly stateless space utopia. As privateers and patriots, '[extending] our free-market values into space' (Kerner, cited in Space Frontier Foundation 2015), NewSpace mining firms would effectively extend state influence 'beyond the line' under the guise of entrepreneurial commerce. It serves as a further reminder that, far from being anarchistic or libertarian, the NewSpace philosophy is distinctly neoliberal. Rather than achieving statelessness on the frontier, the state is in fact fundamental for safeguarding the operation of a market for space resources. The act of authorising private property rights in space constitutes a de facto national claim on those resources.

The benign colonialism?

This comparison between maritime colonialism and space mining is valuable on a politico-legal level, yet it involves some obvious points of contrast. The military technoscience of spacefaring powers is yet to be deployed as a means of supporting resource appropriation or the protection of private property on celestial bodies. Several space lawyers have spoken optimistically, noting the possibility that space will continue to be used predominantly for peaceful uses and that multilateral consensus will prevail as space mining inches closer to reality – there is 'good hope for the eventual prevalence of international law to govern space resource activities' (Masson-Zwaan & Palkovitz 2017, p. 5; see also Freeland 2019, p. 8). However, if we look to the historical entanglement of frontier resource appropriation and impulses to national competitiveness and rivalry, we cannot ignore the possibility of violent, 'primitive' accumulation on the space frontier (Marx 2015 [1887]; Dickens & Ormrod 2007; Marshall & da Rimini 2018). Rather than recognise private property's history of violence, however, the NewSpace narrative has a tendency towards historical deletions (Barthes 1973 [1957]; Messeri 2017). The political mythology of NewSpace self-ascribes benevolence to the colonisers, as part of a familiar 'geo-myth' that presents the frontier as a site of progress.

The violence of property

> Our destiny, beyond the Earth, is not only a matter of national identity, but a matter of national security … Establishing the Space Force is critical to preparing the Department of Defense for the evolving warfighting environments of the twenty-first century.
>
> (President Trump, in 'Space Policy Directive 2019')

When we speculate about violence in outer space – such as state-sanctioned violence that protects corporate property – we might be heading towards the terrain of science fiction. Yet, if the reader finds the prospect of an actual 'Star Wars' entirely implausible, it is worth remembering that the US Congress once allocated over US $3 billion for the Reagan Administration's plans to construct particle beam weapons in space (Gerstenzang 1986). The Strategic Defense Initiative was eventually cancelled, but outer space has of course featured in US military planning ever since the Cold War began. For further examples, we can consider that the United States (in 1985) and China (in 2007) have demonstrated an ability to shoot down satellites (so far deployed against their own space assets). In 2019, the Trump Administration established the US Space Force as a unique branch of the US Armed Services. Russia has maintained its own Space Forces in different guises since 1992. The United States's rival space superpower might prove to be the People's Republic of China, which was recently successful in landing on the far side of the Moon. What role might violence play in the state-corporate enclosure of the off-world mineral commons?

The formation of liberal capitalist states was violent, particularly in processes of enclosure and colonialism. Karl Polanyi's narrative of early capitalism revealed that enclosures involved more than the legal, regulatory and administrative functions of the state. In the vein of other historical sociologists Weber (2008 [1919], p. 127) and Marx (2015 [1887]), Polanyi had identified that the commodification of land was enforced, in large part, through 'individual force or violence' and 'war and conquest' (2001, p. 189). Dominion over land and territory was predicated on conquering the common lands of indigenous populations, or subjugating underclasses within a sovereign territory. There was a nexus between what Weber described as the state's monopoly on 'legitimate' violence (2008, p. 127) and the interests of economic elites. George Orwell described the violence of enclosure on English soil:

> ... the landgrabbers did not even have the excuse of being foreign conquerors; they were quite frankly taking the heritage of their own countrymen, upon no sort of pretext except that they had the power to do so. (1944)

Private property in land is inherently violent. In Marshall and da Rimini's words, 'Without violence and its threat, property borders are vague' (2018, p. 51).

Enclosure involved commoners being forcefully evicted or killed in what Marx described as 'primitive accumulation' – capitalism's 'original sin' (2015 [1887], p. 507). For Marx, primitive accumulation was the 'process that transforms, on the one hand, the social means of subsistence and of production into capital, on the other, the immediate producers into wage labourers' – 'nothing else than the historical process of divorcing the producer from the means of production' (Marx 2015, p. 508). Marx described how the global expansion of capitalism required the destruction and dislocation of indigenous societies, where the development of industrial capitalism in homeland metropoles was fuelled by primitive accumulation in the New World.

> The discovery of gold and silver in America, the extirpation, enslavement and entombment in mines of the aboriginal population, the beginning of the conquest and looting of the East Indies, the turning of Africa into a

> warren for the commercial hunting of black-skins, signalised the rosy dawn of the era of capitalist production. These idyllic proceedings are the chief momenta of primitive accumulation. On their heels treads the commercial war of the European nations, with the globe for a theatre. (Marx 2015, p. 533).

While I have argued that the CLSCA and similar national laws represent a similar 'primitive' or primeval act of appropriation (Schmitt 2003), no social dislocation will result from the CSLCA. Dickens and Ormrod have aptly surmised that commodifying the off-world involves a pre-emptive form of primitive accumulation, 'one not dispossessing anyone already using those resources' (2007, p. 59).

Nonetheless, the CSLCA does raise the question of how space property rights would actually be claimed, protected and enforced in outer space. As preposterous as it may have sounded when President Trump announced his intention to establish a US Space Force, it is in keeping with American exceptionalism. Often in the interests of neoliberal hegemony, the 'supposedly uniquely disinterested moral values of American diplomacy' have involved the United States taking on the role 'as the world's police force' in the global commons (Ó Tuathail & Dalby 1994, p. 10).[5] Department of Defense white papers declare that the Space Force would protect the nation's 'unfettered access to, and freedom to operate in space', ensuring both national security and 'economic prosperity' (DoD 2018, p. 5). Policy recommendations from a recent Heritage Foundation *Mandate for Leadership* volume might be the source of the Trump Administration's interest in policing the off-world commons (Heritage Foundation 2016, p. 27). Tronchetti and Liu note that the Trump Administration has 'taken multiple actions aimed at consolidating US leadership in space' – this has included the prospect of further commercialisation of activities traditionally performed by NASA, and an apparent desire to place weapons in orbit (2018, p. 426). The 'lawful violence' of the state – here, a pre-emptive projection of American might – is acting as 'the steel lining to the velvet glove' of commerce (Polanyi 2001 [1944] , p. 14).

Much like the role of charter companies and privateers in furthering imperial causes, space mining could be used to advance national cosmo-strategic imperatives. US space resources law has frequently been justified to the American political establishment through appeals to 'American leadership in space' (e.g. Planetary Resources 2014; ASD 2016, p. 6; Dunstan & Szoka 2017; Richards 2017). NewSpace entrepreneur Robert Bigelow, whose Bigelow Aerospace was developing inflatable space habitats in partnership with NASA, warned of the threat of China's space programme when testifying before the US Congress (Bigelow 2017). China's development of its own commercial space sector is 'not disconnected from its own military' (as though the US military-industrial complex and 'big aerospace' involved an alternative arrangement) and the US Government needs to 'consider the disruptive strategic role China will play' – particularly if it is 'commercial [space policy] with Chinese characteristics' (Bigelow 2017, p. 5). More than just waving the Stars and Stripes, Bigelow points to the military-strategic priorities of the United States while drawing on American antipathy to communism. As per the Cold War, political-economic ideology and geo-strategy may prove to be intractable elements on the space resources frontier.

If a violent space frontier did materialise, we can really only speculate on the form it would take. Military technologies for the space frontier are highly advanced (although many are likely classified). The Space Shuttle began conducting military missions as early as 1985: these are still classified but were likely conducted for signals intelligence and other military communications or surveillance purposes (Howell 2016). Violence could be projected onto the space frontier in forms yet-to-be realised. 'Space Aggressor' squadrons of the US Air Force presently train troops to prepare for emergent threats against US space assets (Walters 2017). The Air Force's *X-37B* drone spacecraft broke the on-orbit endurance record (718 days) for largely classified purposes in 2017 (Ray 2017). Irrespective of any 'old' and 'new' periodisation, the American military-industrial complex was not abandoned with the Cold War – it remains a key driver of contemporary space commercialisation. Among other examples, the *OSIRIS-REx* spacecraft that has recently arrived at the asteroid 101955 Bennu – it was constructed in partnership with arms and aerospace arms giant Lockheed Martin (which I discuss further in the Epilogue).

None of this is to suggest that space mining will inevitably progress on violent grounds. Mineral resources could be responsibly extracted from asteroids as part of the peaceful and cooperative uses of space envisioned under the OST. It is important, however, that we recognise that this is also a speculative position. Competing narratives of cosmopolitanism and exceptionalism have endured in the American space programme ever since President Kennedy's famous 1962 speech launched the space race.[6] We can see this when space miners pitch the O'Neillian cornucopia to the US political establishment: they claim to want to respect international law and elevate the global standard of living, but 'without constraining the rights and the benefits of the freedom of U.S. commercial enterprise' (Richards 2017, p. 7). As I discussed in relation to the terms of the OST, one actor's freedom can easily preclude an another's ability to exercise their own freedoms. We cannot assume that the exercise of US corporate freedoms in space would necessarily lead towards the peaceful, cooperative use of outer space.

The deployment of state-sanctioned force in the protection of corporate-owned space resources appears explicitly in recent, attempted legislation. The *American Space Commerce Free Enterprise Act of 2017* (ASCFE 2017) was passed by the House in April 2018 (though it progressed no further and its 2019 iteration did not progress to the Senate). This bill asserts that the 'private exploration and use of outer space by nongovernmental entities will further the national security, foreign policy, and economic interests of the United States' (ASCFE 2017, s. 2). It further connects the economic activity of corporate actors with the sovereign power of the United States by stating that:

> The President shall ensure that United States entity exploration and use of outer space, including commercial activity and the exploitation of space resources, is secure from acts of foreign aggression and foreign harmful interference and is given due regard, and the President shall uphold the ownership rights of space objects of United States entities. Space objects certified under this chapter shall receive the full protection of the United States. (ASCFE 2017, s. 80111)

Again, we can only speculate how the President ensures that an asteroid miner is 'secure from acts of foreign aggression', or indeed how or why a foreign power would act aggressively millions of kilometres away from Earth. Nonetheless, Planetary Resources and other space corporations have lobbied for the ASCFE (OpenSecrets 2023i). A press release from Atlas think-tank TechFreedom offers the organisation's support of the ASCFE (TechFreedom 2017). As an example of the 'strong state, free economy' aporia, TechFreedom has praised this legislation as a 'light touch to space regulation' (TechFreedom 2017), despite it making the expansive authorisation that 'the full protection' of the United States be used to secure to space mining operations.

The novelty and expense of owning property on the high frontier obscure what, on Earth, is a truism: the state protects its citizens' rights to private property with recourse to 'legitimate' violence. Internal jurisdictions are tasked by national governments with providing a police force to protect against trespass, theft and damage to private property, while national governments recruit and maintain defence forces that protect territorial sovereignty (and the right to defer policing powers within their jurisdictions). In domestic settings, it is clear that the extractive rights of mining multinationals are protected through the exercise or threat of 'legitimate' violence. Consider the 2016 Standing Rock protests, in which Sioux activists rejected the construction of the Dakota Access Pipeline through their traditional lands due to environmental concerns. This grassroots movement against the powers of mineral sovereignty was met with the deployment of a militarised police force, in which local police employed riot gear, armoured vehicles, rubber bullets and other sophisticated technologies of suppression (Patinkin 2016). The militarisation of police forces across North America presents a challenge to the fundamental liberal democratic right of dissent; here it was being used to safeguard appropriation rights of oil companies against indigenous and environmentalist claims. These events mirror the armed conflicts between the Sioux and the US military during the second half of the 19th century, when military forces were deployed to assist frontier gold miners (not to mention the private armies and navies employed by colonial charter companies).

National militaries are also deployed to protect or enable corporate extractivism in foreign jurisdictions and in the global commons. American military supremacy supported the profitability of US oil services and engineering companies in Iraq, such as Halliburton and Bechtel. China, meanwhile, has previously deployed warships to protect oil rigs in the disputed South China Sea. Perhaps the People's Republic of China will introduce its own mining laws for the off-world – such an act would be symbolically supported by what are the world's second-largest armed forces.

American projections of state power into the oceanic commons could be traced to the end of US isolationism and its turn to 'open imperialism' (Schmitt, 2003, p.292), through US annexations following the 1898 Spanish-American War (Puerto Rico, Guam and the Philippines) – not coincidentally the same period in which expansion on the internal frontier was declared finished (US Census Bureau 2012). Parallels could be drawn between the intermingling of national prestige, technological spectacle and projections of state power inherent in both Roosevelt's Great White Fleet of 1907 and American rocket launches since the Mercury era (1958–1963).

In this light, the passage of the CSLCA is not an isolated political triumph for the NewSpace network, but rather reflects a pattern of both unilateral and multilateral resource imperialisms that the United States has undertaken since WW2.[7] There are no client governments to install in outer space, but the extractive rights of US space miners are pre-emptively guaranteed by the US state's military power as much as they are by US public law. The paradoxical nature of NewSpace's relationship with the US Government is further accentuated when it is entrepreneurs with libertarian tendencies that have prompted this anticipatory projection of state power and might onto the space frontier. The US state is asked to protect the libertarian business that pretends to attack it; the 'rebel alliance' of Han Solo-style entrepreneurs turn out to be part and parcel of the Empire.

'Geo-mythography' and the escape from the 'slaughter bench' of history

The trope of the frontier speaks to both violent appropriation and redemption and freedom. Frontier mythology has a highly emotive resonance: it appeals to individual and collective psyches through the frontier's promise of liberation, salvation and re-birth. As Blouet notes, 'states are clever in promoting ambitions in the cloak of emotional appeals' (1994, p. 285). The European colonial powers claimed theirs was a 'civilising mission' (Said 1995), a valorous project of 'bringing light, faith and trade to "the dark places" of the earth' as they murdered and subordinated indigenous populations on the imperial horizon (Lindqvist 2002, p. 12). Ever since the Apollo programme, outer space has held an important place in the emotional fabric of American national culture.

Political mythologies are not opposed to political rationality – they permeate and are indissociable from them (Dean 2006). Political economist Mitchell Dean has illustrated that 'mythic, poetic and symbolic elements' permeate spatial and cartographic notions of political order (2006, p. 1).

Deploying Connery's term 'geo-mythography' (2001), he describes the mythic foundations of Schmitt's conceptions of *nomos*. For instance, Schmitt begins *The nomos of the earth* by saying: 'In mythical language, the earth became known as the mother of law …' (Schmitt 2003, p. 42). Pagan concepts of the Earth Mother are evident in Schmitt's account, which also drew on his conservative Catholicism in noting the herdsman or shepherd in the etymological roots of *nomos* (ibid, pp. 339–340). Indeed, Schmitt focuses on the *nomos* of medieval Europe's *respublica Christiania*, an empire with Holy Rome at its centre acting as *katcheon* or 'restrainer' of the Antichrist (ibid, pp. 58–62; Dean 2006). The contrasts that Schmitt makes between *terra firma* and *mare libre* arrive at a sort of telluric mythos, his genealogy of spatial law and order invoking the 'consecrated sites' and 'sacred orientations' of landed existence (Schmitt, in Dean 2006, p. 10).

The NewSpace imaginary of course involves a break from the 'Earth Mother' – a point Ormrod has argued while drawing on Freudian psychoanalytics (2007, pp. 266–267) – but geo-myths are nonetheless an important part of their public justifications for space colonisation. 'Manifest Destiny' is a geopolitical discourse that emerged from Enlightenment progress ideology and is evident in many phases of American history and in the NewSpace vision (Parker 2009). Beginning with the 19th-century impulse to 'conquer and civilize the "empty continent"', it was the United States's destiny to continue expanding (Ó Tuathail 1994, p. 159). Like *lebensraum*, which had been inspired by Friedrich Ratzel's visit to frontier America, manifest destiny was a means of justifying imperial expansionism. This geo-mythography was wedded to American exceptionalism: if expansion was America's 'destiny', the violence of expansionism was morally justifiable. The political geographer Gerard Ó Tuathail summarises Manifest Destiny with the following quote from founding father Thomas Paine: 'The cause of America … is in great measure the cause of all mankind' (1994, p. 159).

As has been noted in literature on space colonisation, the idea that humanity needs space to expand on the off-world frontier is a techno-utopian version of Manifest Destiny and American frontier mythologies (Kilgore 2003; Parker 2009). In his essay 'Capitalists in Space' (2009), Parker noted the parallels between off-world expansionism and westward frontiers in American culture. He draws attention to the US historian Frederick Jackson Turner, who had argued that when the westward journey ended on the Pacific Coast and the American frontier was effectively closed, it 'augured badly for the future of the United States. American character was defined by novelty, adaptation and growth, so without this imaginative geography of a frontier, there was a danger of atrophy' (Parker 2009, p. 89). We can here recall Gerard O'Neill's fear that a steady state economy would produce a constriction of innovation and creativity that would be 'abhorrent' (Kilgore 2003, p. 159).

For NewSpace and neoliberalism, Property represents Progress. Yet the notion of private property as inherently virtuous rests upon unstable myths

(Christman 2014). Like American exceptionalism, the valorisation of private property rights in the NewSpace and neoliberal imaginary requires erasing or simply forgetting the violence of enclosure and colonialism. Space writer and policy analyst Rand Simberg produced *Homesteading the Final Frontier* (2012) for the Atlas Network's Competitive Enterprise Institute. He asserts that:

> ... under the view of the universe as a frontier full of potential, the resources that could be developed from it offer great opportunity for human flourishing. Centuries of history demonstrate that the best means of doing that is via the free exchange of goods and services, undergirded by legally enforceable private property rights. (Simberg 2012, p. 4)

In Simberg's view, 'centuries of history' validate private property – and not common property – as the driver of human flourishing. With the ahistoricity characteristic of neoliberalism and neoclassical economics, Simberg sweeps aside centuries of appropriation, displacement and violence that followed in capitalism's imperial wake. The history of private property is tainted with discrimination, coercion and the heavy hand of empire – this is inconsistent with the truth claims of universal beneficence inherent in NewSpace private property advocacy (regardless of how violent or peaceful space colonisation ends up being).

In his *Mythologies* (1957), Roland Barthes explored capitalist myths. His description of the 'privation of history' offers some insight into the erasure of property's violent past in space colonisation narratives. According to Barthes, the privation of history was a myth of estrangement that divorced objects from their history.

> Myth deprives the object of which it speaks of all History. In it, history evaporates. It is a kind of ideal servant: it prepares all things, brings them, lays them out, the master arrives, it silently disappears: all that is left for one to do is enjoy this beautiful object without wondering where it came from. (1973, p. 165)

Severing an object from its history – this is how private property on the frontier is able to sit within NewSpace's humanitarian claims. Consider the following remark from Moon Express' Bob Richards:

> As a country built on the foundations of Earth's frontiers, the United States stands unique in all the world with the opportunity to focus the power of its entrepreneurial history and enterprising vision to open up the space frontier, and in so doing, create a peaceful, prosperous and boundless future for all humanity. (Richards 2017, p.1)

The United States *was* actually built upon 'foundations of the frontier', but only because the expansion of Anglo-American sovereignty involved the imposition of European law upon the foundational *nomoi* of native American law. The (un)settling of the American frontier was ultimately not a 'peaceful, prosperous and boundless' process for all Americans. The privation of property history excises the violence, so that colonial power can be ascribed a measure of 'innocence' (Whyte 2018, p. 237), 'as if one can take the good parts of a metaphor, setting the unseemly ones aside' (Messeri 2017).

In NewSpace representations of property and discussions of space colonisation that appear in neoliberal advocacy (see also Singal 2018), the off-world frontier presents a zone of guilt-free appropriation, an opportunity to escape what Hegel described as the 'slaughter-bench' of history (2001, p. 35). Hegel's *Philosophy of History* described how, in the name of progress, 'the happiness of peoples, the wisdom of States, and the virtue of individuals have been victimized' (ibid, p. 33). Hegel viewed the violence of western civilisation as ultimately worthwhile, if it meant the eventual realisation of Freedom – a teleological account of human history that NewSpace appears to share with Hegel, that 'the History of the world is none other than the progress of the consciousness of Freedom' (2001, p. 33).

For NewSpace libertarians, off-world property represents a paradoxical freedom *from* the empire that is enabled *by* the empire. In their heroic colonisation of the off-world, they are relieved from repressing resistant 'commoners', from negotiating over prior land rights and from managing the ecological impacts of resource exploitation – all that needs to be done is undermine international treaty law. Escaping history, the NewSpace salvationist narrative renders unilateral private property law as commensurate with 'the common interest of all mankind in the progress of the exploration and use of outer space for peaceful purposes' (OST 1967, preamble).

Conclusion

In a 2016 press release, Peter Marquez, Planetary Resources' Vice President of Global Engagement, drew on examples from Europe's colonial history while congratulating Luxembourg in joining the United States as imperial guarantors of off-world resource claims (Planetary Resources 2016b). While likely intended as promotional bluster, the exploitation of space resources was nonetheless framed as a form of a 'benign colonialism'.

Outer space is a frontier that, if settled and exploited, would lack the negative outcomes of terrestrial resource exploitation. Valorising and mythologising private property serves to erase a complex and often violent interrelationship between private property and national sovereignty. Just as the imperial projects of European powers were justified as being 'civilising forces' for the 'barbaric' New World, the supporters of space mining claim we are witnessing an 'enterprising vision … for all humanity' (Richards 2017). Yet, in Marshall and da Rimini's words, property often involves a 'piracy of the strong that gives birth to hierarchy and reinforces it' (2018, p. 51). The CSLCA was thus itself a piratical act of neoliberal appropriation, pre-emptively stealing from the common heritage of humankind.

20th-century assertions of US dominance in the global commons of air, sea and space are being re-animated through the private space economy. This intractable linkage between the sovereign power of the state and the economic power of corporations harkens back to the colonial era and the sovereign claims of the privateer and charter corporation. Colonial mineral sovereignty further underlines the fact that the Manichaean binary of the heroic entrepreneur and the tyrannical state is unrealistic in practice. Perhaps the most significant 'geo-myth' within NewSpace and neoliberal ideology is the notion that economic growth can continue indefinitely. The expansionist, post-limits utopia of NewSpace – empowered by the US state and the Atlas Network – is the focus of the following chapter.

Notes

1 Most of this chapter was first published in an article in which I was sole author (Johnson, M. 2018, 'Privateering on the cosmic frontier? Mining celestial bodies and the 'NewSpace' quest for private property in outer space', in J. Arvanitakis and M.Fredriksson (eds.), *Property, Place and Piracy*, Routledge, Abingdon, pp. 123–139).

2 As a point of revision, space mining start-ups were part of the 'business face' of the broader NewSpace network. In contrast with the utopian thinking elsewhere in NewSpace, the business model for space mining was geared towards more sober, pragmatic projects in the form of extracting water from asteroids, separating it into hydrogen and oxygen for fuel and selling it (through presently non-existent mechanisms for off-world trade) to national space agencies and their 'big aerospace' contractors. However, civil society organisations and several founders of the space mining firms within the broader NewSpace network consider *in situ* resource utilisation as the vehicle for the permanent settlement of other celestial bodies. From O'Neill and the L-5 Society through to SpaceX's proposed Colonial Fleet (Musk 2017, p. 49), NewSpace has consistently treated off-world resource appropriation as the key to 'humanising' the cosmos (O'Neill 1977). I thus treat space mining and space colonisation, the visioneer's contradictory impulses of technical pragmatism and utopianism (McCray 2013), as intractable elements in this chapter.

3 Gorbachev's glasnost and perestroika reform agendas had aimed for more gradual transition from communism to a mixed socialist economy, including reforms that gave work collectives and socialist cooperative greater managerial powers and permitted foreign trade, such as the *Law of the Union of Soviet Socialist Republics on state enterprises* (1987) and the *Law on Cooperatives* (1988). Under Yeltsin, the pace of privatisation increased rapidly.

4 Journalist Janine Wedel (1998) recounts how, from 1991 to 1997, Harvard economists Jeffrey Sachs and Lawrence Summers had guided Yelstin's Minister of Finance, Yegor Gaidar, in pursuing shock therapy by eliminating price controls and subsidies. Anatoly Chubais, who had overseen much of Yeltsin's privatisation agenda, had been entrusted by the Sachs-led Harvard Institute for International Development to receive substantial loans from the United States and European Governments. Working for the US Treasury Department, Harvard's Sachs and Summers "used tens of millions in taxpayer dollars" to help Chubais "deform democracy and economic reform in Russia and helped create a fat-cat oligarchy run amok" (Wedel 1998). While I am unaware any participation of the 'Harvard Boys' in the privatisation of Russian space activity, US Government institutions clearly

played a role in the broader currents of privatisation in which swept through Russian politics during this period.

5 The creation of Space Force was a policy directive that was, at the time, inflected with Trumpian hyperbole and incoherence (see also Tronchetti & Liu 2018 on the uncertainty surrounding recent US space policy). Yet Congressman Ken Kramer (R-CO, 1972–87) had actually proposed a 'US Aerospace Force' as early as 1981 (Michaud 1986, p. 217). Bromberg (1999) also notes that NASA's status as a civilian agency was initially uncertain. Would the Apollo 11 astronauts have gone 'in peace for all mankind' if the Moon landings were conducted by a division of the US Air Force?

6 Discussed in Chapter 2.

7 Examples include the case studies in 'mineral sovereignty' and regime change mentioned in Chapter 4, such as in Chile and the Middle East.

7 Techno-utopianism and post-limits environmentalism

We have discussed how NewSpace projects ideals of individual liberty and economic freedom onto the exotic temporal and spatial horizons of a spacefaring future. Yet the aporia at the heart of NewSpace cosmopolitics is consistent with the neoliberal political project. NewSpace's reliance on the sovereign power of national government and the support of the taxpayer is disguised under pirate fantasies and the valorisation of the entrepreneur and the 'free' market. NewSpace actors have dismissed the claim that space colonisation is an 'escape hatch for the rich' (Musk, in Allen & VandeHei 2018) or that the *Commercial Space Launch Competitiveness Act 2015* (CSLCA) represents 'a [further] step towards American domination and hegemony in space' (Kfir 2016). Does a colonisation project founded on private property really aspire to support the human species, or is it more likely a project in lining the pockets of a select few members? As Shammas and Holen note, NewSpace does not herald the off-worlding of *Gattungswesen,* or the 'species-being' of humanity, but rather a 'specific set of entrepreneurs' venturing forth while 'carrying a particular ideological payload' (2019, p. 5). The cosmopolitan, salvationist rhetoric of NewSpace is discordant with national laws that undermine international laws of the space commons, such as the CSLCA, and their evident support from the neoliberal think-tanks of the Atlas Network.

In this chapter, we will return to another paradox of NewSpace: its post-limits environmental imaginary, where the cosmic frontier offers deliverance from planetary ecological catastrophe. The NewSpace network has appealed to environmental conservation as a justification for off-world migration and industrialism, ever since Gerard O'Neill responded to the predictions of the first *Limits to Growth* report (O'Neill 1977; Meadows et al. 1972). In the words of the Space Frontier Foundation (SFF), the colonisation of the Solar System will 'not only preserve the biosphere of earth by using the resources of space' but will present the opportunity to transport 'life to worlds now dead' (SFF, in Tumlinson 2003, p. 2). The National Space Society (a descendant of the L-5 Society) warns of numerous existential threats to human and non-human life on Earth:

DOI: 10.1201/9781003293613-7

> The human species is encountering increased natural, man-made, and extraterrestrial threats, including disease, resource depletion, pollution, urban violence, terrorism, nuclear war, asteroids, and comets … Many forms of animal and plant life on Earth are suffering increased loss of population and quality habitat because of the growing presence of humans on planet Earth, via expansion, pollution, deforestation, fishing, farming, mining, and promotion of certain species of animals and plants … Space industrialization and settlement provide safety valves to relieve the pressures that cause Earth-bound threats. They also provide escape routes in case of catastrophic man-made or extraterrestrial threats. Humanity has inherited the stewardship of the planet Earth. It will therefore need the vast resources of outer space to reverse the damage it has caused to the Earth's biosphere, and ultimately enhance all life on Earth. (National Space Society 2019)

NewSpace's anticipatory discourse is often eschatological or millenarian in nature: it envisions apocalyptic and world-transformative future events while optimistically positing unrealised space technologies as the source of salvation. A 'rapture of the nerds', to borrow an expression from the more irreverent quarters of science fiction literature (Doctorow & Stross 2012).

How do we interpret NewSpace biopolitics? In the first half of this chapter, I will demonstrate that space mining, as justified through recourse to terrestrial environmentalism, rests upon the 'techno-fix': a mode of problem-solving that defers action on immediate ecological crises through the assumption of future technological progress (Clark & York 2013). Like 'clean coal' or geoengineering, space mining represents a case study in neoliberal environmentalism, where the market is presumed to be superior to the state as an architect of solutions to environmental problems (Mirowski, Walker & Abboud 2013). I will argue that NewSpace biopolitics is actually 'post-biological'. NewSpace techno-utopianism involves an assumption that the biophysical limits of Earth and the human body can be overcome through private sector innovation, such that there is no need for a global steady state economy and the attendant constraints of international law. In this sense, NewSpace eschatology resonates with mystic philosophies like Singularitarianism or noöspherism: hypothesised, future evolutionary stages of humankind in which we transcend our connection to the biosphere (Vernadsky 2012 [1938]; Teilhard de Chardin 1964).

NewSpace's project of 'ecological salvation by space colonisation' is undermined by the inherent elitism of its vision and the way in which the CSLCA and subsequent laws have undermined international laws of the global commons. The irony in the NewSpace 'rapture' is that we can attribute many of the crises facing humanity to the very remedies they have proposed for the off-world: extractive industry and the unyielding, largely unfettered exercise of mineral sovereignty (Walker & Johnson 2018). In the second half of this chapter, I gesture towards more pragmatic and egalitarian alternatives to the NewSpace techno-fix – a pathway towards more inclusive and sustainable futures on Earth and the off-world frontier. For this, we will return to Karl Polanyi and his notion of the 'double movement' – the social and political institutions that can protect against the deleterious effects of neoliberalism (2001 [1944]). Following Nanda and Ris (1976) and Baslar (1998), I explore the public trust doctrine (Sax 1969; Babcock 2019) as a governance regime for the global commons of Earth and as an alternative to the unilateral private property regime heralded by the CSLCA. I argue that if we establish global commons and mineral estates as public trusts, predicated on the protection of intergenerational rights and an ethics of stewardship, we might be able to defend humankind's common heritage on Earth and in space against the tide of neoliberal constitutionalism.

NewSpace biopolitics: planetary crisis meets transcendence fantasy

NewSpace actors have argued that endogenous crises (such as ecological collapse produced by industrial pollution, population growth and resource depletion) and exogenous threats (such as meteor impacts) could be mitigated by opening the space frontier to commercial exploitation and human habitation (Space Renaissance USA 2020 [2011]). The NewSpace philosophy engages with environmental problems through what have been called 'techno-fixes' and anticipates that the fundamental biophysical limits of both the planet and the human body can be transcended through technological innovation (Cooper 2007; Clark & York 2013; Walker & Granjou 2017). Reminiscent of Enlightenment progress ideology, there is a faith-like confidence that technology and the market will inevitably deliver us from evils of our own making – a teleological grand narrative promising a future of infinitude and abundance that Walker (2007) has similarly identified in neoliberal growth theory. Space colonisation is perceived to be humankind's ultimate destiny, where techno-capital will transcend the bonds of Earth and the worthy entrepreneurial elect ascend to pioneer the infinite frontier. I will explore similarities between NewSpace and Singularitarianism, a techno-utopian movement resting on even more 'post-biological' foundations. These two movements have over-lapping social networks and share techno-mystic philosophical tenets. I demonstrate how they appear to draw on the 'noösphere' concept: a teleological account of societal evolution predicated on the triumph of reason (Vernadsky 2012 [1938]) and the transcendence of mortal limits (Chardin 1964). Seen in this light, space mining and colonisation may be a means to escape Earth, but are not going to save it.

The biophysical limits of Earth and NewSpace 'techno-fixes'

NewSpace techno-utopianism posits space colonisation as a means of mitigating the risks of planetary ecological collapse and 'fixing' anthropogenic environmental degradation. In spite of copious technological hurdles, NewSpace philosophy treats such a solution as preferable to regulatory mechanisms. As we explored earlier (Chapter 2), Gerard O'Neill's space utopianism was spurred by the first *Limits to Growth* report (Meadows et al. 1972). O'Neill thought space colonisation could 'protect the biosphere from damage caused by transportation and industrial pollution' (1974, p. 36), while also dismissing the regulatory and governmental mechanisms of the 'steady state' economy as a viable alternative (1977). In the NewSpace paradigm, to work within terrestrial biophysical limits means accepting limits imposed by regulation and any global governance, resource re-distribution or environmental management that it might entail. The SFF, for instance, muse that:

> Five hundred years after the beginning of Age of Enlightenment, society has merely expanded the size of its mental prison, and all current thinking is trapped in the cage of earth and its biosphere. This is a cage in our minds. It is this idea lurking behind such phrases as 'limits to growth' or today's vogue term in social planning circles: 'sustainable growth' … Proponents of this view plan for all of the world's people to live under a global set of rules designed to limit our inevitably increasing damage to the biosphere. They hope to 'manage' human society through treaties and agreements that percolate down to the level of local laws … We can sustain the growth of the human species and the other life of planet Earth only by bursting the bubble. We must open the space frontier. (Tumlinson & SFF 1995).

The SFF is correct in pointing to the fallibility of attempts to achieve 'sustainable growth' on a finite planet (Tumlinson & SFF 1995). There is here a failure to acknowledge that reducing Western patterns of energy and resource consumption is an alternative option to leaving Earth. Responsibility for the Anthropocene is unevenly distributed, and 'we' are not 'inevitably' damaging the biosphere (Walker & Johnson 2018, p. 57). Furthermore, the SFF has previously collaborated with the Cato Institute (Hudgins 2002), who have actively campaigned against environmental law and pollution controls (a deliberate and more literal bursting of the life-supporting atmospheric 'bubble').

It is important to note here that, across NewSpace organisations and their investors, there are divergent views on the most pressing of environmental challenges: climate change. For example, the Space Development Foundation has followed in O'Neill's footsteps by emphasising space-based solar power as a solution to climate change (SDF n.d.). The Lifeboat Foundation, meanwhile, appears to support solar power generation on Earth, rather than solely through O'Neill's highly speculative framework (2020a). Planetary Resources briefly pursued small-scale hybrid power generation through their Planetary Power start-up, which sought to improve access to power in remote communities (CrunchBase 2020). By purchasing and expanding SolarCity and Tesla Motors, SpaceX's Elon Musk fuelled the proliferation of commercial solar panels, storage batteries and electric cars. Alternatively, the political donations made by Jeff Bezos' Amazon.com to climate-denying legislators – and the carbon emissions of the company itself – have likely done more damage to the atmosphere than 'going to space to save Earth' will be able to repair (Mahadevan 2019; Chasan 2019; Bezos, in Blue Origin 2019). Moon Express and Planetary Resources backer Peter Thiel has recently provided $1.7 million in funding for the journal *Inference*, which has started publishing pseudoscientific denials of climate change amongst more credible research papers (Becker 2019). The Founding Declaration of the Mars Society (2020 [1998]) noted how comparative planetology of Earth and Venus illuminates the threat of greenhouse gases. Yet the Society's founder and current president, Dr Robert Zubrin, rejects the science of climate change, pillorying Oreskes and Conway's (2010) *Merchants of Doubt* with his *Merchants of Despair: Radical environmentalists, criminal pseudo-scientists, and the fatal cult of antihumanism* (Zubrin 2013).

Despite the evident interest in deploying technological solutions for climate change on Earth in some organisations, NewSpace's broader environmental imaginary ultimately rests upon a project far more elaborate: space colonisation and the 'off-worlding' of industry. Space industrialisation has featured in NewSpace discourse as a means of displacing carbon-intensive industry on Earth. The science fiction luminary Isaac Asimov had espoused the potential for space industrialisation in reducing atmospheric pollution (1985). Writing in a paper for NASA's Langley Research Center, at a time when the Reagan Administration would vehemently undermine anti-pollution laws, Asimov noted that 'we are in danger of poisoning the entire atmosphere' (1985, p. 88). He nonetheless emphasised techno-utopian solutions: 'when we have a factory in space, any unavoidable pollution that it produces can be discharged into space' (ibid, p. 88). For Asimov, it is only a question of 'when' technological change would render this feasible. Like Karl Polanyi, he deployed William Blake's evocative description of the Victorian workhouses, but was less interested in the historical processes that blanketed London in the poisonous fog of waste output – he thought that by off-worlding polluting factories and mines, 'perhaps Earth can get rid of its "dark satanic mills" … without abandoning industrialisation' altogether (ibid, p. 88).

Asimov's 'space industrialisation' bridges the science fiction inspirations behind NewSpace and the neoliberal commitment to endless economic growth. This environmentalism-through-space industrialisation is perpetuated across the NewSpace network. Harrison Schmitt, the Apollo 17 geologist-astronaut and former board member at the neoliberal Heartland Institute, has argued that the Moon's helium-3 reserves offer an unlimited source of clean energy (2006). Planetary Resources' promotional work frequently claims that space mining could (beneficially) expand extractive industry's resource footprint beyond Earth orbit (Planetary Resources 2012; Orsulak 2018). In a TED Talk, one of the company's executives has combined Asimov's off-worlding of all industrial processes with the O'Neillian vision of orbital megastructures:

> We can move our industrial manufacturing into space. All of it. You see, manufacturing is resource consumption: we use the resources of Earth, we

> turn them into manufactured products … What if we gather and harvest all of our raw materials and resources from deep space, and import them to an orbit manufacturing ring around the planet, and then return only the finished product to the surface? … So if we do this – we reverse the human supply chain, we push all of our mining, our manufacturing, outside of the atmosphere – what have we done? We have now zoned the Earth for residential access only. (Orsulak 2018)

Yet space industrialisation is so far from being realised that it is not a viable solution for preserving Earth as a liveable planet, in light of the stark, short-term imperative of rapid and widespread decarbonisation. Given the expenses of the Apollo Program and the failure of commercial spaceflight to achieve more than the (comparatively unambitious) goal of temporarily re-locating a handful of people off-world at a time, the notion of transporting all polluting industry into outer space is nonsensical. Whilst Orsulak's comments are clearly marketing hyperbole, they are nonetheless emblematic of NewSpace's preference for grandiose long-term visions over less exotic and more politically challenging approaches to address the underlying causes of ecological degradation.

The colonisation of space is a future-projected techno-fix that defers resolution to the underlying causes of environmental degradation by assuming exponential (and beneficial) technological change. In the words of political ecologists Clark and York, proponents of techno-fixes attest that 'there is no need to radically transform the social order, as the market will ensure that a technological fix is created to address each environmental problem' – space mining is another 'technological panacea [that] obscures the anti-ecological tendencies of the capitalist system' (Clark & York 2012, p. 23). NewSpace techno-fixes involve both saving the Earth through the mass migration of people and polluting industry, and a 'Plan B' of quarantining of human and non-human life on other planets – a hedging strategy against planetary catastrophe. If we could transport biodiverse genetic material off-world and somehow propagate it outside the atmosphere – even going so far as to 'terraform' other celestial bodies of the Solar System – we'd be 'backing up the biosphere' and avoiding an ecological equivalent to the Alexandria library fire (Diamandis, in Hoffman 2010). Terraforming projects are an extension of geoengineering and propose manipulating the atmospheres and geochemistry of other celestial bodies (predominantly Mars) in order to recreate life-supporting planets elsewhere in the Solar System.[1] As Cooper notes, 'It is no coincidence that the dream of terraformation has arisen at a moment in history when capitalist modes of production are literally testing the limits of life on earth' (2008, p. 39).

NewSpace can be read as a neoliberal environmentalist project: it offers market-based solutions to problems that have been created by capitalist markets (Mirowski 2009, p. 439). Neoliberal environmentalist discourses hold that 'entrepreneurs will innovate market solutions to address dire environmental problems' (Mirowski, Walker & Abboud 2013, p. 85). NewSpace start-ups are an emblematic example of what Mirowski, Walker and Abboud have called the 'whiz-bang futuristic science fiction side of neoliberalism, seed-financed by inspirational billionaire "thought leaders"' (ibid, p. 85). Yet neoliberal environmentalism is, in practice, an oxymoron: innovations range from the ineffective carbon trading permit through to phantasmic 'clean coal'. The techno-fix approach to environmentalism is evidently more suitable for accumulating capital than for alleviating anthropogenic pressures on a finite planet.

The elitist eschatologies of NewSpace and neoliberalism

NewSpace ideology has clear eschatological characteristics. Eschatology comes from the Greek 'eschatos' or end—it means 'doctrine of last things' (Walker 2007, p. 83). Perhaps the archetypal example of eschatological thought is Christianity's Book of Revelations and the anticipated Day of Judgement. Despite its grounding in the 'hard sciences' of engineering, physics and mathematics – and the 'dismal science' of economic orthodoxy – there is an apocalyptic or millenarian undertone to NewSpace's '*urgent* orientation toward a future of space settlement' (Valentine 2012, p. 1049, italics in original). Yet NewSpace frames this urgency in positive terms through what John Bozemann has termed 'technological millenarianism' – 'the opinion that technology will bring about a new golden age in the near future that will create a substantial, and permanent, fundamental improvement in the human condition' (1997, p. 151).

In addition to the 'capitalogenic' risks discussed above (Moore 2023) and other endogenous risks like nuclear war or rampant artificial intelligence (NSS 2018; Lifeboat Foundation 2020a, 2020b), NewSpace actors often point to exogenous sources of a planetary judgement day. Asteroid impacts feature prominently in attempts to make off-world colonisation seem like an urgent imperative (Kfir 2016), in particular the Chicxulub impact that prompted the Cretaceous–Paleogene extinction event 66 million years ago (the end of the dinosaurs). Gamma-ray bursts (GRBs) are also mentioned as another end of day scenario (NSS 2018). They are brief but massive ejections of highly energised light originating from massive collapsing stars – the energy output of GRB990123, for instance, was estimated as 'one hundred quadrillion times more luminous than the Sun' (NASA 2013). Should Earth happen to be in the path of a nearby GRB, the ozone layer would be eviscerated and the planet scorched with ultraviolet radiation (Gronstal 2016). Fortunately, the likelihood of that happening is low – most identified GRBs have been observed in other galaxies, and none of Earth's neighbouring stars appear on the verge of collapse. Similarly, the risk of 'planet killing' asteroid impacts is significantly lower than localised city or regional-level damage (National Science and Technology Council 2018, pp. 2–4).

Neoliberalism also involves an eschatological dimension. Walker (2007) describes the millenarianism of neoliberalism, where the invisible, god-like hand of the market will deliver abundance and prosperity, so long as it is left unimpeded by government regulation and taxation. 'If enough "deregulation" occurs, ultimately "everyone will become rich"' (Walker 2007, p. 83). Free market capitalism has its own mythic and mystic dimensions. Orthodox economic theories of neoclassical and neoliberal economics offer a cosmological model that seeks to explain the totality of human existence. In Gordon Bigelow's words:

> ... it is economics that offers the dominant creation narrative of our society, depicting the relation of each of us to the universe we inhabit, the relation of human beings to God. And the story it tells is a marvelous one. In it an enormous multitude of strangers, all individuals, all striving alone, are nevertheless all bound together in a beautiful and natural pattern of existence: the market. (in Walker 2007, p. 80).

It is at times a more 'mundane' eschatology, where this anticipation of future prosperity is usually expressed in terms of quarterly GDP figures – but nonetheless it employs 'the millennial sense of expectation oriented toward a future temporal horizon' that we also see in NewSpace eschatology (Walker 2007, pp. 79, 93).

The NewSpace goal is to provide 'citizen access' to space (Spencer, cited in Parker 2009, p. 90), while neoliberalism promises that the benefits of corporate freedoms will 'trickle down' for the rest of humanity. But would the off-world 'rapture' really be open to us all? In Christian eschatology, rewards of immortality and abundance were only granted to the worthy. Neoliberal reforms pursued since the Reagan and Thatcher governments, like tax breaks at the highest income brackets and the resultant disparities in global wealth distribution (in conjunction with paternalistic punishments for the poor), bestow rewards to the 'faithful' captains of industry and their shareholders. The elitist escapism in NewSpace, meanwhile, has some roots in O'Neill's *High Frontier* (O'Neill 1977). O'Neill intended to resolve social conflict through an off-world segregation of interest groups, seemingly an escape from deliberative democracy and political compromise. In his words, the 'space communities would be in contrast to the classical Utopias in part because [the pilgrims] could escape so much more successfully' (O'Neill 1977, p. 198).[2]

> What chance will we have, though, here on an Earth ever more crowded and more hungry for energy and materials, to allow for diversity, for experiment, for groups to try in isolation to find better lifestyles? What chance for rare, talented individuals to create their own small worlds of home and family, as was so easy a century ago in our America as it expanded into a new frontier? (ibid, p. 43)

The O'Neillian project represents a fusing of Francis Bacon's New Atlantis – an autonomous refuge for the intellectual elite – and the Mayflower myth of the virtuous pilgrim colonist. The frontier becomes as a site of social experimentation and escape, but not for everybody.

Peter Diamandis, founder of now defunct company Planetary Resources, has been a vocal prophet of the techno-utopian golden age. His book, *Abundance: The future is better than you think* rails against the bleakness of limits discourse, albeit while acknowledging that 'we are still finding proof of [the Club of Rome reports'] veracity most places we look' (Diamandis & Kotler 2012, p. 7). As with O'Neill, whom he had met while founding the Students for the Exploration and Development of Space organisation, this acknowledgement of limits is drowned out by techno-optimist millenarianism:

> Humanity is now entering a period of radical transformation in which technology has the potential to significantly raise the basic standards of living for every man, woman, and child on the planet. Within a generation, we will be able to provide goods and services, once reserved for the wealthy few, to any and all who need them. Or desire them. Abundance for all is actually within our grasp. (ibid, p. 9)

To take the benefits of technological change beyond the grasp of 'the wealthy few' ... This is a humanitarian impulse at odds with Planetary Resources' role in lobbying the US Congress for the CSLCA, which may result in the benefits of the space harvest accumulating in private hands. Such optimistic, egalitarian rhetoric clashes with the O'Neillian vision and what often appear like zero-g recreations of the 'seastead' or Ayn Rand's 'Galt's Gulch' – the refuge for the virtuously selfish entrepreneur (Rand 2005 [1957]). Much like Christianity's rapture, ascending to the off-world via private property claims will most likely be a reward for the elect.

The mortal limits of the human body

If such an off-world exodus is to eventuate, NewSpace techno-fixes also need to address the biological limits of the human body in the sheer inhospitableness of outer space. The requirements of human life include: a pressurised, breathable atmosphere; ample water, food and gravity; and protection from cosmic and solar radiation. For all these physiological ingredients for human existence, we are fundamentally reliant on the atmosphere, biosphere and magnetosphere, respectively. To use Schmitt's (androcentric) words, 'the human is a son of the earth, and so he shall remain as long as he remains human' (2015, p. 81). To reiterate the difficulty of living outside Earth's protective spheres on the off-world *todesraum* (Chapter 3), we can look to the colossal expense involved in maintaining the *International Space Station* (ISS) – only a small living space within Earth's gravity well.

The vision of space colonisation rests upon an assumption that the hazards of outer space will inevitably be overcome through creativity, innovation and entrepreneurialism. Gerard O'Neill designed vessels that rotated to generate centrifugal force and produce artificial gravity (O'Neill 1974, p. 32). This might mitigate the loss of muscle and bone density caused by microgravity environments (and the need for astronauts to perform 5 hours of exercise per day). It might also help reduce the tendency for internal organs to become more spherical and less effective during extended stays in space (May et al. 2014). Water ice derived from asteroid mining could be chemically separated into oxygen to make breathable air (NSS 2012, p. 15). Another, more speculative solution is to use cyanobacteria to photosynthesise oxygen from carbon dioxide (Worden 2009, p. 23). The lack of a magnetosphere makes human and non-human life vulnerable to carcinogenic mutations produced by galactic cosmic rays and solar energetic particles (National Research Council 2006). K. Eric Drexler, a nanotechnologist, former L-5 Society activist and protégé of O'Neill, had proposed *in situ* manufacturing of protective shielding for spacecraft and habitats using barriers of asteroidal rock and 'soil' (Drexler 1983). The promise of technology means that, for NewSpace, the market will always find solutions to what appear as insurmountable barriers to living off-world.

The techno-libertarian aversion to space bureaucracy seems to downplay the contributions made by public sector technoscience in developing off-world life-supports. Mazzucato's (2013) history of the 'entrepreneurial state' reveals that many core innovations of the ICT industries derived from direct state patronage. In addition to the real achievements of the Apollo Program and the ISS, US Government programmes were equally capable of 'blue sky' musings about how to address the hostility of space. In 1963, NASA commissioned defence contractor United Aircraft to undertake the *Engineering Man for Space: The Cyborg Study* report (Driscoll 1963; Launius 2010). The study took the view that, rather than make space safe for astronauts through habitats, the human body could be engineered to adapt to the space environment. The project investigated 'reducing metabolic demands and attendant life support requirements' through artificial lungs, hearts, and kidneys, while induced hypothermia could act as a metabolic retardant and pathway to suspended animation (Driscoll 1963, p. 76). Ultimately, the project concluded with an acknowledgement that such technologies were 'beyond current capabilities' of the 1960s (Launius 2010, p. 126).

In the decades since, engineering artificial biospheres has proved as challenging as 'cyborg studies'. In 1991, a Texan oil magnate funded the Biosphere II experiment in Arizona, which attempted to house eight people in fabricated, closed ecosystems with only sunlight as an external input. After 15 months, it was apparent that the closed system was unable to produce enough oxygen for the eight people sealed inside, and the experiment was deemed a failure (Launius 2010, p. 125). More recently, Walker and Granjou (2017) describe the European Space Agency's Micro-Ecological Life Support System Alternative (MELiSSA) experiment, which is researching artificial closed-loop biospheres for sustaining astronaut crews on long-distance missions, 'aiming to achieve a complete and continuous conversion of human wastes into edible biomass, drinking water and breathable air' (Walker & Granjou 2017, p. 62). Such a project requires a steady state of 100% recycling and regeneration of life supports (air, water and food), in addition to deep space astronauts' psychological tolerance for these processes during year-long journeys to neighbouring celestial bodies. The closed-loop production systems required by space travel are entirely anathema to NewSpace's prerogatives of infinite extraction and consumption (ibid, p. 61). The central problematic for O'Neillian space environmentalism is that, while industrial capitalism has unintentionally engineered a dying Earth, no one is currently capable of engineering a life-supporting micro-ecology that supports human life in space.

The singularity, neoliberalism and the noösphere: transcending the biosphere and human biology

Neoliberal capitalism's prerogative of infinite accumulation – particularly as manifest in mining – is discordant with NewSpace's ties with the supposed 'knowledge economies' of the information and communication industries. The tech entrepreneur believes himself to deal in incorporeal ideas and 'solutions', not the biophysically irreversible exercise of geological power (Vernadsky, in Guillaume 2014, p. 138). Techno-utopian faith in reason and innovation is not grounded in ecological reality but, rather, technological infinitude. There is an evident tension between disembodied 'knowledge economies' and the Anthropocene, this latest chapter in deep history that is being written by the key agents of extractive capitalism. In the face of planetary crisis and human mortality, movements like NewSpace and Singularitarianism believe in The Promise that the biophysical limits of the Earth and the body will inevitably be overcome.

The concept of the noösphere is helpful for conceptualising this ideational/materialist disjuncture at the core of NewSpace techno-fixes and eschatology. The noösphere is also a helpful framework to explore the mystic and mythological inclinations of techno-utopian movements more broadly. The noösphere concept was articulated, in part, by Vladimir Vernadsky – the progenitor of the Anthropocene concept whom we discussed in relation to the geological power of mineral sovereignty (see Chapter 4, introduction). Like NewSpace precursor Konstantin Tsiolkovsky, Vernadsky was a cosmist philosopher. Siddiqi describes cosmism as a techno-utopian philosophy focused on 'the evolution of both humanity and the universe and the relationship between the two', merging Bolshevik emancipatory imperatives with orthodox Christian concepts of resurrection and immortality (Siddiqi 2008, p. 265). The noösphere was that 'era of reason' that Vernadsky had used to describe human agency as a geological force re-shaping the Earth (Guillaume 2014, p. 138). Davis summarises the Vernadskyian noösphere as the belief that 'planetary evolution was passing from a stage determined by biological laws to one moulded by conscious human activity' (Davis 2015, p. 306). Noösphere translated from Greek as 'mind sphere' or 'thinking stratum' – Vernadsky considered humanity's technoscientific mastery of nature to be 'the final stage of Earth's evolution driven by the powers of interconnected human minds' (Savelyeva 2017, p. 506).

Vernadsky's use of the term – which he first used in a work that introduced a more significant terminological innovation, *The Biosphere* (1926) – owed much to his tenure at the Sorbonne University in Paris. In Paris, he engaged with colleagues such as the mystically inclined mathematician Édouard Le Roy (to whom he credited the term) and the Jesuit palaeontologist Pierre Teilhard de Chardin (Savelyeva 2017, p. 506). Tamar Savelyeva (2017) has charted a genealogy of non-Western sustainability discourses and draws attention to two different strands of 'noöspherism'. For the pioneering geochemist Vernadsky, the noösphere was anthropocosmic in locating human origins 'in the depths of the universe' and it was a 'purely scientific notion' (ibid, pp. 506–507). In Vernadsky's words:

> … we can distinguish an expression of the influence on the structure of the noösphere of two areas of human thought: the sciences common to all reality (physics, astronomy, chemistry, mathematics), and sciences related to the Earth (biological, geological, and humanistic sciences) … Science has a real existence, and like Man himself, is most closely and inextricably bound to the noösphere. The individual is obliterated – 'decomposed' – when he goes beyond the logical grasp of his intellect. (Vernadsky 2012 [1938], pp. 30–31).

Regardless of the primacy of human cognition in the Vernadskyian noösphere, it is nonetheless comparable to the telluric or Earth-bound accounts of political community of Schmitt and Polanyi. As Hamilton and Grinevald describe it, Vernadsky's noösphere was a conceptualisation of 'collective consciousness tethered to the biogeochemical processes' that could be shaped 'by a creature that *belonged* to the evolving biosphere' (Hamilton & Grinevald 2015, p. 65, emphasis added).

Teilhard had also adopted the term in his writing (Teilhard de Chardin 1964), and his work constitutes a second strand of noöspherism (Savelyeva 2017).[3] In contrast to Vernadsky, Teilhard emphasised the spiritual dimensions of this supposed societal evolution towards a noösphere, and it was 'anthropocentric, keeping the human-nature relationship in dominance of the former' (Savelyeva 2017, p. 506). The Teilhardian noösphere appears to have fused the Cartesian mind-over-matter dualism with Christian notions of 'impurity of the flesh'. For Teilhard, the noösphere was an eschatological end goal he called the Omega Point, the 'final maturing and ecstasy of Mankind' (Teilhard de Chardin 1964, p. 127). In his investigation of techno-mysticism, Eric Davis (2015) eruditely summarises the Teilhardian noösphere:

> Teilhard was a global perfectionist who believed that the divine progressively realized itself through the lumbering machinery of history,

> technological as well as natural. Teilhard's mysticism thus fused two contradictory vectors of the Western spirit: the world-denying ascent toward transcendence and the headlong plunge toward the total domination of matter. (Davis 2015, p. 308).

Rather than being tethered to the biosphere, Teilhard's noösphere accentuated human capacity for reason by insisting that the 'thinking stratum' would eventually and inevitably separate itself and exist 'outside and above the biosphere' (Teilhard de Chardin 1964, p. 163).

The teleology of the Teilhardian noösphere resonates more strongly with the escapism and infinitude of NewSpace's space colonisation project. Hamilton and Grinevald argue that Teilhard was not a precursor to the Anthropocene concept, and suggest that:

> If for Teilhard the noösphere represented the power of the whole of humankind's consciousness raised above and purified of its earthly connections, the Anthropocene in the approach of Earth system scientists – for whom explosive human population and its total industrial metabolism have become an accelerating force of nature – has dragged consciousness back into the Earth. (2015, p. 68).

Teilhard's noösphere thus stands in contrast to Vernadsky's embedding of consciousness in the biosphere, or indeed the contemporary political movements that seek to protect Earthly commons. This is clearly not the case for NewSpace advocates of the off-world techno-fix, who prefer to accentuate 'spirits' of innovation and entrepreneurialism (Zubrin 1994; Hudgins 2011). Karl Löwith described teleology as 'an irreversible direction toward a future goal' (1949, p. 54), and this aptly describes NewSpace's assumption of radical technological improvement leading towards a future that is 'better than you think' (Diamandis & Kotler 2012). There is also a teleological dimension to NewSpace understandings of social-ecological relationships (Tumlinson & SFF 1995; Space Renaissance USA 2020 [2011]). Anthropogenic pollution here takes the form of an invisible hand of Malthusian inevitability that no legislative intervention could ever prevent. Again, the 'inevitable' trope neglects the support that NewSpace has received from actors within the Atlas Network, which has organised obstruction to the fortification of environmental consciousness within binding international law.

We can see some philosophical and political overlap between NewSpace and other extropian movements. Davis describes Teilhard's noösphere as 'a kind of theological Extropianism', a 'synthesis of science and spirit' that 'molded together Darwin and the divine' (Davis 2015, pp. 308–309). Contemporary extropianism is a techno-utopian belief system that seeks to problematise the second law of thermodynamics, or the entropy law: that any natural system has an inherent tendency towards the dissipation of useful energy, an inexorable movement towards 'irreversibility, depletion, waste and disorder' (Walker 2007, p. 30). Extropianism, conversely, is defined by its adherents as 'the extent of a living or organizational system's intelligence, functional order, vitality, and capacity and drive for improvement' (Extropy Institute 2005). Like the 'visioneering' of NewSpace (McCray 2013), extropian movements overlap with more sober academic disciplines – the computational and life sciences, for example. Extropians prophesise accumulative improvements in vitality and intelligence in the hope that the human body can be transformed for an era of 'post-humanity'. They draw on an array of scientific knowledges and practices that are diverse in their veracity: cryonics, nanotechnology, life extension, genetic engineering, artificial intelligences and Singularitarianism.

Singularitarianism is an extropian movement that shares similar assumptions and beliefs with NewSpace, and a similar social and financial network. The notion of 'the Singularity' is borrowed from cosmology and mathematics: a point in time and space beyond which exponential change is possible and does not conform to preceding rules and patterns (Shanahan 2015, p. xv). Originating with science fiction writer and mathematician Vernor Vinge, the technological Singularity represented 'the point at which greater-than-human machine intelligence begins rapidly improving itself, bringing an end to human-directed history' (Hughes 2012, p. 763). More recently, Ray Kurzweil, Google's Director of Engineering, has been a preeminent Singularitarian. In his *The Singularity is near: when humans transcend biology* (2005), Kurzweil draws heavily on Moore's Law, the teleological notion of 'accelerating returns' in innovation and computing power.

There is an apocalyptic scenario that many activists and texts have attached to the Singularity, simultaneously lauding human mastery over nature while fearing its obsolescence through or oppression by machine intelligence (Farman 2012). As anthropologist Abou Farman (2012) has noted, Singularitarianism also heralds the communion of humanity with high technology, ushering in a new age of peace, plenty and prosperity. The Singularity is hypothesised to enable extending human lifespans, curing diseases, ending world hunger, bringing people and species back from the dead, and even allowing us to upload human consciousness into computers – leading to immortal 'software-based humans' (Kurzweil 2005, p. 243). The Terasem Movement, for example, synthesise a Singularitarian-NewSpace immortality fantasy, proposing that 'mind files' such as this could be transmitted to across the light-years of interstellar space and human beings reconstituted in new forms by (hitherto undiscovered) advanced technological civilisations (Farman 2012, p. 1081).

Singularitarianism is even more fantastic than NewSpace in its dismissing of the biological. A contempt for the human body – 'the meatsack' – and mortal biology stems from Singularitarian post-humanity. Farman described the movement as attempting to take the self 'beyond the wetness of its human platform' (2012, p. 1084). This is reflective of the inherently androgenic nature of Cartesian dualism, as identified by feminist environmental theorists

(Plumwood 2002). Compared with NewSpace's emphasis on economic liberty, there are more pronounced progressive or socialist blocs within the broader extropian and transhumanist movements. Hughes (2012) details this egalitarian techno-utopian history: from the Marxist bioutopianism of geneticist J.B.S. Haldane that opposed the eugenics movement of the 1920s, through to contemporary 'bioliberal' and 'technoprogressive' members of the World Transhumanist Association, who have called for social democratic measures like improved access to emerging health technologies like bionic ears.[4]

However, Singularitarianism has shifted towards a neoliberal idiom, and the Singularitarian network features some of our recurring characters.[5] With Kurzweil, Planetary Resources CEO Diamandis founded the Singularity University (essentially a start-up 'incubator') in NASA's Ames Research Center in Silicon Valley. Larry Page, co-founder and CEO of Google, had contributed financial support to both Singularity U and Planetary Resources. Elon Musk has recently launched Neuralink, a start-up that researches brain–machine interfaces in the hope of reprogramming our neural code, helping us become one with our software innovations in an 'if you can't beat them, join them' approach to artificial intelligence (Kosoff 2017). Peter Thiel, a financial backer of Planetary Resources and Moon Express, was also a supporter of the Machine Intelligence Research Institute and the life-extension Methuselah Foundation (Hughes 2012). Thiel had funded a libertarian coup of the World Transhumanist Association (now Humanity+), helping to install fellow Seasteader Patri Friedman onto its Board of Directors (Hughes 2012, p. 766).

Through Singularitarianism, we can see the noösphere and the techno-fix resonating with neoliberal thought on an epistemological level (similar to the resonance of the landless NewSpace economy with neoclassical economics' landless model of economic relationships, discussed in Chapter 3).[6] Neoliberalism's deified Market is itself a techno-mystic entity, a private property-based noösphere disembedded from the geosphere and biosphere. In Mirowski, Walker and Abboud's words, neoliberalism goes further than its neoclassical forebear in treating the market as an 'arbiter of truth', a 'self-organising system of distributed knowledge' that is 'smarter than any human being' (2013, p. 83). Hayek's (1950) model of market exchange asserted that it was the transmission and reception of price signals that coordinated buyers and sellers. He theorised the market as an omniscient information processor, allocating resources through the bits and bytes of the price signal in a 'spontaneous order' that was decentralised and superior to the centralised decision-making of the state. This idea of the Market as an omnipotent, autonomous force uncontrollable by the state resonates with the Singularity's mythology of exponential machine superintelligence.

For all of NewSpace's newfangled engineering innovations, its speculative techno-fixes have historical roots as deep as Russian cosmism. As early as the 1920s, the writing of Konstantin Tsiolkovsky (Vernadsky's contemporary) anticipated a future of human spacefaring and articulated a need for new frontiers and emancipation from Earth.

> We are further compelled to take up the struggle against gravity, and for the utilisation of celestial space and all its wealth, because of the overpopulation of our planet. Numerous other terrible dangers await mankind on the Earth, all of which suggest that man should look for a way into the Cosmos. (Tsiolkovsky 1960, p. 372).

Tsiolkovsky simultaneously recognised the finite limits of the Earth while proposing speculative and fantastic possibilities for bypassing these fundamental constraints. Tsiolkovksy emphasised the dangers of a crowded planet, rather than the 'terrible dangers' that await humankind in the sheer hostility of outer space. Given that he was writing well before any humans had ever visited outer space, this rosy view of life on the space frontier can be forgiven. However, the NewSpace network has more recently perpetuated this techno-optimism in spite of the obvious and numerous challenges that need to be overcome if deep space is to be of any use for Earthly environmental imperatives (at least, on a timeframe in which averting planetary ecological catastrophe is remotely possible).

The speculative solutions proposed by NewSpace involve a human and non-human 'species survivalism' that is at odds with the emphasis on individual liberties and personal freedoms that appears in NewSpace discourse, and the instances in which NewSpace has rejected collective obligation in the form of common property and international law. NewSpace environmentalism also sits uneasily with the largely anti-environmentalist Atlas Network, which has continuously sought to capture state sovereignty in order to protect extractive industry from any 'steady state' curtailments of economic growth. If – in Tsiolkovsky's words – humanity ever *needs* to 'look for a way into the Cosmos', the most likely reason will be unbearable changes to the Earth caused by unsustainable processes of industrial capitalism that are directed by those individuals and interest groups profiting from its extension. NewSpace biopolitics reflects what Melinda Cooper has described as 'capitalist delirium', predicated on 'the breakdown and recreation of whole worlds … [The] delirium of contemporary capitalism … is intimately and essentially concerned with the limits of life on earth and the regeneration of living futures – beyond the limits' (Cooper 2007, p. 28). When we consider that investment in NewSpace mining has predominantly arrived from capitalist elites, as opposed to the 'ordinary citizen', it seems more likely that a profit-based colonisation of the off-world represents a chance for deliverance from (rather than resolution to) the 'terrible dangers' that will face those left behind on Earth.

Defending the common heritage of humankind

The paradox of space mining, in a social-ecological sense, is that the Solar System is neither *terra* nor *nullius*. The enclosure of the (presumably abiotic) space commons may not provoke a political animus comparable to the environmental politics of Earth. Yet, as I have argued (Chapters 4 and 5), the undermining of the *res communis* principles of the *Outer Space Treaty* and *Moon Agreement* are reflective of the neoliberal obstruction of cooperative action to preserve Earthly commons and egalitarian socio-economic outcomes. At stake in outer space and on Earth are the rights of future generations to share and benefit from the spaces and resources that should be held in common by the present generation. How can we defend the common heritage of humankind, on Earth and in space? In this section, I revisit Karl Polanyi's *The Great Transformation* (2001 [1944]) and discuss politico-legal counter-movements that offer a social democratic and cosmopolitan alternative to the unilateral private ownership provisions of the CSLCA. I pay particular attention to Joseph Sax's (1969) revitalisation of the ancient Roman public trust doctrine in modern environmental law, as this defence of public or common rights to natural resources presents potential remedies for tragedies of the commons on Earth and in space.

Institutional 'double movements' in response to unilateral space resources law

If we assume that some degree of private and profitable off-world resource appropriation takes place in the future, how might it be directed towards inclusive human futures in space? I will frame this question in terms of the Polanyian 'double movement'. In *The Great Transformation*, Karl Polanyi argued that the essential substance of human society – particularly land and human labour – was transformed into 'fictitious' commodities and made subordinate to the volatility of capitalist markets (2001 [1944], ch.6). While Polanyi investigated the extension of market society, he was equally concerned with ways of shielding society from this extension. He argued that modern economic history involved an 'extension of the market organization in respect to genuine commodities' but 'was accompanied by its restriction in respect to fictitious ones ... a network of measures and policies was integrated into powerful institutions designed to check the action of the market relative to labor, land, and money' (2001, p. 79). Against the tide of commodification, these 'double movements' had partially de-commodified and insulated public goods and the essential qualities of human life from market forces (Polanyi 2001, p. 79). Neither the movement towards commodification nor this protective countermovement was inevitable. As with fictitious commodification, the countermovement necessarily involved political, legal and cultural institutions intervening to protect human society from the competitive logic of the volatile market.

Polanyi provided numerous examples of the 'double movements' that occurred during the ascension of market capitalism, albeit with less attention given to the commodification of land. Counter-movements against the commodification of human beings (in the form of labour markets) included protective measures like trade unions and factory laws that established fair prices and favourable conditions for labour (ibid, p. 81). Central banking and management of money supply would provide 'a buffer between the internal and external economy', offering some protection against the shocks that would follow from fluctuations in the price of 'commodity money' bound to the international gold standard system (ibid, p. 208). Even Tudor and early Stuart monarchs used 'the power of the central government to relieve the victims of the transformation' wrought by rapid enclosure and attempted 'to canalize the process of change so as to make its course less devastating' (ibid, p. 40). *The Great Transformation* was published two decades prior to the cultivation of environmentalism within the Western political consciousness.[7] Nonetheless, Polanyi expressed concern for the protection of 'the integrity of the soil and its resources ... even the climate of the country which might suffer from the denudation of forests, from erosions and dust bowls' (ibid, p. 193). He identified protective movements for nature, like 'land laws and agrarian tariffs [that] were called into being by the necessity of protecting natural resources and the culture of the countryside' (ibid, p. 138).

What might a double movement look like in outer space? What would it be responding to? The *Outer Space Treaty* (OST) may initially appear as a protective countermovement in the Polanyian sense. However, this Treaty was as much a movement against militarisation and state territorial claims as it was a declaration of universal common rights to use and benefit from outer space. The United States pushed negotiations away from the articulation or suppression of economic rights in space, and subsequently the OST was not 'designed to check the actions of the market' (Polanyi 2001, p. 79).[8]

The *Moon Agreement*, however, was clearly part of a double movement. UN declarations and multilateral agreements of the 1970s–1980s – in particular the highly comparable UN *Convention on the Law of the Sea* – declared that certain global commons were the 'common heritage of mankind'. The *Moon Agreement* was a reaction against the prevailing unfairness of the global economy and a pre-emptive movement against the potential over-exploitation of the space commons. Article 4 states, for example: 'Due regard shall be paid to the interests of present and future generations as well as to the need to promote higher standards of living and conditions of economic and social progress' (Moon Agreement 1979, Art. 4). It explicitly addressed the question of private resource exploitation in outer space and was part of a broader socialist countermovement against unequal economic development (the New International Economic Order of the UN's G-77 caucus). Through the limited endorsement of the NIEO and *Moon Agreement* in the most economically advantaged nations, we can see the 'back and forth' of the double movement – a pre-emptive de-commodification movement pushed back by a movement seeking to maintain corporate extractive rights (Block and Somers 2014, p. 220; see also Peck 2013). Even when successful, de-commodification is neither static nor permanent. The ascension of neoliberal international law (e.g. the 'Washington consensus') was itself a countermovement against the initial gains of the NIEO (Bair 2009).

What counter-movements can we see against the CSLCA? Several examples of state-based opposition have appeared in the annual Legal Subcommittee (LSC) meetings of the United Nations Committee on the Peaceful Uses of Outer Space (UNCOPUOS). The Russian submission to the 2016 UNCOPUOS LSC offered the most forthright opposition to the CSLCA, asserting that it manifested 'a total disrespect for international law order' [sic] and was in keeping with 'the notorious doctrine of domination in outer space' (UNCOPUOS 2016, p. 6).[9] Given Russia's annexation of Crimea two years earlier, it is important to note that this comment is coming from a rival space superpower with a propensity to bypass the 'binding' principles of the international legal order when expedient. In the 2017 meeting of the LSC, Belgium (a member state of the European Space Agency) reaffirmed its commitment as a state party to the *Moon Agreement*, while taking aim at the creative interpretations of the OST that have emerged in the wake of the CSLCA (UNCOPUOS 2017, p. 3).[10] Following a proposal from Belgium and Greece at the 2019 UNCOPUOUS LSC, a working group on space resources law was proposed for the recently cancelled 2020 UNCOPUOUS meeting (UNCOPUOS 2019, p. 2).[11] While Belgium and Greece have since become signatories to the Artemis Accords, these past examples underscore that the off-world march of neoliberalism is not guaranteed to be a unidirectional process. However, such opposition to the CSLCA's terms or its unilateral nature also highlights the limits of the Polanyian double-movement concept, given that his analysis was focused primarily on the emergence of new institutions within the nation state (as opposed to counter-proposals to the CSLCA emerging within existing institutions of international law).

Concerns about the CSLCA are not limited to state practice. Academic institutions also voiced concern around the CSLCA, such as the Hague Space Resources Governance Working Group (SRGWG). The principles of the *Moon Agreement* have been perpetuated by the SRGWG, particularly the proposal to establish an 'international regime … to govern the exploitation of the natural resources of the Moon [and other celestial bodies] as such exploitation is about to become feasible' (*Moon Agreement* 1979, Art. 11 at 5). Such a regime was premature when the *Moon Agreement* was opened for signature and it would still be premature in lieu of any actual technologies of commercial space mining. Nonetheless, the Hague SRGWG forum was established in 2016 following the passage of the CSLCA, to be a forum fostering 'dialogue and cooperation between governments, industry, international organizations, academia and civil society on the technical and socio-economic aspects of space resources activities' (The Hague International Space Resources Governance Working Group 2018). The SRGWG was primarily a consortium of universities with space law or engineering departments (headquartered at the International Institute of Air and Space Law at Leiden University, The Hague). The SRGWG also sought stakeholder input: space miners Deep Space Industries and iSpace (Japan) were among the SRGWG's sponsors. The SRGWG's 'Building Blocks' were offered as potential best practice guidelines for future discussions or soft law agreements, and were supported by some state delegations in a 2019 UNCOPUOUS LSC meeting (UNCOPUOS 2019, pp. 33–35).[12]

The SRWG draft building blocks could be considered an attempt at compromise between elite mining firms and the rest of the world. The Working Group's work (and that of the UNCOPUOS deliberations) appear to be valuable first steps towards a social democratic compromise on multilateral grounds, a process that might address the US-first ethos of the CSLCA, while offering a 'third way' alternative to the socialist-capitalist political binary that often animates NewSpace. Block and Somers note that Polanyi 'believed that it is possible to transcend the painful back and forth of the double movement by durably subordinating the economy to social life' (2014, p. 220). The provision of general welfare and an economic basis for individuals' freedom of self-determination need not come at the price of innovation or profitability. Constraints on commodification and resource appropriation do not necessarily engender the yoke of communist totalitarianism.

Outside the SRWG, academics have offered promising policy recommendations for achieving such a balance between developed world elitism and a desire to ameliorate global inequality. For instance, Freeland notes that the *Moon Agreement*'s use of the term 'equitable' does not necessarily 'mean equal, and therefore does not envisage a totally one-sided approach solely for the benefit of developing countries' (Freeland 2017). Baslar (1998) argues that unless private entities exploit off-world mineral resources, *no one* will derive benefits from off-world resources – given that governments appear disinterested in conducting publicly owned mining operations in outer space. He thus suggests a modest 2–3% resource profit tax on off-world mining, payable to some international authority (1998, p. 190). This proposal would represent a globalised version of resource policy from the age of 'royal metals', in which the authority to mine was delegated to joint-stock companies in exchange for royalties payable to state parties uninterested in exploiting the resources themselves (Nef 1964; Walker & Johnson 2018, p. 60). The 'international fund' might resemble a sovereign wealth fund that collected resource rents and distributed them to non-spacefaring countries (as I discussed in Chapter 4; see also Levine 2015).

The CSLCA is a unilateral private property regime that did not impose obligations to pay taxes or rents – it is inadequate for delivering economic benefits outside of the US space industry. Fabio Tronchetti has argued that private space mining would be legal but only if it adheres to the general principles in the OST – this exploitation must take place for the benefit of all nations (2009, p. 235; see also International Institute of Space Law 2016, pp.28–29). This point was also expressed by delegates in the 2019 UNCOPUOS LSC meeting (UNCOPUOS 2019, pp.257–258). Tronchetti proposes a regime that merges the provisions of the *Moon Agreement*, Part XI of the *Law of the Sea Convention* (UNCLOS III) and the International Telecommunications

Union conventions for geostationary orbit (2009, p. 241). Mining licenses would be granted by a democratically elected 'International Space Authority' (Tronchetti 2009, pp. 246–252). Tronchetti proposes that this 'legal regime should not contain any mandatory mechanism obliging States or private operators to share the benefits derived from their exploitative activities' (2009, p. 282). He grounds this opinion in the *realpolitik* of the *Moon Agreement* 'defeat' and considers that the success of any international regime will be dependent on the participation of powerful developed states (ibid, p. 282). Tronchetti concludes by offering more limited policy recommendations for ensuring that off-world resource exploitation proceeded with some commitment to equitability.[13]

Is this a reasonable compromise? My view is that, as per Baslar (1998, p. 190), a global fund that collected and re-distributed revenue from a 'space mining super profit tax' would be preferable to the more limited benefit mechanisms proposed by Tronchetti, though his recommendations are pragmatic in the face of 'strong state' power. Such a fund could be used for developing countries to purchase cargo space on rocket launches – for scientific experiments or remote sensing satellites, for instance – in keeping with the OST's principle that all states should have access to space on a non-discriminatory basis (OST 1967, Art. 1). Any re-distributed resource revenue could also be used for domestic social, economic or environmental outcomes, such as mitigating or adapting to the effects of climate change. Or it could be used for novel purposes, like the global 'universal basic income' proposed by Levine (2015). A fund such as this could act as reparative intergenerational justice: a form of economic compensation for the unjust and often violent exploitation of mineral commonwealths in the past and as a broader acknowledgement of the injustices of Earthly colonialisms and neo-colonialisms (often perpetuated by Western nations that are now in a position to lead the exploration and use of outer space). This would be in keeping with Dickens and Ormrod's suggestion that:

> … rather than being founded on the interests of capital, and individualist fantasies, the humanization of outer space could emphasise collective responsibilities on Earth and try to ensure that any gains made through space exploration were spread throughout to improve the lot of the dispossessed on Earth (as was the original aim of the United Nations Moon Agreement). (2007, p. 190)

Such a fund might be idealistic, but it is less utopian (in the pejorative sense) than imagined trickle-down benefits engendered by mass migration and industrialisation to the off-world.

However, the terrestrial history of mineral sovereignty tells us that even modest constraints imposed on private space mining interests may be undermined through the capture of democratic institutions. Private mining firms that have drawn on the political infrastructure of the neoliberal network have proven adept at hindering policies and governments that protect common interests in common spaces, from counter-movements against the nationalisation of mining operations to concerted lobbying efforts against international agreements that seek to impose limits on atmospheric carbon emissions. The rejection of the *Moon Agreement* is consistent with neoliberal resistance to protective 'double movements' in a host of policy arenas, ranging from the creation of ecological conservation zones and provision of free healthcare to increasing minimum wages or funding for public education. When the interests of mining capital are supported by and even embedded within political institutions (as in the case of 'revolving doors' between industry and public office), a concerted effort will need to be made in domestic and international institutions to push international space law towards anything resembling the ambitions of the *Moon Agreement.* Given the emergent connections between NewSpace and the Atlas Network, any double movement towards the preservation of intergenerational rights in the space commons would likely meet well-funded and well-organised resistance.

The public trust doctrine and the stewardship of global commons

Given the sheer inaccessibility of outer space and its inability to support life, it is largely irrelevant to the 'substance of society' – to use Polanyi's phrase (2001 [1944], p. 75). If we consider the implausibility of the O'Neillian colonisation project and the numerous challenges in establishing profitable mining operations on celestial bodies, the realisation of neoliberal mineral sovereignty on the space frontier is far from certain. Political animus may be lacking from any 'double movements' that attempt to intervene in the marketisation of the cosmos. We are left with a simple question: why does it matter if the space commons are enclosed by the US state in favour of corporate interests?

NewSpace techno-fixes offer the pleasant distraction that space colonisation could address contemporary crises of the global commons. Space mining firms and NewSpace advocacy have linked the space frontier with the fate of the Earthly ecology – I will do the same. However, I will argue here that preserving global commons on Earth *and* in space requires a legal counter-movement against neoliberal constitutionalism (as opposed to its extension) that is predicated on the fortification of intergenerational common and public property rights (as opposed to the further entrenchment of private mining rights in national law). The 'common heritage of mankind' principle bears similarities to the stewardship ethos of the public trust doctrine (Baslar 1998). If celestial bodies and terrestrial global commons were treated as public trusts, they could be preserved for the inheritance of future generations. There is an enormity to this task, given the grounding of off-world mineral rights in the sovereignty of the United States, the possibility that this unilateral move will be emulated by other states committed to preserving the neoliberal international legal order (as has already happened with

Luxembourg), and the fact that these legislative moves are of a piece with the 'rogue state' recalcitrance that has deepened the political impasse on climate change. Yet, in contrast with NewSpace and neoliberal environmentalism, establishing global public trusts for global commons is a goal that is at least grounded in established 'technologies' of environmental law.

How do we resist neoliberal constitutionalism – can state sovereignty be used to protect common interests rather than diminish them? Treating outer space as a global public trust is an intriguing possibility, and legal scholar Kemal Baslar (1998) has previously linked the common heritage principle of the *Moon Agreement* with the public trust project of environmental lawyer Joseph Sax (1969). Sax extended legal understanding of the public trust doctrine from the original ancient Roman focus on tidelands and floodplains. He explored US case law that effectively used this principle in relation to any public lands in which some public institution (federal government, environmental protection agencies and so on) is obligated to act as a trustee. Public trust law involves a public's legal right to natural resources and creates a 'judicially enforceable right which restrains government activities' such that commons 'must be held available for the general public' (Sax 1969, p. 477). A state's failure to protect ecosystems and natural resources as public property represents an abrogation of the responsibility of trusteeship (ibid, pp. 488–489). This would open states and public agencies to litigation.

Baslar makes the argument that the 'common heritage of mankind' principle is essentially a natural law concept (1998, ch. 1). Legal rights to use public trusts are fundamental, self-evident rights of humans, and belong to the class of civil, political and solidarity rights that emerged from modernity and the post-WW2 climate of international co-operation (Baslar 1998, p. 12). Baslar points to other UN declarations of international environmental solidarity, such as the 1972 *Declaration of the UN Conference on the Human Environment* (Stockholm) and the 1992 agreements arising from the UN Conference on Environment and Development (Rio de Janeiro; e.g. Agenda 21). Rather than being a 'principle', 'concept' or legal term of art, the common heritage of mankind needs to be treated as a human right, protected under global public trusts (Baslar 1998).

The public trust doctrine does not prevent private uses of common property but rather requires that any private use is publicly justified. Sax points to the example of a highway being built through public wetlands, where potential damage to local ecosystems might be acceptable with at least '*some* public justification' (1969, p. 496, emphasis in original). A potential scenario in off-world mining might be the irreversible extraction and use of asteroidal water ice in support of a NASA mission to the outer Solar System or the *in situ* construction of Martian habitats. Non-spacefaring or rival spacefaring member states of the UN might find this usage acceptable so long as it was used to support a scientific mission (rather than a colonisation project) in which research findings were publicly available and resulted in technological innovations that were patented under some form of open source license. A scenario such as this would entail usufructuary rights – 'an interest that incorporates the needs of others' (Sax 1969, p. 485) – rather than private rights of exclusive ownership. As a public trust, humankind's common heritage in outer space could still be used at an individual level, but only with public approval and not for commercial exchange under a system of distributed decision-making (as is the case in market capitalism).

The public trust doctrine and common heritage principle are valuable because they underline the necessity of intergenerational rights in the governance of global commons. It is plainly inadequate to treat rights to the global commons as belonging to only the present generation of peoples. Heritage implies inheritance and 'holding in trust' – a more collective understanding of inheritance and bequest than the private philanthropy that funds think-tanks like the Heritage Foundation. If equal rights to freely access and use commons are only bestowed upon those alive today, the present generation's exercise of those rights will prevent future generations from doing the same. George Monbiot (2019) has questioned the UN's Universal Declaration of Human Rights, asserting that it 'is almost meaningless, because there is nothing in the declaration insisting that one generation cannot steal from the next'. Monbiot's phrasing is hyperbolic, considering the importance of this Declaration to national civil rights movements and domestic social welfare policies (among others), but his comment nonetheless accentuates how human rights need to be framed in environmental or intergenerational terms. The Anthropocene can be defined as an intergenerational project in intergenerational theft, from the destruction of essential life-supporting planetary systems to the appropriation of non-renewable resources, like that proposed for the off-world. Monbiot (2019) offers an additional article to the Universal Declaration of Human Rights: 'Every generation shall have an equal right to the enjoyment of natural wealth'. Stewardship and preservation are essential to any commons.

The public-trust doctrine has been deployed as a solution to anthropogenic climate change, opening up the prospect of 'atmospheric trust litigation' – legal action against states unwilling to enact meaningful strategies to reduce carbon emissions. Numerous movements have either proposed creating a public trust for the atmosphere or have drawn on public trust precedents in order to charge nation states with a failure to protect intergenerational rights to an atmosphere capable of supporting human and non-human life. Australian academic Robert Costanza has argued that the atmosphere is one of many natural assets that 'must be held in trust to serve the public good' and that it should be 'every government's responsibility as a trustee to protect these assets as natural capital, and to maintain them for the public's use, not give them away or sell them to private parties' (2016, p. 466). Costanza is part of the Claim The Sky movement, which has proposed an international Atmospheric Trust that could 'collect claims for damages to the atmosphere and invest funds in mitigation, adaptation and compensation' (n.d.).

The 2015 Urgenda climate case involved 886 Dutch citizens launching action against the Dutch Government for failing to protect their rights to the atmosphere. The initial decision in favour of the plaintiffs required the Government to reduce national carbon emissions to 25% of 1990 levels and was recently upheld in the Hague Court of Appeal (Urgenda 2018). In 2015, the *Juliana et al. v. United States, et al.* case was filed by 21 youth climate activists, charging that the US Government's failure to act on climate change represented a failure to protect their constitutional rights to life, liberty and happiness.[14] Public trust law has thus been revitalised during the escalation of our planetary climate emergency.

While public trust litigation may prove to be successful on Earth, these cases highlight the challenges in introducing something similar for outer space. Do global *demoi* have inalienable rights to pristine off-world environments, in the same way they do with a breathable atmosphere? Indeed, who would be the plaintiff in any legal action seeking to enforce the common rights of 'all mankind'?[15] In global commons like the oceans and atmosphere, the necessity of the stewardship ethos and intergenerational rights is clear, but in outer space it is less obvious. No living organism on Earth depends on celestial bodies (excluding the Sun and Moon, of course) for their survival. Moreover, the functioning of the public trust doctrine is clearer when the nation state is the unit of analysis – or, indeed, smaller jurisdictional units, such as the body of Massachusetts and Californian law that Sax drew on (1969).

Yet a stewardship ethos in outer space could be vitally important for future generations. At the risk of descending into NewSpace Malthusianism, the global population is projected to reach 9.7 billion people by 2050 (United Nations Population Division n.d.). Future societies (if not the present generation) will likely deplete key resources on Earth and may *have* to attempt exploiting off-world resources (assuming a circular economy of efficient resource recycling does not eventuate). Lee (2012) links the space commons with the atmospheric commons by pointing to the potential expansion of the hydrogen economy. Hydrogen fuel cells in cars, for instance, produce electric power using water (rather than fossil fuels) and produce no greenhouse gases. However, hydrogen fuel cells are most commonly dependent on platinum as a catalyst, and – as space mining firms and Goldman Sachs have identified (Edwards 2017) – platinum is rare on Earth but abundant in outer space. A private property system of resource exploitation would lead to unequal access and risk over-exploitation of any valuable off-world mineral reserve – and, if NewSpace's more expansive plans eventuated, could be used for *in situ* manufacturing of spacecraft and habitats rather than for the more essential goal of global adoption of zero emissions technologies.

The challenge for achieving justice and equitability in the use of global commons, extra-terrestrial or otherwise, lies in the contrasting enforceability of environmental law and trade or property law. The private property rights of multinational corporations are protected through force, torts law and copious multilateral trade agreements. National governments are committed to economic growth and frequently agree to uphold free trade agreements that ensure the ongoing capital accumulation of multinational corporations, often over common interests or the interests of marginalised social groups.

Environmental law, however, often takes the form of voluntary commitments (both tacitly and explicitly). The Paris Agreement, for example, set only a general goal of limiting global temperature increases to 1.5–2°C above pre-industrial levels, while allowing each nation to determine its own contributions towards achieving this. For a nation to meet the 'obligations' of climate treaties, they might decide to use disingenuous carbon accounting measures (such as 'carry-over carbon credits') or other ineffective decarbonisation policies (such as seed investments for techno-fixes like 'clean coal' or carbon capture technologies that attempt to 'scrub' the atmosphere clean). This contrasts markedly with free trade agreements containing investor-state dispute settlement clauses, where a foreign multinational can seek damages for the loss of *projected* earnings (as opposed to actual earnings or real private property) against national governments. The institutional basis for off-world mining is still being formulated, but it is plausible that the extractive rights of corporate space miners would be protected with greater robustness than would adherence to ratified treaty commitments declaring that the space commons be used 'on a basis of equality' and not be subject to appropriation (OST 1967, Art. 1 and Art. 2).

Moreover, 'rogue states' can simply refuse to ratify these agreements in the first place or withdraw from agreements entirely. This is not a problem unique to international space law. The authority of international treaty law is diminished when powerful state actors choose not to assent to it. The Trump Administration's 2017 withdrawal from the Paris Agreement is a prime example – and the Heritage Foundation have claimed credit for this unilateral 'strong state' move against laws of the global commons (Heritage Foundation 2017). The problems in enforcing rogue state obligations to the international community via the United Nations highlight the challenges in emphasising treaty law as a solution to crises in the commons. As Nanda and Ris (1976) noted, the appeal of the public trust doctrine is its ability to strengthen existing agreements.

In the sphere of international law, the public trust doctrine paradoxically needs to be grounded in state practice, but it also needs to transcend it. Baslar notes how 'common heritage of mankind' declarations used language of the 'universal law of nature' in order to '[convey] a departure from a state-centric international legal system to a human-centric law of mankind' (1998, p. 22). Yet Westphalian notions of sovereign immunity and consent-based international law undermine any international agreement that does not offer terms agreeable to powerful nation states and the interest groups pressuring them. For example, China has flaunted the *Law of the Sea Treaty* in its militarised geoengineering of the Spratley Islands. Moreover, US governments and their allies with neoliberal and neo-imperial foreign policy predilections, such as Australia, have repeatedly disavowed both the competing mineral sovereignties of fossil fuel-producing developing nations and international climate law over a 50-year period. Efforts to uphold the rule of law will inevitably confront the Schmittian paradox: exception to the law is the ultimate source of sovereign power (Schmitt 1985 [1922]).

Conclusion

Comprehensive resolutions to these enduring problems of international law and geopolitics are outside the scope of this book. Schrijver (2016) has described how global commons are 'laboratories' for transboundary problem-solving, necessitating innovative governance mechanisms including 'hard law (treaties, protocols) and international juridical decisions'. Perhaps the anticipatory commoning of the off-world will produce new politico-legal mechanisms that can be of use on Earth. Perhaps we might find lasting resolutions to crises of the planetary commons that can be emulated in space, if mining celestial bodies ever becomes feasible or necessary.

I have highlighted some legal mechanisms that environmental interest groups have deployed to prevent the degradation of global commons, while also arguing that NewSpace's 'planetary conservation through off-world private property' is not among the more plausible options we have for this goal. Space mining and colonisation is a dangerous fantasy, because it presents a grandiose techno-fix as a feasible solution to the wholescale degradation of Earth's capacity to support life. Why bother curtailing anthropogenic pollution on Earth if we can just move to another celestial body elsewhere in the Solar System, 'terraform' it into a new Eden and then – taking the techno-eschatology further – escape this mortal coil entirely by uploading our consciousness into computers? Ultimately, NewSpace seeks freedom, from biophysical limits to growth and from obligations to the common good. Despite NewSpace's rhetoric of environmentalism or cosmopolitanism, the space colonisation project is largely escapist.

Notes

1 Terraforming Mars has featured prominently in NewSpace and planetary science more broadly, such as the work of Carl Sagan (1973) and the blue-sky speculative research conducted at NASA Ames (Cooper 2007).

2 Kilgore (2003, p. 172) notes that, for all the physics and mathematics, O'Neill's project amounted to the most elaborate 'gated community' ever devised. Since he was also concerned with the social unrest and urban crime of 1960s and 1970s America, O'Neill proposed a pilgrimage to the High Frontier that mirrored 'white flight' from inner-city areas. The Lifeboat Foundation has explicitly described their proposed orbital colony as "the ultimate gated community" (Lifeboat Foundation 2020).

3 Davis notes that, as a Jesuit priest with an interest in evolution, Teilhard may have "tap-danced on the thin ice of heresy" – however, given his role in the debunked 'Piltdown man' paleontological discovery, "it would be wrong to accuse Teilhard of practicing science" (2015, pp. 306, 308).

4 Hughes also notes that Kurzweil is more liberal than other Singularitarian figures like Thiel (2012, p. 766); one of his first inventions was a print-to-speech reader for people with visual impairment.

5 Farman (2012, p. 1072) notes how a 'who's who' of West Coast techno-utopians mingled at the early meetings of the L-5 Society, including some Singularitarian forefathers: Freeman Dyson (physicist, space activist and later climate denier), Eric Drexler (molecular nanotechnology), Marvin Minsky (artificial intelligence), Saul Kent (extropianism), Hans Moravec (robotics researcher and transhumanist) and William Sims Bainbridge (Singularitarian and NewSpace historian).

6 The idea of an immortal, digital self seems like an extreme realisation of neoclassical notions of methodological individualism and rationality. Singularitarians believe that the Singularity will make the flesh, blood and emotion of human experience reducible to data and information. Neoclassical economics, meanwhile, offers mathematical abstractions that reduce human interaction to the logic of market exchange.

7 His treatment of land and labour as inseparable (2001, p. 187) resulted in an understanding of land conservation that prioritised the protection of agricultural workers and their communities rather than an environmental ethics in its own right. To use examples prior to the publication of *The Great Transformation,* he appears ignorant of the legislative protection for nature in the form of national parks, which had begun with the creation of the Yellowstone National Park in 1872 and was followed by comparable conservation movements in Australia and Europe from the late 1870s onwards.

8 It is also worth noting that there are significantly fewer progressive or leftist civil society groups that have taken an interest in outer space. The Planetary Society, co-founded by Carl Sagan in 1980, stood in contrast to the activism of the L-5 Society and other libertarian or nationalistic space ideologies that emerged during NewSpace's infancy (Michaud 1986, p. 213). While the Society had taken opposition to the militarisation of outer space and the potential placement of nuclear weapons in space, it appears to have not taken a stance on private property rights or international treaty law (in relation to the *Moon Agreement*, for example). Michaud reports that progressive or 'liberal' (in the popular American meaning of the term) civil society groups were focused predominantly on anti-nuclearization or anti-militarisation agendas, such as Citizens for Space Demilitarization, and often in response to Reagan's 'star wars' Strategic Defence Initiative (1986, p .233). Shukaitis (2009) also describes the (Marxist) Association of Autonomous Astronauts, which was founded in 1995 in similar opposition to US militarisation of space. The JustSpace Alliance is a new civil society group, which is organising inter-disciplinary events around questions of ethics in space exploration (JustSpace Alliance n.d.).

9 U.N. Document: A/AC.105/C.1/2016/CRP.15

10 U.N. Document: A/AC.105/C.2/2017 /CRP.19

11 U.N. Document: A/AC.105/C.2/L.311

12 U.N. Document: A/AC.105/1203

13 Tronchetti's (2009, p. 283) proposals include the requirement that prospective mining licensees submit proposals to the 'International Space Authority' as to how international participation can be promoted through their mineral exploitation (reflecting the governance mechanisms of the International Seabed Authority, which has accepted mining proposals that involved partnerships between developing nations and deep-sea mining firms). He suggests a mining fee be collected by the Authority, and this fee could be increased or reduced depending on the degree of involvement of developing nations (Tronchetti 2009, p. 283)

14 Some links between the space frontier and neoliberal constitutionalism are evident in the *Juliana* case. Former NASA scientist and climatologist James Hansen represented 'future generations' as a plaintiff in the case. Supreme Court Chief Justice John Roberts was instrumental in the neoliberal constitutionalist verdict in the *Citizens United* case – he also supported the Trump Administration in the *Juliana* case by attempting to delay discovery and trial (Rodrigo 2018).
15 In addition to the androcentric and anthropocentric language of the *Outer Space Treaty* and *Moon Agreement*, Baslar notes that the legal personality of 'humanity' is ambiguous as far as legal standing is concerned (1998, p. 70).

8 Epilogue

At the time of writing, NASA's *OSIRIS-REx* spacecraft is travelling through inter-planetary space, having departed from the asteroid 101955 Bennu in March 2021. *OSIRIS-REx* (Origins, Spectral Interpretation, Resource Identification, Security, Regolith Explorer) spent over a year studying Bennu, mapping potential sites where it could briefly touch the asteroid and collect samples (NASA 2018b). *OSIRIS-REx* may prove to be an early 'proof-of-concept' for asteroid mining in its use of landing and sampling technologies and mission design for rendezvous with distant celestial bodies. The principal investigator on the project is Dante Lauretta, who was hired by space mining start-up Planetary Resources as a science advisor (Planetary Resources n.d.-a). NASA hopes that *OSIRIS-Rex* will 'provide a greater understanding of both the hazards and resources in near-Earth space' (NASA 2016, p.4). The spacecraft was built by recurring NASA contractor Lockheed-Martin. On October 22, 2020, *OSIRIS-REx* successfully collected a sample of at least 60 g of loose asteroidal surface material (or regolith), at a cost of over $800 million to the US taxpayer (ibid, p.4; NASA 2020a, 2020b, 2020c). Six years since it left Earth, the spacecraft is nearing the end of a two-and-a-half-year journey home, scheduled to arrive in September 2023 (NASA 2022).

The *OSIRIS-REx* mission highlights the challenges of trying to 'mine' in outer space. For the modest haul of 60 g of off-world 'topsoil', a huge amount of public money and the engineering capability of a 'big aerospace' conglomerate were required. There was no guarantee of success and no possibility of sending a repair crew, should any faults have compromised its mission once it began its high-speed, 2-billion-kilometre journey to Bennu (NASA 2018c). Before a spacecraft can extract (not just collect) minerals from a celestial body, process them into usable metals or fuel and then use them in a manufacturing or refuelling process, significant technological advancements are needed.

Public or private investments rivalling Cold War superpower space budgets may be required if any substantial 'industrialisation' of the Solar System were to take place. Commercially viable space mining will not take place in the next decade, if not much longer. While NASA's crewed missions to the Moon are scheduled to commence in 2024 under the Artemis Program, the establishment of lunar surface habitats is not anticipated to take place until the early 2030s,

DOI: 10.1201/9781003293613-8

assuming these later missions are not delayed (Kshatriya & Kirasich 2022, p.2). Moreover, the nascent space mining industry that emerged in the 2010s has fallen from prominence, amid the challenges of financing such an ambitious project as mining the 'high frontier'. The grandiose O'Neillian dream of wholescale off-worlding of human civilisation and industry is unlikely to occur this century and might be entirely impossible.

However, NewSpace advocacy and the space mining industry have left what may be an important legacy in their wake. There are now legal frameworks for the private ownership of space resources: one that is secured and protected by the military-industrial superpower that is the US; others which have been enacted by Luxembourg, the United Arab Emirates (UAE) and Japan; and an emerging consensus between the US and its allies in the form of the Artemis Accords, which aims to legitimise the commercial appropriation of space resources. Should off-world resource appropriation take place, these legislative instruments have laid the groundwork for actual, rather than anticipatory, claims over the resources of celestial bodies to be realised, thus providing a clear pathway to the future enclosure of the space commons.

Despite the many difficulties in exploring, settling and exploiting the celestial bodies of the Solar System, we should expect interest in off-world resource appropriation to intensify in the coming decades. The global COVID-19 pandemic and mitigating the impacts of anthropogenic climate change have constrained national budgets, and there may be limited appeal for many nations in diverting significant economic resources towards space activity. However, the US-led Artemis Program is seeking to establish a more permanent foothold on the Moon. The Chinese Lunar Exploration Program and the International Lunar Research Station lunar base project, a China-Russia partnership (Wall 2022), exist as alternative projects in what may become another bipolar, off-world superpower rivalry. Should Russia or China pursue similar laws in support of their (possibly state-owned) corporations' interests in commercially profitable space mining, the link between property and national appropriation would be even more pronounced. NewSpace start-ups now attract investment from billionaires like Peter Thiel and Jeff Bezos, illustrating the potential for private wealth to fund space activity where national budgets cannot.

In concluding this book, I will continue to look to the past and the future. What can precedents in capitalist and colonial history tell us about the cosmic frontier? Is there any hope that the off-world will be a site of freedom, emancipation and socio-political renewal, guided by either a libertarian or social democratic philosophy? Will it even be entrepreneurial mining firms that appropriate from celestial bodies and colonise the Solar System? Human space futures may involve forms of politics and law, and power and (in)justice, both different and removed from terrestrial political and economic history. At present, however, the anticipatory, neoliberal challenge to the commons of the cosmos is reflecting problems we face on Earth and thus points us towards some policy and advocacy goals that are far more immediate.

Against 'space exceptionalism': space colonisation in historical perspective

> The aim of all utopias, to a greater or lesser extent, is to eliminate real people. Even if it is not a conscious aim, it is an inevitable result of their good intentions. In a utopia real people cannot exist, for the very obvious reason that real people are what constitute the world that we know, and it is that world that every utopia is designed to replace. (Carey 1999, p.xii)

It is tempting to treat outer space as though it offered human civilisations a clean slate – an escape from the worst parts of our history. The Apollo missions' unifying call, to 'go in peace for all mankind', may have been inspirational but was discordant with the prevailing political climate in which the first steps were made on another celestial body. Since then, members of the NewSpace network have claimed that the colonisation of the Solar System holds much promise for human progress and growth, for political reinvention and experimentation (O'Neill 1977; Zubrin 1994; ASD 2019, p.3; NSS 2019). Yet I have argued here that the NewSpace paradigm would involve bringing disastrous political-economic baggage on the journey off-world. The uniqueness of celestial bodies as a site of politics and culture seems to lead to a sense of 'space exceptionalism', a utopian millenarianism both within and outside NewSpace in which the unscrupulousness of human behaviours on the frontier can be swept under the rug. There is an inherent assumption that off-world societies would inevitably function better than those on Earth, that exploiting and settling a new frontier would somehow negate the capacity for greed, apathy, corruption and violence that plagues our terrestrial existence – indeed, that real people were actually capable of thriving (not just surviving) outside the protective borders of their home planet. Space law itself reflects this dichotomy between Earthly political discord and aspirational off-world harmony, such that achieving consensus on space resources law has thus far been difficult to achieve.

While the exploitation and settlement of the celestial frontier would represent a new chapter in the history of politics, economics and law, I have argued that exploring historical precedent is more useful if we are to speculate on how human spacefaring futures might transpire. Indeed, in the pre-emptive enclosure of the off-world commons, we can see an intermingling of several phases in the genealogy of international law: the mineral sovereign extending powers of lawful appropriation onto the colonial frontier; multilateral declarations of human solidarity, as embodied in the United Nations; and the extra-parliamentary fortification of corporate rights under neoliberal constitutionalism (Purdy 2014; Schneiderman 2013), in which state power is captured to attack multilateral legal agreements and – in this case – establish a legal order amenable to private resource appropriations on the next colonial frontier. If 'going in peace for the benefit of all humankind' is to be more than an evocative phrasing of cosmopolitan aspiration, we need to appreciate the threat that recent legislative and diplomatic manoeuvres pose to the prospect of egalitarian and inclusive futures in space.

It is particularly important, then, to look past NewSpace claims that private ownership rights will be inherently beneficial and to instead consider the elective affinities between NewSpace and neoliberalism (discussed in Chapter 2). While the network is perhaps too diffuse to reduce to a singular ideology, the ideological threads in NewSpace discourse are predominantly on the liberal economic spectrum (Valentine 2012, pp.1047–1048). Centre-right views highlight the bureaucratic inefficiency of NASA and short-termism of national space policy, while a more pugilistic anarcho-capitalist thread portrays governmental oversight of space commerce as authoritarian (*Orphans of Apollo* 2008).

However, there is also a very clear neoliberal component within NewSpace discourses of 'freedom' (Tumlinson 2012; ASD 2016), and these goals of economic liberty have been realised in US space policy. There is now a revised role for NASA and the US state, including to support, fund and purchase from space corporations, while lowering national and international legal barriers that stand in their way (e.g. *NASA Act of 1958*, s.102, as amended under the *NASA Authorization Act, Fiscal Year 1991)*. Presidential Directive on National Space Policy 1988; CSLCA 2015, s.51302; Executive Office of the President 2020). The neoliberal 'international economic order' (Bandow 1985) has produced a staggering degree of socioeconomic inequality since the revolutions of the Thatcher and Reagan governments. In the US, for example, the top income decile's share in national income had risen to 45–50% by 2000–2010 (Piketty 2014, p.24). If the colonisation of the Solar System proceeds on neoliberal terms, we should expect that a share in any economic benefits from the off-world will be limited to all but an elite few.

The NewSpace network and the space property law it has lobbied for cannot be reduced to the exclusive work of Atlas neoliberals. For one, there is support for commercialising space exploration from think-tanks outside of the Atlas Network, such as the Center for New American Security (Zimmerman, in Shammas & Holen 2019, p.6). Neoliberalisation is a process that is uneven and incomplete: this much is true for both NewSpace and NASA. While I have highlighted some definitive movements in the neoliberalising of NASA, it is hard to imagine a scenario where American space science and engineering became entirely commodified or privatised under the neoliberal agenda for scientific research, as described by Lave, Mirowski and Randalls (2010), for example. The scientific knowledge gained from planetary science and astronomy may never become private property in the same, marketable way that knowledge from the life sciences has in the age of corporate biotechnology, among others. Nor would NASA, a public sector institution so deeply embedded in the modern American consciousness, likely be fully privatised and managed by market forces in a manner consistent with neoliberal policy in carceral, health or energy policy, for example.

While NewSpace civil society and start-up culture is predicated on harnessing the state to provide commercial incentive for space settlement, other organisations interested in space exploration or colonisation may lobby to push space policy back towards a Keynesian or social democratic focus. Further sociological research into the broader constellation of 'space enthusiast' organisations could explore the contemporary extent of alternative political-economic ideologies within the movement to settle outer space.

These caveats aside, my focus on NewSpace's links with Atlas neoliberalism helps to avoid treating this contemporary articulation of 'space enthusiasm' ideographically, as though recent events in space resources law were a discrete sideshow to the broader political and economic currents that have transformed the political economy of the US and, subsequently, much of the world. Through Peter Thiel's Founders Fund, at least one Atlas member was an investor in space mining start-ups – including Planetary Resources, the firm that spearheaded lobbying for the CSLCA's passage into US law (Planetary Resources n.d.-a). The voice of the NewSpace network has been amplified through the political infrastructure of Atlas think-tanks, in the form of policy advocacy (e.g. Dunstan & Szoka 2017) and the legislative work of Atlas' political allies on Capitol Hill (e.g. Rohrabacher 2002; Congressional Record 2015b, H3517). The pathway to the CSLCA was established through the US's non-ratification of the *Moon Agreement*, and this defeat can be partly attributed to the aligned opposition of the Reagan Administration, Heritage Foundation and L-5 Society against the post-NIEO laws of the global commons. An awareness of potential Atlas engagement with future space activity is essential for any researchers, scientists, engineers, activists and civil society groups who are genuinely interested in inclusive human futures in outer space. Atlas funding or support for an off-world policy goal that claims to be in humankind's interests should be met with profound scepticism.

I have argued that the vision of space colonisation espoused by NewSpace is ultimately predicated on benefits for the individual, not the collective (Chapter 3). NewSpace has repeated Locke's natural rights argument, which falsely presumed that everyone has 'the opportunity to be part of the appropriation process' – as though different nations, firms and individuals have an equal opportunity to appropriate the mineral resources of space (Pilchman 2015, p.142). Lockean or neoliberal attempts to 'naturalise' market economies falsely demarcate political and economic spheres. This line of argument suits space miners need to demarcate private and national appropriation as per the *Outer Space Treaty*, more than it does any claims to beworking in the interests of humanity. As Polanyi (2001[1944]) argued, capitalist markets are supported by democratic institutions – they should thus be directed towards democratic ends.

Yet neoliberalism involves the privatisation of politics itself and a NewSpace mining start-up effectively purchased a law that suited their commercial interests. The passage of the CSLCA illustrates that – through their lobbying outlays – Planetary Resources captured state power in order to make legislative interventions into the space commons that I believe undermine international law (Chapter 4). In the CSLCA, US state sovereignty undermines international laws of the global commons on behalf of corporate extractivism, a story that resonates with our current impasse over international collective agreement on limiting carbon emissions. In the case of the CSLCA, the recent history of extra-parliamentary mineral sovereignty is being brought to bear on the future of the space commons (Walker & Johnson 2018).

My historicisation of private property rights has also demonstrated that to allocate mining rights on celestial bodies is to assert sovereignty over those sites of resource extraction. I have paid particular attention to how national resource ownership laws contravene the OST's 'non-appropriation principle', that celestial bodies or their contents are 'not subject to national appropriation by claim of sovereignty, by means of use or occupation, or by any other means' (1967 Art.2). In addition to this, such laws run afoul of other assertions of collective rights, responsibilities and obligations that are expressed in the commons 'constitution' of the OST (Chapter 5). Establishing a mining site would impinge on global rights to freely access 'all areas of celestial bodies' (OST 1967, Art.1). One party's non-renewable use of mineral resources would prevent 'use by all States without discrimination of any kind' (OST 1967, Art.1). Profit-based exploitation would take place under the competitive and depletory logic of market capitalism, entirely incommensurate with the declaration that the use of outer space should occur 'for the benefit and in the interests of all countries, irrespective of their degree of economic or scientific development' (Art.1).

If national resource ownership laws are accepted as consistent with the principles and terms of the OST, it represents a dangerous precedent in international space law. It paves the way for additional countries to emulate the US and eventually establish a form of neoliberal multilateral law that makes delivering 'benefits to all countries' and peoples even harder to achieve (Schneidermann 2013). Narrower multilateralism in this form could potentially insulate space mining from the diplomatic and legal fora of the UN and the democratic chambers of its member states. This is being realised in state practice, multilateral agreement or international diplomatic opinion in the form of the Artemis Accords. There are numerous scenarios where demarcating the space economy from Earthly democracy could be problematic.

One further potential scenario is a private multilateral agreement that includes only the actors capable of space mining. Some writers have argued that private international law and the use of supranational arbitration courts are a valuable next step for space resources law, a project which would circumvent questions of international politico-legal consensus (Salter & Leeson 2014; Hertzfeld, Weeden & Johnson 2016). For example, a country might wish to impose resource super profit taxes on publicly funded space mining start-ups, but could instead face legal action for loss of expected profit under an investor-state dispute settlement mechanism.

The institutional, administrative and judicial frameworks that govern off-world mining rights are still evolving. No company or country has successfully extracted extra-terrestrial minerals and we can only speculate on the precise material, economic and politico-legal forms that property in space resources would take. However, for a national government to grant its citizens the right to exploit extra-territorial resources is to claim authority over those resources, extending sovereign powers of lawful appropriation onto the frontier commons (Chapter 6). Should space mining ever eventuate, there is the realistic possibility (consistent with terrestrial resource imperialism) that the claims of American space miners could be protected through American military supremacy, against the claims of rival state or non-state actors (the national space agencies or state-owned corporations of China and Russia, for instance). Rather than fulfilling the libertarian space pirate myth or representing an escape from the violent history of private property, space mining might bear a closer resemblance to the age of European colonialism, where states delegated authority to their commercial vanguards and property was enforced through the force of law *and* threat of violence.

Hypotheses of off-world resource imperialism aside, could there ever be a synergy between NewSpace's desire for political-economic freedoms and the bypassing of ecological constraints? The NewSpace and neoliberal myth of endless economic growth belies the fact that the limits of the human organism will inevitably travel off-world. This is the central problematic for NewSpace and its eschatology of permanent human colonisation of the cosmos (Chapter 6). Technologies of artificial 'minimal biospheres' are in their infancy, and recreating life-supporting environments in deep space entails utter technological dependence (Walker & Granjou 2017). Can we *really* extend the 'law of the land' and categories of sovereignty and property onto a frontier devoid of land, in the sense of the grounded, life-supporting ecosystems in which human societies are embedded? Conservative jurist Carl Schmitt had explored the elemental contrasts between land and sea (2015 [1954]). The maritime existence enabled by technologies of seafaring was entirely different to the telluric existence of the home, 'the space in which the ship moves is other than the space of the landscape' (2015, p.73). Outer space brings new meaning to his statement that 'technology encloses the humans more than it opens new space to them' (ibid, p.80).

In search of new frontiers: the uncertain futures of the space mining industry and techno-utopian democracy

Neoliberalism is predicated on the capture of state sovereignty to create and protect corporate freedoms – whether the freedom to appropriate the minerals of the commonwealth, freedom from environmental protection law or freedom to shift capital to off-shore jurisdictions. These freedoms, while enabled by the state sovereignty often decried by NewSpace and techno-libertarians, represent an escape fantasy: the flight from social democracy and the principle of the common heritage of humankind, and an escape from a dying Earth. If an actual escape from Earth is to materialise, however, it will likely involve a different cast of characters than the start-ups that I have discussed. To an extent, the preceding account represents a brief snapshot in space history: the abrupt rise and (potential) fall of the space mining firm. Reflecting the boom and bust of Silicon Valley start-up culture, the nascent space mining industry has encountered financial difficulties.

With backers like Larry Page and James Cameron, Planetary Resources made a grand entrance into the NewSpace commercial landscape in 2012. In 2015, the company successfully lobbied for the resource ownership provisions of the CSLCA – this may prove to be NewSpace's biggest political triumph. By 2018, however, Planetary Resources announced some significant setbacks. Interest from 'a mining company that was in line to lead a fresh funding round' failed to materialise (Boyle 2018a) and, shortly afterwards, staff layoffs resulted in 'the company being down to around 10 employees' (Messier 2018). By August 2018, the firm company began 'auctioning off hundreds of items from its headquarters … ranging from industrial-strength CNC machine tools and 3-D printers to laptops and folding chairs' (Boyle 2018b). In October 2018, the company was purchased by Consensys, a blockchain company owned by Ethereum co-founder Joe Lubin (Planetary Resources 2018). From space mining to cryptocurrency 'mining', it is a turn of events highlighting the sheer challenge of industrialising the Solar System.

Deep Space Industries (DSI), too, has been purchased by another space firm. In January 2019, DSI was purchased by the Bradford Space group, a US-owned and European-based space manufacturing firm. As with Planetary Resources' acquisition, the intellectual property for the new space technologies developed by DSI has been passed onto a larger firm. The technologies might be put towards more modest applications, such as DSI's propulsion technologies being used in low-Earth orbit (Bradford Space 2019). These corporate acquisitions may represent a shot-in-the-arm for space mining, but it remains to be seen whether the new owners of Planetary Resources and DSI will make any new investments in space mining technology. Maybe Luxembourg's deep public coffers will make new investments in space mining and continue the financial connection between the off-world and the 'off-shore'; perhaps the loss of €25 million via Planetary Resources will discourage them from doing so.

The Moon Express brand remains in the space resources landscape – its broader business interests in lunar landing technologies provide it with a more immediate revenue stream. The company was selected as one of nine companies in NASA's Commercial Lunar Payload Services contracts programme – they will be eligible to bid for contracts to sell lunar delivery services to NASA, as part of a $2.6 billion pool of public funds available through to 2028 (NASA 2018a, 2018b, 2018c). iSpace (based in Japan and Luxembourg and funded in part by the Japanese government) appears to be their largest competitor for access to the presently non-existent space resources market.

As far as techno-libertarian movements are concerned, the quest for an 'escape from politics' – as Peter Thiel describes it (2009) – will need to look to

Earthly frontiers, in the short-term at least. Outer space or cyberspace (as per Singularitarianism) may prove a post-biological fantasy that is eternally out-of-reach. There appears to be a convergence between the settlement of the aquatic frontier and – in a recent development – the medium of cryptocurrency. Patri Friedman of the Atlas-affiliated Seasteading Institute has put forth the case for start-up countries: 'permanent autonomous zones on land or at sea intended to accelerate economic development and to serve as laboratories for voluntary political experiments' (Friedman 2018). Cryptocurrency, he argues, will eventually produce 'profound political change' by reducing 'nation-state revenue (and thus power)' and fostering new technologies of governance, such as ICT-enabled deliberative democracy (Friedman 2018). We can see here the persistent dream of the 'sovereign individual' – the anarcho-capitalist elite – rising from the ashes of global political-economic upheaval (Davidson & Rees-Mogg 1999).

The CLSCA is a case study in the privatisation of a republic once led by a 'government of the people, by the people and for the people' – yet Friedman is here portraying cryptocurrency as a techno-fix for democracy. In this regard, the new owners of Planetary Resources have made an interesting remark; according to Ethereum co-founder Joe Lubin:

> Bringing deep space capabilities into the ConsenSys ecosystem reflects our belief in the potential for Ethereum to help humanity craft new societal rule systems through automated trust and guaranteed execution. And it reflects our belief in democratizing and decentralizing space endeavors to unite our species and unlock untapped human potential. (in Planetary Resources 2018)

Ethereum – as an open-source cryptocurrency platform – might herald new 'societal rules' of great potential for the increasingly enclosed digital commons. But it would be remiss to treat the decentralisation of currency as being essential to the revitalisation of democracy. If democracy itself is to be further decentralised and arbitrated through technologies of market exchange, the further concentration of corporate power (and further transference of this power into the political sphere) is an equally plausible outcome.

NewSpace discusses democratisation largely in terms of reducing the cost of being a participant in space exploration and settlement (e.g. Beck, cited in Shammas & Holen 2019, p.3; Space Renaissance USA 2020 [2011]). The claim is that through the entrepreneurship of tech start-ups and the incentive of private property ownership (and the 'light touch' of the state apparatus and taxpayers' purse), space travel and habitation can be transformed into something more efficient, thus more affordable, and thus accessible to a greater number of people. Elon Musk's Mars colonisation blueprint, for instance, rests upon bringing the cost of travel to the Red Planet down to that of a 'median house price in the United States, which is around $200,000' (Musk 2017, p.47).

> "Not everyone would want to go. In fact, probably a relatively small number of people from Earth would want to go, but enough would want to go who could afford it for it to happen. People could also get sponsorship. It gets to the point where almost anyone, if they saved up and this was their goal, could buy a ticket and move to Mars ... " (ibid, pp.47–48)

The most publicised plan for pursuing the large-scale settlement of outer space rests upon pioneers who can reach what is (for many) the increasingly out-of-reach goal of outright home ownership.

Yet, future sailors on the cosmic seas may discover alternate political forms that are even more exclusionary and authoritarian, beyond NewSpace 'democracy' and neoliberal constitutionalism. Other than a seat on Musk's Colonial Fleet, what would $200,000 purchase for his Martian colonisers? Is the fare also the price of admission into the Martian political community, or does that privilege rest with the 'early adopters' or those able to pay exorbitant 'surge pricing' if a planetary ecological apocalypse starts to materialise? Will Martian-produced food, water, habitation and fuel be distributed to each according to their needs and from each according to their ability? Or are further expenses likely if establishing life-supporting artificial ecosystems prove as costly and unrealisable as they have on Earth? Does the initial expense of accessing this off-world democracy include a return flight? Or will off-world colonies produce new classes of impoverished workers and indentured labourers, sweating in their spacesuits to afford a ticket back home? Will it even produce a new class of robotic labourers, bestowed with forms of artificial intelligence that do not require recognition of fundamental political rights or freedoms? As a potential site of political change and experimentation, we should not assume the off-world will deliver the innovations that we need or want.

Justice, equality and stewardship: the future of the global commons

These speculations about off-world politics rest upon the assumption that space colonisation and mining will actually take place. Even if a legal order of neoliberal mineral sovereignty were enacted on the space frontier, questions about resource exploitation in outer space may not engender the same ethical and political concerns as terrestrial mining or neo-colonialism. Unlike the 'new world' on the frontiers of European empire at the dawn of global capitalism, there is no indigenous *nomos* to be displaced through brute force and subjugation. Nor is off-world mining likely to threaten fragile ecologies (if we ignore the possibility of discoveries in exobiology). Future political-economic approaches to NewSpace could further explore the potential social and environmental consequences of space mining, because the egalitarian and intergenerational policy considerations prompted by off-world enclosure may suffer from a lack of political will (outside the legal and diplomatic chambers of the United Nations, at least).

The pristine environments of the Solar System bring into stark relief the scale of enclosure and over-exploitation of environments on Earth. Celestial bodies may represent the 'final frontier' for resource appropriation, but they cannot support life as we know it. From the methane lakes and cryovolcanism of Titan to the geysers of water vapour extending into space from the south pole of Enceladus and the sub-surface oceans of Europa – these are dynamic and fascinating environments, but it is likely that most of the off-world commons will be eternally out-of-reach from the processes of accumulation, depletion and pollution that have brought Earth to widespread ecological emergency. Off-world commons are a unique case study in the history of enclosure, but – the discoveries of exoplanetology pending – it is the life-supporting Earth that is unique in the history of the observable universe, or at least in our cosmic neighbourhood. Preserving it is our only feasible option in the age of the Anthropocene.

The oceans are increasingly unable to support marine life. An atmosphere capable of maintaining planetary temperatures at a level that makes Earth habitable for all species is slipping through our fingers. Great swathes of the South American and Australian continents have been set ablaze in recent years. Recent prerogatives of 'restarting the economy' look set to return anthropogenic carbon emissions to their pre-pandemic levels. One perverse outcome of planetary temperature increases is that melting sea ice has made gas and oil reserves on the deep seabed more accessible. Several countries and corporations might look to prolong fossil fuel combustion by exploiting the Arctic Circle – a new mineral commons that can be enclosed and burned to the detriment of global commons of the seas and skies.

While the NewSpace quest for private property rights in space may seem novel, it essentially masks a much bigger problem: that our supposedly democratic institutions appear better equipped to serve private interests at the expense of those things we hold in common on Earth. In Chapter 4, I deployed a research methodology that might be of use to activists and scholars seeking to understand and critique the role of neoliberal actors in domestic and international politics. By using a number of public information sources – specifically, Congressional records and lobbying data – I was able to describe the passage of the CSCLA into US public law. In this process, I was indebted to the online tools developed by the Center for Responsive Politics (e.g. OpenSecrets 2023a), a civil society organisation advocating for greater transparency in American democracy. Scholars investigating neoliberal influence on local political life might find similar tools in their local jurisdictions that let them identify neoliberal actors involved in similar attacks on democracy and the commons – such as in the 'citizens' hub' of Guardian Media's *Transparency Project* (Guardian Australia 2019).

It is also worth highlighting the value of a 'networked' approach to the study of neoliberalism (Mirowski & Plehwe 2009) and mineral sovereignty (Walker & Johnson 2018, p.64). My research has teased out some new fields of inquiry for sociologists and historians interested in the connection between neoliberal political networks and NewSpace. Further research is needed to uncover additional connections to those I have established; perhaps future projects looking at the cross-pollination of NewSpace and neoliberalism could be augmented with additional forms of data collection. Understanding the broader impact of the neoliberal network in diverse policy arenas can take scholarship and activism beyond a more general critique of the 'forces of capitalism' and into an analysis that points to particular nodes and agents of neoliberalism that are directly responsible for the undemocratic or anti-environmental laws we are faced with. Such an approach might underscore the imperatives for particular 'double movements' (Polanyi 2001), such as strengthening disclosure laws for campaign contributions or closing specific 'revolving doors' between political office and private industry (such as those that undermine protective action in Earth's commons).

There are doubtless more policy recommendations that could address the depth and breadth of the challenges we face under planetary ecological emergency, but they are largely outside the scope of this book. Establishing global commons as global public trusts may serve as a means to strengthen *existing* agreements that seek to protect them on behalf of present and future generations (Nanda & Ris 1976). Furthermore, as Dahlin and Fredriksson (2017) have identified, the act of resistance to enclosure and extractivism is itself an act of commoning, or 'working in common'. Dahlin and Fredriksson describe how 'multiple singularities' can establish 'arenas where diverse movements can coexist and interact' (2017, p.271; Hardt & Negri 2004). Facing a common enemy in the global commons, a diverse array of interest groups might be able to discover further 'common ground for interaction and collaboration that can encompass large differences between the collaborating actors' (2017, p.271).

Despite the enormity of these challenges, building political coalitions that are predicated on collective rights and responsibilities offers a more promising and inclusive utopia than the NewSpace project of off-world environmentalism and trickle-down democracy. In closing, I will turn to Cynthia Selin's description of the 'sociology of the future', how '...stories of the future are potent sources of legitimization, inspiration and construction...' (2008, p.1880). Contrary to the rising tide of youth climate action, NewSpace is telling a story that there is in fact a 'Planet B' and claims that a highly speculative and market-based project is a means of reaching it. This fantasy is now grounded in the sovereign authority of the world's reigning space superpower and is supported by one of the world's wealthiest tax havens. For NewSpace and neoliberalism, outer space represents a frontier of guilt-free expansion and a means of avoiding the curtailment of economic growth and personal freedoms on Earth. However, these eschatological and environmentalist justifications for space mining are grounded in a faulty sense of inevitability.

What might be an alternate story for us to tell about the future, something more pragmatic than the fantasies of NewSpace or less foreboding that the ongoing fortification of neoliberal constitutionalism? Can we arrive at a new *nomos* of the Earth and off-Earth that is instead predicated on the global and intergenerational solidarity rights and stewardship ethos envisioned under the common heritage principle? In the wake of the Global Financial Crisis and the Great Depression before it, neoliberal actors recognised the importance of never letting 'a serious crisis go to waste' (Mirowski 2013). As planetary ecological collapse looms large on the immediate temporal horizon, we might now strengthen democratic and cosmopolitan ideals in our politico-legal institutions, with an even greater sense of urgency and a greater commitment to the things we need to hold in common.

References

Abrahamian, A.A. 2017, 'How a tax haven is leading the race to privatise space', *The Guardian*, 15 September, viewed 9 August 2023, <https://www.theguardian.com/news/2017/sep/15/luxembourg-tax-haven-privatise-space>.

Abrahamian, A.A. 2019, 'How the asteroid-mining bubble burst: A short history of the space industry's failed (for now) gold rush', *MIT Technology Review*, 26 June, viewed 14 August 2023, <https://www.technologyreview.com/2019/06/26/134510/asteroid-mining-bubble-burst-history/>.

Agamben, G. 2005, *State of Exception*, trans. K. Attell, University of Chicago Press, Chicago.

Aldrin, E.E. & Jones, R. 2002, 'Changing the space paradigm: Space tourism and the future of space travel', in E.L. Hudgins (ed.), *Space: The Free-Market Frontier*, Cato Institute, Washington, DC, pp. 177–192.

Allen, M. & VandeHei, J. 2018, 'Elon Musk: there's a 70% chance that I will personally go to Mars', *Axios on HBO*, 26 November, viewed 9 August 2023, <https://www.axios.com/elon-musk-mars-space-x-14c01761-d045-4da0-924b-322fb6a109ce.html>.

Alliance for Space Development 2016, *Citizens' Space Agenda*, National Space Society, Washington, DC, viewed 9 August 2023, <https://space.nss.org/media/Citizen-Space-Agenda-August-2016-Blitz-Talking-Points.pdf>.

Alliance for Space Development 2017, *Citizens' Space Agenda: 2017 August Home District Blitz*, ASD, Washington, DC, viewed 14 August 2023, <https://space.nss.org/wp-content/uploads/August-Blitz-2017-Talking-Points-draft.pdf>.

Alliance for Space Development 2019, *Citizens' Space Agenda 2019*, ASD, Washington, DC, viewed 9 August 2023, <https://allianceforspacedevelopment.org/wp-content/uploads/2016/04/ASD-2019-Objectives.pdf>.

'American Space Commerce Free Enterprise Act of 2017' (ASCFE), U.S. House of Representatives, H.R. 2809, 115th Congress (2017).

'American Space Commerce Free Enterprise Act of 2019', U.S. House of Representatives, H.R. 3610, 116th Congress (2019).

'American Space Technology for Exploring Resource Opportunities In Deep Space Act (ASTEROIDS Act)', U.S. House of Representatives, H.R. 5063, 113th Congress (2014).

Ames, M. 2013, *Meet Charles Koch's Brain*, Not Safe For Work Corporation, Las Vegas.

Andrews, S.J. 2014, 'Modernity, law and the violence of piracy, property and the state', in M. Fredriksson & J. Arvanitakis (eds.), *Piracy: Leakages from Modernity*, Lilwin Books, Sacramento.

Armitage, D. 2004, 'John Locke, Carolina, and the *Two Treatises of Government*', *Political Theory*, vol. 32, no. 5, pp. 602–627.

The Artemis Accords: principles for cooperation in the civil exploration and use of the Moon, Mars, comets and asteroids for peaceful purposes, adopted 13 October 2020, viewed 14 August 2023, <https://www.nasa.gov/specials/artemis-accords/img/Artemis-Accords-signed-13Oct2020.pdf>.

Arvanitakis, J. & Fredriksson, M. 2016, 'Commons, piracy, and the crisis of property', *TripleC*, vol. 14, no. 1, pp. 132–144, viewed 9 August 2023, <http://www.triple-c.at/index.php/tripleC/article/view/680>.

Asimov, I. 1985, 'Our future in the cosmos – space', in J. Burke, J. Berman & I. Asimov (eds.), *The Impact of Science on Society*, SP-482, NASA Langley Research Center, Hampton, VA, pp. 79–96.

Atlas Network 2019, *Seasteading Institute*, Atlas Network, Arlington, VA, archived website, viewed 9 August 2023, <https://web.archive.org/web/20190326112609/https://www.atlasnetwork.org/partners/global-directory/seasteading-institute>.

Atlas Network 2023, *Our Mission*, Atlas Network, Arlington, VA, viewed 9 August 2023, <https://www.atlasnetwork.org/our-mission>.

Austrian Economic Center 2015, *Annual Gala: Peter Thiel Awarded by the Austrian Economic Center*, AEC, Vienna, viewed 9 August 2023, <https://www.austriancenter.com/annual-gala-peter-thiel-awarded-by-the-austrian-economics-center/>.

Ax, J. 2018, 'SpaceX launches first U.S. national security space mission', *Reuters*, 24 December, viewed 9 August 2023, <https://www.reuters.com/article/us-space-spacex-launch-idUSKCN1OM0D9>.

Bainbridge, W.S. 1976, *The Spaceflight Revolution: A Sociological Study*, Wiley, New York.

Babcock, H. M., The Public Trust Doctrine, Outer Space, and the Global Commons: Time to Call Home ET, 2019, vol. 69, no .2, *Syracuse Law Review*, pp. 191–262.

Bair, J. 2009, 'Taking aim at the new international economic order', in P. Mirowski & D. Plehwe (eds.), *The Road from Mont Pèlerin: The Making of the Neoliberal Thought Collective*, Harvard University Press, Cambridge, MA, pp. 347–385.

Bandow, D. 1980, 'Across-the-Board Tax Cuts – But not freedom', *Reason*, August, Reason Foundation, Los Angeles, viewed 9 August 2023, <https://reason.com/1980/08/01/across-the-board-tax-cutsbut-n/>.

Bandow, D. 1982, 'Developing the mineral resources of the seabed', *Cato Journal*, vol. 2, no. 3, pp. 793–821.

Bandow, D. 1985, 'Totalitarian Global Management: The UN's War on the Liberal International Economic Order', *Cato Institute Policy Analysis*, no.61, Cato Institute, Washington, DC, viewed 9 August 2023, <https://object.cato.org/pubs/pas/pa061.pdf>.

Barbrook, R. & Cameron, A. 1996, 'The Californian ideology', *Science as Culture*, vol. 6, no. 1, pp. 44–72.

Barnatt, C. 2014, 'Rather than desecrate the Artic, should business mine the moon?', *The Guardian*, 27 August, viewed 9 August 2023, <http://www.theguardian.com/sustainable-business/blog/2014/aug/27/arctic-business-mining-moon-space-sustainability>.

Barthes, R. 1957, *Mythologies*, trans. A. Lavers, republished 1973, Paladin, London.

Baslar, K, 1998, *The Concept of the Common Heritage of Mankind in International Law*, Kluwer Law International, The Hague.

Basu, A. & Kurlekar, A. 2016, 'Highway to the danger zone: United States legislative framework regulating the commercial space sector', *Astropolitics*, vol. 14, no. 1, pp. 44–70.

Becker, A. 2019, 'A science journal funded by Peter Thiel is running articles dismissing climate change and evolution', *Mother Jones*, 29 January, viewed 9 August 2023, <https://www.motherjones.com/environment/2019/01/a-science-journal-funded-by-peter-thiel-is-running-articles-dismissing-climate-change-and-evolution/>.

Bell, D. 1973, *The Coming of Post-industrial Society: A Venture in Social Forecasting*, Basic Books, New York.
Bennett, J.T. 1981, 'The second space race', *Reason*, 1 November, Reason Foundation, Los Angeles, archived website, viewed 9 August 2023, <http://reason.com/archives/1981/11/01/the-second-space-race/>.
Benton, L. & Straumann, B. 2010, 'Acquiring empire by law: From Roman doctrine to early modern European practice', *Law and History Review*, vol. 28, no. 1, pp. 1–38.
Berlin, I. 1969, *Two Concepts of Liberty*, Oxford University Press, Oxford.
Bhala, R. 1999, 'The myth about stare decisis and international trade law (part one of a trilogy)', *American University International Law Review*, vol. 14, no. 4, pp. 845–956.
Bigelow, R.T. 2017, Statement of Robert T. Bigelow, Founder and President, Bigelow Aerospace, LLC, *Reopening the American Frontier: Reducing Regulatory Barriers and Expanding American Free Enterprise in Space*, before the U.S. Senate Committee on Commerce, Science, and Transportation, Subcommittee on Science, Space, and Competitiveness, 115th Congress (26 April 2017).
Billingham, J. & Gilbreath, W. 1977, *Space Resources and Space Settlements*, SP-428, NASA Ames, Moffett Field, CA, viewed 9 August 2023, <https://ntrs.nasa.gov/api/citations/19790024054/downloads/19790024054.pdf>.
Bjørnvig, T. 2013, 'Outer space religion and the overview effect: A critical inquiry into a classic of the pro-space movement', *Astropolitics*, vol. 11, pp. 4–24.
Blackstone, W. 1893, 'Book the second: of the rights of things', in *Commentaries on the Laws of England in Four Books, vol.1*, J.B. Lippincott Co., Philadelphia, re-published 2019, Liberty Fund, viewed 9 August 2023, <http://oll.libertyfund.org/titles/blackstone-commentaries-on-the-laws-of-england-in-four-books-vol-1>.
Blasko, A. 2004, *Reagan and Heritage: A Unique Partnership*, weblog, 7 July, The Heritage Foundation, Washington, DC, viewed 9 August 2023, <https://www.heritage.org/conservatism/commentary/reagan-and-heritage-unique-partnership>.
Block, F. 2001, 'Introduction', in K. Polanyi (ed.), *The Great Transformation*, Beacon Press, Boston, MA, pp. xviii–xxxviii.
Block, F. & Somers, M.R. 2014, *The Power of Market Fundamentalism: Karl Polanyi's Critique*, Harvard University Press, Cambridge, MA.
Block, W. & Huebert, J.H. 2008, *Environmentalists in Outer Space*, weblog, 1 March, Foundation for Economic Education, New York, viewed 9 August 2023, <https://fee.org/articles/environmentalists-in-outer-space/>.
Blouet, B.W. 1994, 'Geopolitics revisited', *Journal of Geography*, vol. 93, no. 6, pp. 285–288.
Blue Origin 2019, *Going to Space to Benefit Earth*, videorecording, YouTube, viewed 9 August 2023, <https://www.youtube.com/watch?v=GQ98hGUe6FM>.
Blue Origin 2022, *Blue Origin Successfully Completes 22nd Mission to Space*, press release, 4 August, viewed 14 August 2023, <https://www.blueorigin.com/news/ns-22-mission-updates>.
Bodin, J. 1576, *Six Books of the Commonwealth*, trans. M.J. Toohey, republished 1967, Basil Blackwell, Oxford.
Bolden, C. 2014, 'American companies selected to return astronaut launches to American Soil', *NASA Blogs*, weblog, NASA, Washington, DC, viewed 9 August 2023, <https://blogs.nasa.gov/bolden/2014/09/16/american-companies-selected-to-return-astronaut-launches-to-american-soil/>.
Bollier, D. 2002, *Silent Theft: The Plunder of Our Common Wealth*, Routledge, New York.
Bollier, D. & Watts, T. 2002, *Saving the Information Commons: A Public Interest Agenda in Digital Media*, New America Foundation, Washington, DC, viewed 9 August 2023, <https://dlc.dlib.indiana.edu/dlc/bitstream/handle/10535/19/Pub_File_866_1.pdf?sequence=1&isAllowed=y>.

Bottomley, S. & Bronitt, S. 2018, *Law in Context*, 4th edn., The Federation Press, Sydney.

Boulding, K.E. 1966, 'The economics of the coming spaceship Earth', in H. Jarrett (ed.), *Environmental Quality in a Growing Economy*, John Hopkins University Press, Baltimore, MD.

Boyle, A. 2018a, 'Amid departures, Planetary Resources is holding out hope for an asteroid mining comeback', *GeekWire*, 25 June, viewed 9 August 2023, <https://www.geekwire.com/2018/amid-departures-planetary-resources-holds-hope-asteroid-mining-comeback/>.

Boyle, A. 2018b, 'Financially strapped planetary resources gets set to auction off equipment at HQ', *GeekWire*, 7 August, viewed 9 August 2023, <https://www.geekwire.com/2018/planetary-resources-auction/>.

Bozeman, J. 1997, 'Technological millenarianism in the United States', in T. Robbins & S.J. Palmer (eds.), *Millennium, Messiahs and Mayhem*, Routledge, New York, pp. 139–158.

Bradford Space n.d., *Locations*, Bradford Space Inc., San Jose, CA, viewed 9 August 2023, <https://www.bradford-space.com/locations>.

Bradford Space 2019, *Bradford Space Group Acquires Control of Deep Space Industries, Inc.*, press release, 2 January, Bradford Space Inc., San Jose, CA, archived website, viewed 16 August 2023, <https://web.archive.org/web/20191031223138/http://bradford-space.com/news2019-01-02.php>.

Brandt-Erichsen, D. 1994, 'Brief History of the L-5 Society', *Ad Astra*, Nov–Dec, National Space Society, Washington, DC, archived website, viewed 15 April 2019, <https://web.archive.org/web/20190727143126/https://space.nss.org/brief-history-of-the-l5-society/>.

Bromberg, J.L. 1999, *NASA and the Space Industry*, John Hopkins University, Baltimore, MD.

Bromley, D.W. 1991, *Environment and Economy: Property Rights and Public Policy*, Basil Blackwell, Oxford.

Brown, W. 2015, 'Law and legal reason', in *Undoing the Demos: Neoliberalism's Stealth Revolution*, Zone Books, New York, pp. 151–173.

Bryson, B. 2005, *A Short History of Nearly Everything*, Transworld Publishers, London.

Buchanan, J. & Tullock, G. 1962, *The Calculus of Consent*, University of Michigan Press, Ann Arbor, MI.

Burnett, N. 1981, 'The Ex-Kennecott Lobbyist and the Scuttled Sea Law', *Washington Post*, 22 March, viewed 9 August 2023, <https://www.washingtonpost.com/archive/opinions/1981/03/22/the-ex-kennecott-lobbyist-and-the-scuttled-sea-law/4cf8d117-6365-4fd2-857a-7a910527361e/>.

Butler, S.M., Sanera, M. & Weinrod, W.B. 1984, *Mandate for Leadership II: Continuing the Conservative Revolution*, Heritage Foundation, Washington, DC.

Caffentzis, G. 2005, 'The petroleum commons: Local, Islamic and global', *Alternatives*, vol. 4, no. 1 & 2, pp. 108–123.

Cahill, D. 2014, *The End of Laissez-faire? On the Durability of Embedded Neoliberalism*, Edwards Elgar, London.

Callahan, G. 2007, *How Free Society Could Solve Global Warming*, Foundation for Economic Education, New York, 1 October, viewed 9 August 2023, <https://fee.org/articles/how-a-free-society-could-solve-global-warming/>.

Carey, J. 1999, 'Introduction', in J. Carey (ed.), *The Faber Book of Utopias*, Faber, London, pp. xi–xxvi.

Castree, N. 2010, 'Neoliberalism and the biophysical environment: A synthesis and evaluation of the research', in *Environment and Society: Advances in Research*, 1, pp. 5–45.

Chasan, E. 2019, 'Amazon's new environmental report will show how bad two-day shipping is', *Bloomberg*, 21 February, viewed 9 August 2023, <https://www.bloomberg.com/news/articles/2019-02-20/amazon-amzn-agrees-to-reveal-carbon-footprint-in-2019>.

Christman, J. 2014, *The Myth of Property: Toward an Egalitarian Theory of Ownership*, Oxford University Press, Oxford.

Cicero n.d., *De Officiis*, trans. W. Miller, 1913, William Heinemann, London & The Macmillan Co., New York.

Cirillo, R. 1980, 'The "socialism" of Léon Walras and his economic thinking', *The American Journal of Economics and Sociology*, vol. 39, no. 3, pp. 295–303.

Claim the Sky n.d., *Claim the Sky*, viewed 9 August 2023, <http://claimthesky.org/>.

Clark, B. & York, R. 2012, 'Techno-fix: ecological rifts and capital shifts', in A. Hornborg, B. Clark & K. Hermele (eds.), *Ecology and Power: Struggles over Land and Material Resources in the Past, Present and Future*, Routledge, Abingdon, pp. 23–36.

Coase, R. 1960, 'The problem of social cost', *Journal of Law and Economics*, vol. 3, pp. 1–44.

Cohen, M.R. 1927, 'Property and sovereignty', *Cornell Law Review*, vol. 13, no. 1, pp. 8–30.

Collis, C. 2009, 'The geostationary orbit: A critical legal geography of space's most valuable real estate', in D. Bell & M. Parker (eds.), *Space Travel and Culture: From Apollo to Space Tourism*, Wiley-Blackwell/Sociological Review, Malden, MA, pp. 47–65.

Colman, T. 2010, 'Gold in Britain: Past, present and future', *Mercian Geologist*, vol. 14, no3, pp. 173–180.

Commercial Space Launch Act 1984. U.S. Congress, Pub.L. 98-575.

Congressional Record 2015a, *Statement of Rep. Donna Edwards*, House of Representatives, vol. 161, no. 79, 21 May.

Congressional Record 2015b, *Statement of Rep. Dana Rohrabacher*, House of Representatives, vol. 161, no. 79, 21 May.

Connery, C.L. 2001, 'Ideologies of land and sea: Alfred Thayer Mahan, Carl Schmitt, and the shaping of global myth elements', *Boundary 2*, vol. 28, no. 2, pp. 173–201.

Cooper, J.C. 1951, 'High altitude flight and national sovereignty', *International Law Quarterly*, vol. 4, pp. 411–418.

Cooper, L.A. 2003, 'Encouraging space exploration through a new application of space property rights', *Space Policy*, vol. 19, pp. 111–118.

Cooper, M. 2005, *Pre-empting emergence: The biological turn in the war on terror*, Working Paper no. 6, Global Biopolitics Research Group, University of East Anglia.

Cooper, M. 2007, 'Life, autopoeisis and debt', *Distinktion: Journal of Social Theory*, vol. 8, no. 1, pp. 25–43.

Cooper, M. 2008, *Life as Surplus: Biotechnology and Capitalism in the Neoliberal Era*, e-book, University of Washington Press, Seattle, WA.

Copulos, M.R. 1985, 'Commercial obstacles to the commercial use of space', *Backgrounder*, no.413, The Heritage Foundation, Washington, DC, viewed 9 August 2023, <http://s3.amazonaws.com/thf_media/1985/pdf/bg413.pdf>.

Cornish, C. 2017, 'Interplanetary players: A who's who of space mining', *Financial Times*, 19 October, viewed 9 August 2023, <https://www.ft.com/content/fb420788-72d1-11e7-93ff-99f383b09ff9>.

Cosgrove, D. 2001, *Apollo's Eye: A Cartographic Genealogy of the Earth in the Western Imagination*, John Hopkins University Press, Baltimore, MD.

Costanza, R. 2016, 'Hold atmosphere in trust for all', *Nature*, vol. 529, p.466.

Crawford, A.P. 1986, 'An "industrial policy" for space?', in *Policy Analysis*, no.69, Cato Institute, Washington, DC.
Cristi, R. 1984, 'Hayek and Schmitt on the rule of law', *Canadian Journal of Political Science/Revue Canadienne de science politique*, vol. 17, no. 3, pp. 521–535.
Crunchbase 2019a, Planetary Resources, Crunchbase, San Francisco, data viewed 29 September 2019, <https://www.crunchbase.com/organization/planetary-resources/company_financials>.
Crunchbase 2019b, Moon Express, Crunchbase, San Francisco, data viewed 29 September 2019, <https://www.crunchbase.com/organization/moon-express-inc/company_financials>.
Crunchbase 2019c, Deep Space Industries, Crunchbase, San Francisco, data viewed 29 September 2019, <https://www.crunchbase.com/organization/deep-space-industries---dsi/company_financials>.
Crunchbase 2019d, iSpace, Crunchbase, San Francisco, data viewed 29 September 2019, <https://www.crunchbase.com/organization/ispace-technologies-inc-/company_financials>.
Crunchbase 2020, Planetary Power, Inc., Crunchbase, San Francisco, viewed 30 September 2019, <https://www.crunchbase.com/organization/planetary-power#section-overview>.
Crutzen, P.J. 2002, 'Geology of mankind', *Nature*, vol. 415, no. 6867, p.23.
Cruz, T. 2018, *Sen. Cruz: Prematurely Canceling NASA Programs for Political Reasons Costs Jobs and Wastes Billions of Dollars*, press release, 17 May, viewed 9 August 2023, <https://www.cruz.senate.gov/newsroom/press-releases/sen-cruz-and-lsquoprematurely-cancelling-nasa-programs-for-political-reasons-costs-jobs-and-wastes-billions-of-dollars-and-rsquo>.
Dahlin J. & Fredriksson, M. 2017, 'Extracting the commons', *Cultural Studies*, vol. 31, no. 2–3, pp. 253–276.
Davidson, J.D. & Rees-Mogg, W. 1999, *The Sovereign Individual: Mastering the Transition to the Information Age*, Touchstone, New York.
Davidson, K. 1999, *Carl Sagan: A Life*, Wiley, New York.
Davis, E. 2015, *Techgnosis: Myth, Magic, and Mysticism in the Age of Information*, North Atlantic Books, Berkeley, CA.
Dean, M. 2006, 'A political mythology of world order: Carl Schmitt's *Nomos*', *Theory, Culture & Society*, vol. 23, no. 5, pp. 1–22.
Dean, M. 2014, 'Rethinking neoliberalism', *Journal of Sociology*, vol. 50, no. 2, pp. 150–163.
Dembling, P.G. & Arons, D.M. 1967, 'The evolution of the Outer Space Treaty', *Journal of Air Law and Commerce*, vol. 33, pp. 419–456.
Deep Space Industries 2015, *U.S. Makes Space History: President Obama Signs Law Enabling Commercial Exploration and Use of Space Resources*, press release, 25 November, Bradford Space Inc., archived website, viewed 9 August 2023, <https://web.archive.org/web/20191025132420/http://deepspaceindustries.com/u-s-makes-space-history/>.
Deep Space Industries 2016, *Building an Unlimited Future: Deep Space Industries 2016 Prospectus*, DSI, Moffett Field, CA.
Deep Space Industries 2018, *Who We Are*, Bradford Space Inc., archived website, viewed 9 August 2023, <https://web.archive.org/web/20180209035307/http://deepspaceindustries.com/company>.
Deep Space Industries 2019, *Advanced Space Resource Utilization Technology Projects Supported by New NASA Awards to Deep Space Industries*, Bradford Space Inc., archived website, viewed 9 August 2023, <https://web.archive.org/web/20191031203039/http://deepspaceindustries.com/advanced-space-resource-utilization-technology-projects-supported-by-new-nasa-awards-to-deep-space-industries/>.

DeGroot, G.J. 2006, *Dark Side of the Moon: The Magnificent Madness of the American Lunar Quest*, New York University Press, New York.

Denis, G., Alary, D., Pasco, X., Pisot, N., Texier, D. & Toulza, S. 2020, 'From new space to big space: How commercial space dream is becoming a reality', *Acta Astronautica*, vol. 166, pp. 431–443.

Department of Defense 2018, *Final Report on Organizational and Management Structure for the National Security Space Components of the Department of Defense*, DoD, Washington, DC.

Deudney, D. 1982, *Space: The High Frontier in Perspective*, paper 50, Worldwatch Institute, Washington, DC.

Devlin, H. 2019, 'First green leaf on moon dies as temperatures plummet', *The Guardian*, 17 January, viewed 9 August 2023, <https://www.theguardian.com/science/2019/jan/16/china-first-cotton-plant-on-moon-dies-change-4-lander>.

Diamandis, P. & Kotler, S. 2012, *Abundance: The Future Is Better than You Think*, Free Press, New York.

Dickens, P., & Ormrod, J. S. 2007, *Cosmic Society: Towards a Sociology of the Universe*, Routledge, Abingdon.

Doctorow, C. & Stross, C. 2012, *The Rapture of the Nerds*, Tor Books, New York.

Donnelly, S. 2016, *Leaving London: The Road to Cambridge*, London School of Economics, viewed 9 August 2023, <https://blogs.lse.ac.uk/lsehistory/2019/09/26/leaving-london-the-road-to-cambridge/>.

Doran, C. 2012, *Making the World Safe for Capitalism: How Iraq Threatened the US Economic Empire and Had to Be Destroyed*, Pluto Press, London.

Douthit, N. 1992, 'The Hudson's Bay Company and the Indians of Southern Oregon', *Oregon Historical Quarterly*, vol. 93, no. 1, pp. 25–64.

Drexler, K.E. 1983, 'The asteroidal manifesto or, is the Moon really the next logical step?' *L-5 News*, February, National Space Society, Washington, DC, viewed 14 August 2023, <https://space.nss.org/l5-news-the-asteroidal-manifesto/>.

Driscoll, R.W. 1963, *Engineering Man for Space: The Cyborg Study*, excerpts, Report NASw-512, United Aircraft report to NASA (OART) Biotechnology and Human Research, NASA Historical Reference Collection, NASA, Washington, DC.

Dula, A. 1979a, 'Free enterprise and the proposed Moon Treaty – Part I', *L-5 News*, November, National Space Society, Washington, DC, pp. 1–2, viewed 14 August 2023, <https://space.nss.org/wp-content/uploads/L5-News-1979-10.pdf>.

Dula, A. 1979b, 'Free enterprise and the proposed Moon Treaty – Part II', *L-5 News*, November, National Space Society, Washington, DC, pp. 3–7, viewed 14 August 2023, <https://space.nss.org/wp-content/uploads/L5-News-1979-11.pdf>.

von der Dunk, F. 2011, 'The origins of authorisation: Article VI of the outer space treaty and International Space Law', *Space, Cyber, and Telecommunications Law Program Faculty Publications*, vol. 66, pp. 1–19.

von der Dunk, F. 2012, 'Regulating the final frontier', *The Futurist*, September–October, p.20.

von der Dunk, F. 2020, *The Artemis Accords and the Law: Is the Moon 'back in business'?*, University of Auckland, 2 June, viewed 9 August 2023, <https://www.thebigq.org/2020/06/02/the-artemis-accords-and-the-law-is-the-moon-back-in-business/>.

Dunstan, J.E. 2002, 'Toward a unified theory of space property rights: Sometimes the best way to predict the weather is to look outside', in E.L. Hudgins (ed.), *Space: The Free-Market Frontier*, Cato Institute, Washington, DC, pp. 223–243.

Dunstan, J.E. & Szoka, B. 2017, 'Written Testimony of James E. Dunstan & Berin Szoka', *Reopening the American Frontier: Exploring How the Outer Space Treaty Will Impact American Commerce and Settlement in Space*, before the U.S. Senate Committee on Commerce, Science, and Transportation, Subcommittee on Science, Space, and Competitiveness, 115th Congress (23 May 2017).

Dyson, F. 1972, 'The world, the flesh and the devil. The Third J.D. Bernal Lecture', in J. Carey (ed.) 1998, *The Faber Book of Utopias*, Faber, London, pp. 463–471.
Dyson, F. 1993, 'Gerard kitchen O'Neill', *Physics Today*, vol. 46, no. 2, pp. 97–98.
Edwards, J. 2017, 'Goldman Sachs says space-mining for platinum with asteroid-grabbing spacecraft is 'more realistic than perceived', *Business Insider*, 6 April, viewed 14 August 2023, <https://www.businessinsider.com.au/goldman-sachs-space-mining-asteroid-platinum-2017-4?r=US&IR=T>.
Egger, J.B. 1994, 'The contributions of W.H. Hutt', *The Review of Austrian Economics*, vol. 7, no. 1, pp. 107–138.
Ehrlich, P. 1971, *The Population Bomb*, Ballantine Books, New York.
Elden, S. 2013, 'Secure the volume: Vertical geopolitics and the depth of power', *Political Geography*, vol. 34, pp. 35–51.
Ellis, T. 2016, 'Contesting the High Frontier: Professor Gerard K. O'Neill, Lieutenant General Daniel O. Graham and the future of American space-capitalism', paper presented to the Royal Geographical Society, 2 September, viewed 14 August 2023, <https://www.academia.edu/28288730/Contesting_The_High_Frontier_Professor_Gerard_K_ONeill_Lieutenant_General_Daniel_O_Graham_and_the_Future_of_American_Space_Capitalism>.
Engels, F. 1887, *Condition of the Working Class in England*, republished 1998, Marxists Internet Archive, viewed 14 August 2023, <https://www.marxists.org/archive/marx/works/download/pdf/condition-working-class-england.pdf>.
Executive Office of the President [Trump White House] 2020, *Executive Order on Encouraging International Support for the Recovery and Use of Space Resources*, 6 April, White House, Washington, DC, viewed 14 August 2023, <https://trumpwhitehouse.archives.gov/presidential-actions/executive-order-encouraging-international-support-recovery-use-space-resources/>.
Extropy Institute 2005, *Prologue: What is the Purpose of the Principles of Extropy?*, Extropy Institute, viewed 14 August 2023, <http://www.extropy.org/About.htm>.
Exxonsecrets.org, n.d., *Organizations in Exxon secrets database*, Greenpeace, viewed 11 January 2019, <https://exxonsecrets.org/html/listorganizations.php>.
Farman, A. 2012, 'Re-enchantment cosmologies: Mastery and obsolescence in an intelligent universe', *Anthropological Quarterly*, vol. 85, no. 4, pp. 1069–1088.
Fassbender, B. 2003, 'Sovereignty and constitutionalism in international law', in N. Walker (ed.), *Sovereignty in Transition*, Hart, Oxford, pp. 115–143.
Faure, G. & Mensing, T.M. 2007, *Introduction to Planetary Science: The Geological Perspective*, Springer, Dordrecht, London.
Federal Law No. 12 of 2019 On the Regulation of the Space Sector, United Arab Emirates, issued 19 December 2019, Official Gazette, no. 669, p.111, viewed 14 August 2023, <https://space.gov.ae/Documents/PublicationPDFFiles/SpaceSectorFederalLaw_EN.pdf>.
Federal Procurements Data System 2023a, 'Planetary Resources' in *Contract Search*, General Services Administration, Washington, DC, data produced on 20 March 2023, <https://www.fpds.gov/common/jsp/FPDS.jsp>.
Federal Procurements Data System 2023b, 'Deep Space Industries' in *Contract Search*, General Services Administration, Washington, DC, data produced on 20 March 2023, <https://www.fpds.gov/common/jsp/FPDS.jsp>.
Federal Procurements Data System 2023c, 'Moon Express' in *Contract Search*, General Services Administration, Washington, DC, data produced on 20 March 2023, <https://www.fpds.gov/common/jsp/FPDS.jsp>.
Finney, B.R. & Jones, E.M. 1985, 'Introduction', in B.R. Finney & E.M. Jones (eds.), *Interstellar Migration and the Human Experience*, University of California Press, Los Angeles, CA, pp. 3–13.

Finch, E.R. 1979, 'L-5 Board of Directors member, Hon. Edward R. Finch Jr., speaks out in favor of the Moon Treaty', L-5 News, vol.4, no. 11, National Space Society, Washington, D.C., archived website, viewed 4 February 2024.

Fischer, K. 2009, 'The influence of neoliberals in Chile before, during and after Pinochet', in P. Mirowski & D. Plehwe (eds.), *The Road from Mont Pèlerin: The Making of the Neoliberal Thought Collective*, Harvard University Press, Cambridge, MA, pp. 305–344).

Fitzmaurice, A. 2014, *Sovereignty, Property and Empire 1500-2000*, Cambridge University Press, Cambridge.

Flomenhoft, G. 2018, 'Historical and empirical basis for communal title in minerals at the national level: Does ownership matter for human development?', *Sustainability*, vol. 10, no. 6, 1958.

Forbes 2023, *The Real-time Billionaires List*, Forbes Media, viewed 16 August 2023, <https://www.forbes.com/real-time-billionaires/#432b0d253d78>.

Foundation for Common Land 2016, *Rights of Common*, FCL, Carlisle, archived website, viewed 16 August 2023, <https://web.archive.org/web/20180124055849/https://foundationforcommonland.org.uk/rights-of-common>.

Foust, J. 2013, 'Bigelow report calls for use of COTS model for cislunar transportation', *NewSpace Journal*, 12 November, viewed 16 August 2023, <http://www.newspacejournal.com/2013/11/12/bigelow-report-calls-for-use-of-cots-model-for-cislunar-transportation/>.

Freeland, S. 2017, 'Common heritage, not common law: How international law will regulate proposals to exploit space resources', *Questions of International Law*, 30 January, viewed 16 August 2023, <http://www.qil-qdi.org/common-heritage-not-common-law-international-law-will-regulate-proposals-exploit-space-resources/>.

Freeland, S. 2019, 'The Legacy of the Moon Agreement, Revisited: Context, Opportunities and Risks', presentation slides, *IISL/ECSL Symposium*, 1 April, International Institute of Space Law and European Centre for Space Law, Vienna, viewed 16 August 2023, <https://www.unoosa.org/documents/pdf/copuos/lsc/2019/symp-06E.pdf>.

Free Radical Productions 2008, *Orphans of Apollo*, Free Radical Productions, viewed 16 August 2023, <http://www.orphansofapollo.com/>.

Friedman, M. 1962, *Capitalism and Freedom*, University of Chicago Press, Chicago.

Friedman, M. 1993, 'Why government is the problem', *Essays in Public Policy*, no.39, Hoover Institution Press, viewed 16 August 2023, <https://www.hoover.org/sites/default/files/uploads/documents/friedman-government-problem-1993.pdf>

Friedman, P. 2018, 'Beyond democracy: Could seasteads and cryptocurrencies replace the nation state?', *Spectator*, 10 November, viewed 16 August 2023, <https://www.spectator.co.uk/article/beyond-democracy-could-seasteads-and-cryptocurrencies-replace-the-nation-state//>.

Friedrich, C. 1955, 'The political thought of neo-liberalism', *The American Political Science Review*, vol. 49, no. 2, pp. 509–525.

Fuller, R.B. 1969, *Operating Manual for Spaceship Earth*, Southern Illinois University Press, Carbondale, IL.

Gabrynowicz, J.I. 2004, 'Space law: Its cold war origins and challenges in the era of globalization', *Suffolk University Law Review*, vol. 37, pp. 1041–1065.

Gabrynowicz, J.I. 2014, 'Written testimony of Joanne Irene Gabrynowicz', *Exploring our Solar System: The Asteroids Act as a key step – Hearing on H.R. 5063*, before the U.S. House of Representatives Committee on Science, Space, and Technology, Subcommittee on Space, 113th Congress (10 September 2014).

Gabrynowicz, J.I. 2017, 'Title IV of the 2015 U.S. Commercial Space Launch Competitiveness Act', presentation slides, *IISL/ECSL Symposium*, 27 March, International Institute of Space Law and European Centre for Space Law,

Vienna, viewed 16 August 2023, <http://www.unoosa.org/documents/pdf/copuos/lsc/2017/symp-05.pdf>.

Gabrynowicz, J.I. 2019 [unpublished], 'Answers to Questions Submitted for the Record by Chairwoman Kendra S. Horn', *A review of NASA's plans for the International Space Station and future activities in low Earth orbit*, before U.S. House of Representatives Committee on Science, Space and Technology, Subcommittee on Space and Aeronautics, 116th Congress (10 July 2019).

Gacek, C.M. & Malone, J.L. 1992, 'Guidelines for the U.N. Environmental Conference', *Backgrounder*, no. 874, The Heritage Foundation, Washington, DC, viewed 16 August 2023, <http://s3.amazonaws.com/thf_media/1992/pdf/bg874.pdf>.

Galbraith, J.K. 1970, 'Economics as a system of belief', *The American Economic Review*, vol.60, no.2, Papers and Proceedings of the Eighty-second Annual Meeting of the American Economic Association (May, 1970), pp.469–478.

Gangale, T. 2009, *The Development of Outer Space: Sovereignty and Property Rights in International Space Law*, Praegar, California.

Genovese, T.R. 2017, 'The New Right Stuff: Social Imaginaries of Outer Space and the Capitalist Accumulation of the Cosmos', Masters dissertation, Northern Arizona University.

Gerstenzang, J. 1986, '"Star Wars" leads all defence costs: Anti-missile program fast becoming a solidly entrenched part of budget', *Los Angeles Times*, 13 July, viewed 16 August 2023, <https://www.latimes.com/archives/la-xpm-1986-07-13-mn-20681-story.html>.

Gill, S. 2002, 'Constitutionalizing inequality and the clash of globalizations', *International Studies Review*, vol. 4, no. 2, pp. 47–65.

Gilroy, P. 2004, *After Empire: Multiculture or Postcolonial Melancholia*, Routledge, London.

Gluckman, H. 1978, 'We have friends in Congress', *L-5 News*, vol. 3, no. 3, National Space Society, Washington, DC, p.5, viewed 16 August 2023, https://web.archive.org/web/20191001000000*/https://space.nss.org/media/L5-News-1978-03.pdf.

Gorove, S. 1969, 'Interpreting article II of the Outer Space Treaty', *Fordham Law Review*, vol. 37, no. 3, pp. 349–354.

Government of the Grand Duchy of Luxembourg 2016, *SpaceResources.lu: New Space Law to Provide Framework for Space Resource Utilization*, press release, 3 June, viewed 16 August 2023, <https://gouvernement.lu/fr/actualites/toutes_actualites/communiques/2016/06-juin/03-spaceresources.html>.

Graham, D.O. 1982, 'Defense and development on the high frontier', *Imprimis*, vol. 11, no. 6, viewed 16 August 2023, <https://imprimis.hillsdale.edu/defense-and-development-on-the-high-frontier/>.

Granjou, C., Walker, J. & Salazar, J.F. 2017, 'The politics of anticipation: On knowing and governing environmental futures', *Futures*, vol. 92, pp. 5–11.

Gray, K. 1991, 'Property in thin air', *Cambridge Law Journal*, vol. 50, no. 2, pp. 252–307.

Grearson, J. & Bennett, J.C. 2019, *The Economics of Space: An Industry Ready to Launch*, Reason Foundation, Los Angeles, CA.

Grewal, D.S. & Purdy, J. 2014, 'Introduction: Law and neoliberalism', *Law and Contemporary Problems*, vol. 77, no. 1, pp. 1–23.

Gronstal, A. 2016, 'How deadly would a nearby gamma ray burst be?', *News and Discoveries*, Astrobiology at NASA, viewed 16 August 2023, <https://astrobiology.nasa.gov/news/how-deadly-would-a-nearby-gamma-ray-burst-be/>.

Grotius, H. 1609, *Mare Liberum*, re-published 2004, Liberty Fund, IN.

Gruss, M. 2016, 'Bezos to donate Heinlein Prize winnings to student group', *SpaceNews*, 14 September, viewed 16 August 2023, <https://spacenews.com/bezos-to-donate-heinlein-prize-winnings-to-student-group/>.

Guardian Australia 2019, *The Transparency Project*, series, Guardian News and Media Limited, viewed 16 August 2023, <https://www.theguardian.com/australia-news/series/the-transparency-project>.

Guillaume, B. 2014, 'Vernadsky's philosophical legacy: A perspective from the Anthropocene', *Anthropocene Review*, vol. 1, no. 2, pp. 137–146.

Gump, D. 2018, 'Space resources belong to those who show up', *LinkedIn Pulse*, 11 June, viewed 16 August 2023, <https://www.linkedin.com/pulse/space-resources-belong-those-who-show-up-david-gump?articleId=6411742535911243776>.

Gunther, M. 2017, 'Climate converts: the conservatives who are switching sides on warming', *Yale Environment360*, 30 March, Yale School of Forestry and Environmental Studies, New Haven, CT, viewed 16 August 2023, <https://e360.yale.edu/features/climate-converts-the-conservatives-who-are-switching-sides-on-climate-change>.

The Hague International Space Resources Governance Working Group 2017, *Draft Building Blocks for the Development of an International Framework on Space Resource Activities*, International Institute of Air and Space Law, Leiden University, The Hague, viewed 16 August 2023, <https://www.universiteitleiden.nl/binaries/content/assets/rechtsgeleerdheid/instituut-voor-publiekrecht/lucht--en-ruimterecht/space-resources/draft-building-blocks.pdf>.

The Hague International Space Resources Governance Working Group 2018, *Recent Developments*, International Institute of Air and Space Law, Leiden University, The Hague, archived website, viewed 16 August 2023, <https://web.archive.org/web/20180726162853/https://www.universiteitleiden.nl/en/law/institute-of-public-law/institute-for-air-space-law/the-hague-space-resources-governance-working-group#first-face-to-face-meeting>.

Haley, A.G. 1956, 'Basic concepts of space law', *Jet Propulsion*, vol. 26, no. 11, pp. 951–957.

Hall, D. 2013, *Land*, Polity Press, Cambridge.

Hall, R.D. & Shayler, D.J. 2003, *Soyuz: A Universal Spacecraft*, Praxis Publishing & Springer-Verlag, Chichester.

Hamilton, C. & Grinevald, J. 2015, 'Was the Anthropocene anticipated?', *The Anthropocene Review*, vol. 2, no. 1, pp. 59–72.

Hampson, J. 2017, *The Future of Space Commercialization*, research paper, 25 January, Niskanen Center, Washington, DC, viewed 16 August 2023, <https://republicans-science.house.gov/sites/republicans.science.house.gov/files/documents/TheFutureofSpaceCommercializationFinal.pdf>.

Harcourt, B. 2011, *The Illusion of Free Market: Punishment and the Myth of Natural Order*, Harvard University Press, Cambridge, MA.

Hardin, G. 1968, 'The tragedy of the commons', *Science*, vol. 162, no. 3859, pp. 1243–1248.

Hardt, M. & Negri, A. 2004, *Multitude: War and Democracy in the Age of Empire*, The Penguin Press, New York.

Harland, D.M. 2005, *The Story of Space Station Mir*, Praxis Publishing & Springer-Verlag, Chichester.

Harmes, A. 2012, 'The rise of neoliberal nationalism', *Review of International Political Economy*, vol. 19, no. 1, p.59–86.

Harper, D. 2019, 'Colony', *Online Etymology Dictionary*, viewed 16 August 2023, <https://www.etymonline.com/word/colony>.

Hartwich, O.M. 2009, 'Neoliberalism: The genesis of a political swearword', in *CIS Occasional Paper*, no.114, Centre for Independent Studies, Sydney.

Harvey, D. 1981, 'The spatial fix – Hegel, von Thunen, and Marx', *Antipode*, vol. 13, no. 3, pp. 1–12.

Harvey, D. 2004, 'The 'New' imperialism: Accumulation by dispossession', *Socialist Register*, vol. 40, pp. 63–87.
Hayek, F.A. 1950, 'The use of knowledge in society', *American Economic Review*, vol. 35, no. 4, pp. 519–530.
Hayek, F.A. 1981, 'The best book on general economics in many a year', *Reason*, December, Reason Foundation, Los Angeles, CA, viewed 19 August 2023, <https://reason.com/1981/12/01/the-best-book-on-general-econo/>.
Hayek, F.A. 1986, *The Road to Serfdom*, Routledge, London.
HBC Heritage 2016, *Royal Charter of the Hudson's Bay Company*, Hudson's Bay Company, viewed 16 August 2023, <http://www.hbcheritage.ca/things/artifacts/the-charter-and-text#>.
Heatherly, C.L. (ed.) 1981, *Mandate for Leadership: Policy Management in a Conservative Administration*, The Heritage Foundation, Washington, DC.
Hegel, G.W.F. n.d., *The Philosophy of History*, trans. J Sibree, republished 2001, Batoche Books, Kitchener.
Heinrich, T. 2002, 'Cold War Armory: Military contracting in Silicon Valley', *Enterprise & Society*, vol. 3, June, pp. 247–284.
Heller-Roazen, D. 2009, *The Enemy of All: Piracy and the Law of Nations*, MIT Press, Cambridge, MA.
Henson, H.K. & Henson, C.M., 1975, 'Closed ecosystems of high agricultural yield', in *Princeton University Conference Meeting no. 127 on Space Manufacturing Facilities*, May, Princeton, N.J.
Henson, H.K. 1979, 'Space Forts or "where are you Obi Wan Kenobi?"', *L-5 News*, vol. 4, no. 6, National Space Society, Washington, DC, viewed 16 August 2023, URL: https://space.nss.org/media/L5-News-1979-06.pdf.
Henson, H.K. 1980, 'L5 News: Bulletin from the Moon Treaty front', *L-5 News*, January, National Space Society, Washington, DC, viewed 16 August 2023, <https://space.nss.org/l5-news-bulletin-from-the-moon-treaty-front/>.
Heritage Foundation 2016, *Blueprint for Reform: A Comprehensive Policy Agenda for A New Administration in 2017*, Heritage Foundation, Washington, DC, viewed 16 August 2023, <http://thf_media.s3.amazonaws.com/2016/BlueprintforReform.pdf>.
Heritage Foundation 2017, *Heritage Research Impacts Trump's Decision to Withdraw from Paris Climate Deal*, Heritage Foundation, Washington, DC, viewed 16 August 2023, <https://www.heritage.org/impact/heritage-research-impacts-trumps-decision-withdraw-paris-climate-deal>.
Hertzfeld, H.R., Weeden, B. & Johnson, C.D. 2016, 'Outer space: Ungoverned or lacking effective governance?: New approaches to managing human activities in space', *SAIS Review International Affairs*, vol. 36, no. 2, pp. 15–28.
Higginbotham, J. 2002, 'Private possibilities in space', in E.L. Hudgins (ed.), *Space: The Free-Market Frontier*, Cato Institute, Washington, DC, pp. 142–150.
Hilzenrath, D.S. 2005, '$200,000,000: Telecom tycoon used international financial labyrinth', *Washington Post*, 18 April, viewed 16 August 2023, <http://www.washingtonpost.com/wp-dyn/articles/A61202-2005Apr17.html>.
Hilzenrath, D.S., Leonnig, C.D. and Noguchi, Y. 2005, 'Tax case defendant says money was to do good', *Washington Post*, 4 March, viewed 16 August 2023, <https://www.washingtonpost.com/archive/politics/2005/03/04/tax-case-defendant-says-money-was-to-do-good/b3e4830f-3d6d-4b39-8a0f-731be1f9467d/>.
HitRecord on TV 2014, *RE: SPACE*, HitRecord Films, Los Angeles, CA.
Hobe, S. & de Man, P. 2017, 'National appropriation of outer space and state jurisdiction to regulate the exploitation, exploration and utilization of space resources', *Zeitschrift fur Luft- und Weltraumrecht [German Journal of Air and Space Law]*, vol. 66, no. 3, pp. 460–475.

Hoffman, P. 2010, 'Big think interview with peter diamandis', *Big Think*, 5 April, viewed 16 August 2023, <https://bigthink.com/videos/big-think-interview-with-peter-diamandis>.

Hohler, S. 2015, *Spaceship Earth in the Environmental Age, 1960-1990*, Pickering & Chatto, London.

Hopkins, M. 1982, 'L-5's inevitable victory', *L-5 News*, September, National Space Society, Washington, DC, viewed 16 August 2023, <https://space.nss.org/l5-news-l5s-inevitable-victory/>.

House Committee on Science, Space and Technology 2015a, *Report, Together with Minority Views [to accompany H.R. 2262]*, report 114-119, 114th Congress, Library of Congress, Washington, DC, viewed 16 August 2023, <https://www.congress.gov/congressional-report/114th-congress/house-report/119>.

House Committee on Science, Space and Technology 2015b, *Report, Together with Minority Views [to accompany H.R. 1508]*, report 114-153, 114th Congress, Library of Congress, Washington, DC, viewed 16 August 2023, <https://www.congress.gov/congressional-report/114th-congress/house-report/153>.

Howell, E. 2016, 'Classified Shuttle missions: Secrets in space', *Space.com*, 27 October, viewed 16 August 2023, <https://www.space.com/34522-secret-shuttle-missions.html>.

Hudgins, E.L. 1998, *Martian Law*, 15 August, Cato Institute, Washington, DC, viewed 16 August 2023, <https://www.cato.org/publications/white-paper/martian-law>.

Hudgins, E.L. 2001, 'National Aeronautics and Space Administration', in Crane, E.H. and Boaz, D. (eds) *Cato Handbook for Congress*, Cato Institute, Washington, DC, pp. 377–388.

Hudgins, E.L. 2002 (ed.), *Space: The Free Market Frontier*, Cato Institute, Washington, D.C.

Hudgins, E.L. 2006, *Ocean of Profits*, weblog, 9 May, Atlas Society, Kingwood, TX, archived website, viewed 16 August 2023, <https://web.archive.org/web/20160819204216/http://atlassociety.org/commentary/commentary-blog/4799-ocean-of-profits>.

Hudgins, E.L. 2011, *America's Pioneer Spirit: Government vs. New Frontiers*, weblog, 10 February, Atlas Society, Kingwood, TX, viewed 16 August 2023, <https://atlassociety.org/commentary/commentary-blog/4379-america-s-pioneer-spirit-government-vs-new-frontiers>.

Hudson, A. 2000, 'Offshoreness, globalization and sovereignty: A postmodern geo-political economy?', *Transactions of the Institute of British Geographers*, vol. 25, no. 3, pp. 269–283.

Hudson, M. 2003, *Super Imperialism: The Origins and Fundamentals of U.S. World Dominance* 2nd edn., Pluto Press, London.

Hufford, D. B. 1983, 'Ideological rigidity vs. political reality: A critique of Reagan's Policy on the Law of the Sea', *Yale Law & Policy Review*, vol. 2, pp. 127–166.

Hughes, J.J. 2012, 'The politics of transhumanism and the techno-millenial imagination, 1626-2030', *Zygon*, vol. 47, no. 4, pp. 757–776.

Hyde Price, W. 1906, *The English Patents of Monopoly*, Harvard University Press, Cambridge, MA.

Intergovernmental Panel on Climate Change 2023, *Climate Change 2023: Synthesis Report – Summary for Policymakers*, IPCC, Geneva.

International Institute of Space Law 2016, *Does international space law either permit or prohibit the taking of resources in outer space and on celestial bodies, and how is this relevant for national actors? What is the context, and what are the contours and limits of this permission or prohibition?*, background paper, IISL Directorate of Studies, Paris, viewed 16 August 2023, <http://iislweb.space/wp-content/uploads/2020/01/IISL_Space_Mining_Study.pdf>.

International Telecommunications Union 1992, Constitution and Convention of the International Telecommunications Union, ITU, Geneva.

Isaac, B.L. 2012, ‘Karl Polanyi’, in J.G. Carrier (ed.), *A Handbook of Economic Anthropology*, 2nd edn., Edward Elgar, Cheltenham, pp. 13–25.

Israel, B. 2019, ‘Space resources in the evolutionary course of space lawmaking’, *AJIL Unbound*, vol. 113, pp. 114–119.

iSpace Inc. n.d., *About us*, iSpace, Tokyo, viewed 16 August 2023, <https://ispace-inc.com/aboutus/>.

Jakhu, R.S. 2006, ‘Legal issues relating to the global public interest in outer space’, *Journal of Space Law*, vol. 32, pp. 31–110.

Jakhu, R.S., Pelton, J.N. & Nyampong, Y.O.M. 2017, *Space Mining and Its Regulation*, Springer Praxis Books, Switzerland.

Jazeel, T. 2011, ‘Spatializing difference beyond cosmopolitanism: Rethinking planetary futures’, *Theory, Culture & Society*, vol. 28, no. 5, pp. 75–97.

Johnson, R.D. & Holbrow, C. (eds) 1975, *Space Settlements: A Design Study*, SP-413, NASA Ames, Moffett Field View, CA, viewed 16 August 2023, <https://ntrs.nasa.gov/api/citations/19770014162/downloads/19770014162_update.pdf>.

Johnson, S. 2015, ‘Interview with Jeffrey Manber’, *International Space Station – Oral History Project*, 4 August, NASA Johnson Space Center, Huston, TX, viewed 16 August 2023, <https://historycollection.jsc.nasa.gov/JSCHistoryPortal/history/oral_histories/ISS/ManberJ/ManberJ_8-4-15.htm>.

Johnson, J. 2018, ‘“Unions Are Lying, Cheating Rats”: Leaked video reveals Amazon’s Belligerent anti-worker tactics’, *Common Dreams*, 27 September, viewed 16 August 2023, <https://www.commondreams.org/news/2018/09/27/unions-are-lying-cheating-rats-leaked-video-reveals-amazons-belligerent-anti-worker>.

Jones, R. 2018, ‘How Gina Rinehart bought the IPA’, *Independent Australia*, viewed 16 August 2023, <https://independentaustralia.net/politics/politics-display/how-gina-rinehart-bought-the-ipa,11749>.

Just Space Alliance n.d., *Our Work*, Just Space Alliance, viewed 16 August 2023, <https://justspacealliance.org/work>.

Kantorowicz, E. 1957, *The King's Two Bodies: A Study in Mediaeval Political Theology*, Princeton University Press, Princeton, NJ.

Kecskemeti, P. 1950, *The Satellite Rocket Vehicle: Political and Psychological Problems*, RM-567, RAND Corporation, Santa Monica, CA.

Kelsen, H. 1967, *Pure Theory of Law*, University of California Press, Berkeley, CA.

Kennedy, J.F. 1962, *Address at Rice University on the Nation's Space Effort*, 12 September, John. F. Kennedy Presidential Library, Boston, MA, viewed 16 August 2023, <https://www.jfklibrary.org/learn/about-jfk/historic-speeches/address-at-rice-university-on-the-nations-space-effort>.

Keohane, N.O. 2009, Cap and trade, rehabilitated: Using tradable permits to control U.S. Greenhouse Gases, *Review of Environmental Economics and Policy*, vol. 3, no. 1, pp. 42–62.

Kero, G. 2014, ‘State invests K327m’, *The National*, 25 April, Port Moresby, viewed 16 August 2023, <https://www.thenational.com.pg/state-invests-k327m/>.

Keynes, J.M. 1936, *The General Theory of Employment, Interest and Money*, Macmillan, London.

Kfir, S. 2016, ‘Is asteroid mining legal? The truth behind Title IV of the Commercial Space Launch Competitiveness Act of 2015’, *LinkedIn Pulse*, 21 April, viewed 16 August 2023, <https://www.linkedin.com/pulse/asteroid-mining-legal-sagi-kfir>.

Kfir, S. & Perry, I.B. 2017, ‘Title IV of the U.S. Commercial Space Launch Competitiveness Act of 2015: A critical step forward in facilitating the development of a viable space infrastructure’, *New Space*, vol. 5, no. 3, pp. 163–169.

Kilgore, D.D. 2003, *Astrofuturism: Science, Race and Visions of Utopia in Space*, University of Pennsylvania Press, Philadelphia, PA.

Klein, N. 2007, *The Shock Doctrine: The Rise of Disaster Capitalism*, Allen Lane, London.

Kochetkov, Y. 2000, Photo of Proton rocket with Pizza Hut logo, in Agence France-Presse, *Proton set to make pizza delivery to ISS*, 8 July, viewed 16 August 2023, <http://www.spacedaily.com/news/pizzahut-00b.html>.

Kokalitcheva, K. 2020, 'Varda Space raises $9 million for manufacturing in space', *Axios*, 8 December, viewed 16 August 2023, <https://www.axios.com/2020/12/08/varda-space-9-million-manufacturing-space>.

Konkin, S.E. 1998, *History of the Libertarian Movement*, The Anarchist Library, viewed 16 August 2023, <https://theanarchistlibrary.org/library/samuel-edward-konkin-iii-history-of-the-libertarian-movement>.

Kosoff, M. 2017, 'Elon Musk wants to merge your brain with a computer', *Vanity Fair*, 28 March, viewed 16 August 2023, <https://www.vanityfair.com/news/2017/03/elon-musk-neuralink-investment>.

Kramer, W.R. 2014, 'To humbly go: Guarding against perpetuating models of colonization in the 100-year starship study', *Journal of the British Interplanetary Society*, vol. 67, pp. 180–186.

Kshatriya, A. & Kirasich, M. 2022, *Artemis I-IV mission overview/status*, presentation slides, 31 October, NASA Advisory Council, viewed 16 August 2023, <https://www.nasa.gov/sites/default/files/atoms/files/nac_october_2022_artemis_final_rev_b.pdf>.

Kunstadter, C. 2014, *COMSTAC Business/Legal Working Group (BLWG) – September 2014*, presentation slides, XL Insurance, archived website, viewed 16 August 2023, <https://web.archive.org/web/20220207015415/https://www.faa.gov/about/office_org/headquarters_offices/ast/advisory_committee/meeting_news/media/2014/sep/Chris_Kunstadter.pdf>.

Kurzweil, R. 2005, *The Singularity is Near: When Humans Transcend Biology*, Viking Books, New York.

Lardinois, F. 2014, 'Google wins rights to lease Moffett Field, will restore Hangar One', TechCrunch, 2 October, viewed 16 August 2023, <https://techcrunch.com/2014/02/10/google-wins-right-to-lease-moffett-field-will-restore-hangar-one/>.

Launius, R.D. 2000, 'The historical dimensions of space exploration: Reflections and possibilities', *Space Policy*, vol. 16, pp. 23–38.

Launius, R.D. 2003, 'Perfect world, perfect societies – The Persistent Goal of Utopia in Human Spaceflight', *Journal of the British Interplanetary Society*, vol. 56, pp. 338–349.

Launius, R.D. 2010, 'Can we colonize the solar system? Human biology and survival in the extreme space environment', *Endeavour*, vol. 34, no. 3, pp. 122–129.

Lave, R., Mirowski, P. and Randalls, S. 2010, 'Introduction: STS and Neoliberal Science', *Social Studies of Science*, vol. 40, no. 5, pp. 659–675.

Lee, R.J. 2012, *Law and Regulation of Commercial Mining of Minerals in Outer Space*, Springer, Dordrecht.

Lerner, J. 2002, 'When bureaucrats meet entrepreneurs: The design of effective 'public venture capital' programmes', *The Economic Journal*, vol. 112, pp. 73–84.

Lerner, J., Leamon, A. & Speen, A. 2016, 'Venture capital activity in the low-earth orbit sector, in P. Besha & A. MacDonald (eds.), *Economic Development of Low Earth Orbit*, NASA, Washington, DC.

Levine, N. 2015, 'Democratize the universe', *Jacobin*, March, viewed 11 January 2019, <https://www.jacobinmag.com/2015/03/space-industry-extraction-levine/>.

Lewin, T. 1931, 'The history of government property in minerals in the United States', *St Louis Law Review*, vol. 16, no. 3, pp. 245–252.

Lewis, J.S. 1997, *Mining the Sky: Untold Riches from the Asteroids, Comets and Planets*, Helix Books, Reading, MA.
Lewis, M. 2000, *The New Thing: A Silicon Valley Story*, W.W. Norton, New York.
Lifeboat Foundation 2020a, *Blog – Solar Power*, Lifeboat Foundation, archived website, viewed 16 August 2023, <https://web.archive.org/web/20200630042321/https://lifeboat.com/blog/category/solar-power>.
Lifeboat Foundation 2020b, *About*, Lifeboat Foundation, archived website, viewed 16 August 2023, <https://web.archive.org/web/20200630051654/https://lifeboat.com/ex/about>.
Lindqvist, S. 2002, *Exterminate All the Brutes*, trans. J. Tate, Granta Publications, London.
Linklater, A. 2015, *Owning the Earth: The Transforming History of Land Ownership*, Bloomsbury, London.
Lippman, W. 1938, *The Good Society*, Allen & Unwin, London.
Littlewood M. 2021, 'Space offers true spirit of enterprise that the critics should not dismiss', *The Times*, 18 October, viewed 16 August 2023, <https://www.thetimes.co.uk/article/space-offers-true-spirit-of-enterprise-that-the-critics-should-not-dismiss-nncwq0mjt>.
Locke, J. 1690, *Second Treatise of Government*, published online 2005, Project Gutenberg Literary Archive Foundation, Salt Lake City, UT.
Loi du 20 juillet 2017 *sur l'exploration et l'utilisation des ressources de l'espace* [Law of 20 July 2017 on the Exploration and Use of Space Resources], Official Gazette of the Grand Duchy of Luxembourg, no.674, 28 July 2017.
Lowe, R. 2022, *Space Invaders: Property Rights on the Moon*. Adam Smith Foundation, London, UK.
Löwith, K. 1949, *Meaning in History: The Theological Implications of the Philosophy of History*, University of Chicago Press, Chicago.
Lucas, A. 2018, 'Revealed: The extent of job-swapping between public servants and fossil fuel lobbyists', *The Conversation*, 5 March, viewed 16 August 2023, <https://theconversation.com/revealed-the-extent-of-job-swapping-between-public-servants-and-fossil-fuel-lobbyists-88695>.
Lunar Embassy 2024a, *Lunar Embassy*, homepage, viewed 4 February 2024, <https://lunarembassy.com/>.
Lunar Embassy 2024b, *Declaration of Galactic Government*, viewed 4 February 2024, <https://lunarembassy.com/declaration-galactic-government/>.
Luxembourg Space Agency 2019, *Space Resources*, Government of the Grand Duchy of Luxembourg, Luxembourg, viewed 16 August 2023, <www.spaceresources.public.lu/en/faq.html#positioning>.
Luxembourg Space Agency 2022, *Bradford Deep Space Industries*, LSA, Luxembourg, viewed 16 August 2023, <https://space-agency.public.lu/en/expertise/space-directory/bradford_dsi.html>.
Luxinnovation 2017, *Ten good reasons to choose Luxembourg*, Government of the Grand Duchy of Luxembourg, Luxembourg, archived website, viewed 22 May 2020, <https://web.archive.org/web/20200828193032/https://space-agency.public.lu/dam-assets/publications/other/10reasons-10-17-web.pdf>.
Lyons, J. 2014, 'Miners' strike: Margaret Thatcher was prepared to declare state of emergency and use 4,500 troops to break unions', *Mirror*, 3 January, viewed 16 August 2023, <https://www.mirror.co.uk/news/uk-news/miners-strike-margaret-thatcher-prepared-2981964>.
MacLean, N. 2017, *Democracy in Chains: The Deep History of the Radical Right's Stealth Plan for America*, Viking, New York.
Machine Intelligence Research Institute 2021, *Top Contributors*, 13 November, MIRI, Berkeley, viewed 16 August 2023, <https://intelligence.org/topcontributors/>.

Mahadevan, A. 2019, *How Big Is Amazon's Carbon Footprint?*, The Poynter Institute, St. Petersburg, FL, viewed 16 August 2023, <https://www.poynter.org/tfcn/tfcn-feature/2019/how-big-is-amazons-carbon-footprint/>.

Mailer, N. 1970, *Of a Fire on the Moon*, Little, Brown & Co, Boston.

Maine, H. 1917, *Ancient Law: Its Connection to the History of Early Society*, republished 2007, Project Gutenberg Literary Archive Foundation, Salt Lake City, UT.

Malinowski, B. 1984, *Argonauts of the Western Pacific: An Account of Native Enterprise and Adventure in the Archipelagos of Melanesian New Guinea*, Waveland Press, Prospect Heights, IL.

Malm, A. & Hornborg, A. 2014, 'The geology of mankind? A critique of the Anthropocene narrative', *Anthropocene Review*, vol. 1, no. 1, pp. 62–69.

Malone, J.L. 1983, 'The United States and the Law of the Sea after UNCLOS III', *Law and Contemporary Problems*, vol. 46, no. 2, pp. 29–36.

Mansfield, B. 2007, 'Neoliberalism in the oceans: 'rationalization', property rights, and the commons question', in N. Heynen, J. McCarthy, S. Prudham & P. Robbins (eds.), *Neoliberal Environments: False Promises and Unnatural Consequences*, Routledge, Abingdon, pp. 63–73.

Markusen, A.R., Deitrick, S., Campbell, S. & Hall, P. 1991, *The Rise of the Gunbelt: The Military Remapping of Industrial America*, Oxford University Press, New York.

'Margaret Mead and L-5', *L-5 News*, December, no.4, National Space Society, Washington, DC, viewed 16 August 2023, <https://space.nss.org/wp-content/uploads/L5-News-1975-12.pdf>.

Marquez, P. 2017, 'Statement of Peter Marquez, Vice President for Global Engagement, Planetary Resources', *Reopening the American Frontier: Exploring How the Outer Space Treaty Will Impact American Commerce and Settlement in Space*, before the U.S. Senate Committee on Commerce, Science, and Transportation, Subcommittee on Science, Space, and Competitiveness, 115th Congress (23 May 2017).

Marshall, J. & da Rimini, F. 2018, 'Unreal property: Anarchism, anthropology and alchemy', in J. Arvanitakis & M. Fredriksson (eds.), *Property, Place and Piracy*, Routledge, Abingdon, pp. 50–64.

Mars Society 2020, *Founding Declaration*, The Mars Society, Lakewood, CO, viewed 16 August 2023, <https://www.marssociety.org/founding-declaration/>.

Marx, K. 1887, *Capital: A Critique of Political Economy, Volume I*, republished 2015, Marxists Internet Archive (2015), viewed 16 August 2023, <https://www.marxists.org/archive/marx/works/download/pdf/Capital-Volume-I.pdf>.

Masson-Zwaan, T. & Palkovitz, N. 2017, 'Regulation of space resource rights: Meeting the needs of States and private parties', *Questions of International Law*, 30 January, viewed 16 August 2023, <qil-qdi.org/regulation-space-resource-rights-meeting-needs-states-private-parties/>.

May, C., Borowski, A., Martin, D., Popovic, Z., Negishi, K., Hussan, J.R., Gladding, P., Hunter, P., Iskovitz, I., Kassemi, M., Bungo, M., Levine, B. & Thomas, J. 2014, 'Affect of microgravity on cardiac shape: comparison of pre- and in-flight data to mathematical modeling', *Journal of the American College of Cardiology*, vol. 63, no. 12, A1096.

Mazo, J. 2009, 'Moon over Manhattan', *Survival*, vol. 51, no. 2, pp. 225–236.

Mazzucato, M. 2013, *The Entrepreneurial State: Debunking Public vs. Private Sector Myths*, Anthem Press, London.

McCray, P.W. 2013, *The Visioneers: How a Group of Elite Scientists Pursued Space Colonies, Nanotechnologies, and A Limitless Future*, Princeton University Press, Princeton, NJ.

McCarthy, J. & Prudham, S. 2004. Neoliberal nature and the nature of neoliberalism. *Geoforum*, 35, 275–283.
McCurdy, H.E. 2011, *Space and the American Imagination*, John Hopkins University Press, Baltimore, MD.
McDougall, W. 1997, *The Heavens and the Earth: A Political History of the Space Age*, John Hopkins University Press, Baltimore, MD.
McKay, M.F., McKay, D. & Duke, M.B. (eds.) 1992, *Space Resources – Overview*, SP-509, NASA Lyndon B. Johnson Space Center, Houston, TX, viewed 16 August 2023, <https://www.lpi.usra.edu/lunar/strategies/SP509-Overview.pdf>.
Meadows, D.H., Meadows, G., Randers, J. & Behrens, W.W. 1972, *The Limits to Growth*, Universal Books, New York.
Messeri, L. 2017, 'We Need to Stop Talking About Space as a "Frontier"', *Slate*, 15 March, viewed 16 August 2023, <https://slate.com/technology/2017/03/why-we-need-to-stop-talking-about-space-as-a-frontier.html>.
Messier, D. 2018, 'Planetary Resources Holding On, Seeking New Funding', *Parabolic Arc*, 26 June, viewed 16 August 2023, <http://www.parabolicarc.com/2018/06/26/planetary-resources-holding-seeking-funding/#more-65275>.
Michaud, M.A.G. 1986, *Reaching for the High Frontier: The American Pro-space Movement, 1972-84*, Praeger, New York.
Miller, J. 1982, 'State Department investigating $100,000 fee', *New York Times*, 10 March, viewed 16 August 2023, <https://www.nytimes.com/1982/03/10/world/state-department-investigating-100000-fee.html>.
Minca, C. 2005, 'The return of the camp', *Progress in Human Geography*, vol. 29, no. 4, pp. 405–412.
Mirowksi, P. 2002, *Machine Dreams: Economics Becomes a Cyborg Science*, Cambridge University Press, Cambridge, MA.
Mirowksi, P. 2009, 'Postface: defining neoliberalism', in P. Mirowski & D. Plehwe (eds), *The Road from Mont Pèlerin: The mAking of the Neoliberal Thought Collective*, Harvard University Press, Cambridge, MA, pp. 417–446.
Mirowksi, P. 2013, *Never Let a Serious Crisis Go to Waste: How Neoliberalism Survived the Global Financial Crisis*, Verso Books, New York.
Mirowksi, P. & Plehwe, D. (eds.) 2009, *The Road from Mont Pèlerin: The Making of the Neoliberal Thought Collective*, Harvard University Press, Cambridge, MA.
Mirowski, P., Walker, J. & Abboud, A. 2013, 'Beyond denial', *Overland*, Autumn, no. 210, pp. 80–86.
Mitchell, T. 2009, 'Carbon democracy', *Economy and Society*, vol. 38, no. 3, pp. 399–432.
Monbiot, G. 2019, 'Capitalism is destroying the Earth. We need a new human right for future generations', *The Guardian*, 15 March, viewed 16 August 2023, <https://www.theguardian.com/commentisfree/2019/mar/15/capitalism-destroying-earth-human-right-climate-strike-children>.
Montague, D. 2002, 'Stolen goods: Coltan and conflict in the Democratic Republic of Congo', *SAIS Review*, vol. 22, no. 1, pp. 103–118.
Mont Pèlerin Society n.d., *Statement of Aims*, MPS, archived website, viewed 16 August 2023, <https://web.archive.org/web/20210630180513/https://www.montpelerin.org/statement-of-aims/>.
Moon Express n.d., *Moon Express – Redefining Possible*, homepage, viewed 16 August 2023, <http://moonexpress.com/>.
Moore, J.W. 2010, '"This lofty mountain of silver could conquer the whole world": Potosí and the political ecology of underdevelopment, 1545-1800', *The Journal of Philosophical Economics*, vol. IV, no. 1, pp. 59–103.
Moore, J.W. 2017, *Capitalism in the Web of Life: Ecology and the Accumulation of Capital*, Verso Books, New York.

More, T. 1551, *Utopia*, republished 2005, Project Gutenberg Literary Archive Foundation, Salt Lake City, UT.

Moore, J. W. 2023 Our capitalogenic world. *Annales Universitatis Paedagogicae Cracoviensis. Studia Poetica*, 11, 97–122.

Muncy, J., Tumlinson, R.N. & Werb, B. 2002, 'Structure of the space market: Public and private space efforts', in E.L. Hudgins (ed.), *Space: The Free-Market Frontier*, Cato Institute, Washington, DC, pp. 215–222.

Murphy, R.P. 2005, *A Free Market in Space*, blog, 1 January, The Mises Institute, Auburn, AL, viewed 16 August 2023, <https://mises.org/library/free-market-space>.

Musk, E. 2017, 'Making humans a multi-planet species', *New Space*, vol. 5, no. 2, pp. 46–61.

Nanda, V.P.J. & Ris, W.R. 1976, 'The public trust doctrine: a viable approach to international environmental protection', *Ecology Law Quarterly*, vol. 5, no. 2, pp. 291–319.

National Aeronautics and Space Administration Act of 1958, U.S. Congress, Pub.L 85-568, (1958).

National Aeronautics and Space Administration Authorization Act, Fiscal Year 1991, U.S. Congress, Pub.L. 101-611, (1990).

National Aeronautics and Space Administration 1972a, 'AS-17-148-22727', photograph, *Apollo 17 Image Library*, NASA, Washington, DC, viewed 16 August 2023, <https://www.hq.nasa.gov/alsj/a17/as17-148-22727.jpg>.

National Aeronautics and Space Administration 1972b, 'AS-17-152-23274', photograph, *Apollo 17 Image Library*, NASA, Washington, DC, viewed 16 August 2023, <https://www.hq.nasa.gov/alsj/a17/AS17-152-23274HR.jpg>.

National Aeronautics and Space Administration 1997, 'NASA Civil Service Workforce Employment Trend', *Pocket Statistics*, NASA, Washington, DC, archived website, pp. 27–28, viewed 22 February 2019, <https://web.archive.org/web/20221206031835/https://history.nasa.gov/pocketstats/sect%20D/CS%20Trend.pdf>.

National Aeronautics and Space Administration 2007, *Blue Marble – Image of the Earth from Apollo 17*, NASA, Washington, DC, viewed 16 August 2023, <https://www.nasa.gov/content/blue-marble-image-of-the-earth-from-apollo-17>.

National Aeronautics and Space Administration 2009, *NASA Ames Becomes Home To Newly Launched Singularity University*, press release, 4 February, viewed 16 August 2023, <https://www.nasa.gov/centers/ames/news/releases/2009/09-11AR.html>.

National Aeronautics and Space Administration 2010, *NASA Awards Contracts For Innovative Lunar Demonstrations Data*, press release, 15 October, NASA, Washington, DC, viewed 16 August 2023, <https://www.nasa.gov/home/hqnews/2010/oct/HQ_10-259_ILDD_Award.html>.

National Aeronautics and Space Administration 2013, *Gamma-ray Bursts*, NASA Goddard Space Flight Center, Greenbelt, MD, viewed 16 August 2023, <https://imagine.gsfc.nasa.gov/science/objects/bursts1.html>.

National Aeronautics and Space Administration 2016, *OSIRIS-REx Asteroid Sample Return Mission*, press kit, NASA, Washington, D.C, viewed 16 August 2023, <https://www.nasa.gov/sites/default/files/atoms/files/osiris-rex_press_kit.pdf>.

National Aeronautics and Space Administration 2018a, *NASA Announces New Partnerships for Commercial Lunar Payload Delivery Services*, press release, 30 November, NASA, Washington, DC, viewed 23 August 2023, <https://www.nasa.gov/press-release/nasa-announces-new-partnerships-for-commercial-lunar-payload-delivery-services>.

National Aeronautics and Space Administration 2018b, *OSIRIS-REx Mission Operations*, 4 December, NASA, Washington, DC, viewed 23 August 2023, <https://www.nasa.gov/content/osiris-rex-mission-operations>.

National Aeronautics and Space Administration 2018c, *OSIRIS-REx Arrives at Bennu*, press release, 4 December NASA, Washington, DC, viewed 23 August 2023, <https://www.nasa.gov/feature/goddard/2018/osiris-rex-approach>.

National Aeronautics and Space Administration 2020, *NASA's OSIRIS-REx Spacecraft Collects Significant Amount of Asteroid NASA*, press release, 24 October, Washington, DC, viewed 23 August 2023, <https://www.nasa.gov/press-release/nasa-s-osiris-rex-spacecraft-collects-significant-amount-of-asteroid>.

National Aeronautics and Space Administration 2021, *Mike Gold, Former Associate Administrator for Space Policy and Partnerships*, 11 December, NASA, Washington, DC, archived website, viewed 23 August 2023, <https://web.archive.org/web/20220320043857/https://www.nasa.gov/feature/Michael_Gold>.

National Aeronautics and Space Administration 2022, *1st NASA Asteroid Sample Return Mission on Track for Fall '23* Delivery, 15 October, NASA, Washington, DC, viewed 23 August 2023, <https://www.nasa.gov/feature/goddard/2022/1st-nasa-asteroid-sample-return-mission-on-track-for-fall-23-delivery>.

National Aeronautics and Space Administration 2023, *Voyager 1*, NASA, Washington, DC, viewed 23 August 2023, <https://solarsystem.nasa.gov/missions/voyager-1/in-depth/>.

NASA Advisory Council Regulatory and Policy Committee 2019, *Star Laws: Rise of Space Resources*, presentation slides, 31 October, NASA, Washington, DC, archived website, viewed 23 August 2023, <https://web.archive.org/web/20200108205317/https://www.nasa.gov/sites/default/files/atoms/files/regulatory_policy_committee_report.pdf>.

NASA Office of Inspector General 2021, *NASA's Management of the International Space Station and Efforts to Commercialize Low Earth orbit*, 30 November, Report No. IG-22-005, NASA, Washington, DC.

National Commission on Space 1986, *Pioneering the Space Frontier: An Exciting Vision of Our next Fifty Years in Space*, report of the US National Commission on Space, Bantam Books, New York, Toronto, viewed 16 August 2023, <https://history.nasa.gov/painerep/begin.html>.

National Research Council of the National Academies 2006, *Space Radiation Hazards and the Vision of Space Exploration*, Ad Hoc Committee on the Solar System Radiation Environment and NASA's Vision for Space Exploration: A Workshop, Space Studies Board, Division on Engineering and Physical Sciences, National Academies Press, Washington, DC.

National Space Society 2009, *White Paper – Rejecting the Law of the Sea Treaty (LoST)*, 13 March, NSS, Washington, DC, viewed 16 August 2023, <https://space.nss.org/wp-content/uploads/National-Space-Society-LoST-WhitePaper.pdf>.

National Space Society 2012, *Milestones to Space Settlement: an NSS Roadmap*, NSS, Washington, DC, viewed 16 August 2023, <https://space.nss.org/media/NSS-roadmap.pdf>.

National Space Society 2018, 'Part Six: Additional Expansion and Greater Sustainability of Human Civilization', *NSS Roadmap to Space Settlement*, 3rd edn., NSS, Washington, DC, viewed 16 August 2023, <https://space.nss.org/nss-roadmap-to-space-settlement-3rd-edition-2018-part-6/>.

National Space Society 2019, *NSS Statement of Philosophy*, NSS, Washington, DC, viewed 16 August 2023, <https://space.nss.org/nss-statement-of-philosophy/>.

National Science and Technology Council 2018, *National near-Earth Object Preparedness Strategy and Action Plan*, Interagency Working Group for Detecting and Mitigating the Impact of Earth-bound Near-Earth Objects, National Science and Technology Council, Washington, DC.

Nef, J.U. 1964, *The Conquest of the Material World*, University of Chicago Press, Chicago.

Nesbit, J. 2017, 'Google's true origin partly lies in CIA and NSA research grants for mass surveillance', *Quartz*, 8 December, viewed 16 August 2023, <https://qz.com/1145669/googles-true-origin-partly-lies-in-cia-and-nsa-research-grants-for-mass-surveillance/>.

Northrup Grumman 2019, *Northrop Grumman to Demonstrate Robotic Manufacturing in Space*, press release, 16 July, Northrup Grumman, viewed 16 August 2023, <https://news.northropgrumman.com/news/releases/northrop-grumman-to-demonstrate-robotic-manufacturing-in-space>.

Novak, J. & Moran, A. 2011, *Submission to Inquiry into the Mineral Resource Rent Tax Bill 2011 and Related Bills*, Institute for Public Affairs, Melbourne, VIC.

Nozick, R. 1974, *Anarchy, State and Utopia*, Basic Books, New York.

O'Connell, M. 2018, 'Why Silicon Valley billionaires are prepping for the apocalypse in New Zealand', *The Guardian*, 15 February, viewed 16 August 2023, <https://www.theguardian.com/news/2018/feb/15/why-silicon-valley-billionaires-are-prepping-for-the-apocalypse-in-new-zealand>.

Oduntan, G. 2015, 'Who owns space? US asteroid mining act is dangerous and potentially illegal', *The Conversation*, 25 November, viewed 16 August 2023, <https://theconversation.com/who-owns-space-us-asteroid-mining-act-is-dangerous-and-potentially-illegal-51073>.

Office of Management and Budget 2023, 'Table 4.2 – Percentage distribution of outlays by agency: 1962-2023', *Historical Tables*, OMB, Washington, DC, viewed 4 March 2023, <https://www.whitehouse.gov/wp-content/uploads/2023/03/hist04z2_fy2024.xlsx>.

Office of Technology Assessment 1995, *U.S.-Russian cooperation in space*, US Government Printing Office, Washington DC, report OTA-ISS-618.

Offworld n.d., *Offworld's Master Plan*, Offworld, Inc., Pasadena, CA, viewed 16 August 2023, <https://1f6c02f4-027c-4917-9b03-6af235b97a03.filesusr.com/ugd/3823cc_8d3542f245784b9fb0a48194e383cde2.pdf>.

On the Commons 2017, *Wrapping Our Legal Minds Around the Global Commons: Res Nullius, Res Communis, and Res Divini Juris*, weblog, 16 February, On The Commons, Minneapolis, viewed 16 August 2023, <http://www.onthecommons.org/wrapping-our-legal-minds-around-global-commons-res-nullius-res-communis-and-res-divini-juris>.

Organisation for Economic Co-operation and Development 2014, *The Space Economy at a Glance 2014*, OECD Publishing.

Olson, V.A. 2013, 'NEOcology: The solar system's emerging environmental history and politics', in D. Jørgensen, F.A. Jørgensen & S.B. Prichard (eds.), *New Natures: Joining Environmental History with Science and Technology Studies*, University of Pittsburgh Press, Pittsburgh, PA.

O'Neill, G.K. 1974, 'The colonization of space', *Physics Today*, vol. 27, no. 9, pp. 32–40.

O'Neill, G.K. 1977, *The High Frontier: Human colonies in outer space*, Morrow, New York.

Open Secrets 2023a, *Client Profile: Planetary Resources*, data aggregated for 2014-2018, Open Secrets, Washington, DC, viewed 12 December 2023, <https://www.opensecrets.org/lobby/clientsum.php?id=D000071317&year=2014>.

Open Secrets 2023b, *Rep. Derek Kilmer – Washington District 06, OpenSecrets.org*, Open Secrets, Washington, DC, viewed 12 December 2023, <https://www.opensecrets.org/members-of-congress/contributors?cid=N00034453&cycle=2014&recs=100&type=I>.

Open Secrets 2023c, *Clients Lobbying on H.R.5063: American Space Technology for Exploring Resource Opportunities In Deep Space Act*, Open Secrets, Washington, DC, viewed 12 December 2023, <https://www.opensecrets.org/lobby/billsum.php?id=hr5063-113>.

Open Secrets 2023d, *Client Profile: Planetary Resources, lobbyist data for 2014*, Open Secrets, Washington, DC, viewed 12 December 2023, <https://www.opensecrets.org/lobby/clientlbs.php?id=D000071317&year=2014>.

Open Secrets 2023e, *Koch Industries: Summary*, Open Secrets, Washington, DC, viewed 12 December 2023, <https://www.opensecrets.org/orgs/summary.php?id=d000000186>.

Open Secrets 2023f, *Clients Lobbying on H.R. 1508: Space Resource Exploration and Utilization Act of 2015*, Open Secrets, Washington, DC, viewed 12 December 2023, <https://opensecrets.org/lobby/billsum.php?id=hr1508-114>.

Open Secrets 2023g, *Clients Lobbying on H.R.2262: U.S. Commercial Space Launch Competitiveness Act*, Open Secrets, Washington, DC, viewed 11 December 2023 <https://www.opensecrets.org/lobby/billsum.php?id=hr2262-114>.

Open Secrets 2023h, *Moon Express: Client Summary, Data Aggregated for 2014-2018*, Open Secrets, Washington, DC, viewed 11 December 2023, <https://www.opensecrets.org/federal-lobbying/clients/summary?cycle=2014&id=D000089333>.

Open Secrets 2023i, *Clients Lobbying on H.R. 2809: American Space Commerce Free Enterprise Act of 2017*, Open Secrets, Washington, DC, viewed 12 December 2023, <https://www.opensecrets.org/lobby/billsum.php?id=hr2809-115>.

Open Secrets 2023j, *Dana Rohrabacher, 2012*, Open Secrets, Washington, DC, viewed 16 August 2023, <https://www.opensecrets.org/members-of-congress/dana-rohrabacher/contributors?cid=N00007151&cycle=2012&recs=100&type=I>.

Open Secrets 2023k, *Dana Rohrabacher, 2014*, Open Secrets, Washington, DC, viewed 16 August 2023, <https://www.opensecrets.org/members-of-congress/dana-rohrabacher/contributors?cid=N00007151&cycle=2014&recs=100&type=I>.

Ormrod, J.S. 2007, 'Pro-space activism and narcissistic phantasy', *Psychoanalysis, Culture & Society*, vol. 12, no. 3, pp. 260–278.

Ormrod, J.S. 2009, 'Phantasy and social movements: An ontology of pro-space activism', *Social Movement Studies*, vol. 8, no. 2, pp. 115–129.

Orphans of Apollo 2008, Motion Picture, Free Radical Productions.

Orsulak, J. 2018, *Manufacturing in Space could Save Life on Earth*, 3 January, TEDx Talks, viewed 16 August 2023, <https://www.youtube.com/watch?v=2JfVzMvLEn8>.

Orwell, G. 1944, 'As I Please', *Tribune*, 18 August, republished online (n.d.), viewed 16 August 2023, <https://www.telelib.com/authors/O/OrwellGeorge/essay/tribune/AsIPlease19440901.html>.

Oreskes, N. and Conway, E.M. 2010 *Merchants of Doubt: How a Handful of Scientists Obscured the Truth on Issues from Tobacco Smoke to Global Warming*. Bloomsbury Press,New York.

Ostrom, E. 1990, *Governing the Commons: The Evolution of Institutions for Collective Action*, Cambridge University Press, Cambridge.

Ostrom, E. 2012, *The Future of the Commons: Beyond Market Failure and Government Regulation*, Institute for Economic Affairs, London.

Ó Tuathail, G. 1994, 'Manifest destiny', in J.V. O'Loughlin (ed.), *Dictionary of Geopolitics*, Greenwood Press, Westport, CT, pp. 158–159.

Ó Tuathail, G. & Dalby, S. 1994, 'American exceptionalism', in J.V. O'Loughlin (ed.), *Dictionary of Geopolitics*, Greenwood Press, Westport, CT, pp. 8–10.

Pace, S. 2017, 'Space development, law and values', presented to *IISL Galloway Space Law Symposium*, 13 December, International Institute of Space Law, Washington, DC, viewed 16 August 2023, <https://spacepolicyonline.com/wp-content/uploads/2017/12/Scott-Pace-to-Galloway-Symp-Dec-13-2017.pdf>.

Parker, M. 2009, 'Capitalists in Space', in Parker, M. & Bell, D. (eds.), *Space Travel and Culture: From Apollo to Space Tourism*, Blackwell, Oxford, pp. 83–97.

Patinkin, J. 2016, 'Standing Rock tribe protests over North Dakota pipeline', *Al Jazeera*, 29 October, viewed 16 August 2023, <https://www.aljazeera.com/indepth/

inpictures/2016/10/north-dakota-native-americans-protest-pipeline-161028150518748.html>.

Peck, J. 2013. For Polanyian economic geographies. *Environment and Planning A: Economy and Space*, vol. 45, pp. 1545–1568.

Pepis, S., Evans, J. & de Jong, P. 2018, 'The valuation of startups in new markets: An applied case in asteroid mining', *International Journal of Business and Social Science*, vol. 9, no. 4, pp. 10–16.

Perry, I.B. 2017, 'Law of space resources and operations on celestial bodies: Implications for legislation in the United States', *Astropolitics*, vol. 15, no. 1, pp. 1–26.

Phan, T.T. 2021, 'Peter Diamandis: "The world's biggest problems are the world's biggest business opportunities"', *The Hustle*, 29 September, viewed 16 August 2023, <https://thehustle.co/peter-diamandis-q-and-a-trung-phan/>.

Philpott, D. 2014, 'Sovereignty', in E.N. Zalta (ed.), *The Stanford Encyclopedia of Philosophy*, Summer 2014, viewed 16 August 2023, <http://plato.stanford.edu/archives/sum2014/entries/sovereignty>.

Piketty, T. 2014, *Capital in the Twenty-first Century*, trans. A. Goldhammer, Harvard University Press, Cambridge, MA & London.

Pilchman, D. 2015, 'Three ethical perspectives on asteroid mining', in J. Galliot (ed.), *Commercial Space Exploration: Ethics, Policy and Governance*, Ashgate, Surrey & Vermont, pp. 135–147.

Planetary Resources (n.d.-a), *Team*, Planetary Resources, Redmond, WA, archived website, viewed 16 August 2023, <https://web.archive.org/web/20200615032323/https%3A%2F%2Fwww.planetaryresources.com%2Fcompany%2F>.

Planetary Resources (n.d.-b), *Timeline*, archived website, viewed 16 August 2023, <https://web.archive.org/web/20181003201559/https://www.planetaryresources.com/company/timeline/>.

Planetary Resources (n.d.-c), *Brian Israel*, archived website, viewed 16 August 2023, <https://web.archive.org/web/20200927163621/https://www.planetaryresources.com/team/brian-israel/>.

Planetary Resources 2012, *Planetary Resources, Inc. Announces Agreement With Virgin Galactic For Payload Services*, press release, 11 July, Planetary Resources, Redmond, WA, archived website, viewed 16 August 2023, <https://web.archive.org/web/20170626214655/http://www.planetaryresources.com/2012/07/planetary-resources-inc-announces-contract-with-virgin-galactic-for-payload-services/>.

Planetary Resources 2013a, *Bechtel Partners With Planetary Resources For Space Initiative*, press release, 16 April, Planetary Resources, Redmond, WA, archived website, viewed 16 August 2023, <https://web.archive.org/web/20201112020451/https%3A%2F%2Fwww.planetaryresources.com%2F2013%2F04%2Fbechtel-partners-with-planetary-resources-for-space-initiative%2F>.

Planetary Resources 2013b, *Planetary Resources names Peter Marquez as Vice President for Global Engagement*, press release, 10 June, Planetary Resources, Redmond, WA, archived website, viewed 16 August 2023, <https://web.archive.org/web/20200615031659/https%3A%2F%2Fwww.planetaryresources.com%2F2013%2F06%2Fplanetary-resources-names-peter-marquez-as-vice-president-for-global-engagement%2F>.

Planetary Resources 2014, *Planetary Resources' Letter to Members of Congress Regarding H.R. 5063 – the ASTEROIDS Act*, press release, 10 September, Planetary Resources, Redmond, WA, archived website, viewed 16 August 2023, <https://web.archive.org/web/20201124003831/http%3A%2F%2Fwww.planetaryresources.com%2F2014%2F09%2Fplanetary-resources-letter-members-congress-regarding-h-r-5063-asteroids-act%2F/>.

Planetary Resources 2016a, *Planetary Resources and the Government of Luxembourg Announce €25 Million Investment and Cooperation Agreement*, press release, 3 November, Planetary Resources, Redmond, WA, archived website, viewed 16 August 2023, <https://

web.archive.org/web/20200615031504/https%3A%2F%2Fwww.planetaryresources.com%2F2016%2F11%2Fplanetary-resources-and-the-government-of-luxembourg-announce-e25-million-investment-and-cooperation-agreement%2F>.

Planetary Resources 2016b, *The Second Age of Exploration Has Begun … In Space*, 16 November 2016, archived website, viewed 16 August 2023, <https://web.archive.org/web/20200615031606/https%3A%2F%2Fwww.planetaryresources.com%2F2016%2F11%2Fthe-second-age-of-exploration-has-begun-in-space%2F>.

Planetary Resources 2018, *ConsenSys Acquires Planetary Resources*, press release, 31 October, Planetary Resources, Redmond, WA, archived website, viewed 16 August 2023, <https://web.archive.org/web/20190624152253/https://www.planetaryresources.com/2018/10/consensys-acquires-planetary-resources/>.

Plehwe, D., Walpen, B. & Neunhöffer, G. 2006, *Neoliberal Hegemony: A Global Critique*, Routledge, Abingdon.

Plehwe, D. 2009, 'Introduction', in P. Mirowski & D. Plehwe (eds.), *The Road from Mont Pèlerin: The making of the neoliberal thought collective*, Harvard University Press, Cambridge, MA, pp. 1–42.

Plumwood, V. 2002, *Environmental Culture: The Ecological Crisis of Reason*, Routledge, Abingdon.

Polanyi, K. 1944, *The Great Transformation*, republished 2001, Beacon Press, Boston, MA.

Polanyi-Levitt, K. & Mendell, M. 1987, 'Karl Polanyi: His life and times', *Studies in Political Economy*, 22, pp. 7–39.

Policante, A. 2015, *The Pirate Myth: Genealogies of an Imperial Concept*, Routledge, Abingdon.

Poole, R.W. 2002, 'Is this any way to run space transportation?', in E.L., Hudgins (ed.), *Space: The Free-Market Frontier*, Cato Institute, Washington, pp. 53–66.

Pop, V. 2000, 'Appropriation in outer space: The relationship between land ownership and sovereignty on the celestial bodies', *Space Policy*, vol. 16, pp. 275–282.

'Presidential Directive on National Space Policy' 1988, 11 February, NASA Historical Reference Collection, NASA, Washington, DC, archived website, viewed 16 August 2023, <https://web.archive.org/web/20190714112603/https://www.hq.nasa.gov/office/pao/History/policy88.html>.

'Presidential Space Policy Directive' 2019, *President Donald J. Trump is Establishing America's Space Force*, 19 February, White House, Washington, DC, viewed 16 August 2023, <https://trumpwhitehouse.archives.gov/presidential-actions/text-space-policy-directive-4-establishment-united-states-space-force/>.

Purdy, J. 2014, 'Neoliberal constitutionalism: Lochnerism for a new economy', *Law and Contemporary Problems*, vol. 77, pp. 195–213.

Quiggin, J. 2015, *Locke's Theory of Just Expropriation (crosspost from Crooked Timber)*, weblog, 20 April, viewed 16 August 2023, <https://johnquiggin.com/2015/04/20/lockes-theory-of-just-expropriation-crosspost-from-crooked-timber/>.

Quirk, J. 2018, *Peter Thiel speaks for 6 minutes about Seasteading*, 25 September, The Seasteading Institute, San Francisco, CA, viewed 16 August 2023, <https://www.seasteading.org/31937-2/>.

Rand, A. 1957, *Atlas Shrugged*, republished 2005, Penguin, New York.

Ratiner, L. n.d., *Detailed Career History for Leigh Ratiner, 1987-Present*, Leigh Ratiner, archived website, viewed 16 August 2023, <https://web.archive.org/web/20170417045521/http://ratiner.com/Leigh_Ratiner/Detailed_Career_Chronology.html>.

Ratiner, L.S. & Wright, R.L. 1978, 'The billion dollar decision: Is Deepsea mining a prudent investment?', *University of Miami Inter-American Law Review*, vol. 10, no. 3/4, pp. 713–773.

Ray, J. 2017, 'X-37B spaceplane returns to Earth and makes autopilot landing in Florida', *Spaceflight Now*, 7 May, viewed 16 August 2023, <https://spaceflightnow.com/2017/05/07/x-37b-spaceplane-returns-to-earth-and-makes-precision-autopilot-landing/>.

Raz, J. 1979, *The Authority of Law: Essays on Law and Morality*, Clarendon Press, Oxford.

Reagan, R. 1984, 'Address Before a Joint Session of the Congress on the State of the Union', 98th Congress, *The American Presidency Project*, University of California, Santa Barbara, viewed 16 August 2023, <https://www.presidency.ucsb.edu/documents/address-before-joint-session-the-congress-the-state-the-union-4>.

Rees, W.E. 1999, 'The built environment and the ecosphere: A global perspective', *Building Research and Information*, vol. 27, no. 4, pp. 206–220.

Reiffel, L. 1959, *A Study of Lunar Research Flights – Vol. 1*, Air Force Special Weapons Center, document ID: AD425380, Defense Documentation Center for Scientific and Technical Information, Alexandria, VA.

Reisman, A. 2013, 'Meet the right-wing Mars guru', *Vice*, 22 February, viewed 16 August 2023, <https://www.vice.com/en_us/article/wnnaj4/the-right-wing-mars-guru-robert-zubrin-interview>.

Reuters 2021, *Amazon Acknowledges Issue of Drivers Urinating in Bottles in Apology to Rep. Pocan*, 4 April, Reuters, viewed 16 August 2023, <https://www.reuters.com/article/us-amazon-com-workers-pocan-idUSKBN2BQ0DC>.

Review of Human Spaceflight Plans Committee 2010, *Seeking a Human Spaceflight Program Worthy of a Great Nation*, NASA, Washington, DC.

Richards, B. 2017, 'Statement of Robert (Bob) Richards, Founder and CEO, Moon Express', Inc, *Reopening the American Frontier: Exploring How the Outer Space Treaty Will Impact American Commerce and Settlement in Space*, before the U.S. Senate Committee on Commerce, Science, and Transportation, Subcommittee on Science, Space, and Competitiveness, 115th Congress (23 May 2017).

Robinson, E. 1976, 'Movement into space: A view from two worlds', *L-5 News*, no. 16, pp. 6–11, National Space Society, Washington, DC, viewed 16 August 2023, URL: https://space.nss.org/media/L5-News-1976-12.pdf.

Robinson, G.S. & White, H.M. 1986, *Envoys of Mankind: A Declaration of First Principles for the Governance of Space Societies*, Smithsonian Institution Press, Washington, DC.

Rodrigo, C.M. 2018, 'Chief justice halts discovery, trial in youth climate lawsuit', *The Hill*, 19 October, viewed 16 August 2023, <https://thehill.com/regulation/court-battles/412350-chief-justice-roberts-halts-discovery-in-youth-climate-lawsuit>.

Rohrabacher, D. 2002, 'Zero Gravity, Zero Tax', in E.L. Hudgins (ed.), *Space: The Free-Market Frontier*, Cato Institute, Washington, pp. 213–214.

Rose, C.M. 2003, 'Romans, roads, and romantic creators: Traditions of public property in the information age', *Law and Contemporary Problems*, vol. 66, no. 1/2, pp. 89–110.

Rose, D.B. 2013, 'Common property regimes in Aboriginal Australia: Totemism revisited', in P. Larmour (ed.), *The Governance of Common Property in the Pacific Region*, ANU E Press, Canberra, pp. 127–143.

Roth, S. 2014, The eye-patch of the beholder: Introduction to entrepreneurship and piracy. *International Journal of Entrepreneurship and Small Business*, 22, 399.

Rothbard, M. 1980, 'Viewpoint: From Cuban to American Socialism', *Reason*, December, Reason Foundation, Los Angeles, CA, viewed 16 August 2023, <https://reason.com/1980/12/01/from-cuban-to-american-sociali/>.

Rowan, R., 2018, *Enclosing the Cosmos: Neoliberalism, Extraction & Colonization in the Age of 'NewSpace'*, University of Zurich, viewed 16 August 2023, <https://www.zhdk.ch/veranstaltung/34493>.

Sagan, C. 1973, 'Planetary engineering on Mars', *Icarus*, vol. 20, pp. 513–514.
Sagan, C. 1994, *Pale Blue Dot: A Vision of the Human Future in Space*, Ballantine Books, New York.
Said, E. 1995, *Orientalism*, Penguin Books, London.
Salter, A.W. & Leeson, P.T. 2014, 'Celestial anarchy: A threat to outer space commerce', *Cato Journal*, vol. 34, no. 3, pp. 581–596.
Sandoval, C. 1997, 'Theorizing white consciousness for a post-empire world: Barthes, Fanon, and the rhetoric of love', in R. Frankenberg (ed.), *Displacing Whiteness: Essays in Social and Cultural Criticism*, Duke University Press, Durham and London, pp. 86–106.
Sarsfield, L.P. 2002, 'The arrival of tomorrow: NASA in the 21st century', in E.L. Hudgins (ed.), *Space: The Free-Market Frontier*, Cato Institute, Washington, DC, pp. 29–51.
Savelyeva, T. 2017, 'Vernadsky meets Yulgok: A non-Western dialog on sustainability', *Educational Philosophy and Theory*, vol. 49, no. 5, pp. 501–520.
Sax, J. 1969, 'The public trust doctrine in natural resource law: Effective judicial intervention', *Michigan Law Review*, vol. 68, pp. 471–566.
Scheraga, J.D. 1987, 'Establishing property rights in outer space', *Cato Journal*, vol. 6, no. 3, pp. 889–903.
Scheuerman, W. 1997, 'The unholy alliance of Carl Schmitt and Friedrich A. Hayek', *Constellations*, vol. 4, no. 2, pp. 172–188.
Schmitt, C. 1922, *Political Theology: Four Chapters on the Concept of Sovereignty*, republished 1985, MIT Press, Cambridge & London.
Schmitt, C. 1950, *The Nomos of the Earth in the International Law of the Jus Publicum Europaeum*, trans. G.L. Ulmen, republished 2003, Telos Press, New York.
Schmitt, C. 1954, *Dialogues on Power and Space*, trans. A. Kalyvas and F. Finchelstein, republished 2015, Polity Press, Cambridge.
Smith, N. 1994, 'Bowman, Isaiah', in J. O'Loughlin (ed.), *Dictionary of Geopolitics*, Greenwood Press, CT, pp. 23-24.
Schmitt, H.H. 2006, *Return to the Moon: Exploration, Enterprise, and Energy in the Human Settlement of Space*, Praxis Publishing, New York.
Schneidermann, D. 2013, *Constitutionalizing Economic Globalisation: Investment Rules and Democracy's Promise*, Cambridge University Press, Cambridge.
Schrijver, N. 2016, 'Managing the global commons: Common good or common sink?', *Third World Quarterly*, vol. 37, viewed 16 August 2023, <https://www.tandfonline.com/doi/full/10.1080/01436597.2016.1154441>.
Selin, C. 2008, 'The sociology of the future: tracing stories of technology and time', *Sociology Compass*, vol. 2, no. 6, pp. 1878–1895.
SES 2021, *SES Extends Long-Term Partnership with Sky*, press release, 25 February, SES, Luxembourg, viewed 16 August 2023, <https://www.ses.com/press-release/ses-extends-long-term-partnership-sky>.
SES n.d. '1988', in *Our History*, SES, Luxembourg, viewed 16 August 2023, <https://www.ses.com/about-us/our-history>.
Shammas, V.L. & Holen, T.B. 2019, 'One giant leap for capitalistkind: private enterprise in outer space', *Palgrave Communications*, vol. 5, no. 10, pp. 2–9.
Shanahan, M. 2015, *The Technological Singularity*, MIT Press, Cambridge, MA.
Shany, Y. 2005, 'Toward a general margin of appreciation doctrine in International Law?', *European Journal of International Law*, vol. 16, no. 5, pp. 907–940.
Sharp, T. 2022, 'How big is the Moon?', 8 February, *Space.com*, viewed 16 August 2023, <https://www.space.com/18135-how-big-is-the-moon.html>.
Sheppard, A. 2013, '10 Things we learned from Peter Diamandis's Reddit AMA', *Popular Mechanics*, 18 October, viewed 16 August 2023, <https://www.popularmechanics.com/science/health/a11986/10-things-we-learned-from-peter-diamandis-reddit-ama-16051944/>.

Shukaitis, S. 2009, 'Space is the (non) place: Martians, Marxists, and the outer space of the radical imagination', *The Sociological Review*, vol. 57 (1_suppl), pp. 98–113.
Siddiqi, A.A. 2008, 'Imagining the Cosmos: Utopians, mystics, and the popular culture of spaceflight in Revolutionary Russia', *Osiris*, vol. 23, no. 1, pp. 260–288.
Sikor, T. and Lund, C. 2009, 'Access and property: A question of power and authority', *Development and Change*, vol. 40, no. 1, pp. 1–22.
Simberg, R. 2012, *Homesteading the Final Frontier: A Practical Proposal for Securing Property Rights in Space*, Issue Analysis 2012, no.3, Competitive Enterprise Institute, Washington, DC.
Simon, J. & Kahn, H. (eds.) 1984, *The Resourceful Earth: A Response to Global 2000*, Blackwell, Oxford and New York.
Singal, J. 2018, 'Is it racist to refer to space "colonization"?', *Reason*, 16 August, Reason Foundation, Los Angeles, CA, viewed 16 August 2023, <https://reason.com/2018/08/16/is-it-racist-to-refer-to-space-colonizat/>.
Sloterdijk, P. 2013, *In the World Interior of Capital: Towards A Philosophical Theory of Globalisation*, Polity, Cambridge.
Smith, A. 1776, *An Inquiry into the Nature and Causes of the Wealth of Nations*, electronic book, republished 2001, Electric Book Company, London.
Smith, S. 2018, 'A space law primer for Colorado lawyers – Part 1: International space law', *Colorado Lawyer*, March, pp. 48–56, viewed 16 August 2023, <https://www.cobar.org/Portals/COBAR/Repository/TCL/March2018/FEATURES_SPACE_LAW.pdf>.
Smith, M. 2020, 'NASA unveils 'Artemis Accords'', SpacePolicyOnline.com, website, 15 May, viewed 11 December 2023, https://spacepolicyonline.com/news/nasa-unveils-artemis-accords/
Smoking Gun Memo $1000 Reward n.d., archived website, viewed 16 August 2023, <https://orphansofapollo.wordpress.com/smoking-gun-memo/>.
Sowers, G.F. 2017, 'Testimony of Dr. George F. Sowers Jr., Professor, Space Resources, Colorado School of Mines', *Private Sector Exploration of the Moon*, before the U.S. House of Representatives Committee on Science, Space, and Technology, Subcommittee on Space, 115th Congress (7 September 2017).
Space Development Foundation n.d., *Projects*, SDF, Maryland, viewed 16 August 2023, <http://www.spacedevelopmentfoundation.org/wordpress/projects/>.
'Space Exploration, Development, and Settlement Act of 2016', U.S. House of Representatives, H.R.4752, 114th Congress (2016).
Space Frontier Foundation 2006, *Unaffordable and Unsustainable: NASA's Failing Earth-to-orbit Transportation Strategy*, 25 July, SFF, Silver Spring, MD, archived website, viewed 16 August 2023, <https://web.archive.org/web/20220316111211/http://highfrontier.org/oldarchive/Archive/Jt/Space%20Frontier%20NASA%20ESAS%20LV%20Critique.pdf>.
Space Frontier Foundation 2008, *NewSpace 2006*, SFF, Silver Spring, MD, archived website, viewed 16 August 2023, <https://web.archive.org/web/20180814165916/http://archive.spacefrontier.org/Events/NewSpace2006/>.
Space Frontier Foundation 2015, *Space Frontier Foundation Celebrates Milestone Bill for Commercial Space Industry*, press release, 25 November, SFF, Silver Spring, MD, viewed 27 September 2019, <https://web.archive.org/web/20200927222540/http://newspace.spacefrontier.org/press-releases/>.
Space Frontier Foundation 2019, *This is Why You Need Permission to Go to the Moon*, weblog, SFF, Silver Spring, MD, viewed 16 August 2023, <https://web.archive.org/web/20220125041441/https://newspace.spacefrontier.org/2019/05/04/2056/>.
Space Frontier Foundation 2023a, *About Us*, SFF, Silver Spring, MD, viewed 13 June 2023, <https://space-frontier.org/about-us/>.
Space Frontier Foundation 2023b, *History of NewSpace*, SFF, Silver Spring, MD, viewed 22 March 2018, <https://space-frontier.org/our-history/>.

Space Renaissance USA 2020, *The Space Renaissance Manifesto*, ratified 24 July 2011, Space Renaissance USA, Woodside, NY, viewed 16 August 2023, <https://usa.spacerenaissance.space/manifesto/>.
'Space Resource Exploration and Utilization Act of 2015', U.S. House of Representatives, H.R. 1508, 114th Congress (2015).
'Space Resource Exploration and Utilization Act of 2015', U.S. Senate, s.976, 114th Congress (2015).
The Space Show 2017, *Walt Anderson*, The Space Show, Tiburon, CA, viewed 16 August 2023, <https://www.thespaceshow.com/guest/walt-anderson>.
Steffen, W., Rockström, J., Richardson, K., Lenton, T.N., Folke, C., Liverman, D., Summerhayes, C.P., Barnosky, A.D., Cornell, S.E., Crucifix, M., Donges, J.F., Fetzer, I., Lade, S.J., Scheffer, M., Winkelmann, R. & Schnellnhuber, H.J. 2018, 'Trajectories of the Earth System in the Anthropocene', *Proceedings of the National Academy of Sciences of the United States of America*, vol. 115, no. 33, pp. 8252–8259.
Steinberg, A. 2011, 'Space policy responsiveness: The relationship between public opinion and NASA funding', *Space Policy*, vol. 27, pp. 240–246.
Steinberg, P.E., Nyman, E. & Caraccioli, M.J. 2012, 'Atlas swam: Freedom, capital, and floating sovereignties in the Seasteading vision', *Antipode*, vol. 44, no. 4, pp. 1532–1550.
Stevens, H. 2003, 'Fundamental physics and its justifications, 1945-1993', *Historical Studies in the Physical and Biological Sciences*, vol. 34, no .1, pp. 151–197.
Stirn, A. 2020, 'Do NASA's lunar exploration rules violate space law?', *Scientific American*, 12 November 2020, viewed 16 August 2023, <https://www.scientificamerican.com/article/do-nasas-lunar-exploration-rules-violate-space-law/>.
Storr, C. 2021, "Space is the only way to go': The evolution of the extractivist imaginary of international law', in S. Chalmers & S. Pahuja (eds.), *Routledge Handbook of International Law and the Humanities*, Routledge, Abingdon, 16 August 2023, 290–301
Stutt, A. 2019, 'Nautilus Minerals officially sinks, shares still trading', *Mining.com*, 26 November, viewed 16 August 2023, <https://www.mining.com/nautilus-minerals-officially-sinks-shares-still-trading/>.
Sykes, M.V. 2014, 'Statement of Mark V. Sykes, CEO and Director, Planetary Science Institute, *Exploring our Solar System: The Asteroids Act as a key step – Hearing on H.R. 5063*, before the U.S. House of Representatives Committee on Science, Space, and Technology, Subcommittee on Space, 113th Congress (10 September 2014).
Teachout, Z. 2014, 'Neoliberal political law', *Law and Contemporary Problems*, vol. 77, pp. 215–237.
Tea Party in Space 2014a, *Core Values*, Tea Party in Space, archived website, viewed 16 August 2023, <https://web.archive.org/web/20180831045902/http://www.teapartyinspace.org/?page_id=8>
Tea Party in Space 2014b, *Platform*, Tea Party in Space, archived website, viewed 16 August 2023, <https://web.archive.org/web/20190621143900/http%3 A%2 F%2 Fteapartyinspace.org%2F%3Fpage_id%3D10>.
TechFreedom 2015, *Congress Should Fix Space Property Rights Bill*, press release, 19 May, TechFreedom, Washington, DC, archived website, viewed 16 August 2023, <https://web.archive.org/web/20230523142303/https://techfreedom.org/congress-should-fix-space-property-rights-bill/>.
TechFreedom 2017, *Light Touch to Space Regulation under New House bill*, 8 June, TechFreedom, Washington, DC, archived website, viewed 16 August 2023, <https://web.archive.org/web/20230425214354/https://techfreedom.org/light-touch-to-space-regulation-under-new-house/>.
Teilhard de Chardin, P. 1964, *The Future of Man*, trans. N. Denny, Collins, London.
'Telegram from the mission to the United Nations to the Department of State' 1981, in A.O. Poster (ed.), *Foreign Relations of the United States 1981-1988*, vol. XLI,

Global Issues II, document 130, Government Printing Office, Washington, DC, viewed 16 August 2023, <https://history.state.gov/historicaldocuments/frus1981-88v41/d130>.

The Planetary Society 2022, 'Space Policy Edition: Mike Gold on Crafting the Artemis Accords', Planetary Radio, podcast, 2 September, The Planetary Society, Pasadena, CA, viewed 11 December 2023, https://www.planetary.org/planetary-radio/artemis-accords-mike-gold

Thiel, P. 2009, 'The education of a libertarian', *Cato Unbound*, 13 April, Cato Institute, Washington, DC, archived website, viewed 16 August 2023, <https://web.archive.org/web/20230726093827/https://www.cato-unbound.org/2009/04/13/peter-thiel/education-libertarian/>.

Thompson, E.P. 1993, *Customs in Common*, Penguin, London.

Thoreau, H.D. 1862, *Walking*, republished 2008, Project Gutenberg Literary Archive Foundation, Salt Lake City, UT.

Thorpe, F.N. (ed.) 1909, *The Federal and State Constitutions, Colonial Charters, and Other Organic Laws of the State, Territories, and Colonies Now or Heretofore Forming the United States of America*, Government Printing Office, Washington, DC, republished 2019, Liberty Fund, viewed 16 August 2023, <http://oll.libertyfund.org/titles/thorpe-the-federal-and-state-constitutions-7-vols>.

Tierney, J. 1999, 'Martian chronicle', *Reason Magazine*, February issue, Reason Foundation, Los Angeles, viewed 16 August 2023, <https://reason.com/1999/02/01/martian-chronicle/>.

Time Magazine 1947, *Foreign Relations: Lippman's Cold War*, 22 September, viewed 16 August 2023, <https://content.time.com/time/subscriber/article/0,33009,798120-1,00.html>.

Tronchetti, F. 2009, *The Exploitation of Natural Resources of the Moon and Other Celestial Bodies: A Proposal for a Legal Regime*, Martinus Nijhoff Publishers, Leiden and Boston.

Tronchetti, F. 2015, 'The Space Resource Exploration and Utilization Act: A move forward or a step back?', *Space Policy*, vol. 34, pp. 6–10.

Tronchetti, F. & Liu, H. 2018, 'The Trump administration and outer space: Promoting US leadership or heading towards isolation?', *Australian Journal of International Affairs*, vol. 72, no. 5, pp. 418–432.

Tronchetti, F. & Liu, H. 2021a, 'The White House Executive Order on the recovery and use of space resources: Pushing the boundaries of international space law?', *Space Policy*, vol. 57, no. 101448, pp 1–8.

Tronchetti, F. & Liu, H. 2021b, 'Australia's signing of the Artemis Accords: a positive development or a controversial choice?', *Australian Journal of International Affairs*, vol. 75, no. 3, pp 243–251.

Trudeau, A.G. 1959, *Project Horizon: Volume 1 – Summary and Supporting Considerations*, United States Army, viewed 16 August 2023, <https://history.army.mil/faq/horizon/Horizon_V1.pdf>.

Tsiolkovsky, K. 1960, *The Call of the Cosmos*, trans. P. Zvezdam, Foreign Languages Publishing House, Moscow.

Tumlinson, R.N. & Space Frontier Foundation 1995, '5. The lie of sustainable growth', *The Frontier Files*, SFF, Silver Spring, MD, archived website, viewed 16 August 2023, <https://web.archive.org/web/20151022173152/https://spacefrontier.org/1995/01/the-lie-of-sustainable-growth/>.

Tumlinson, R.N. 2003, 'Testimony of Rick Tumlinson, Founder, Space Frontier Foundation', *The Future of NASA*, before Senate Committee on Commerce, Science and Transportation, 108th Congress, (29 October 2003), viewed 2 October 2019, <https://www.govinfo.gov/content/pkg/CHRG-108shrg20898/pdf/CHRG-108shrg20898.pdf>.

Tumlinson, R.N. 2012, 'Government and space: Lead, follow, and get out of the way', *HuffPost*, 1 August, viewed 16 August 2023, <https://www.huffpost.com/entry/government-and-space-lead_b_1556312?guccounter=1&guce_referrer=aHR0cHM6Ly93d3cuaHVmZnBvc3QuY29tL2F1dGhvci9yaWNrLXR1bWxpbnNvbg&guce_referrer_sig=AQAAAK25XERpcHYTuIr-u8fF1ylCYX6ZvUuUX8R2-ZcrT3D5LeWQCiZ62mMVMa7C-cyPEmOpPWXDMnfE460ecmeTvHjSf3SP0ZqnVGAZYstR11sCA3wzvMMwWTUuUIArRaYkLXFBjbM9GFRt9MWIe5QIjw9i_LPwqGut_1wBcVUBO90->.

United Nations 1959, 'The Antarctic Treaty', Washington, *United Nations Treaty Series*, vol.402, no.5778, opened for signature 1 December 1959, entered into force 23 June 1961.

United Nations 1963, 'Treaty Banning Nuclear Weapon Tests in the Atmosphere, in Outer Space and Under Water', Moscow, *United Nations Treaty Series*, vol.480, no.6964, opened for signature 5 August 1963, entered into force 10 October 1963.

United Nations 1967, 'Treaty on Principles Governing the Activities of States in the Exploration and Use of Outer Space, including the Moon and Other Celestial Bodies' (OST), New York, *United Nations Treaty Series*, vol. 610, No. 8843, opened for signature 27 January 1967, entered into force 10 October 1967.

United Nations 1979, 'Agreement Governing the Activities of States on the Moon and Other Celestial Bodies', New York, *United Nations Treaty Series*, vol. 1363, no. 23002, opened for signature 18 December 1979, entered into force 11 July 1984.

United Nations 1982, 'United Nations Convention on the Law of the Sea', New York, United Nations Treaty Series, vol. 1833–35, opened for signature 10 December 1982, entered into force 16 November 1994.

United Nations 1992, 'Constitution and Convention of the International Telecommunications Union (with annexes and optional protocol)', Geneva, United Nations Treaty Series, vol. 1825, concluded on 22 December 1992.

United Nations 1994, Convention on the Law of the Sea (UNCLOS). Montego Bay, United Nations Treaty Series, vol. 1833 and vol.1904, opened for signature 10 December 1982, entered into force 16 November 1994.

U.N. Committee on the Peaceful Uses of Outer Space 1966, Report of the Legal Subcommittee on its fifth session, U.N. Doc. A/AC.105/35, Annex.III (16 September 1966).

U.N. Committee on the Peaceful Uses of Outer Space 2016, Reviewing opportunities for achieving the Vienna Consensus on Space Security encompassing several regulatory domains – Working paper submitted by the Russian Federation, fifty-third session of the Scientific and Technical Subcommittee, U.N. Doc. A/AC.105/C.1/2016/CRP.15, (16 February 2016).

U.N. Committee on the Peaceful Uses of Outer Space 2017, Contribution from Belgium to the discussion under UNCOPUOS Legal Subcommittee on item "General exchange of views on potential legal models for activities in exploration, exploitation and utilization of space resources, fifty-sixth session of the Legal Subcommittee", U.N. Doc A/AC.105/C.2/ 2017/CRP.19 (28 March 2017).

U.N. Committee on the Peaceful Uses of Outer Space 2019a, Report of the Legal Subcommittee on its fifty-eighth session, U.N. Doc. A/AC.105/1203, (1–12 April 2019).

U.N. Committee on the Peaceful Uses of Outer Space 2019b, Proposal for the establishment of a working group for the development of an international regime for the utilization and exploitation of space resources - Working paper by Belgium and Greece, fifty-eighth session of the Legal Subcommittee, U.N. Doc. A/AC.105/C.2/L.311, (1-12 April 2019).

U.N. Conference on the Human Environment 1972, Report of the United Nations Conference on the Human Environment, U.N. Doc. A/CONF.48/14/Rev.1, Stockholm (5–16 June 1972).

U.N. General Assembly 1958, *Question on the Peaceful Use of Outer Space*, G.A. Res. 1349 [XIII] (13 December 1958).
U.N. General Assembly 1961, Resolution on International Cooperation in the Peaceful Uses of Outer Space, G.A. Res. 1721 [XVI] (20 December 1961).
U.N. General Assembly 1974, *Declaration on the Establishment of a New International Economic Order*, G.A. Res. 3201(S-VI), (1 May 1974).
U.N. General Assembly 2017, Declaration on the fiftieth anniversary of the Treaty on Principles Governing the Activities of States in the Exploration and Use of Outer Space, including the Moon and Other Celestial Bodies, G.A. Res 72/78 (7 March 2017).
United Nations Population Division n.d., 'Data story highlights', *UN Population Division Data Project*, viewed 7 February 2024, <https://population.un.org/dataportal/home?df=6d8a43ab-98b1-43b4-b243-503e700f9ea4>.
United Nations Statistics Division 2016, 'Global commons', *Environment Glossary*, archived website, viewed 16 August 2023, <https://web.archive.org/web/20221031061117/https://unstats.un.org/unsd/environmentgl/gesform.asp?getitem=573>.
United Nations Intergovernmental Conference on Marine Biodiversity of Areas Beyond National Jurisdiction 2023, *Draft Agreement under the United Nations Convention on the Law of the Sea on the Conservation and Sustainable Use of Marine Biological Diversity of Areas Beyond National Jurisdiction*, resumed 5th session, 4 March, viewed 16 August 2023, <https://www.un.org/bbnj/sites/www.un.org.bbnj/files/draft_agreement_advanced_unedited_for_posting_v1.pdf>.
'UN Moon Treaty falling to US opposition groups'1982, *L-5 News*, March, National Space Society, Washington, DC, viewed 16 August 2023, <https://space.nss.org/l5-news-un-moon-treaty-falling-to-us-opposition-groups/>.
Urgenda 2018, *Urgenda Wins Historic Climate Case in Hague Court of Appeal*, press release, 9 October, Urgenda, Amsterdam, viewed 16 August 2023, <http://news.smart.pr/urgenda/press-release-urgenda-wins-historic-climate-case-in-court-of-appeal>.
US Census Bureau 2012, *Following the Frontier Line, 1790 to 1890*, 6 September, viewed 16 August 2023, <https://www.census.gov/dataviz/visualizations/001/>
'U.S. Commercial Space Launch Competitiveness Act', U.S. House of Representatives, H.R. 2262, 114th Congress (2015).
'U.S. Commercial Space Launch Competitiveness Act', U.S. Senate, s.1297, 114th Congress (2015).
'U.S. Commercial Space Launch Competitiveness Act of *2015*' (CSLCA), U.S. Congress, Pub.L. 114-90 (2015).
U.S. House of Representatives 1974, 'Appendix B: Manned Space Flight Fiscal Year 1974 Program, Questions and Answers for the Record', *H.R. 4567: 1974 NASA Authorization, Hearings before the Subcommittee on Manned Spaceflight of the Committee on Science and Astronautics*, 93-466, 93rd Congress, Government Printing Office, Washington, DC.
U.S. House of Representatives 2014, 'Cosponsors', *H.R. 5063: ASTEROIDS Act*, 113th Congress (2013-2014), Library of Congress, Washington, DC, viewed 16 August 2023, <https://www.congress.gov/bill/113th-congress/house-bill/5063/cosponsors?q=%7B%22search%22%3 A%5B%22ASTEROIDS+Act%22%5D%7D&r=1&s=7>.
U.S. House of Representatives 2015a, 'All actions', *H.R. 2262: U.S. Commercial Space Launch Competitiveness Act*, 114th Congress (2015–2016), Library of Congress, Washington DC, viewed 16 August 2023, <https://www.congress.gov/bill/114th-congress/house-bill/2262/all-actions?q=%7B%22search%22%3 A%5B%22commercial+space+launch%22%5D%7D&s=4&r=2>.
U.S. House of Representatives 2015b, 'Cosponsors', *H.R. 1508: Space Resource Exploration and Utilization Act of 2015*, 114th Congress (2015–2016), Library of Congress, Washington DC, viewed 16 August 2023, <https://www.congress.gov/bill/

114th-congress/house-bill/1508/cosponsors?q=%7B%22search%22%3 A%5B%22space +resource+exploration%22%5D%7D&r=1&s=3>.
U.S. Office of Technology Assessment 1988, *Copper: Technology and Competitiveness*, OTA-E-367, September, U.S. Government Printing Office, Washington, DC.
U.S. Senate 2015a, 'Cosponsors', S.976: Space Resource Exploration and Utilization Act of 2015, 114th Congress (2015–2016), Library of Congress, Washington, DC, viewed 16 August 2023, <https://www.congress.gov/bill/114th-congress/senate-bill/976/cosponsors?q=%7B%22search%22%3 A%5B%22 S.976%22%5D%7D&r=1&s=5>.
U.S. Senate 2015b, 'Cosponsors, *S.1297: U.S. Commercial Space Launch Competitiveness Act*', 114th Congress (2015–2016), Library of Congress, Washington, DC, viewed 16 August 2023, <https://www.congress.gov/bill/114th-congress/senate-bill/1297/cosponsors?q=%7B%22search%22%3 A%5B%22 s.1297%22%5D%7D&r=1&s=3>.
Valentine, D. 2012, 'Exit strategy: Profit, cosmology, and the future of humans in space', *Anthropological Quarterly*, vol. 85, no. 4, pp. 1045–1068.
Van Horn, R. 2009, 'Reinventing monopoly and role of corporations: The roots of Chicago law and economics', in P. Mirowski & D. Plehwe (eds.), *The Road from Mont Pèlerin: The making of the neoliberal thought collective*, Harvard University Press, Cambridge, MA, pp. 204–237.
Van Horn, R. & Mirowski, P. 2009, 'The rise of the Chicago School of Economic and the Birth of Neoliberalism', in P. Mirowski & D. Plehwe (eds.), *The Road from Mont Pèlerin: The Making of the Neoliberal Thought Collective*, Harvard University Press, Cambridge, MA, pp. 139–178.
Vernadsky, V.I. 1926, *The Biosphere*, trans. D.B. Langmuir, republished 1998, Copernicus, New York.
Vernadsky, V.I. 1938, 'Excerpts from scientific thought as a planetary phenomenon', trans. W. Jones, *21st Century Science and Technology*, Spring-Summer 2012, pp. 16–31.
Villaneda, R. 2009, 'The galactic purchase of a Russian space station', *Palos Verdes Peninsula News*, 2 April, archived website, viewed 16 August 2023, <https://web.archive.org/web/20190926055210/https://www.pvnews.com/news/city_news/the-galactic-purchase-of-a-russian-space-station/article_52702e5e-1a01-56f7-9778-a51816e5ccbf.html>.
Vinx, L. 2013, 'Carl Schmitt and the analogy between constitutional and international law: Are constitutional and international law inherently political?', *Global Constitutionalism*, vol. 2, no. 1, pp. 91–124.
Wainscott, J. 2017, *Advocating for Commercial Space*, 9 February, Space Frontier Foundation, Arlington, VA, archived website, viewed 16 August 2023, <https://web.archive.org/web/20211208122502/http://newspace.spacefrontier.org/2019/05/04/2034/>.
Waldron, J. 2016, 'Property and ownership', in E. Zalta (ed.), *Stanford Encyclopedia of Philosophy* (Winter 2016 edition), viewed 16 August 2023, <http://plato.stanford.edu/archives/win2016/entries/property/>.
Walker, J. 2007, Economy of Nature: A Genealogy of the Concepts of 'Growth' and 'Equilibrium' as Artefacts of Metaphorical Exchange between Natural and the Social Sciences, PhD thesis, University of Technology, Sydney.
Walker, J. 2013, 'Worlds to endure: Weathering disorder from Arnhem Land to Chicago', *Global Networks*, vol. 13, no. 3, pp. 391–409.
Walker, J. & Granjou, C. 2017, 'MELiSSA the minimal biosphere: Human life, waste and refuge in deep space', *Futures*, vol. 92, pp. 59–69.
Walker, J. & Johnson, M. 2018, 'On mineral sovereignty: Towards a political theory of geological power, *Energy Research and Social Science*, vol. 45, pp. 56–66.
Walker, J. 2020, *More Heat than Life: The Tangled Roots of Ecology, Energy and Economics*, Palgrave Macmillan, Singapore.

Wall, D. 2014, *The Commons in History: Culture, Conflict, and Ecology*, MIT Press, Cambridge, MA & London.
Wall, M. 2022, 'Not just Artemis: China and Russia plan to put boots on the moon, too', *Space.com*, 4 September, viewed 9 August 2023, <https://www.space.com/china-russia-moon-base-ilrs>.
Wallerstein, I.M. 1974, *The Modern World-system: Capitalist Agriculture and the Origins of the European World-economy in the Sixteenth Century*, Academic Press, New York.
Walters, G. 2017, '"Space aggressors" are training US forces for extraterrestrial conflict', *Seeker*, 23 May, viewed 16 August 2023, <https://www.seeker.com/space/space-aggressors-train-us-forces-for-extraterrestrial-conflict>.
Waluchow, W. 2017, 'Constitutionalism', in E. Zalta (ed.), *Stanford Encyclopedia of Philosophy* (Winter 2017 edition), viewed 7 August 2018, <https://plato.stanford.edu/entries/constitutionalism/>.
Wasser, A. & Jobes, D. 2008, 'Space settlements, property rights, and international law: could a lunar settlement claim the lunar real estate it needs to survive?', *Journal of Air Law and Commerce*, vol. 73, pp. 37–78.
Weber, M. 1919, 'Politics as vocation', in J. Dreijmanis & G.C. Wells (eds.) 2008, *Max Weber's Complete Writings on Academic and Political Vocations*, Algora Publishing, New York, pp. 126–166.
Wedel, J.R. 1998, 'The Harvard Boys do Russia', *The Nation*, 14 May, viewed 16 August 2023, <https://www.thenation.com/article/world/harvard-boys-do-russia/>.
Weeks, E. 2012, *Outer Space Development, International Relations and Space Law: A Method for Elucidating Seeds*, Cambridge Scholars Publishing, Newcastle.
Weil, E. 2000, 'American megamillionaire gets Russki space heap!', *The New York Times Magazine*, 23 July, viewed 16 August 2023, <https://www.nytimes.com/2000/07/23/magazine/american-megamillionaire-gets-russki-space-heap.html>.
Weiss, E.M. 2006, 'Telecom mogul guilty of tax scam', *Washington Post*, 9 September, viewed 16 August 2023, <http://www.washingtonpost.com/wp-dyn/content/article/2006/09/08/AR2006090801126.html?noredirect=on>.
White, W. 1998, 'Real property rights in outer space', paper presented to the *40th Colloquium on the Law of Outer Space*, International Institute of Space Law, republished Space Settlement Institute, New York, viewed 16 August 2023, <http://www.space-settlement-institute.org/Articles/research_library/WayneWhite98-2.pdf>.
White, W. 2002, 'The legal regime for private activities in outer space', in E. Hudgins (ed.), *Space – The Free Market Frontier*, Cato Institute, Washington, DC, pp. 86–111.
The White House 2023, Fact Sheet: Strengthening U.S. International Space Partnerships, Washington, DC, viewed 11 February 2024.
Whyte, K.P. 2018, 'Indigenous science (fiction) for the Anthropocene: Ancestral dystopias and fantasies of climate change crises', *Environment and Planning E: Nature and Space*, vol. 1, no. 1-2, pp. 224–242.
Wingfield, N. 2018, 'Amazon chooses 20 finalists for second headquarters', *The New York Times*, 18 January, viewed 16 August 2023, <https://www.nytimes.com/2018/01/18/technology/amazon-finalists-headquarters.html>.
Winstanley, G. 1649, *The True Levellers Standard Advanced: Or, The State of Community Opened, and Presented to the Sons of Men*, republished n.d., Marxists Internet Archive, viewed 16 August 2023, <https://www.marxists.org/reference/archive/winstanley/1649/levellers-standard.htm>.
Worden, S.P. 2009, 'Settling the solar system', *Mars Quarterly*, vol. 1, no. 3, pp. 22–26.

Young, A. 2014, 'The commercial race back to the Moon', *The Space Review*, 9 June, viewed 9 August 2023, <https://www.thespacereview.com/article/2527/1>.

Zalik, A. 2015, 'Trading on the offshore: Territorialisation and the ocean grab in the international seabed', in K. Ervine & G. Fridell (eds.), *Beyond Free Trade*, Palgrave Macmillan, London, pp. 173–190.

Zubrin, R. 1994, 'The significance of the Martian frontier', *Ad Astra*, September/October, National Space Society, Washington, DC, viewed 16 August 2023, <https://space.nss.org/the-significance-of-the-martian-frontier-by-robert-zubrin/>.

Zubrin, R. 1996, *The Case for Mars: The Plan to Settle the Red Planet and Why We Must*, The Free Press, New York.

Zubrin, R. 2013, *Merchants of Despair: Radical Environmentalists, Criminal Pseudo-Scientists, and the Fatal Cult of Antihumanism*, Encounter Books, New York.

Zucman, G. 2015, *The Hidden Wealth of Nations: The Scourge of Tax Havens*, University of Chicago Press, Chicago.

de Zwart, M. 2022, 'The impact of the Artemis Accords on resource extraction', in V. Hessel, J. Stoudemire, H. Miyamoto & I.D. Fisk (eds.), *In-space Manufacturing and Resources: Earth and Planetary Exploration Applications*, Wiley-VCH, Weinheim, Germany, pp. 351–368.

Index

Note: Italicized page numbers indicate figures.

For Product Safety Concerns and Information please contact our EU
representative GPSR@taylorandfrancis.com
Taylor & Francis Verlag GmbH, Kaufingerstraße 24, 80331 München, Germany

www.ingramcontent.com/pod-product-compliance
Ingram Content Group UK Ltd.
Pitfield, Milton Keynes, MK11 3LW, UK
UKHW020150200926
475702UK00016B/2641
* 9 7 8 1 0 3 2 2 7 6 6 2 5 *